We Who Love to Be Astonished

We Who Love to Be Astonished

Experimental Women's Writing
and Performance Poetics

edited by
LAURA HINTON AND CYNTHIA HOGUE

THE UNIVERSITY OF ALABAMA PRESS
Tuscaloosa and London

Copyright © 2002
The University of Alabama Press
Tuscaloosa, Alabama 35487-0380
All rights reserved
Manufactured in the United States of America

2 4 6 8 9 7 5 3 1
03 05 07 09 10 08 06 04 02

Typeface: Minion and Goudy

∞
The paper on which this book is printed meets the minimum requirements of American
National Standard for Information Science–Permanence of Paper for Printed Library
Materials, ANSI Z39.48–1984.

Library of Congress Cataloging-in-Publication Data

We who love to be astonished : experimental women's writing and performance poetics / edited
by Laura Hinton and Cynthia Hogue.
    p.   cm. — (Modern and contemporary poetics)
Includes bibliographical references and index.
    ISBN 0-8173-1094-0 (alk. paper)—ISBN 0-8173-1095-9 (pbk. : alk. paper)
    1. American literature—Women authors—History and criticism. 2. Women and literature—
United States—History—20th century. 3. American literature—20th century—History and
criticism. 4. Experimental fiction, American—History and criticism. 5. Experimental poetry,
American—History and criticism. 6. Postmodernism (Literature)—United States. I. Hinton,
Laura. II. Hogue, Cynthia. III. Series.
    PS151 .W36 2001
    810.9′9287′0904—dc21
                2001002381

British Library Cataloguing-in-Publication Data available

For Susan Hardy Aiken, feminist scholar and mentor *extraordinaire,* cherished friend

As for we
who "love to be
astonished"
        . . . There is no solitude.
      It buries itself in veracity. It is as if
one splashed in the water lost by one's tears.
                —Lyn Hejinian, *My Life*

Contents

Acknowledgments

Grateful acknowledgment is given to the following sources for permission to reprint material:

From "The Disappeared" by Kathleen Fraser, copyright © 1994 by Kathleen Fraser. Used by permission. Kathleen Fraser, excerpts from "WING," "Now that the Subjunctive is Dying," "What I Want," "These labdanum hours," "Giotto: Arena," "Etruscan Pages," "when new time folds up," from *il cuore: the heart* © 1997 by Kathleen Fraser, Wesleyan University Press by permission of University Press of New England.

"Asterisk: Separation at the Threshold of Meaning in the Poetry of Rae Armantrout," by Ron Silliman. Reprinted from A WILD SALIENCE: THE WRITING OF RAE ARMANTROUT, ed. Tom Beckett, Bobbie West, and Robert Drake (Cleveland: Burning Press). Copyright © 1999 by Ron Silliman. "Generation" by Rae Armantrout from THE EXTREMITIES (Berkeley: The Figures), copyright © by Rae Armantrout, 1978. "A Pulse" by Rae Armantrout from MADE TO SEEM (Los Angeles: Sun & Moon), copyright © by Rae Armantrout, 1995. "Locks" by Rae Armantrout from *NECROMANCE* (Los Angeles: Sun & Moon), copyright © by Rae Armantrout, 1991.

From COLLECTED POEMS by Wallace Stevens. Copyright 1923 and renewed 1951 by Wallace Stevens. Reprinted by permission of Alfred A. Knopf, a Division of Random House, Inc.

From *The Descent of Alette* by Alice Notley. Copyright © 1996 by Alice Notley. Used by permission of Penguin Books USA Inc.

From *Empathy* by Mei-Mei Berssenbrugge, copyright © by Mei-Mei Berssenbrugge. Used by permission.

From *Tree Tall Woman* by Harryette Mullen, copyright © 1980 by Harryette

Mullen. From *Trimmings* by Harryette Mullen, copyright © 1991 by Harryette Mullen. Used by permission.

Passages from *The Woman Who Fell from the Sky*. Reprinted from *The Woman Who Fell from the Sky*, by Joy Harjo, by permission of the author and W. W. Norton & Company, Inc. Copyright © 1994 by W. W. Norton & Company, Inc.

From *Le Spleen de Paris* by Charles Baudelaire, ed. by Claude Pichois, copyright © 1975 by Gallimard: Editions Pléiade. Used by permission.

From *Paris Spleen* by Louise Varèse, Translator. Copyright © 1947 and renewed in 1970 by New Directions. Reprinted by permission of New Directions Publishing Corp.

"Indian Fort" from John Underhill, *News From America*. Courtesy of the John Carter Library at Brown University.

From A KEY INTO THE LANGUAGE OF AMERICA by Rosmarie Waldrop, copyright © 1994 by Rosmarie Waldrop. Reprinted by permission of New Directions Publishing Corp.

From *Animal Instincts* by Carla Harryman, copyright © 1989 by Carla Harryman. Used by permission.

From *And for Example* by Ann Lauterbach. Copyright © 1994 by Ann Lauterbach. Used by permission of Viking Penguin, a division of Penguin Putnam Inc.

From *MARS* by Norma Cole, copyright © 1994 by Norma Cole. From *MOIRA* by Norma Cole, copyright © 1995 by Norma Cole. From *Desire & Its Double* by Norma Cole, copyright © 1998 by Norma Cole. Used by permission.

From *The Nonconformist's Memorial*, copyright © 1993 by Susan Howe. Reprinted by permission of New Directions Publishing Corp. From *The Birthmark: Unsettling the Wilderness in American Literary History* by Susan Howe, copyright © 1993 by Susan Howe, Wesleyan University Press by permission of University Press of New England. From *The Europe of Trusts* by Susan Howe, copyright © 1990 by Susan Howe. Used by permission.

From *Arcade,* by Erica Hunt and Alison Saar, copyright © 1996 by Kelsey Street Press. Used by permission.

From *Dictée* by Theresa Hak Kyung Cha, copyright © 1995 by The Regents of the University of California. Used by permission.

From *Iovis* by Anne Waldman, copyright © 1993 by Coffee House Press. Used by permission.

From *Intermission* by Tracie Morris, copyright © 1998 by Tracie Morris. From *Chap-t-her Won: Some Poems by Tracie Morris,* copyright © 1992 by Tracie Morris.

From *Coagulations: New and Selected Poems,* copyright © 1984 by Jayne Cortez.

Introduction
Oppositions and Astonishing Contiguities

Laura Hinton and Cynthia Hogue

> *Whereas Modernist poetics was overwhelmingly committed, at least in the-ory, to the "natural look," . . . we are now witnessing a return to artifice, but a "radical artifice" . . . less a matter of ingenuity and manner, of elaboration and elegant subterfuge, than of the recognition that a poem or painting or performance text is a made thing—contrived, constructed, chosen. . . . At its best, such construction empowers the audience by altering its perceptions of how things happen.*
>
> —Marjorie Perloff

> *One troubling aspect of privileging language as the primary site to torque new meaning and possibility is that it is severed from the political question of for whom new meaning is produced. . . . I would suggest that it is important to think how writing can begin to develop among oppositional groups, how writ-ing can begin to have social existence in a world where authority has become highly mobile, based less on identity and on barely discerned or discussed re-lationships.*
>
> —Erica Hunt

In the introduction to her seminal study of postmodern poetry, *Radical Artifice: Writing Poetry in the Age of Media*, Marjorie Perloff reveals the roots of the post-modernist avant-garde in modernist formal concerns.[1] She does so in order to raise the issue of audience, and the possibility of affecting the process whereby it perceives the text in and of the world. Like the modernist avant-garde, post-modern writers refuse realism's dream of the transparent transmission of knowl-edge. And like the modernist avant-garde, too, the postmodern avant-garde con-sciously employs artifice as a means of realizing—or concretizing—that refusal.

But many of the modernists, Perloff reminds us, aspired to make their poetic language seem natural. What distinguishes the postmodern avant-garde is its refusal to naturalize the language of the text. Postmodern poetics foregrounds the text's ability to explore the material and signifying possibilities of the language medium.[2] Experimental writing today urges readers to apprehend "the world through a lens that would subvert, at their linguistic-perceptual root, habits of consciousness comfortable with the predominant cultural givens," as Marianne DeKoven has put it.[3]

Erica Hunt raises a concern that Perloff also raises but does not pursue: for whom are the avant-garde writing? Hunt reminds us in her essay, "Notes for an Oppositional Poetics," that the roots of what she terms "oppositional writing" today (writing produced by writers of color, feminist writers, and/or experimental writers) lie in the politicized literature of earlier eras: in abolitionist, pacifist, populist, labor, women's, and civil rights movements. Oppositional writing is, according to Hunt, produced by those whose cultural positioning has caused them to resist and question—to oppose—dominant structures of power, of white, class, and/or gender privilege. Rather than "the dream of a common audience," to adapt Adrienne Rich's well-known phrase, Hunt interrogates the subject positions for readers as well as writers of the avant-garde. She warns that the "ideal reader is an endangered species, the committed reader has an ideological agenda both open and closed." The danger for such committed audiences of oppositional writing is that they can harden into positions opposing each other, rather than establishing areas of shared concerns. Then, readers and writers alike can be easily marginalized by dominant culture.

Hunt proposes an alternative approach: finding or building the interconnections among the various audiences of oppositional writers—a textual and social practice that she terms "contiguity." This practice is one that "acknowledges that the relationships among groups who share an interest in changing the antidemocratic character of the social order is not as oblique as their individual rhetoric would represent." Contiguity suggests new reading and writing practices, new syntheses, which would "consider the variance between clusters of oppositional writing strategies with respect for what has been achieved by each and a sense of the ground that holds it in place."[4] The advantage of contiguity as a textual practice is that it acknowledges common ground: the shared political and aesthetic interests among various schools, and cultures of writers and readers. The advantage of contiguity as a social practice is that it maintains and respects the integrity of these same groups' oppositions and differences, at the same time as their exchange and dialogue in a public forum fosters a broadening sense of community—intellectual, political, and social, as well as artistic.[5]

In an essay on the complexities of writing today aptly entitled, "Bewilderment," Fanny Howe argues that a poetry of "bewilderment" is "close to dream-construction": "It cracks open the dialectic and sees myriads all at once." It is an error, Howe contends, to believe that there is only one form in which to view a subject. Such a view leads to painful disputes, and reminds her that, as a Kabbalistic rabbi once said, "in the Messianic age people will no longer quarrel with others but only with themselves." This, Howe observes, "is what poets are doing already."[6] Critics, too, we might add, as recent debates about poetic aesthetics might suggest.[7]

Charles Altieri has usefully characterized such debates as arising from the ethical desire of postmodern artists both to extend modernist formal resistance to realist ideals and marketplace values, and to offer more plausible ways than those suggested by postmodern theory in the imagining of alternatives to mainstream culture. Countering realism has entailed treating art less as a mode of referring directly to the world than as a syntactic mode of feeling and thinking, which projects investments not bound to dominant social structures. But how does one keep the resistance to realism from becoming a modernist formalism, blind to historical forces and refusing to take responsibility for the political conditions created by those forces?

As a cultural space for diversity has emerged, issues of difference in mainstream culture have tended to be confined to a poetics of identity politics, which renders inaudible and invisible formally innovative work challenging dominant paradigms of representation and reception. "Consequently," Altieri asserts, "the very factors that allow the art its cultural currency also considerably weaken its capacity to make substantial modifications in received ideas."[8] As Altieri (following Charles Bernstein, among others) has explored, the problem for postmodernism has been how to confront what remain today deeply disturbing political forces through an art that does not embody its political content in conventional formal models, which may reinforce—rather than transform—conventional thinking.[9]

In this volume, we have collected critical essays on innovative women's writing that directly and variously engages in addressing what Altieri terms "postmodernism's problem." The assumption upon which we based this collection, that there is no one formal model that resolves this problem, follows from Hunt's compelling argument to create places—interfaces—where writings of differing oppositional textual and aesthetic practices meet. The volume thus is conceptualized as a metaphoric and textual common ground among audiences, so that innovative writing can begin to have a greater "social existence in the world," to recall Hunt's words in the quotation with which we opened.

We Who Love to be Astonished explores the contiguities and interconnections among cross-generic women's avant-garde writings; it seeks to do so without losing their historical specificity. The collection brings together critical essays on works by diverse, and diversely experimental, American women writers. It seeks not only to promote dialogue among schools of experimental poetry and fiction, but also to cross formal thresholds and boundaries among this volume's diverse pool of literary critics, many of whom are also experimental poets and/ or fiction writers. While the essays published here examine writings by experimental women who innovate through cultural hybridization, the volume itself also innovates through a similar crossing of borders, by a contiguous mapping of critical paths. We include essays, for instance, about writings that engage in poetry-prose hybrids, all of which experiment in language, but many of which experiment, also, in visual referents or performance sound—re-enunciating the body-in-performance in the process. We include, as well, essays about works whose formalist concerns grow out of the "Language" school (in both its West and East coast contingents), as well as essays about poetry and fiction emerging out of the more ethnically diverse populist traditions, sprouting up among Southwestern "Tex-Mex" border communities and New York's "village" cultures alike. The writers of these works—Denise Chávez, Mei-Mei Berssenbrugge and Tracie Morris, to name a few—are rarely found in conversation with one another, because of aesthetic but also political, regional, and ethnic differences.

In her introduction to the notable anthology of experimental women's writing, *Moving Borders: Three Decades of Innovative Writing by Women,* Mary Margaret Sloan asserts that the "task of an anthology editor is to draw a boundary around a number of writers." In order to represent the rich multiplicity of experimental writing by American women today, we have set up critical borders that we neither fix neatly nor see hardening into place. To echo Sloan, the lines we have drawn should "be seen as provisional, as arbitrary as a political boundary is to topography, in short as a border that may be moved."[10] In assembling our collection of essays, we also note the provisional nature of this work. There is clearly an on-going need for more work, for other contiguous, inclusive (and yet different) critical anthologies on the topic of experimental women writers. The need to acknowledge—indeed, to expand—the connections continues.[11]

In the way of contiguity, we hope to provide in *We Who Love to Be Astonished* suggestions as to how one might configure many varieties of feminist thought— and, likewise, the way in which such varieties of feminist thought form words and letters on a page for the particular women writers whose works we discuss. Promoting dialogue, realigning and also shifting borders of all kinds, we seek to break, and play within, the once irreconcilable divide between those who theorize about women's writing and those who focus purely upon its formalist concerns. It is never easy to read gendered awareness into what are, necessarily, formal-linguistic structures. In asserting that women's postmodern writing plays with the notion of gender (as opposed to gendering "a common language"), we follow Rachel Blau DuPlessis's crucial argument for a feminist reception of such work.[12] Hence, the origin of our title in an often-repeated phrase from Lyn Hejinian's neo-Steinian hybrid poetry-prose text, *My Life:* "We who 'love to be astonished'": a phrase uttered as the speaker of this radical poetry-novella constructs a woman writer's life-in-process. Altering the generic landscape of the bildungsroman, the autobiography, and the romance, *My Life* offers an "astonished" female subject, who herself posits "astonishing" new subjects: a new language and vision about her gendered body and voice; and the making and unmaking of signs that represent her (in all senses of the phrase).

Buried in the etymological roots of the word "astonish," however, among its now-obsolete connotations, is the capacity "to stun . . . stupefy" an *opponent,* "to shock one out of *his* wits . . . bewilder" (emphasis added). Something of this oppositional force that the word once conveyed resides in the astonishing agencies of women's avant-garde literatures, as these writers have sought experimentally to investigate the role of gender in the making of formal, material, and psychoanalytic structures upon which all texts are based. The current usage of "astonish" suggests the less agonistic, more sublime implications of "to stun" (or, as Howe has put it, to bewilder): "*to astonish* . . . to give a shock of wonder by the presentation of something unlooked for or unaccountable; to amaze, surprise greatly." In reading this definition through gendered and racialized lenses, we contend that the women writers whose works are considered in this volume reveal what we call a feminist proclivity: to astonish by presenting what previously remained not only unseen but *unlooked for* in mainstream culture. In their verbal innovations, these writers investigate racial-sexual differences in material society that dominant constructs cover up, creating women's texts that proffer ways of seeing the unseen, looking at the unlooked at. As Ron Silliman, AnaLouise Keating, and Kathleen Crown contend respectively in their essays on Rae Armantrout, Chavez, and Morris in this volume, these writers both question and investigate existing ways of knowing. They suggest radically edged epistemological paradigms.

A love to *be* astonished becomes a love *to* astonish in these women's texts, as women who have taken up avant-garde writing approaches—like Lorine Niedecker from the 40's and 50's, and Kathleen Fraser and Harryette Mullen in the present—gain increasing recognition. Conversely, "we who 'love to be astonished'" are "we," the readers of these women's writing. "We" are *writerly* readers, to borrow from Roland Barthes's useful distinction between classic and experimental texts. And "we," invited in by the open hermeneutic climate, become contingent producers of our own texts. "We," the writers, of this volume love to astonish—by means of our own writings about women's experimental works.

For the volume entitled, *We Who Love to Be Astonished* is, in fact, our own political statement of opposition to the assimilation of difference into conventions of thinking. It is also our effort to form contiguities. This volume offers for the first time a series of critical essays devoted to American women's postmodern writing, a collection which contiguously places writings about women's works now well acknowledged alongside writings about women's works previously overlooked. It also places essays about white women's innovative writings in dialogue with essays about women writers of color. Until recently, major anthologies devoted to innovative writing have under-represented the contributions of women and/or writers of color, an oversight Sloan's recent *Moving Borders* has begun to correct.[13] Commenting on the under-representation of experimental women's poetics in criticism, Linda A. Kinnahan has asserted that we need to rethink the implications of gender in relation to theory, history, and the new literary tradition. Kinnahan suggests that an "obscuring of these relations has produced, in the past, obviously masculine-centered readings of innovative writing in this century, whether intentionally or not."[14] If critical anthologies focusing on experimental writing have included few essays about women's work (or essays only about the same experimental women writers), other anthologies that address the critical need to assess women's writing have not focused solely upon innovation as a topic.[15]

Historically, we have needed a volume that critically evaluates women's specific contributions to the burgeoning tradition of postmodern experimentation. Creative and critical interest in experimental women's writing is growing, if one is to judge by a recent crop of stimulating forums and conferences on this topic in recent years. During the spring of 1999 alone, three major conferences took into account the specific role women have played in the production, publishing, and teaching of experimental works.[16] And that same spring, Kathleen Fraser resurrected out of a 1980's journal the electronic journal *HOW(ever) 2*, devoted primarily to the topic of women's innovative writing. *HOW(ever) 2*, in short time, has become a central forum for commentaries on gender and experimentation. *We Who Love to Be Astonished* grows out of these astonishingly recent contiguities of cultural thought. It grows out of the on-going contiguous weave of academic and activist feminisms, which seek to hear and to know women's strategies and voices.

The volume is organized into four parts, reflecting some of the cross-generic and differing structural concerns that the various contributors take up in their essays. Although investigating a poetics of marginality (to adapt the title of Fraser's foundational essay on the topic), this collection is distinguished by its refusal to reproduce taxonomies of social marginalization and critical segregation by racial categorization. Rather, as editors, the organizational model we have adopted is characterized by Hunt's notion of contiguity. To create "new . . . syntheses . . . between clusters of oppositional writing strategies," as Hunt has suggested, we have arranged essays in order to foster dialogue, explore interfaces and thresholds, especially among white writers and writers of color too rarely considered together. Through this conceptual arrangement, we hope to augment new reading practices.

The first two sections, "Formal Thresholds" and "In the Margins of Form," identify the multiple ways in which women of various cultural backgrounds have been exploring their relationship to inherited formal traditions. The first section looks at how innovative women writers have reconceived the forms of dominant culture—often from a "place/within silence," to quote Armantrout. In doing so, they have opened up what we term, for the purposes of this volume, new formal thresholds. They explore other ways of knowing, hearing, seeing and being.

Eileen Gregory examines Fraser's persistent commitment to the practice of writing as "investigation." The space of genuine discovery in a Fraser poem begins in uncertainty, risk-taking, and accident. Fraser's "re:searches," Gregory contends, comprise a palimpsest of historical evidence taking shape in a progressively generative linguistic exploration. As Ron Silliman observes, Armantrout, too, dwells in her poetry on the processes of knowing and perception, rather than the fixed meanings we try to impose on a poem. In deft close readings, Silliman examines Armantrout's characteristic gesture toward silence—the breaks in her exemplary sequential poems that are marked by asterisks, and which make her poems structurally disjunctive at the segment level. Such parataxis is, for Armantrout's work, fundamental to perception. It enables her to hold readers at what Silliman has termed a threshold of meaning, just at the impulse to turn perception to sign—that "place / within silence" which both contains and exceeds language.

The last two essays in this section treat specific generic innovations, exploring their attempts to refigure cultural tropes of being and emotion within a traditional (however revised) generic frame. Susan McCabe considers Alice Notley's *The Descent of Alette*, contending that this experimental feminist epic enters the male-dominated genre in order to re-imagine gender assumptions embedded like barbed wire at its aesthetic borders. The resulting heroic female subject pursues an ecstatic search for new ways of being, McCabe asserts. If *Descent* elaborates upon a faith in poetry's ability to expand formal boundaries, Berssenbrugge's poetry elaborates upon a paradox that Charles Altieri explores as ontological inquiry. He asks to what degree such an experimental poetry, one which demands what he calls "intricate acts of self-reflection," also can create in the reader an engaged affective response. Berssenbrugge's dense lyrics, with their self-conscious stylistic surface, refuse standard assumptions about how emotional intensity—what Altieri suggests we experience as "intimacy"—is best staged.

If the first section focuses upon writers who explore thresholds of meaning and formal edges, the second section is comprised of essays on writers who formally reverse the center/margin structure of dominant American culture, often in order to question received notions of community: ethnic, tribal, national. Chávez's experimental fiction, like the poetry of Armantrout and Notley in section one, employs silence, absence or emptiness, marked by formal breaks in the narratives. As AnaLouise Keating observes, Chávez's *Menu Girls* is reft with self-other divisions, lacunas of cultural and personal loss that Chávez refuses to cover over. Her ambiguous, fragmented, unstable text illustrates one vital aspect of multicultural thinking, one that resonates contiguously with other formal projects in this volume: the challenge to existing knowledge structures. Focusing on textual depictions of Chicana alienation, Keating analyzes the way in which Chávez seeks to expand representational practices and restructure underlying knowledge systems. Cynthia Hogue makes a related argument about Mullen's work. Tracing the roots of Mullen's experimental poetry back to her early contributions to the Black Arts movement, Hogue then examines Mullen's attempts to write beyond the epistemological "frame of whiteness." In marginalizing whiteness and centralizing black experience, Mullen's early work reverses the movement in the literature of passing from the "not-white margins" to the "white center." In what she terms Mullen's revisionary "border work," Hogue contends that the border between these two oppositional identities is rendered fluid, permeable to an exchange of culturally ordered signs and assumptions.

The next two essays, by Jonathan Monroe and Lynn Keller, both take up Rosmarie Waldrop's *A Key into the Language of America* (the title of non-conforming colonist Roger Williams' dictionary of the Narragansett language) from differing, dialogical perspectives. Monroe raises an issue that resonates with our passage above from Hunt. "What kind of communities," he asks, "do experimental poetries envision and what kind of poetries do these communities call for in return?" By discussing Waldrop's work in conjunction with a recent collection by Muscogee poet Joy Harjo, Monroe is able to investigate the roles innovative poetry can play in negotiating intersections of language, nationality, post-coloniality, and community reception, as well as gender. Keller's formalist analysis focuses on three elements fundamental both to Waldrop's experimentalism and the formal concerns of this section: the productive tension between an interest in patterns and their disruption; a preoccupation with emptiness-as-generative; and Waldrop's feminist scrutiny of her own position as at once privileged (as white) and marginalized (as a woman and poet).

The final essay in this section, by poet and playwright Carla Harryman, itself experiments with the very disruption of rules and patterns—what Harryman terms "constraints" and "restraints"—that both she and Keller contemplate. Such rules do govern the experimental text, but as Harryman contends, they are rules "of thought, not of literary convention." Looking at Hejinian's and Acker's work, as well as her own, Harryman argues that it is the intellectual position that "allows the difficult text to come into being at all." The intellectual position both enables and limits the exploratory complexity of these texts.

The third section of this collection takes up the issue of visuality, in a variety of its political and formal possibilities. Charles Borkhuis's essay on Norma Cole and Ann Lauterbach, a former painter and an art critic respectively, begins this section, in a study of these two women poets' complex responses to image-making. Borkhuis calls attention to both the problem and the challenge of vision for writers steeped in both post-structural philosophies and postmodern poetries. On the one hand, vision and visuality, and the ocularcentrism they imply, create a deep distrust. On the other, poets like Cole and Lauterbach have rejected the too-easy binarism that polarizes the visual from verbal expression. Borkhuis investigates the way both Cole and Lauterbach at once employ and critique the visual, renovating the image in a form he terms "the critical lyric."

The next essay in this section examines the role of the fetish in constructing descriptive vision, particularly in the fantastical visual descriptions of the postmodern romance. Laura Hinton reminds us that the romance is an historically female, as well as American, narrative genre—whose ambivalent relation to realism gives it a complex fetishistic resonance, based in themes of castration and loss of representation. Hinton suggests that Fanny Howe's *The Lives of a Spirit* and Hejinian's *My Life* both play with the fantastical possibility of self and world through the present but absent structure of the visual fetish. In Howe's poetry-novella, fetishism is embraced through excessive descriptions. In Hejinian's *My Life*, the classic fetishistic oscillation between self and other, presence and absence, is rejected—and the text is given entirely over to the play of language.

More concrete but no less theoretical uses of vision are central concerns in two following essays. How one might begin to read the typography of words—or their lack—on the material page in the concrete poetry of Susan Howe is a topic addressed by Alan Golding. Typographical design and the deployment of words produces an image, Golding notes; it is an image that then opens up significant ellipses, gaps, and erasures in Howe's texts, a *non*-image highly symbolic for a feminist poet obliquely commenting upon patriarchal language systems. Linda A. Kinnahan's essay examines the visual messages produced in *Arcade*, by poet Hunt and visual artist Alison Saar. A verbal-visual collaboration that juxtaposes poetry with a series of provocative woodcuts, *Arcade* creates a circulation of images that reveals the regulatory roles of race and gender in commodity culture. The dual, interacting images in *Arcade* call attention to the organization of the female body through commodified forms, particularly of the African-American woman's body in a visual, racialized regime. Through what Kinnahan calls the "contiguous" representations of verbal and visual signifiers, Hunt and Saar create a hybridity that enunciates a body too often used in service of the modern power structure.

Particularly at issue in Kinnahan's essay is the bodily aspect of vision that ignites and serves, as well as explores, the formation of power in this Foucaultian analysis. The fourth section of the volume further explores the role of the body as material and performing referent in women's poetics. Continuing some of Kinnahan's Foucaultian observations, Elisabeth A. Frost studies the visual and verbal images permeating the hybrid texts of Korean-American writer Theresa Hak Kyung Cha. Considering the role of the body in light of both visual and verbal referents, Frost examines the photographs, word images, and other linguistic signifiers (for example, both Western and Chinese medical diagrams) that ambivalently signify and "perform" this body: as a body politic, in all the implications of that term. In *Dictée*, verbal-visual images comment on the ambivalent relationship the body has to making signs. The body is both a material legible "object" and inherently illegible—as sign-maker.

While Frost demonstrates how Cha experiments with the materiality of both body and text, in ways particularly marked by gender, a following essay by Nicole Cooley demonstrates that the body *is* a text, as well as a signifier of pain, in punk-fiction writer Acker's last works. Cooley interprets two of Acker's final fictive pieces—Acker died of breast cancer in 1997—as testimonies to the power of the body to generate text, and as pseudo-autobiographical reflections on the painful experience of disease. Acker's usual foregrounding of the materiality of the body, Cooley notes, is even more accentuated in her later works, "Eurydice in the Underworld" and "The Gift of Disease," in which Acker experiments with relations between the body in pain and the body as signifier, also critiquing Western practices of medicine. Acker's texts are always bodily performances, Cooley suggests; they probe the concepts of authenticity and autobiography, subjectivity and the material body, calling into question any privileged mapping of either the female body or the literary self.

The next essay also interrogates the mapping of the body and the self in poetic-performative contexts. Heather H. Thomas's piece suggests that the performative qualities in Anne Waldman's mythopoetic epic *IOVIS* is an Ackeresque literary-collage and *tour-de-force,* in which the epic hero as feminist bard calls into question the traditional constructions of the self, and the traditional ways in which identity has been institutionalized by mainstream poetics. Choreographing a myriad of dictions, rituals, and poetic forms, the latter of which include chants, dreams, arguments, and letters, Waldman's *IOVIS* speaker takes on a variety of performative personae and masks, enhanced, Thomas notes, by Waldman's own live performances. Waldman may seek to literally lift the poet's "voice" off the page, through a ritual and performative use of vocalization, body, music and gesture, in the meantime calling into question the binarisms associated with socialized gender roles. Her poetry suggests that even language on the page can act as both body and bodily performance.

Two final essays, about African-American women artists, examine the acts of literal performance generated by the new spoken-poetry revolution. Tracie Morris's spoken poetry, which incorporates sonic improvisations, is analyzed by Kathleen Crown. In performance in New York City cafés, Morris incorporates features of African-American oral discourse into her poetic language, which creates activist, feminist affirmations of her community. In doing so, she suggests the way in which the spoken word, often criticized as too immediate and transparent, creates a new postmodern epistemology by reincorporating lost languages and cultural knowledge. Also studying performance poetry, Aldon Lynn Nielsen considers the method underlying Jayne Cortez's jazz poetry performances. For Cortez, Nielson suggests, a poem both is and is a response to a musical performance; the poem becomes a synchronic integration of sound and music, voice and word. Reading closely Cortez's performance piece "I See Chano Pozo," Nielsen charts in this jazz poem two genealogies: one that follows the Cuban influence on jazz from its New Orleans inceptions, through Bop and the Buena Vista Social Club; and another that is "literary," recalling Latin American *modernismo,* carving a different trajectory than that of later international modernism, and leading to the Negritude Caribbean poets who would influence the Harlem Renaissance.

Cortez's performance poetry—not unlike that of Morris—is a "capillary network," to borrow that phrase from Nielsen, one that contains and conveys the history of African-American language and lore. Through this network, Cortez's poetry is connected to jazz invention, and a larger twentieth-century artistic legacy. Finally, the poem by Rachel Blau DuPlessis, "Draft 48: Being Astonished," which closes this volume as an afterword, is conceptually cross-generic—a "capillary" summary, we might say, that comments upon and performatively networks the collection as a whole. It both enacts the very hybridity that it theorizes, and embodies the claim of this volume: that art itself offers rich ways of thinking about the cultural relevance of the arts.

We Who Love to Be Astonished—as a volume of contiguous and competing essays—offers its own "capillary network," one that extends a community of discourses once held in strict opposition. In assembling these essays, we have created linguistic and artistic networks that also are cross-over sequences of contiguous threads—threads bearing not only formal instruction and cultural history, but also aesthetic practices and political tools. Astonishing as that might seem, such threads work to make a tight new weave, and help to reframe the way in which we speak about the avant-garde in general. It is our hope that this volume will reconfigure the patterns by which we will receive experimental poetry and fiction to come.

PART I
FORMAL THRESHOLDS

"A Poetics of Emerging Evidence": Experiment in Kathleen Fraser's Poetry

Eileen Gregory

It is radium giving off that light. It is the glowing evidence that she has been seeking. It is like nothing that has come before it.[1]

In her essay "The Tradition of Marginality," Kathleen Fraser delineates the path that led to her increasingly strong public advocacy of experimental women writers, culminating in her founding of the journal *HOW(ever)* in 1983. This story takes as its beginning the image of Madame Curie, as Fraser came as a child to imagine her through the 1944 film starring Greer Garson. This figure of the untraditional (woman) scientist as an analogue for the experimental (woman) poet—"searching for that element which had not yet been imagined or named" (*Translating* 26)—allows a way of seeing a continuity within Fraser's ever more adventurous career. In her poetry, beginning with the first volume, *Change of Address* (1966), the sense of search—accepting the inevitability of change and the challenge of the new—is always present, the idea of the "text as a speculative journey, a process . . . in which [the woman writer] does not know what the limits will be ahead of time."[2] With each new volume one finds shifts and sometimes ruptures with previous styles. An assessment of Fraser's long and multiple engagement in the life of writing is now easier because of the recent publication of her selected poems, *il cuore : the heart: Selected Poems 1970–1995*,[3] and a collection of essays, *Translating the Unspeakable: Poetry and the Innovative Necessity.* A reading of this career renders the sense of life practice and poetic practice continuously under examination, the writer's steady wait for "the glowing evidence," whatever evidence is manifest within a process constantly open to change.

The basic link between Fraser's project and Madame Curie's is the notion of experiment. Fraser of course shares the notion of an experimental practice with a number of contemporary poets, but this broad identification may obscure sharply specific aspects of her work. She takes very seriously the scientific model of Madame Curie, the mode and the language of empirical investigation, consistently returning to a technical terminology—of evidence, observation, notation, record, method, proof—both in her essays on writing and in the poetry itself. Though this language roots Fraser within experimental poetries descending from early modernists,[4] it also defines speculative aspects of her writing that could use further emphasis.

"Experiment" implies, first, the notion of detached consciousness, discrete observation, judgment and speculation. This blue coolness is crucial to Fraser's poetics: the line, she claims, "[notates] the moving path of a poet's discovering intelligence" (*Translating* 141). And she persistently admires a quicksilver mobility in the practice of other poets: the "investigating intelligence" of Charles Alexander,[5] for instance; and in Lorine Niedecker, the "movement of her own thought, how this response might be located in *her* poetry" (*Translating* 112). About Wallace Stevens she notes: "It is the construction of what he discovers and how he knows, through attentive observation, multiplied by the sound and velocity of what he imagines" (*Translating* 12). Fraser speaks of Barbara Guest's "mercurial engagement," associating this perspective with the Italian concept of *distacco*, "a little emotional distance that may be taken from a situation or conversation." It is a moment of "cool observation" such as that allowed in the step backward taken by a painter to assess the effect of a crucial brush stroke (*Translating* 125). Fraser's remarks locate in these poets a propelling curiosity and continual self-reflexiveness—the poem as the record of an engaged intelligence and of emerging structures of thought.

Though experiment implies deliberation, it also implies uncertainty. "The tension builds through endless failures in the lab," Fraser says of the film story of Madame Curie, "as she uses what has been proposed by traditional scientific method thus far, then finally discards it to consult the further reaches of her imagination for what might work" (*Translating* 26). This willingness to let go of—or deliberately to defy—prescribed ordinations and to enter into uncertain verbal and formal play is a constant emphasis in Fraser's writing: "Repeating *the known* is acquisitive; it surrenders, as a collector does, to 'good things,' rather than hazarding uncertain territory; it narrows the range of attentiveness, neglects the unacknowledged" (*Translating* 205). Though resistance to the bounds of the known and the certain propels Fraser's work, one should note that *knowing* and *ascertaining* remain very compelling needs—though pursued at the edges and on the wires.

To these emphases one must add the aspect of Fraser's experimentation indicated in the title of her selected poems: *il cuore : the heart*. In the context of contemporary experimental poetries—heavily inflected with theory and conceptual explanations of innovation—this title may be seen as a gesture of rebellion and provocation. Fraser does *not* mean here an affiliation with conventional lyric qualities or with the subjective lyric "I," nor does she invoke any kind of intellectual naivete. Nevertheless, the title *is* meant to distinguish her project from conceptually-driven poetic practices, and to insist upon its rootedness in desire, pleasure, emotional difficulty, affection, sensuous response. The image on the cover of *il cuore*—an abstract painting by Jo Ann Ugolini—speaks to the form of the "heart" in Fraser's poetry. It is a primitive line-image of the features of a face, against a background of blue/purple and black. The empty, iris-less eyes are set apart within a rectangular frame, and painted in contrasting, bold colors, red on the right, green and white on the left: two eyes *as* two chambers of the heart, as two distinct pulsations of life. The roughly drawn mouth seems to be uttering something, indicated in lines going down and outward. This is a contemporary version of the classical Dionysus mask, though it also gives the impression of ephemeral, scrawled graffiti on the walls of an (Italian) city, since the words "*il cuore*" appear above the image as though stenciled on a poster. It is a sober and disturbing image, in its suggestion of great emotional depth and, at the same time, impermanence and fragmentation.

Fraser's reference in a recent interview to "a poetics of emerging evidence"[6] highlights a persistent practice, at once empirical and experiential: to establish figuratively a kind of deliberate laboratory space, the writer assuming a position of speculative observation, the poem noting the "evidence" generated within these imaginative parameters and projecting its implications. Though the sites of investigation vary greatly in Fraser's poetry, one can nevertheless note two large contexts which she persistently engages. The first, especially present in poetry of the sixties and seventies, is the laboratory arena of erotic relationship; another, emerging particularly in her late poetry through her part-time residence in Rome, is a concern with the cultural artifact of the city and the complexity of historical layering. Each of these contexts is especially significant in offering a "structure of difficulty"[7] analogous to the difficulties—the trust, danger, and labor—of the experiment of writing. In both these contexts, *knowing, finding*—working through manifold evidence toward provisional clarification—is a thematic concern enacted at the level of syntax and form.

The evidence subject to analysis in Fraser's early poetry arises out of relationships, friendship and sexual intimacy. The latter is the main site of analysis, in Fraser's words, "the needs and doubts and paranoid suspicions around romantic love—its old doxology of sexual images and expectations confined by the very structure of love-language as we knew it" (*Translating* 39). Much of this frankly erotic early poetry—culminating in *New Shoes* (1978)—has not been extensively discussed in feminist terms, one suspects because it emerged at the same time as

Adrienne Rich's popular articulation of a radical lesbian feminism, *The Dream of a Common Language* (1978). Nevertheless, the male-female relationship—its duplicities, its ties to threadbare social and poetic conventions, its painful challenges to identity and authority, its possibilities for irony and satire, for intricate encodings, for sensuous extravagance—is a major location of Fraser's feminist poetic explorations. As Linda Kinnahan has persuasively argued, the aim of Fraser's inquiry in this context is, in part, a criticism of patriarchal power structures as imbedded in language and convention, and an affirmation of the prerogatives of a marginal female position.[8] But the erotic relationship is a primary site not only for critique but for a constructive, speculative experiment, wherein the emergence of the new, the possible made actual, is an animating belief. The final section of *New Shoes,* entitled "Now That the Subjunctive Is Dying," signals such a belief, the shift from the hypothetical to the real, as in the words of the concluding title poem: "not what might be, but learning / each seam of you" (*il cuore* 34). In this poetry, the risk and the possibilities for success within the erotic bond are an analogue for the possibilities of formal experimentation. "We are after difficulty," begins "Notes Preceding Trust," and "There are shifts we learn / to trust behind their split seconds." A relationship is a kind of experimental poem constructed in concert. Even trivial conversation mimics the daring of experiment, where a new or concealed territory may suddenly emerge through a decisive linguistic gesture: "a very fast lane of traffic / the intentional chance taken when, without looking, // I swerved our conversation's reserve with similar behavior."[9]

A recent prose poem by Fraser, "Soft Pages," arrives within the first lines at this meditation: "This was not about desire or choice—the two preferred categories of explanation for my life, in conscious moments of trying to make sense (or at least an admirable clarity) of things—but about dropping into a place after that."[10] The poems surrounding erotic relationship carry the charge of this ethical trajectory, desire and choice themselves in the process of becoming apparent. The initial poem in *il cuore,* "What I Want"—first in a series entitled "Six Uneasy Songs" (dated 1972)—represents such a process of emotional discrimination, propelling and propelled by poetic exploration.

> Because you are constantly coming to begin,
> I suggest solutions and
> am full of holes. See through me
> when my back is turned.
>
> A hotel is the notion of entrance
> by thought. Your love is

constantly a solution,
criminally full
of no difference
when my back is turned.

I read your thoughts because
you are constantly changing and
coming through me
when my back is turned. And

I want something
for something, constantly.
Coming. (*il cuore* 3)

The poem is itself a syntactical experiment, something like a postmodern villa-
nelle, with words and phrases repeated in shifting contexts. In the accretional
small shocks of this displacing echo, Fraser has indicated, she aimed "to under-
mine any single understanding" of certain words.[11] The echoing serves to expose
the "uneasy" apprehension of betrayal and duplicity. Fullness, for instance, is as-
sociated with void: "full of holes," "criminally full / of no difference." The pain-
ful permeability of the self—"See through me," "coming through me"—is accen-
tuated in the refrain suggesting treachery: "when my back is turned." The most
resonant echo is in the word "constantly." It means first "repeatedly" ("constantly
coming to begin"), with the sense of fruitless re-initiation; it then means "in-
variably" ("Your love is // constantly a solution"), here suggesting an ever-present
option for the obliteration of choice. The third use presses the irony within the
situation of erotic duplicity: "you are constantly changing"—invariably vari-
able. The last use is the only one suggesting an ordinary moral sense of the word:
"And // I want something / for something, constantly. / Coming." The word here
carries the other usages in the poem—repeatedly, invariably—but it also suggests
a permanence rooted in self, a recognition of the constancy of desire itself, aris-
ing precisely out of frustration with illusory gestures. This last line, too, com-
municates the nervy edge of frustration and desire, in both erotic and lexical
contexts. The difference between the first and last use of "constantly/coming" is
precisely this tense, estranging linguistic event, pushing and distorting bound-
aries to find an opening.
      A later poem, from *Notes Preceding Trust* (1987), makes clear that for Fraser
poetic experiment is fundamentally linked with the experiment of desire and
intimacy. "These labdanum hours" (*il cuore* 78) enacts and records an activity of
finding and making, in which the subtlest recognitions within desire require an

attentiveness and tenacity like that of writing itself. The first lines drop us into a search already underway: "You couldn't find it in the bird's weight / pulling an arc through the twig. You must // catch yourself somewhere or fall anywhere." And the pivotal question arising within this meditation reiterates the search: "What can you find in this // that is yours, wholly? A belief, / not to be divided into silken strands // in air." The poem constitutes this exploratory effort of finding, the lover/poet gradually awakening to the presence of "the helper" with "her rags and tools," who "[w]ith tenacity . . . hangs on to the dimming / vision." The mysterious time alluded to in the title, "labdanum hours," refers to the alternate dimension of consciousness both in erotic intimacy and in the process of poetic making. In the same way, the "belief, / not to be divided into silken strands // in air" represents a mysterious commitment belonging to both arenas. The stunning last line—"You were the lightest of all the silver-white metals"—is praise for the tactile, erotic, but reflective grace arriving in "these labdanum hours." But it suggests an alchemical finality of some kind, coming after a tenacious opus of desire and of imaginative making. The lover/poet from the beginning has been trying to find this phrase, which arrives as discovery and surprise. And the poem itself has exactly this quality of mercurial subtlety, as it probes an unnameable apprehension.

Fraser's recent writing engages more consciously a method begun in earlier series, beginning, perhaps, with the "Magritte Series" in *New Shoes:* to set up deliberately a lexical and formal context and to note the generated evidence: thus, "Four voices telling stories about dark and light," and thus "re:searches / (fragments after Anakreon)"; and thus "Five letters from one window, San Gimignano, May 1981." In these the laboratory arena is clearly delineated. With this increasing self-consciousness about the act of experiment comes an enlargement of the sphere of observation and analysis, coincident with Fraser's residence part of the year in Italy beginning in the early 1980s. Living in Rome, Fraser says in a recent interview, "has given me a much more living sense of history, and perhaps of the human habitation of myth . . . the 'livingness' of architecture, of historic events."[12]

Fraser's experimentation has never been bolder than in these recent poems. As Carolyn Burke points out: "While the theme of openness to the motions of the mind had long been key in her poetics, it was not until its means of expression joined form and content in this radically new work that Fraser's preeminence became apparent."[13] The four long poems in *When new time folds up*— "Etruscan Pages," "Giotto : Arena," "frammenti romani," and "when new time folds up"—as well as the more recent "WING," operate in one form or another through a textual, spatial layering of "evidence," which Fraser herself and Cynthia Hogue have associated with H.D.'s concept of palimpsest.[14] At the same time, however, the experiment in these poems is more powerfully than ever a line-sketch of *il cuore*. In fact, Jo Ann Ugolini's image of the heart—a kind of post-modern tragic mask—figures with sharp accuracy the emotional seriousness of Fraser's recent writing, as well as the sense of an improvised, rough, impure urban form. One of the most insistent figural and formal explorations of recent poetry is, indeed, the urban space of European cities.

The ragged and layered city represents another "structure of difficulty" analogous to that of the poem, in particular as it suggests the experience of "layered or constellated time" that Fraser has sought to investigate in her poetry.[15] Several poems replicate formally the complex experience of fragment and ruin, of broken-up and palimpsestic time that Fraser refers to in her comments on Rome. Many of these recent poems are, in fact, tied to Rome: "Etruscan Pages," written in "Trastevere (Rome), once called *Litus Etruscus*"; "when new time folds up," drawing from a circular path of travel, "Rome—Berlin—Wannsee—Rome"; and "WING," structured, in part, according to streets in Rome (Via Tasso, Via Vanvitelli, Via della Penitenza).[16] The city serves as an arena where the poet excavates the surfaces of the present, finding evidence of the missing and dead. In a sense, then, some of these poems are not only concerned with palimpsestic layering, but also with the loss and catastrophe residing within ruin and fragment. They are like H.D.'s imaginative engagement of the shattered city in the poems of *Trilogy*, where "ruin opens / the tomb" and where "through our desolation, / thoughts stir, inspiration stalks us / through gloom."[17] H.D. is revisited in this late poetry not only in providing a model of technical innovation—as Hogue has made clear[18]—but also in presenting an imaginative engagement with the devastations of this century.

These recent poems, even more than earlier ones, suggest the sober and dark qualities of *il cuore:* the experience of grief is evident in many of them, as both context and theme. In poems such as "frammenti romani" and "Giotto : Arena," Fraser finds pleasure in the "marks and evidence of events" of life in Rome or of art in Padua,[19] manifesting the sensuous exuberance and formal/syntactical playfulness that have always characterized her poetry. Even these poems, however, have an edge. "Gesture of damp gnawing grief" surfaces in "Giotto" (133), which is predicated upon the artist's (and the poet's) acceptance of the risk of accurate human notation. And "frammenti romani" concludes its exploration of tactile/verbal pleasures with an edge: "what is mortal / in this body."[20] But in other poems—such as "Etruscan Pages," "when new time folds up," and "WING" —the engagement with "marks and evidence of events" is darker in its implications. The author's notes to "Etruscan Pages" and to "WING" given in *il cuore* (196) suggest that with these poems a private grief has been crystallized by particular external encounters. But with all these poems, the feeling of loss is complex and manifold, coming from an awakened sense of history—the destruction of the civilization and language of the Etruscans, the residual memory of the Holocaust in both "when new time folds up" and "WING." Here, indeed, "new time folds up": the process of the poem, excavating the past, unfolds the pain of loss, but then folds it back in, so that, though hidden and unresolved, it forms part of the amalgam of the present.

Fraser's complex engagement in "Etruscan Pages" with the Etruscan *necropoli* of the Maremma, the coastal region north of Rome, represents an imaginative recovery of an ancient people accessible only through the images within their grave-houses. Hogue has insightfully explored the formal experimentation of the poem, which "posits 'herself' as site of an excavation . . . analogous to an archeological dig" and which employs the page as the deposit of disparate evidence of this exploration. Hogue calls this innovation "a revitalizing method of lexical juxtaposition/recasting and a formal coincidence of history, letters, languages, signs, normative grammatical and syntactical structures into a new space."[21] Indeed, the poem is so technically arresting that one only gradually grasps the feeling that compels the whole investigation. The poem opens with a sense of haunting—"In the ravine, a presence"—and it comes back again and again to the image of the stone bed, the "place they lay the dead one," the "places we longed for / where the dead lived under us" (*il cuore* 98, 99). This inexplicable longing compels research, conversations with friends, visits to an Etruscan museum; it generates dreams. And these "findings" are folded into the poem. The gradual recovery and exposure of the images of exuberant life within the small houses of the dead allow the poet to gain a complex proximity to the experience of grief. "Grief is simple and dark // as this bridge or hidden field / where something did exist once // and may again, or / your face receding behind the window // a possible emptying" (117).

The modern city requires another form of excavation—a reading of the hodgepodge surfaces to arrive at what is concealed in the poverty of craft and the despair of material expediency. In a recent poem, "The Disappeared,"[22] as in "Etruscan Pages," the meditation focuses upon architectural detail:

> entablature, missing elements, details
> that found the architect's practice

<><>

> a disappeared part   spirit to doorway's cornice
> column of all these unravelled cities

              (client more than satisfactory and anyway we are
                            overwhelmed   useless)

            run-after city   *all this belonged to us*
      we walked through the streets arm-in-arm

In this reading of architectural language in the constantly reconstructed city, poetic practice replicates the "architect's practice"—the lines as entablature here, or elsewhere in the poem as fragmented elements, column and wall.[23] The "missing," the "disappeared part," the sign of "all these unravelled cities," resides only as traces, obliterated and distorted architectural elements, within the overriding contemporary attention to surface and economy. This represents something like a loss of language, such as that of the Etruscans; beneath the lines of "plastic value," one can still read "canonical elements of the classical / language   even here, in the point of   disappearance . . ." With that loss of architectural language (here the "classical language" intrinsic to Rome) comes the loss of the place inhabited in memory: "*all this belonged to us / we walked through the streets arm-in-arm.*"

It is as though the imagination, alerted in the Maremma sites to "the places . . . where the dead lay under us," is haunted by the buried life of the city. Obliterated in the surface language are the vitality and pleasure to which memory attaches itself—"*all those green parrots gone wild*"—like the vivid images drawn within the houses of the dead in Vulci and Tarquinia. The poet's reading of architectural elements—here in words forming a wall—reveals absences beneath the surface:

    Deep signs in the form of our cities' exhausted daily craftsmen never reached
    Silence of the noisy and forced Houses with littered causeways Submerged city
    roughly put aside with slight regret Ecstatic tolerance for the shiny missing dead

This meditation on the contemporary city driven by material expediency touches upon a complex sense of unease: suppression of craft, a certain ruthlessness and carelessness of attention, distaste for memory disguised as consciousness of history. The reading of surface incongruities generates a fragmentary awareness of the "submerged city"—not nostalgically rooted in any historical paradigm (classical or baroque or fascist), but in the possibility of simple human "ownership"— "*all this belonged to us*"—the possibility of a space for the untamed particular, "parrots slashing / through curved light bent and wrinkled // in the beloved unadorned."

Other reflections on the contemporary city in "when new time folds up" and "WING" are, once again, simultaneous with formal experimentation. And, as much as any poems in *il cuore*, these carry the form of Ugolini's fragmented image of the heart, an image at the threshold between private and public experience. These poems are in some senses companion pieces: both set in contemporary Rome but enlarged in reference to modern European history, specifically the Holocaust. But thematically and formally—one might say—they represent the two sides of the Dionysus mask. In "when new time," the compulsive and disintegrative rubble of daily life is rendered as disturbing, tilted-forward-and-falling lineation; in "WING," the constructive and transformative agency of change figured in art is rendered at times in the form of strictly shaped geometrical segments.[24]

"when new time folds up" might also bear the title of one of Fraser's early poems: "Uneasy Songs." The form and lineation of these curtal sonnets—a half-line short of sonnet form, and usually a syllable or two short of sonnet line-length—reflects a sense of the contemporary moment. Here is the opening sonnet, entitled "understood and scrupulous":

I would have stayed at home as   rehearsal
                                                                          food
if a bystander plated in gold,
understood and scrupulous among
metal bowls, but a doctor goes
to the Gymnasium where scale is   in key
brick to the heart and air com-
pletely empties itself, without
gender'd regard, thus I tried
my luck as "you," in neutral,
running with you as we talked,
inside the blue grape hyacinth   represses
where nature reproduces its
mechanical force, *rughetta*
wild in tomb grass, (*il cuore* 138)

The just-too-shortness of each line propels one vertiginously into the next, and the just-too-shortness of the sonnet as a whole—each last half-line ending with a comma—also throws one forward to the next in the series. At the same time, the lines shift and slide abruptly from one facet of consciousness to another; Fraser calls this a kind of enjambment of perceptions, without "a linear or logical development."[25] The form succeeds brilliantly in creating a kind of temporal claustrophobia, refusing to the reader any point of pause or deliberation, and rather giving the impression of imbalance, compulsion, relentlessness of forward movement—"a certain uneven panic" (139) as time crazily folds up, line by adumbrated line. In keeping with this sense of confinement, and with the violence alluded to in the poems, some fragmentary words and phrases are blasted to the right margin, a visualization, in Fraser's words, of "a condition of rubble and disintegration in the language."[26]

The syntactical play in the poems resembles that in the early poem "What I Want," in that words and phrases are repeated from one poem to another with disturbing shifts of context, so that eventually certain irrepressible images and questions emerge as points of serious engagement in the series. The figure in the first poem of the woman doctor insecure in her own authority, falling back upon clinical detachment, becomes a reiterated motif finally associated with the position of the poet herself: "small body / . . . runs / for stethoscope sanction" (140); "never sensing her struggle for / authority" (141); "caught in rescuing / the authority of her task" (150); "In the authority of my task" (151). So, too, in the first poem, the "heart" crushed by oppressive scale and impersonality becomes a motif: "where scale is brick to the heart"; "heartbeat crumpled neatly / on white card" (139); then the word "crumpled" is repeated, suggesting this sense of private poverty in the context of overmastering authority.

More broadly, this first poem opens questions that gain increasing seriousness as the scenes jump recurrently to Wannsee, where Hitler contrived the "Final Solution," to images from the German concentration camps, and, back in Italy, to the murder of Judge Falcone in Palermo by the Mafia, and, throughout, to images of the rubble of buildings. The opening poem initially poses the choice of remaining "a bystander plated in gold, / understood and scrupulous"—the choice to be the eternal, disengaged attendant. But a similar detachment of the doctor in this initial poem resembles the objectivity of those directing Jews in the camps: "Come forward five at a time" (144). In contrast, the poet chooses a more difficult witness position, testifying to the vulnerability of the heart, of "*rughetta* / wild in tomb grass" that stands as "resistance" to nature's "mechanical force." In later sonnets, she refuses the position of bystander, engaging images of the terror of those in the camps, the courage of Falcone confronting the Mafia: "decision to / persist, no *kinder* even, passion / vigilant, this *amore per la vita*" (147). The sonnet sequence enacts the ruthlessness and pathological distraction that seems to compel contemporary life (Rome, Berlin, Wannsee, Palermo). But in so doing the poet confirms a role of moral accountability in acknowledging repressed layers of violence and vulnerability: "In the authority of my task, a city's constant / and hidden remorse beneath construction" (151).

The powerful recent poem "WING" continues this emphasis upon the "authority of her task," and it also leads us back to a consideration of Fraser's consistent orientation and practice. Taking cues from contemporary artwork, from a contemplation of the iconography of angels, and from her own personal mourning,[27] Fraser in this poem reflects upon the startling emergence of the New out of a matrix of contingencies and accidents. She figures the construction of the New in art is a coming-into-body of the angel—the ancient messenger who breaks through the mundane and shatters its boundaries. What she considers here is not the angel as a metaphysical concept, but the angel's wing as a constant sign in iconography of the mortal particularities out of which dreams of annunciation and epiphany come. The wings particularize themselves out of the complex needs, desires, and pain of the human.

The prolonged, suspended opening lines themselves give the sense of startling emergence:

The New comes forward in its edges in order to be itself;

its volume by necessity becomes violent and three-dimensional
and ordinary, all similar models shaken off and smudged

as if memory were an expensive thick creamy paper and every
corner turned now in partial erasure,

even bits of pearly rubber, matchstick and lucent plastic
leaving traces of decision and little tasks performed

as if each dream or occasion of pain had tried to lift itself
entirely away, contributing to other corners, planes and
accumulated depth (*il cuore* 184)

These lines make clear the emphasis within Fraser's experimental poetics: that "the New" in art is more than a matter of technical sophistication; rather, it is a complex, arduous embodiment, coming into being in the context of memory, pain, and mysterious urgency. The wing—this figure for the New—bears the marks and evidence of events: it "is not static but frayed, layered, fettered, furling and / stony," tattered, intricate, mobile and rigid. However transcendent the angel as concept, the constantly imagined wing points to the contingencies of the mortal being; it is "attached to its historic tendons; more elaborate / the expansive ribcage, grieving, stressed, yet // marked midway along the breastbone with grains of light" (184). Attachment, rather than detachment, is the characteristic of the wing, its claim to truth: "Even the New is attached or marked by attachment // the shimmer of wing, which claim may tell us everything / in a white blink" (188).

These opening lines also point to another aspect of Fraser's poetics: that art, poetry, represents "traces of decision and little tasks performed." This ethical dimension of choice and acceptance of claims—the claims of others, the claims of the life of writing—is central to Fraser's work and career, tying together the earliest poetry with the latest, uniting the discrete experiments in individual volumes with her teaching and with her public advocacy of women's experimental writing. The "glowing evidence" of the New for which Fraser waits has shifted over time in its character and shape, but her late writing in particular shows an expansiveness and depth of discovery. The last page of Fraser's selected poems (193), a shape form of an angel's wing composed of accumulated fragmentary words and phrases from "WING," presents another figure of *il cuore*. The descending or diminishing wing repeats a phrase signaling loss: "forward edge itself to be volume by necessity as if by partial erase." The ascending wing counterbalances this diminishment with acts of attention, "lucent decision and little tasks of pain had tried to lift." This concluding image is evidence both of Fraser's experimentation, her insistence upon the "New [coming] forward in its edges," and of the rootedness of that experiment in contingencies, in "the wing not static but frayed, layered, fettered, furling and / stony."

Asterisk: Separation at the Threshold of Meaning in the Poetry of Rae Armantrout

Ron Silliman

By comradeship and publication history, Rae Armantrout has long been associated with the tendency characterized as language poetry. Yet she has sometimes been read as a border case or problematic instance of the phenomenon. Implicit within the question "Why don't women do language-oriented writing?"—the title of her best-known critical piece, first published in 1978, a response to something that had even then already been asked of her more than once—are two interlocking presumptions: that Rae Armantrout doesn't "do" language-oriented writing, and that she nonetheless has a relationship to that literary movement that empowers her to speak with insight and privilege concerning its internal terms and conditions. Twenty years ago, Armantrout punctured the balloon of that curious logic by noting that a wide range of women writers—her list may be a little overly expansive, just to reinforce the point—do investigate various issues of language in their poetry. Armantrout then went on to discuss in somewhat greater detail the work of Susan Howe, Carla Harryman and Lyn Hejinian, three women closely linked to langpo in its heroic phase.

Although Armantrout wrote that the work she preferred is "ambi-centric" (as if a concern for language needed to be balanced by one also for the world, as though language were not a part of reality but a competing realm), she was silent in the essay about her own work and its relationship to either language or the movement that came to be identified by that term. That silence, indeed silence itself, turns out to be a characteristic Armantrout gesture.

Perhaps I should use a different tense—*is turning out to be a characteristic Armantrout gesture.* Armantrout's use of silence, of gaps, breaks and the unsaid over time has evolved. Her poems today are more apt to come in numbered sections or with the not quite ubiquitous asterisk that leaps out from her books, cleaving segment from segment.

If we divide Armantrout's work into two periods of roughly 14 years each,

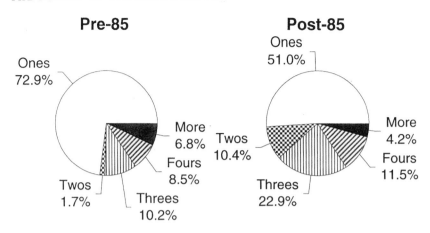

Fig. 1

we discover—in addition to the fact that Armantrout, unlike many poets, has picked up the pace of production as she has matured, having written and published 99 poems after *Precedence*, compared with just 60 combined in her first three books[1]—that the likelihood that a poem will have multiple sections, either numbered or divided by asterisks, rises nearly 81 percent. The chart (Figure 1) groups the poems of each period by the number of sections: onesies, twosies, et cetera.

The first thing one notices about a poem that arrives at its conclusion in segments, particularly when it is short,[2] is its constructedness. It is difficult to feign the simple, single voice of the writing workshop monologue if in fact the work in front of the reader arrives visibly in pieces. Wallace Stevens understood as much and thus, with a few specific exceptions such as "Like Decorations in a Nigger Cemetery," his numbered works were often the ones to most heavily rely on the first person singular (and sometimes plural) or, as in "Esthétique du Mal," "he." Had Armantrout been one of the high modernists, her sense of the section might have been much closer to the geotechtonic plates of which one is sometimes reminded when reading, say, the ambitious early works of Eliot (especially Eliot as edited by Pound).

Even in the shortest works, Armantrout's instinct for a poetry of edges, a jagged indeterminacy, leaps out. Consider Stevens again, with an early poem, "Life Is Motion":

In Oklahoma,
Bonnie and Josie,
Dressed in calico,
Danced around a stump.

They cried,
"Ohoyaho,
Ohoo" . . .
Celebrating the marriage
of flesh and air.[3]

Compare this work with one of Armantrout's earliest efforts, "Generation":

We know the story.

She turns
back to find her trail
devoured by birds.

The years; the
undergrowth[4]

At first glance, both poems look straightforward enough. Reading closer, how-ever, reveals depths not immediately apparent in each. For Stevens, much de-pends upon "Ohoyaho," which may or may not be a Native American lyric and, if it is, may or may not be "authentic," depending on whose authenticity (Stevens's or that of Bonnie and Josie) the reader envisions to be at stake. Are the two fig-ures children or adults, native or Anglo? How the reader answers those questions will determine which nuances appear in the hinge word, "marriage."

Armantrout's poem similarly relies upon the reader's interpretation of a de-tail not given. The title suggests that the "years" of the third stanza represent precisely the crumbs "devoured by birds," and that "She" in turn cannot re-turn to her youth. But, by both punctuation and stanzaic grouping, "The years" is linked not to the devoured trail but to a completely different detail—"the / undergrowth"—a phrase that doesn't so much undercut the initial reading as it does twist it, invoking both the visual forest scene of "trail" and the passage of time not as a disappearance but as the past's obliteration through the accumula-tion of sheer detail.

Each poem resonates with the undecidable. In one sense, Armantrout's writ-ing is more economic than that of Stevens: if his opening, "In Oklahoma," isn't intended to suggest an almost cartoon sense of "the West," setting up in advance the Native American aura that will surround the "nonsense" calling five and six lines later (just as "calico" seems to set up "childhood"), then his writing is casual to the point of sloppiness. If it is intended to achieve these effects, then it's Stevens thinking and attitudes that come across as questionable.

Armantrout's poem, in contrast, leaves the reader with a sense of incompletion and awkwardness that invokes the emotions of panic and loss "She" feels discovering that there can be no road back. Right at what should have been the moment of closure, Armantrout has complicated the poem's narrative machinery and deliberately left it hanging. It's a more powerful, more disturbing effect, but one achieved by robbing the poem of a value that someone like Stevens would find essential to his sense of craft.

Only at the moment of ellipsis itself does "Life Is Motion" demonstrate anything even remotely like a gap between statements. An image is presented, against which a homily is offered.[5] Only in his next to last line—where its absence serves to underscore the key term in the poem—does Stevens forego terminal punctuation. Punctuation in fact serves to balance and order the lines.

Just two of Armantrout's six lines have terminal punctuation, each a stanza closing period. In what was an almost obsessive device of her early work—only six of the 32 poems in *Extremities* conclude with punctuation—she uses an absence of any period in the final line after the deliberately gaudy semicolon in theone immediately above to leave the reader off-center, unsettled at the end. Punctuation is utilized to create balance in this piece and others of that period in order for Armantrout to send it spinning off wildly by the poem's end.

If anything, "Generation" unravels closure by reversing the order of expectation, starting with a moment of maximum containment: the assertion of a tale we all already know. The second strophe presents a single detail specifying *which* story. This detail, one gesture, provides character, movement, context, and history—the past is troubled, the future bleak—an economy of information that is virtually Armantrout's signature.

As "Ohoyaho" demonstrates, in the short poem it is the word, phrase or trope that stands out of place, unexplained, "unmotivated" as the Russian formalists would have put it, that in actuality organizes the reader's experience. In "Generation," this same function is served by "The years"—the phrase can be read as referring to any number of things, although only the title itself directly implies time.[6] This link is what brings the title literally into the poem—as distinct from Stevens's homily. But Armantrout undercuts the phrase immediately, yoking "the / undergrowth" to it with an aggressive semicolon, ending the next to last line on the article, leaving the final word and line hanging.

I read "undergrowth" as a deliberately vulnerable term, alluding back both to the story of the trail through the forest—no forest has been mentioned, although it seems clearly implied by the second stanza—*and* to "The years." The phrase situates itself between these two decidedly different schema, the depicted tale and a temporal theme, refusing to resolve itself in favor of one or the other. What is being said about time? That one can't go back? It may be as simple as that, and

yet the air of claustrophobia given off by what feels like a broken ending drives
these two discursive lines together with great force.

"Generation" is a characteristic Armantrout piece in that it offers only the
most minimal narrative or figurative context for the work—it seems perfectly
reasonable to argue, for example, that time is the subject of this poem and that
the story we know is in fact the metaphor. Figure and ground seem as reversible
here as in the image that oscillates between a candlestick and the silhouettes of
two faces. It is precisely the presence of two thematic lines, neither of which
directly addresses the other, that gives this poem its motive energy. It's as if each
theme inhabits the other: the reader feels the energy demanded settling into a
sense of which is which. Having read this poem literally hundreds of times over
a quarter of a century, I still sense my disquiet at having to "make sense," at
feeling forced to choose which line to treat as the theme and which as the com-
ment upon it. That disquiet is deliberate on Armantrout's part.

I wanted to begin with a reading of a piece that uses no visible marks for its
gaps as a means of having a point of comparison for other works that do. Here
is "A Pulse," chosen at random, from *Made to Seem:*

Find the place
in silence
that is a person

or like a person
or like not
needing a person.
*

After the heart attack
she fills her apartment
with designer accents—

piece by piece.
*

This is a bed,
an abiding
at least,

close to *lastly,*
but nicer.
*

Light changes:

Separation
anxiety refers
to this

as next
tears itself off.
*

A hospital calendar
shows the sun going down
on an old-time
round, lime-green
diner.
*

Just a quick trip back
to mark the spot
where things stop
looking familiar.[7]

Again, an almost archetypal Armantrout work in which a simple surface covers vertical silos of meaning rendered even more dizzying for their combination of depth and economy. The first of its six sections initially seems to offer three choices. But, as Armantrout's readers have come to expect, relatively little is as straightforward as it appears. To begin, the reader is asked to identify a physical location within temporality and to identify this with three possibilities. But the possibilities are not at all equivalent. The contrast between the first pair—"is a person // or like a person"—plays rather gently with our recognition that there can, literally speaking, be no such place "in silence" and that what are being offered here are a series of figures: the metaphor of the first option, an equation in the world, replaced in the second by an equation in language, a simile. The next line—"or like not"—prepares us for a twist, but not at all the twist that's coming: "needing a person." Armantrout, with the insertion of a single term, transforms the section into something infinitely more complicated and ambivalent. The section, if not the entire poem (about which it's much too early to speak), suddenly is not about time or space, as such, but about need, which invokes a wide range of possible reactions, including loneliness and loss. How is "a person" like "not / needing a person"? Is this a statement of fulfillment or isolation? Up to this point we are given no clues. The title, "A Pulse," suggests both the presence of a person —the way a doctor might recognize one—and a temporal phenomenon not unlike the problem stated in the first part of this section: we distinguish the pulse through rhythm, each one separated by precisely that "place / in silence" between beats. How, between beats, might we recognize the presence of a person or something "like a person"?[8]

There are any number of alternative potential narratives that might explicate at least the context in which we are intended to read the first section. Armantrout breaks the poem with an asterisk before offering any, and then in the next section appears to offer the simplest explanation possible—a heart attack. The event itself is figured in the past tense, a beat we've already missed, offering instead the narrative of a woman—the first moment of gender in the poem—as she "fills an apartment." At one level, this depiction presents an absolutely narrative moment, a character in action. At a second level, however, this line offers not one, but two almost intangible puns that refer back to the first section. Silence, after all, like "not / needing a person," is an empty state, an absence. "Fills" is exactly how one might respond to such isolation, literally an "apart ment."

The connotative reverberations here are delicious enough that we don't even need to know that "apartment" is setting up the consonants p and t for a critical role later in the poem. Yet what is the apartment being filled with but "designer accents." And how? "Piece by piece," a phrase that resists telling us too much, such as what pieces of what, while both echoing the rhythm of a heart beat and characterizing the progress of the poem itself. Even in the plainest depiction, we find Armantrout writing to the reader on several dimensions simultaneously. She makes it look so easy!

The third section presents the reader with a completely different scene, figured by a single object with no context whatsoever. The poem now proceeds along what the linguist Jakobson would have called a euphonic[9] path, not that far from the rhetorical one that the first section initially appeared to take: "a bed" leads to "an abiding," "at least" to "lastly." Here consonants predict consonants, while vowels offer variation, a dance of difference. "Bed" is a term that could mean anything, an object that can be found in an apartment, a setting in which a pulse itself might be taken, a place where one might, or might not, need a person. All of these meanings are active, perceptible but not fixed. An adjectival phrase used here in the nominative, "an abiding" may follow from "a bed" as sound,[10] but it presents a very different set of connotations. The three definitions offered for "abiding" by the Random House Dictionary of the English Language are "continuing without change; enduring; steadfast," terms of continuity that clash with the concept of a pulse, sequential alternations of beat and silence. "An abiding" suggests acceptance, one possible way of reading "not / needing a person." It is this connotation of acceptance that I hear in "at least," the next line, emphasized by italics. The use of "close to" in the next line calls attention to the linguistic strategy of the section as it takes to "lastly," one of the—if not the— most opaque terms in this text. What does it mean to be abiding lastly? An adverb to describe an adjective used as a noun, the construction is so self-consciously awkward as to bring the reader up short. One possible reading would be "at last," while a very different interpretation would be "at the end." Armantrout's use of "but nicer" in the last line of this section shifts our interpretation part of the way toward the latter interpretation, but certainly not decisively. She wants us to be aware of the more grim interpretation, but resists the idea of fixing our reading.

Another asterisk moves us to the next section. By now, the reader is aware that the poem is in no way a straightforward narrative, although it is manifestly evident that linkages are taking place on many levels at once. There is a sense of ongoing coherence but nothing in the way of determinate direction. We cannot at this point imagine where the poem might end up, even as we are entertaining many possible directions. Armantrout seems to me unique in her ability to delay this sense of directedness in her work without losing the tangible evidence of internal connectivity many readers require as a prerequisite for their trust. Even poets who work with a much larger canvas—Olson, for example—would by now have committed themselves not simply to a unitary sense of visual shape on the page (our first recognition of form), but to many, if not most (if not all) of the primary terms of the work, and would have done so in such a way that the process of reading the latter half of the poem, in fact of reading the latter half of most poems, is largely a question of the reader's following the predictable trail of crumbs as the poet works through the problems he or she has already set out, an end game not unlike chess.

Each section in "A Pulse," at least thus far, reads as though it were its own separate canvas, aimed at a subject that may or may not be identified in the title. As with the bed of the previous section, the first line here also provides us with what appears to be a detail: "Light changes." Again we have an assertion of time described indirectly as though that in itself constituted narrative motion. As with the designer accents of the second section, light is something that occurs only as a conjunction—it demands a light source and objects to be illuminated (which can be as large as the sky or as small as some point on my desk). We recognize light not so much in itself as in its effects.

So it is only as the section unfolds that we begin to realize that the first line can be read another way, one in which "changes" is a plural noun, something distinct, say, from "heavy changes." As in the poem "Generation" nearly twenty years earlier, Armantrout uses internal punctuation with this first line's colon as a deliberately gaudy device; she starts the next strophe with a capital letter where not only is one not needed, but its use also contrasts directly with her use of capitalization in the previous sections—"Separation" is all the more cleaved from the first phrase, even as it remains a part of the same sentence. Immediately in the next line—"anxiety refers"—we recognize that the noun before was in fact an adjective, one that invokes every kind of grammatical twist we have thus far come across: one it takes us right back to is the use of "not" in the initial segment, both for its own sense of anxiety and for the use of a linebreak to alter expectation. And just as this line begins with a broken subject, it closes with a snapped predicate, enjambed at every margin, rendering it perhaps the least stable line in the poem, the one we are most apt to glide right past. "Separation / anxiety refers / to this," the stanza continues, an anaphoric harking back to "light changes," but also to the metalinguistic nature of language, yet another instance of Armantrout's wry humor, readable even as an allusion to the magazine once edited by Barrett Watten and Bob Grenier. What is driven almost from view here is the persistent question of *separation from what?* Once again Armantrout has written around something without precisely naming it, a strategy of omission that she foregrounds in the following stanza, "as next / tears itself off." I don't think there is any way to read the first word in that second line as a noun, even as we've anticipated one there, which turns our attention back to "next," and changes it from adjective into noun. The broken aspect of the line ending redoubles our sense of the cleavage described next.

Armantrout's sense of how far she can let the reader move toward a purely abstract writing can be tested by the fifth section, a magnificent single sentence stanza that is the most visual segment of the work. Like a painting by Edward Hopper, the scene is frozen: nothing more happens than the depiction of a scene on a calendar. Yet Armantrout ratchets up the prosodic axis of the poem, packing it with an extraordinary sequence of *o* sounds, rhyming "time" and "lime" so that the following "green" virtually leaps off the page—our first moment of color in the text—leading to the curiously situated final term "diner," the third object (after "hospital calendar" and "sun") in this one stanza. The *d* of "diner" is set up by the two terminal *d* sounds of "old" and "round" (just as they were set up by "down" earlier), so that we hear the difference of the word starting, rather than closing, on the hard sound, rendering the liquid *r* all the more audible. Similarly, "diner" takes the *d* away from its association with the vowel *o*, pulling forward the long *i* from "time" and "lime," accenting the difference with the *e* of "green." After the explicit invocation of "hospital" in the first line, it's impossible not to hear the echo of "die" in "diner." That echo pulls the pulse, the heart attack, even separation anxiety all into place. The reader at this moment may well assume that the subject of the poem is death.

The reader would not be that far off—death or its anticipation is at least the context. Armantrout has yet another piece to play before "A Pulse" is done. Like the fifth segment, this section also occurs as a single stanza heavily structured by the organization of consonants, in this case *k*, *p*, and *t*. Hard sounds are everywhere and the first twelve words are each exactly one syllable long, a device that readers with historical memory will associate with the late Lew Welch. Seven of the twelve words even end with a hard stop.[11] Long vowels have virtually disappeared from the first three lines, with only the slightest echo lingering in "to." After the trio of terminal *k* sounds, the reversal of consonants between "spot" and "stop" sets up the final line, which sounds radically different: here there is only one hard consonant, a *k* contained between the double *o* and long *i* sound of "looking." Liquids are everywhere.

Looking is of course what so much of this poem has been about: identifying that "place / in silence," adding designer accents, changing light and the hard-edged depiction of the calendar. "Light changes," as the line said, a point beyond which one cannot exactly return. That point, the pulse, is precisely a moment of separation, an apart / ment. This is in fact why (and how) the least stable line in this poem is the closest thing to a topic sentence, the credo of the text: "anxiety refers."

It would, I suppose, be possible to tell some version of this "tale" in a normative, continuous narrative. We can imagine how some very similar point could be made in the poetry of a Mark Doty, a Robert Hass, even conceivably a Philip Levine. Yet of course it could never have been the same poem. The form of the work in Armantrout's hands embodies an anxiety over nextness without reducing it to a demonstration of structure as theme. The poem is disjunctive at the level of the segment. The relation of one to the next is paratactic—yet like parataxis in the hands of any great postmodern practitioner, that democracy of units is by no means arbitrary in its order. Remove any of the six segments and you have an entirely different work. Put them into a different sequence and the actual articulation of the poem would dissolve.[12] As much as fire or any other unilateral physical process, "A Pulse" is a demonstration of time as motivated direction. Time itself, the poem seems to argue, has meaning.

"Locks," from *Necromance,* is a poem that uses numbers to segregate its four sections.

1
Place things
in relation
when I want them
permanent.

Curved
rose vine, a
standing wave.

2
Traffic
in surplus meaning
quite heavy of late.

Bulbs light up
on the cactus-shaped
                    facade.

3
Binary
alterations which
appear
to undulate,

sounded as if from
successive landings.

4
When to notice
something further
is to take a sacrament.

Ritual switch.
Photos of lighthouses
line the walls
        of banks.[13]

Armantrout has written privately "I think of the numbers, when they occur, as separating more completely than the asterisks."[14] While the asterisk is invariably situated midway between two segments of a work—this is true not just for Armantrout—numbers bond to the section that follows, an attachment that lends them a pseudo-naming function. The segment is thus more completely bracketed.[15] Without submitting "Locks" to the same sort of close reading given to "Generation" and "A Pulse," it seems evident enough that the poem may be more relaxed than the other two, even as it makes excellent use of very similar devices and strategies, not the least of which is the pun in the title between that object which fixes something into place "permanent" and those "ritual switches" such as we find in canals that toggle one to another, further condition, "successive landings," resisting precisely the permanence identified as desire in section

1. If there is a greater segregation of individual sections in "Locks" than in "A Pulse," it is because the referential dimension of the piece is far less focused: the lighthouse photo on the bank wall may be no less tacky than the bulbs on the "cactus-shaped / facade"—and it is certainly possible to read "standing wave" as an allusion to the classic Japanese painting that has become every editorial cartoonist's knee-jerk characterization of the Asian monetary crisis—but their point of commonality, American kitsch, is as vast a discursive terrain as exists.

Even if we turn to a work whose title seems to proclaim its disjunctiveness, such as "Entries: look," from *Precedence*,[16] we find in fact while its six numbers may create a greater sense of space between individual sections, elements within them absolutely bind the text together, in this case a "voice" constructed entirely from capital letters that shows up in four of the poem's segments, with questions and commands such as "ARE YOU SICK OF ME?" and "DON'T LOOK AT ME LIKE THAT!" Reminiscent of a shrill tone that sometimes turns up in the writing of Hannah Weiner, these comments, always tabbed in away from the left margin, provide the work with a continuity that is inescapable. Indeed, continuity in "Entries: look" seems synonymous with paranoia.

Armantrout's poetry, whether in its more serious modes or even in a lighter poem such as "Locks," often focuses or turns on questions of order. The title *Precedence* admits as much. In the range between what at least appears to be a completely happenstance accumulation of "occasional" verse—Ted Berrigan's "Tambourine Life," Robert Creeley's *Pieces* or Robert Grenier's aggressively arbitrary shuffle-the-cards approach to the box Sentences—and the strict expository ordering of George Oppen's "Of Being Numerous," Armantrout, like Lyn Hejinian or Barrett Watten, comes down on the side of organization. But sequencing serves Armantrout differently than it does someone like Oppen, even if, as was also true for Oppen, the use of segments is a way for a writer whose instinct is for the short form to build up a larger text. Oppen states his themes clearly either in his titles or at the beginning of poems. Armantrout is almost always indirect. For Oppen, the poem itself is an elaboration or demonstration, and segmentation in his work is at least as much about balance and pacing as it is a mechanism to shift scene and discourse.[17] For Armantrout, the structure is almost always in the opposite direction—we have to actually read the poem in order to gain some sense what it may be "about."

I'm deliberately comparing Armantrout here with some of the finest writers of the century in order to make it clear that such emphases aren't a matter of a better or worse way to write poetry. Rather, it's a question of sensibility. If, as is now apparent, what was known, however unwillingly, as language poetry was a series of different tendencies tied together loosely by an indebtedness to the New Americans of the post-WW2 period and an attention to the role of language in the construction of meaning; what seems today of greater interest and import is how those tendencies increasingly differentiate themselves as these writers go forward in time. Armantrout is quite clearly a poet for whom parataxis is a fundamental condition of perception. But her writing, as it continues to evolve, has little if anything in common with some other highly paratactic poets—for example, Bruce Andrews. It is not merely that Armantrout (although she has demonstrated, at least briefly, an ability to turn up the volume in her text to a degree we associate with Andrews) doesn't go for the in-your-face assault that is Andrews's preferred designer accent, but rather that in her divisions between sections she identifies a place within meaning—a suspension—that seems not to be capable of articulation in any other way. It is that moment when, during any experience that is new and undigested, details flood in, awaiting the gestalt organization of data into something recognized and subject to being categorized, an instant that is privileged by parataxis. Often, as in "A Pulse," each section will arrive at a threshold only to have the segment stop right there as the poem shifts to an entirely new scene and discourse. Connotation seems about to break into denotation *and yet.* . . . To accomplish this requires a certain degree of holding meaning back—the same impulse is implicit even in an unsectioned work such as "Generation." What is being "depicted" in such gaps is not the leap from segment to segment, but rather the moment before, that condition of readiness and anticipation. Often it feels exactly like anxiety, which, as we know, automatically *refers* as its mechanism of escape. But where Andrews seems to want us to feel anxiety as a condition imposed by external sources, and where referral and shifting in his work are rapid-fire, Armantrout repeatedly holds us right at the point before the leap, forcing the reader to pay attention to the impulse within, that "place / within silence."

Alice Notley's Experimental Epic: "An Ecstasy of Finding Another Way of Being"

Susan McCabe

Alice Notley's *The Descent of Alette* was first published in its entirety in a some-what obscure work, *The Scarlet Cabinet: A Compendium Books*, containing writing also by Douglas Oliver (Scarlet Editions, 1992). While a portion of the long poem appeared in Notley's *Selected Poems* (1993), it has only recently become more widely available in the present complete edition.[1] Notley is most often thought of in connection with her late husband Ted Berrigan (who died in 1983), both poets positioned as belonging to the so-called second generation of New York School poets (among their poetic predecessors and mentors were Frank O'Hara, James Schuyler, Kenneth Koch and John Ashbery). Throughout Notley's impressive and prolific career of over sixteen volumes of poetry, she has marked herself as writing in the American grain of the idiomatic, spontaneous and anti-academic. This reputation obscures how the poet's experimentation often emerges with a feminist perspective. The slow surfacing of *Descent*, Notley's most ambitious work to date, is perhaps due to Notley's overt combination of experimental use of epic form along with an unabashed feminism, an element more understated in her earlier work.

This essay will examine how Notley explicitly *enacts* the aesthetic and generic question of whether or not women can write the epic. In the process, she explores the enmeshment of poetic and bodily forms. Breaking into what has been a per-vasively masculinist realm, Notley's poem, in the tradition of Dante's *Inferno*, depicts a purgatorial descent which spans four books. An idiosyncratic, poten-tially distracting use of quotation marks as her primary grammatical device (which I will need say much more about later) reflects her double position as a woman poet: she reveals how quotation usually signals citational authority, but here it ruptures the line, thus fragmenting image and narrative, unsettling epic voice and legitimacy.

Instead of featuring a male epic hero, the work follows Alette in her quest to "confront" "& vanquish" the Tyrant, a figure who loosely yet distinctly represents manifold manifestations of patriarchy. Alette's descent takes her from the more recognizable world of the subway system ("Down" "is now the only way" "to rise" 26) to the baroque circuitry of a "deeper," "unilluminated place," a network of very fleshly caves or grottoes (she enters one after another as if entering a series of flickering cinemas) in the second book; by the penultimate book, after she has undergone and witnessed various transmutations of bodily form, she comes into contact with "our" decapitated "first mother" as well as a father/guide in the form of an owl (once a man, whose death liberated him into "an ecstasy" "of finding" "another way" / "of being" 102) in order to plunge in the fourth book into the lowest depth of the Tyrant's basement apparently to uproot his power and dominance.

Notley's poetic project fuels itself by a kind of ecstatic search for new ways of being, reimagined ways of inhabiting a gendered world. Indeed, the break into the epic has serious stakes in connection with embodiment. Notley reuses the epic form to look for a new corps, both in the sense of the corpse of the exclusively male epic and of the reimagined outlines of her self-fashioned poetic body. The poem relies upon descent, and upon the choice to leave the subway "for another," "deeper," "unillumined place," "where all is" / "uncharted" (41). With this self-proclaimed pioneering, Notley manages a difficult duet: to be almost uncompromisingly philosophical and intensely ludic, an element that she distinctively employs to undermine the high seriousness of traditional epic. For instance, Alette and a companion in Book Two detach their sex organs and insert them into malleable clay walls: in this characteristically ribald, fantastical passage, Alette's post-sexual confusion ("I couldn't think" "at all" "Was formless" "was in chaos" 57) makes her anxious to retrieve her vagina. While sex here seems integral to identity, the text struggles with the timely question of whether or not sexuality and gender are constructed, and, therefore, reconstructable. While there are many lyric epics by male writers (including T. S. Eliot, Hart Crane and Ezra Pound) in the twentieth century, these texts do not use lyricism to question the masculinist biases of epic form.

Along with the pairing of the philosophical with the ludic, Notley also undermines the polarization between narrative and lyric prominent in recent poetry criticism. As Susan Stanford Friedman has articulated, post-structuralists "Barthes, Kristeva, Cixous all variously associate narrative" with "repressive social order that the lyric and the poem can potentially disrupt."[2] In searching out a new textual body for the epic, Notley doesn't abandon narrative, but as Friedman suggests about other women's long poems, enters into a "dialectical play between narrative and lyric" in part because of the "need for narrative based in traditional Western exclusions of women from subjectivity and from the discourses of both myth and history."[3] The poet must, in these terms, "enter" these excluding realms and refashion them from within.

Notley's experiment is then two-fold: genre and form must be reworked and reembodied as the necessarily simultaneous reworking of so-called narrative content, those elements familiar to us from epic that contribute to structuring and maintaining social and gender relations. And the constitution of these relations extends back further than the Dantean journey and quest so resonant here. The Odyssean hero, for instance, is endowed with the ability to move and to act, to overthrow obstacles, to aggressively supplant enemies, and to defeat those fatal attractions that threaten to reduce masculine power and mobility. These characteristics belong to the epic apparatus that traditionally scripts women as acted-upon rather than as actors. Notley's work qualifies as experiment because so few texts have managed by the end of the twentieth century to devise a female "hero" or to reuse epic as feminist or, more significantly, to radically question the constrictive modes of embodiment and gender imbricated in epic claims. In undertaking to regenerate old forms and plots, to put them in critical quotation, she takes on a monumental task. She takes on both the Homeric and Oedipal heroes, who while not interchangeable, belong to a foundational and dominant narrative model that foregrounds male desire; furthermore, in revising her epic, she undermines Plato's legacies of female disembodiment that install and reify the centrality of the male hero in post-Homeric long poems.

Notley's book opens in medias res, placing readers immediately into the mysterious, the strangely familiar:

"One day, I awoke" "& found myself on" "a subway, endlessly"
"I didn't know" "how I'd arrived there or" "who I was" "exactly"
"But I knew the train" "knew riding it" "knew the look of"
"those about me" "I gradually became aware—" "though it seemed"

 as that happened" "that I'd always" "known it too—" "that there was"
"a tyrant" "a man in charge of" "the fact" "that we were"
"below the ground" "endlessly riding" "our trains, never surfacing"
"A man who" "would make you pay" "so much" "to leave the subway" (3)

The text persuades us of piecemeal consciousness through incantatory but fragmented repetition; her imagery dazzles with the tender pyrotechnics in the segment: "A mother" "& child" "were both on fire, continuously"; when separated by an intrusive "fireproof" figure, we see the mother as she "floated" / "a flower-like" "a red flower" "its petals" "curling flames" / "She cradled" "seemed to cradle" "the burning flower of" "herself gone" (10). (This language is reminiscent of H.D.'s revisionary "Eurydice" who "at least / has the flowers of [herself]" by transforming her loss and underworld.)[4]

Such imagery of the dissolving self or ego is of a piece with Notley's resourceful wide-ranging methods in her remaking the epic. Her Spenserian phantasmagoria that verges on contemporary science fiction contributes to the experience of being dis-placed from masculinist tradition as she breaks into it, as she looks for other ways of being. Breaking in is not only a matter of gaining foothold in a literary genre, but here is a matter of interrogating the very basis of tradition and poetic form. In this way, she creates a dislocated and dislocating voice, "a sort of ecstasy of desolation" (to use H.D.'s phrase from her earlier feminist epic, *Helen in Egypt*).[5] Again, I want to emphasize how Notley's experimentalism pivots upon her shaking up our established notions of a hero's identity. *Descent* bravely takes on what has become one of the central conundrums within feminism over the last two decades and which has yet to be settled: how to enter a pervasively masculinist discourse and have it reflect women's particular and erased concerns and identities? Notley demonstrates that we may participate in a "master" discourse in order to revise it using the "master's tools." Her text exemplifies the way narrative does not have to remain in the province of the masculine.

In the middle of Book One, Alette confronts this overarching dilemma for aesthetics through the figure of a weeping "hysterical" artist:

"In a station" "I saw" "a woman crying" "She stood against"
"the wall" "looking dirty" "& exhausted," "crying quietly"
"I asked her who she was" "& why" "she was crying" "She
      said: 'I'" "am a painter" "I have been trying" "to find"

"a form the tyrant" "doesn't own—" "something" "he doesn't
      know about" "hasn't invented, hasn't" "mastered" "hasn't
      made his own" "in his mind" "Not rectangular," "not a
      sculpture" "Not a thing at all—" "he owns all things,"

"doesn't he?" "He's invented" "all the shapes" "I'm afraid he's"
"invented mine," "my very own" "body'" ("she was hysterical")
"'Did he invent me?" "I want" "to do something like
      paint air" "Perhaps" "I even want to" "invent air" "I've

painted" "thin transparent" "pieces" "of plastic" "They—"
"the pictures on them—" "always turn" "rectangular," "circular"

"I once painted" "on bat's wings" "I caught a bat" "painted
colors on" "let it loose &" "watched the air change . . . "

"He owns form," "doesn't he?" "The tyrant" "owns form'" (25)

Form in this context is not only aesthetic but bodily. And form, in the domain
of the phallic, is a philosophical trope that goes back at least as far as Plato's
Timeaus where the feminine becomes linked with all that cannot be named, with
what cannot have a form, and what therefore cannot possess a body. In Plato's
cosmogony, the feminine is posited as matter; at the same time, women are ul-
timately excluded from matter as they are foreclosed from the possibility of pos-
sessing form. Judith Butler analyzes Plato's conflation of femininity with a re-
ceptacle, otherwise called the "chora," which stands as "the receiving principle"
by which "a form can be said to generate its own sensible representation."[6] The
receiving principle, in short, can never participate in either the material or uni-
versal Forms. As Butler further puts it, "the receiving principle" is "only to be
entered, never to enter."[7] I expand on this because it seems extremely pertinent
to Notley who forthrightly addresses this exclusion at the core of "phallogocen-
trism" and its implications for poetics: can "form" and embodiment, snugly in
the province of masculine privilege, be remapped along lines other than the phal-
lic? Can the feminine be allowed to "enter" materiality and form?

Notley explores the possibility of "entering" epic form even if she is com-
pelled to reject aspects of that tradition. Even as an experimental woman lyri-
cist, she is caught up, implicated in tradition: she still must cite tradition and *be
cited by it*. This partly explains Notley's obsessive experimental use of quotation
marks (that have multiple effects beyond her note to read them as providing a
musical score). These quote marks highlight the text's interest in how women are
"scored," the crisis of Alette articulated in the first book: "To be steeped in" "the
authority" // "of" "another's mind" "the tyrant's mind" "Life of bits & pieces"
(4); Alette's mind is in bits and pieces in part because she recognizes that her
language is not her own, may never be her own no matter how she steals it.
Women's speech could be said to be all quotation within patriarchy. Encased in
the tyrant's body, Alette's language is imprisoned by quote marks. But again they
do more than this. They distract, trouble, question and astonish. To put "of," for
instance, on its own, to put "the authority" in quotation is to charge the words
with their citationality, their arbitrariness. They allow us to take the measure of
each bit and piece.

It might be argued that the poem could have produced a similarly fractured
text through parsing each quoted phrase into short lines (in the manner of Wil-
liams or Creeley), that the poem could have been segmented without risking

alienating or unnecessarily distracting the reader through lyric subversion. But this feature of consecutive phrases in quotes, measured most often as if in a traditional quatrain, calls attention to the space between what is quoted as well as to the space within *what can be quoted* that, like her body and epic itself, must be dismembered for transformation to take place. Thus one of the text's urgent pleas: what *isn't* borrowed? What is not owned or formed by patriarchy? Notley's active cutting into the line and our expectations for line breaks are attempts to interrupt our paradigms of naming and identity reified as immutable and universal, and to shatter the cohesion of those master narratives or mythic structures that map us unthinkingly into social bodies.

The text can't but come with its accreted meanings, allusions to other texts. Alette has, after all, left the academy, pointing to the time "before / [she'd] willingly" "walked away from" "that upper world," "had left" / "a university —" (21). Even as she mentions a library where "[t]he books were decayed matter" (21), in the very rejection of the library lies an embedded history of this very trope from the famous library arson in Williams's *Paterson*. In other words, we can't entirely (nor perhaps should we) discard the literary tradition we emerge from. We write, and write over, but this always implies that there is something to change and veil. How then to enter more deeply, to touch the edge of our postmodern "always already" (a phrase invoked throughout), and to question it as with her soldier asking as an echoic amnesiac born "on heroin": "When I was born," "I was born now" "When I was born," "I'm not allowed" // "to remember if I was" "the little baby" "the little boy" "Was I the cub" / "for an instant?" "Or was I" "already" "a soldier . . . " (15); or later: "Thus a woman" "may be" "already dead" "born dead" (60). Patriarchy is all-encompassing even if one thinks that one has escaped it as with the "crazed woman" who delusively believes that there is "[n]o place no" "place" "except me" "No place" // "except under" "this shawl" (14). Notley's text reveals the doomed nature of this "no place" as it cuts itself off from all relations. In other words, *Descent* does not suffer from proposing a too-easy solution to the dilemma of being within an apparently "always already" tradition.

Notley's fragmentation presents the female body, or the body bound by patriarchy, as a scarred one. Scoring becomes scarring. Experimental poetry breaks new ground; in itself such a venture seems anachronistic in a postmodern frame, yet Notley uses this framing to make us aware, startlingly and astonishingly, that we can risk having a feminist epic, seemingly an oxymoron. To astonish derives from the phrase "to turn to stone"; Medusa is our anti-hero in such business. But as Teresa de Lauretis argues, women have been excluded from narrative and desire, and have been assigned such fatal positions as Medusa's or the Sphinx's, both characters who "have survived inscribed in hero narratives, in someone else's story, not their own," who "are figures or markers of positions—places and topoi—through which the hero and his story move to their destination and to accomplish meaning."[8] The Oedipus story of psychoanalysis derives from Sophocles as *the story* of desire with "the hero as mover of the narrative, the center and term of reference of consciousness" and becomes "paradigmatic of all narratives."[9] De Lauretis reveals how the social structuring of sexual difference emerges through narrative by turning to Jurij Lotman's semiotic work on plot typology where he pinpoints "'a pattern of mythical narratives'" as "'entry into a closed space, and emergence from it'"; the term "woman" in this model is the "closed space" and as such conflates with other images of confinement: cave, grave, house, womb, and as de Lauretis emphasizes, "[i]n this mythical-textual mechanics, then, the hero must be male" and thus "the obstacle, whatever its personification, is morphologically female and indeed, simply, the womb."[10] By choosing the genre of epic and by making her hero female, Notley unhinges this dominant narrative thrust. And significantly her hero must notably "enter" many spaces.

But it is obviously not enough just to insert a female agent or actor to renegotiate the intractable Oedipal model of desire and plot. Notley interrogates the notion of space itself, scrutinizing the boundary between her subject Alette and the spaces she enters. Because she enters them so fluidly and in such rapid succession they lose the rigidity of obstacles to be overcome; the subject and its objects are not so finely distinguished. In part this comes from Notley's insistence that poetic form is itself a body to be reshaped. For instance, and pertinently here given the above discussion of closed spaces, the following scene shows Alette's becoming "eye" ("I saw" "a black flower"), undoing distinctions between inside and outside:

"As I looked at it" "it seemed" "to enlarge" "As I came nearer,"
"as if" "by my attention" "it enlarged more" "& I entered it,"
"I was it, for a time" "was that black blood crushed velvet" "velvet
    womb, I guessed" "womb of Hell" "I was womb" ("was I

    also dead?") "& inside it" "inside me" "in the center"
"was a seed that was" "an eye" "a small eye" "a blue eye"
"pale blue" "And smaller," "its black pupil" "Look"
"inside the pupil" "Inside the pupil's the" "black flower," "again"

"enormous" "crushed velvet" "black blood" "But
    whose eye" "whose" "would it be?" "If it was mine," "whose
    was that," "who" "would I be?" "Did it matter" "to me?" "Since really I"
"was womb?" "blood-black." "And would always" "again"

"become that" (29)

After three ghost quatrains and sapphic end line, she asserts both the always already "again" and the endless potential to become. Significantly, she inverts her own body, discarding the phallic for the gynocentric wound. And like H.D.'s Eurydice who maintains that "before [she] is lost" again through Orphic decree, "Hell must open like a red rose / For the dead to pass."[11] Alette similarly occupies a liminal space: she is both inside a "womb of Hell" and *is* one. The metonymic movement from the hymenal flower to the eye to the womb enacts a disorientation of identity ("who" "would I be?") that, while troubling, discounts a singular, bounded body and ego.

While Alette has a "fear of losing" "my I," "fear of personal" "extinction" (58) and must enter, at one point, a face that "was a black hole" that becomes her own (59), it is such loss of self that allows her to belong to a more communal identity. Quotes within quotes remind us that the voice of Alette is multiple; unlike traditional epic heroes, she does not travel alone: "We were caught up" "in movement" "in ongoingness" "& in ongoingness" / "of voices" (4). The train of Book One loses form and so do the bodies that inhabit it; descent is necessary in order to see paradigms of patriarchy as made, "as man-made," to see how our vision and our bodies are constructed and therefore can be, with difficulty, metamorphosed and recreated.

Alette's experience of bodily dissolution belongs to Notley's attempt to undo the existing body, an undoing that accelerates in Book Two as her hero visits a series of caves. Notably many of the passages begin "I entered a cave" (51, 57, 60, 61, 63, 64, 68, 69, 70, 71, 74, 75, 76, 77, 78, 79, 80, 81); Book Two ends with "I exited" but throughout she is entering and exiting spaces, without apparent progress, in quick succession. It is, in fact, the *process of movement* (entering and exiting) that most represents the power of Alette as atypical epic hero. As Page duBois points out, women are frozen inactive figures in Homer's *Odysssey,* paradigmatically epic; only the "hero moves across the epic landscape defining himself as he goes, encountering fixed female creatures of various sorts, and then moving beyond them.[12] While women may inflict their horrors and threaten castration they are, finally, without the capacity to mobilize and, therefore, to define their own destinies. (In the recent German film *Run Lola Run,* Tom Tykwer attempts to break this paradigm; displacing our expectations, Lola is on the move, in literal speedy traversal of the city, while her boyfriend remains mostly in one place waiting for her rescue of him).[13]

Women are traditionally excluded from "Ideal Forms" (as Butler has theorized); through Alette's movement between and through caves in a frenetic, disrupted and alinear narrative, Notley refutes Plato's "allegory of the cave" as it especially encodes women as living in the shadows of intellect and most bereft (along with poets) of the means to access ideality. She establishes a metonymy of caves—grottoes—cinemas, the latter reinforced by multiple references throughout to screens and filmic imagery. Such reference suggests that "projected" images, self-referential to Notley's filmic poetics, are transmutable, potentially the means by which to alter those Ideal Forms, only arbitrarily installed as permanent. One instance of "a dark cave" cinema occurs as Alette once again dissolves, becoming "a single small thing" "a cell of 'I' afloat"; and then almost instantaneously feels enlarged: "And those feelings" "seemed to work a change" / "on the darkness:" "a jagged" "turquoise line" "shot out from me" // "& unfurled downward" "into a sheet of" "white light" "like an airy" "movie screen" "& then I saw" "on that quasi-screen" "this scene:" (64). The scene unfolds an unexpected hybrid body (one of many in this text): "a strange mermaid a" "girl child" "with tangled black hair" "who had a / man's" "hairy chest" "& a fish's" "lower body" (64). (Notice how line breaks do not only occur with closed quotes, and quoted material doesn't abide by our expectations, such as in the phrase "a strange mermaid a.")

The Tyrant of this text is a pale, gelatinous figure, cartoonishly indomitable; he is dangerous, in part, because of his innocuousness, his pernicious and banal self-duplication. Notley makes his body the ultimate in incorporating, potentially containing and engulfing all other bodies. During Alette's final descent into his basement in the last book, he procures a series of dioramas, microcosms of worlds she had witnessed in the previous sequences, one even with herself in miniature riding a subway car; he reminds her: "'I keep telling you,'" "I keep telling you:'" "all" "'exists in me'" (125). Is there no outside to this body? This, then, is Alette's crisis, and of the epic itself. Even after the Tyrant's apparent death, the text asks: "Must we continue" "to live in" "this corpse of him?" (148) Perhaps Notley's Tyrant is too easy a target—too encompassingly oppressive; but somehow this quality is also the characterization's strength, its mythic resonance. If made more specifically human, he would, perhaps, become paradoxically too embodied: the text strategizes, after all, escape from the Tyrant's constrictive form through a reimagining of corporeality.

If Alette is literally *inside* the body of the Tyrant, there seems to be no outside. The imperative of the text is to turn the inside out, to discover how to alter the skin—the surface—and then the heart (figured at one point as the arterial map of the subway underground). Form is fluid, not fixed as traditional poetics might have it. A poem of this length, with its vertical movement downwards into dreams, is necessary for such transformation. Alette realizes she must "'probe being's depth . . . '" "Before I try to" "change its surface—" (109). Reveling in the power of metamorphoses, she vigorously tries out different morphologies, not stopping at one, not stopping with division. A startlingly surreal instance of such morphing occurs in a sequence where Alette manages to enter an eye (are we in a Magritte painting?) outlined by "white ink—" // "many times" "the size of" "a whole body" (46) and then discovers that her limbs have multiplied: "I looked plural" (47).

Notley's caves have soft walls, become fluid abodes that represent plural bodies and "an ecstasy" "of finding" "another way" / "of being" (102). In a passage referred to earlier where Alette makes the attempt, for instance, to remove (with a male companion) her genitals, attaching them to "fleshy walls" (57), she screams in horror at their momentary formlessness. While Notley reveals the longing for a singular gendered identity, aligning the drive for rigid ego boundaries with Enlightenment values of reason as well as with the Cartesian split between body and mind, she challenges our Western cultural tradition's denigration of the body, what Elizabeth Grosz aptly calls "somatophobia."[14] At best the body is a site of reproductivity, but even then the body we inherit from Plato leaves woman out of the scene; as I have recounted from Butler, the womb-like chora does not touch or influence what it reproduces: it is merely the container, the receptacle. Inverting Athena's emergence from Zeus's brain, the tyrant enters Alette's brain: "He sank down" "into my head" "to my thoughts" / "which instantly" "separated" (note this word's isolation) so that her "[t]houghts felt / efficient" (12). This text is a search for an embodied existence without the "separations"; yet the text simultaneously enacts, through splicing quotation, the divisions produced by patriarchy in the text's body, cutting up what might otherwise be complacently and seamlessly imbibed. According to the logic of this text, women are part of the tyrant's body primarily because they have incorporated patriarchal paradigms and are, therefore, not easily disentangled from them.

There is no place for women, as duBois underscores, in Plato's community of philosophers, and Sappho is virtually erased, usurped as prominent thinker; she suggests how Sappho's "aphrodisia," her interest in the sensory and the bodily in the rites of Aphrodite, constitute an alternate kind of "sophia," one not present in Plato's drive to negate or subsume the body into the abstract call of transcendent spirit or reason.[15] Notley's project relies upon reclaiming an aesthetics that might accommodate a somatic "sophia," or wisdom. Yet the text cannot be made fully coherent, but rather posits a body in bits and pieces as a means of reimagining it. Think of the following composite: "a black snake," "which I took to be" "a female—" "she wore" / "a gold fillet" "the shape of" "delicate grasses" "& tiny flowers—" (52). Rather than providing clearly determined boundaries, this visual gestalt presents this garlanded body as splintered collage, the quotation marks both interrupting and permitting fluid, shifting reassemblage. Indeed, Alette keeps losing her body and getting it back (in getting it back it could never be the same) or confronting other estranged figures or bodies; these caves, or grottoes of the grotesque, push us to the extremes of malleable identity.

The so-called "first mother" becomes a site of such extremity, and part of Notley's circumvention of the paradigmatic oedipal narrative and search for paternal origin of our culture. When Alette meets a uniformed man looking for "their" father, she angrily remarks that such a task "would be easier" "much easier" than her search for the mother (7). In Book Three, Alette recognizes a headless body:

> "I didn't" "want to look" "but" "of course I had to:" "this headless"
> "woman" "was a living personage," "whose hands moved slightly,"
> "whose feet shifted" "As I looked at her" "I was filled with" "an oceanic"
> "sorrow," "staring at her gruesome neck," "its black well" "I knew she was"
>
> "the one I sought," "our mother," "first woman" (89)

Hélène Cixous has asserted that women "*only keep [their heads] on condition that they lose them*—lose them, that is, to complete silence, turned into automatons, decapitation is part of women's condition or legacy under patriarchy."[16] This "first woman" clings to this headlessness, "afraid" "[she'll] lose [her] power" "to speak from" "deep inside [her]" (98), but with the accuracy and seamless dream quality of a fairy-tale, Alette converts a "silvery broad axe" to a cloth that will wrap around the neck wound and restore the head without erasing the mark of wounding, and the first woman becomes the prototypic creator: "'As I / say a word,' she said—" "'As - I - say - a - word,'" "she said again" / "but in a" "staccato way," "'a - new - star - appears'" (99). Later, as part of Alette's ritual journey she views her own corpse, the most uncanny of things, in an extraordinarily vivid out-of-body trance ("My face was gone" "My flesh was gone" and "I sat beside" "my skeleton," 112). In the liminal wash of "original" shapes ("I saw amoebas" "swell & divide," 112), she reassumes her body, recognizing how we "put on" our very contingent physical form (as with our sex, our gender): "My bones" "were full //of knowledge," "the history" "of the planet" "As I put them on" (112). Alette re-experiences an incipient "skin ego" as further evidence of the importance of the corporeal self: "I felt skin" "begin to grow on me," "grow on me" "again" (113).

  In her note to the text, Notley tells us that her quotation marks function to slow down our reading: "they're there, mostly, to measure the poem." This device scores her work as a made thing, stitched and as part of her interruptive strategy, as if what lived between segments were as significant as what speaks within them. The marks become dismaying, halting signals for the fact that we can't hope for an intact, cohesive narrative (why would we want to?) that assures and comforts. Instead Notley dramatizes the entrance of the female voice into narrative as the violation that it is. In a text that uses other punctuation so sparingly and offers in fairly unconvoluted syntax what might be mistaken for linear narrative, such singular punctuation becomes puncturation (indeed almost painful for the reader's eyes). The gaps produce successive breaks that reflect the text's search for voice—the repressed feminine that exceeds measurement, and its rejection of a delusively unfractured Enlightenment rationality. Alette, after all, realizes of the Tyrant: "He owns enlightenment" "all enlightenment" and that she "must resist it" (37). The text resists "enlightenment" as it relies on the surreal, on the necessary descent into darkness and dream.

Descent becomes an overt rejection of Enlightenment values of reason and light in favor of the richer experiences of the unillumined underground: "Something" "is still alive in there," "has power" (17); "Down here it is" "a more desperate" / "decay" (21); "I had become" "unreason" (20); "the light" "was a lie" (22). There is power in Notley's Ovidian transformation, in recognizing the ability of the body to mutate, to transform if only in dreams. And it is dream-consciousness (in defiance of Enlightenment) that allows for suspension and uncertain boundaries. The quicksilver quality of events within dreams questions limits of all kinds. Notley has written on the primacy of dreams for this poem and for the future of poetry:

> Dream is the ocean into which all twentieth century forms are being dumped. . . . The final dissolution & rebirth is taking place in darkness: & what will be born probably hasn't been seen yet, because no one has walked straight into the dark & stayed awhile. To break & recombine language is nothing. To break & recombine reality, as Dream always does do, might be something.[17]

Thus narrative must return to the unknown darkness; it is not a matter of mere surface experiment. If we are not sure by the end of the poem whether the Tyrant has truly been overcome, he has certainly become the regenerative stuff of dreams. Alette, very much a new epic hero, declares:

> "'I'm killing no one" "You are not real" "You said so" "yourself'" "I
>   said" "'Forms in dreams . . . '" "forms in dreams . . . '" "I searched within"
> "for right words" "'I will change the" "forms in dreams'" (144)

As Alette observes in the last poem, a multiple, repressed, underground corpus is being raised:

> "all the

> lost creatures" "began to" "emerge" "Come up from" "below the subway"
> "From the caves &" "from the dark woods" "I had visited" "they emerged"
> "I watched through" "tears of clarity" "many" "forms of being" (148)

Descent astonishes as fantastical and feminist epic, compelling through its use of the uncanny, through our discovering disconcerting resemblances within the strange, as with a Circean subway car of "suited . . . animals—" "men, actually," / "in business suits" (8); or one of mostly women in "pantyhose," "grown-up shoes," / & "makeup" who endlessly "perform actions" "without objects" / "As if in pantomime" "Without papers" "without machines" (19); or with the car of orphaned beggars emaciated only to their voices (somehow Alette synesthetically *sees* their voices) as they haunt and echo: "Spare? Spare any?" "Spare any mothers?" / "fathers? . . . "Spare a / new" "new body?" "body?" (18); or of the veteran (who turns out to be Alette's brother) incanting in Notley's remarkably plain lyricism of both ecstasy and desolation: "'When I was born,' "I was born now" "fully grown," "on heroin" "When I / "was born" "fully grown" "in the universe" "of no change" "nothing" "grows / up from" (15).

The familiar figures that Alette meets in her descent all seem in need of new bodies (apparently the impoverished homeless or the mechanized stenographers are not alone in this). *Descent* showcases multiple bodily mutations such as the "streamlined" "leglessness" of a mermaid girl (64), or Alette's "entire" "body" "burst open" "like a seam" (65), or a woman who "was protoplasmic-" "looking—" "But rather beautiful" (87). Yet what the soldier, "not allowed" "to remember when [he] was" "the little baby," is a body "before" that is not inundated by patriarchal control, by the battlefield. Thus while the text mourns for a lost "first mother," it intelligently posits the limits of such remembering of the maternal. Notley's quotation marks reveal an ongoing unhealed sense of rupture as well as an immersion within the always already patriarchal. This experimental poem attests to the possibility of creating anew even as Notley finds herself implicated in the very forms she wants to overcome. The poet "enters" the epic genre in order to dismantle the stark boundaries of the mode; by entering again and again, she invents a female actor and gives her a body, powerful in its mutability. Bodily form becomes coextensive with aesthetic form. Thus the crisis of the woman painter searching for "a form the tyrant" "doesn't own—" (25) is ultimately a microcosm of Notley's "ecstasy of desolation," her anguished exploration and displacement of fixed corporeality. In the process, she reveals how aesthetics (in this case the epic form) figures forth our cultural tropes of gender and embodiment; and in order to refigure one domain we must refigure the other. What Williams said in praise of Marianne Moore, that she was "difficult to quote convincingly," here becomes almost viscerally experienced.[18] *Descent* is a poem so upsetting to tradition that it demands a new body; it requires of us a belief in art's ability to stretch and expand the established boundaries of form, to paint, as it were, on the bat's wing.

Intimacy and Experiment in Mei-Mei Berssenbrugge's *Empathy*

Charles Altieri

When I first decided to write a book developing ways of talking about the affects in lyric poetry, I eagerly told my friend Heather McHugh about the decision. I assumed that a poet would be glad to see a critic renouncing interpretation for a more affect-oriented perspective, so I expected her to sustain the imaginary version of myself leading me to elicit her approval in the first place. Instead she seemed dismayed, for reasons that working on my book has finally led me to understand, probably better than I have come to understand the emotions. She realized that there are few topics more distorted by the effort to think well of oneself than discoursing on the emotions, and she had seen enough of what critics do to poems when they are pursuing that goal. For where emotions are, there will be perhaps our greatest temptations to confuse the versions of ourselves that we want to have with what authors actually do or with what happens as we experience both persons and texts.

Yet there seems to me no alternative but to risk everything McHugh feared. Emotion is now a cutting edge topic in the humanities, bringing not only the drawbacks McHugh saw so clearly but also creating a distinctive problem for those who care about poets who take on difficult projects. When topics draw everyone's attention, we tend to let basic formulations of them provide allegorical keys for reading a wide body of materials. And that mode of generalization makes it all too easy to ignore what is most demanding and challenging in particular writers. So I turn to Mei-Mei Berssenbrugge's *Empathy* because this text insistently repudiates the now standard allegorical framework yet makes very strong appeals to be engaged for its affective intensities. Therefore I hope that concentrating on Berssenbrugge will help us appreciate some of the pressures requiring some contemporary poets to try new kinds of experiments. And the better we see how these experiments engage these pressures, the more likely we are also to appreciate the possibility of taking fresh tacks in our efforts to understand the personal and interpersonal dynamics that circulate around affective energies.

Here I cannot dwell at length on the theoretical issues involved. Suffice it to say that most theorists now concentrating on emotions dwell on the importance of framing them within narratives and treating our investments in emotions as means of making discriminations and establishing the salience necessary for supple and accurate practical judgments. For these theorists the emotions have become the allies of an enlightened rationality, at the cost of letting their intransigent as well as their aesthetic, self-sustaining qualities drift away as irrelevance or mere immaturity.[1] Resisting that cost then offers powerful reasons for attempting to make it new. Poets have both the need and the resources for rendering aspects of affective life sharply opposed to this version of enlightenment. Berssenbrugge in particular devotes considerable energies to exploring aspects of the emotions that become articulate in the lyric's ways of resisting narrative. For she finds in that resistance a range of needs and powers shaping human desires that nonetheless do not have a substantial place within these contemporary theories.

Because she resists Englightenment models, Berssenbrugge's treatment of affective life turns out to have a good deal in common with standard postmodern concerns for mobility, fluidity, and indeterminacy. But stressing these similarities in such standard abstract terms would seriously diminish the force of her experiments. For she has a commitment to description and denotation completely at odds with orthodox pomo. Her poetry does not avoid the referential power of language—it suffuses that power with an excess of investment that makes clear the limitations of what Englightenment thinking at its best can accomplish. Such denotative language ties us to the physical world, but it also expresses a multisurfaced set of affective engagements of that world that are anchored in description but not reducible to it. Berssenbrugge the poet shaping distinctive affective states cannot be separated from Berssenbrugge the implicit theorist linking postmodern mobilities to the referential commitments of contemporary science. And Bersenbrugge the lyric poet cannot be separated from the apparently anti-lyric flirtation with the seductions of objectivity. No wonder then that we have to use what often seems an outdated language of experiment if we are to bring together the energies of Berssenbrugge's refusals with the forms of power articulated in her actual renderings of affective intensities. She seeks ways to force us back from narrative and drama to the more elemental phenomenological aspects characterizing how language helps make it possible for us to connect to a world beyond the ego.

In order to foreground these phenomenological relations Berssenbrugge has to evade the two obvious poles for gathering lyrical energy—the rendering of subjective need and the articulating of how the world rewards what language can make of our efforts to pay attention to objects. Instead she treats as primary the need to identify with a condition of possibility for moving between the ego and the world that I am going to call a distinctive "imaginative site." By "imaginative site" I mean something close to what critics like Kenneth Burke meant by "attitude," the articulation of dispositions toward the world which allows us to reflect on the kinds of emotions and lines of connection that might follow if we identify fully with the speaking presence of the text. But I prefer the rubric "imaginative site" because that foregrounds the constructed nature of the attitude and calls attention to the need for readers to occupy a particular ground if the text is to have exemplary force. The early Auden's characteristic site was a generalized process of self-examination addressed to readers who were offered the possibility of viewing their own engagements in cultural life through his distanced yet engaged eyes. At the other pole, Hopkins made the extremes of ecstasy and anxiety his entries into poetic speech, and his readers were invited not to speculate on their cultural lives but to reach for the moment beyond what practical concerns are likely to mask.

Berssenbrugge's characteristic site in *Empathy* combines two basic affective orientations along lines that I hope to show open into significant value stories. The most fundamental of these orientations for me is her attempt to focus directly on the desire for intimacy—with herself, with other people, and with the reader as an extension of both those projections—while struggling against pressures to theatricalize or thematize or otherwise flatten intimacy into idea and the dynamics of person into the elements we attribute to character. Accompanying and sharpening that effort is a corresponding fascination with the idea of empathy as a mode of organizing imaginative energies and disposing affective intensities. I think we have to ask why she entitles her book *Empathy* in order to make it her preferred imaginative vehicle for such intimacy. Why stress empathy rather than, say, sympathy? And why make the term so abstract in her title—without any preposition or object, so that it comes to represent a state in its own right?

It is important to realize that intimacy need not be a basic instrument for lyric feeling. Many lyrics are content to provide articulate accounts of emotions that retain their distance from us. Some even challenge us to try provisional identifications that require us to assume stances resisting or defamiliarizing our desires to achieve intimacy with the poet. Think for example of Williams's short lyrics or Yeats's imperious ones, or Plath's paranoid projections. But many lyrics use defamiliarization as a means of invoking from readers new realizations of how flexible and intense their powers of achieving intimacy are. And most lyrics, even Yeats's imperious ones, use rhythm and metaphor and concision to bring bodies into play and to establish familiarity over time. Berssenbrugge knows all this, but as Yeats might say, she is not content. She sees the thematizing of intimacy as the displacing of its dynamics into clear subject-object polarities. And she seems to think that too easy an entrance into psychological discourse blinds us to where and how in the psyche poems may want to live. It may not be enough to think in terms of psychological subjects because that presupposes an organizing unit much more abstract than the actual synthetic processes attaching psyche to world. So Berssenbrugge must develop her own version of the paradox fundamental to the modernist lyric. For intimacy to appear in its most elemental properties poetry has to risk a level of difficulty and flatness that for many readers will preclude there being any intimacy at all.

Stressing the experimental energies in Berssenbrugge also helps us avoid a second debilitating tendency in contemporary criticism—the disposition among critics identifying with the avant-garde to rely on an imaginatively crippling binary opposition that honors experiment almost exclusively as a radical attitude toward the poem's language while relegating values like intimacy to the reactionary egocentricity of an enervated romanticism. Only those experiments are honored as progressive and worthy of academic attention which focus on subject positions rather than on subjects, on the absorptive materiality of the signifier rather than on its evocativeness, and on the work of resistance to social forces rather than on the phenomenology of affective life. Yet this binary simply does not hold for many of the most interesting contemporary poets who consider their work a radical departure from dominant contemporary styles. In addition to Berssenbrugge one could cite writers like Ann Lauterbach and Lyn Hejinian, and one could turn to Rob Kaufman's effort to make analogous cases for poets like Michael Palmer and Norma Cole.[2] In all these cases experimenting with the language of lyric remains deeply committed to challenging dominant contemporary cultural values in the service of the developing emotional intensities and exploring their consequences.

Now it is time for particulars; so I call your attention to how the first two sections of Berssenbrugge's "Honeymoon" configure the intimacy she pursues. The critique of representation directly opposes the now dominant models for what we seek in our expressions of the emotions, yet it manages to provide a gorgeously denotative framework equally at odds with most contemporary experimental poetry:

Though relations with oneself and with other people seem negotiated in
    terms secretly confirmed
by representation, her idea of the person's visibility was not susceptible to
    representation. No matter

how emphatically a person will control his demeanor, there will be perspec-
        tives she cannot foresee or
direct, because there is no assignable end to the depth of us to which repre-
        sentation can reach,
the way part of a circle can be just the memory of a depth. The surface inside
        its contour,
like the inside of a body emits more feeling than its surroundings, as if
the volume or capacity of relations would only refer to something inside, that
        I can't see,
that the other person and I keep getting in the way of, or things in the land-
        scape while they are driving,
instead of the capacity being *of* your person. The volume of a bright cotton-
        wood could be almost
a lack of volume or a lack of space inside the tree, the way a membrane is the
        entrance of an organism.
Here the person and the yellow tree would resemble the flesh of yellow fruit.

There are dimensions of an assessment of human relations, which go before
        and after our relation to the picture
as allegorical to what the picture is of, to what she sees or says about you as
        what her attachment to you
is *of,* so a narrow shadow of the cloud on a red cliff may just mark the plane
        of a line of print across
what you see, that could represent a perspective, as if some particular part
        were not turned toward you,
the way a fold can become a particular object or seam, like relations with
        oneself
or with another person. The fold is the shadow of a heavy eyelid on a cheek.
        My feeling for it
is like the flash in the rearview mirror of a pick-up as I pass it in the dark,
my fixation on *my* body's opacity.[3]

Like Lacan, Berssenbrugge wants to challenge the essentially visual, pictorial
ways that we now take as central to imagining closeness with other people. For
her the visual confines feelings to an essentially "mystical" mode in which we are
constantly drawing inferences from particulars. In the place of that visuality she
projects a "conjectural" model of feeling (38). Conjecture differs from interpre-
tation because it is an ongoing process of constant mobile adjustments content
with a series of imaginative leaps. Conjecture here is opposed to the synthetic

building of hypotheses by combining sets of signs in accord with received vocabularies for what counts as expressivity. Conjecture is metaphor that knows it has to remain analogically positioned toward what its chain of metonymic "like"s bring into play as circumferences for the self's sense of its placements. So, with Lacan, Berssenbrugge stresses the ways that efforts at representation and self-representation seem to elicit intimacy but in fact block access to many dimensions of the psyche that might enable intense closeness between people. The ideals of representation prove as frustrating as they are seductive. For the basic role of representation is to provide a stable object promising to assuage anxieties over what we actually desire and how we want to be understood. But suppose that both our desires and our intelligibility to others cannot be fully realized within such stabilities. If that is so, then we purchase self-confidence at the cost of entering self-protective illusions.

And suppose that our desires are severely distorted by the same visual imperatives because they project an outside and an inside, with the outside then somehow having to express or symbolize what cannot be seen but can apparently be given a definitive psychological space to inhabit. Ideals of representation foreclose what counts as depth and block possible perspectives that might give access to the traits most profoundly characterizing us as persons.

Lacan offers for this critique of representation his mirror stage and his brilliant analysis of how and why we project imaginary versions of ourselves as subjects. Berssenbrugge adds to that mix an insistence that we examine how the ideal of visibility forms and deforms the logics of distribution shaping what we invest in as subjective identities. How we conceive visibility as emotionally charged will also shape how we characterize the invisible as well as how we establish links between the two. In our culture, she suggests, we formulate these links primarily in the epistemic terms we have inherited from the success of Enlightenment science. We rely on a tight but problematic connection between how ideals of representation function for empiricist practices and how they function for our visions of what it means to know and to get close to other human beings. We want to be knowable in almost the same way that we feel we have confident grasps of what objects are and we understand using these objects to perform various tasks. Correlatively, we want this visibility supplemented by something invisible, something hidden that confers on us a depth and a mystery making us different from objects. Then our humanity consists largely in our efforts to bring this depth to the surface by making visible or expressing in a world of objects what makes us subjects. We are most human when we can communicate by bringing the invisible into pictures that we construct of ourselves and of others.

This logic has substantially affected contemporary American culture's ideas about lyric poetry. The dominant styles over the past forty years at least have made intimacy with the audience a basic ideal, and have based that intimacy on two basic principles. The first locates the source of the poet's power to communicate in his or her ability to make visible for an audience what the poet can represent as most intense or most focused in his or her inner life. At one pole such work continues confessional ideals (Gerald Stern or Alicia Ostriker); at the other, now more popular pole, it offers as the locus of intimacy the engaged reflexive distance that poets like Robert Hass and Frank Bidart present as they reconstruct the subtle and elemental emotional moments and patterns basic to their affective lives. The second alternative takes a more rhetorical stance. Rather than focus on the poet's efforts at personal expression it concentrates on constructing dramatic scenes that build towards emotional climaxes, with the event projected as a means of providing a symbolic embodiment of emotions that the entire audience is led to share. By virtue of the surrogate situation a basic emotion takes dramatic form, and as we participate in that form we become visible to each other.

These alternatives seem to me to provide the backdrop motivating Berssenbrugge's experiments because the models of representation and expression on which they rely prove terribly confining—both as dramatic events and as rhetorical means of engaging audiences. Persons remain objects with predicates about mystery vaguely attached to them. And responders are forced into roles that are far too monocular. In her view rich intimacy requires gaining access to "perspectives" that an agent "cannot see or direct." And it involves realizing how temporality modifies, extends, and complicates our experiences of intimacy. So both spatial and temporal access to other persons is best achieved if we can imagine ourselves as cubist painters bringing multiple overlapping perspectives together as a kind of parallax view projecting beyond what can only be dimly realized in specific images. Moreover we best attune our reflexive lives to these others, as well as to our own needs and desires, if we replace the idea of an invisible core lurking below the visible surface by a notion of spirit as simply an extension of bodies into something like auras of energy and processes of attunement. Spirit becomes manifest as the folding and unfolding of surfaces that we produce as we engage in various relationships. That is why Berssenbrugge stresses the sublime passage between the volume of a bright cottonwood and "a lack of volume or lack of space inside the tree." Light flattens the tree, combining figures of pure space with figures of entry that require no penetration. Analogously that is why Berssenbrugge's own flat descriptions flow so easily and often incomprehensibly into complicated physical analogies, since attachment is an alignment of surfaces as they keep morphing into different possible forms. Finally, that is why at the end of the poem she concentrates on what is involved in treating the goal of the honeymoon as learning to treat the other as "the color of a seam, not a doll" (75):

> She creates a dark flank of a mountain, a person's thoughts or feelings, passing
>   across the person, concealing the person.
> She wonders what the body would reveal, if the cloud were transparent.
> It pervades the creation of a motive, like the action of a heart. (76)

Here Berssenbrugge's understanding of empathy helps explicate what the site of intimacy involves. Suppose one were to ask what attitude it takes for this person to understand herself or for an audience to engage her. One would have to accept the fact that "the person" is always concealed, like a mountain beneath clouds. But what conceals also reveals, in this case by eliciting a sense of conjecture about the body beneath the cloud, so that questions of motive are now inseparable from registering such strange conjunctions of the purely physical and the densely metaphorical.

No wonder then that Berssenbrugge's title *Empathy* calls attention to so abstract a form of that quite common mode of response to other persons. This title does not project any particular object of empathy. Nor, for that matter can we identify a particular subject experiencing the empathy. The title offers empathy as a state that can fluctuate between what subjects feel and what objects elicit, each readily folding into its opposite. And the title suggests a sharp opposition to sympathy, relegating sympathy to states that impose conventional emotional plots, establish a suffering ego, and afford the beholder a satisfying, self-regarding relation to the plot so constructed. Rather than give empathy a dramatic context, Berssenbrugge asks us to reflect upon this potential interchangeability, this floating possibility for subject and object to occupy the same space. To engage the mode of agency that situates itself in relation to flanks of mountains and then lets related metaphors unfold one has to locate subjectivity not in any identifiable dramatic agent but in the specific modes of care that get articulated by the fluid, intricately expanding chain of associations.

As her title poem sets the stage, engaging this fluidity requires opening oneself to a "feeling of mystery" that "adheres to his or her manner of asking / where is the space, instead of what space it is" (57). Where sympathy defines what the space is, empathy attunes itself to a manner of asking that is itself distributed between what the agent's manner makes visible and the mode of questioning elicited for a responder. So by the end of "Empathy" the speaker can define intimacy in terms that give priority to modes of response that can be content to treat persons in terms of the "parts" that give them luminosity. Keeping these parts in relation in turn requires reading against all our tendencies to turn process into substance:

> Be that as it may, real and constant luminosity of the parts can create
> a real self who will remain forever in the emotion of a necessary or real person.
> To deny this is to deny the struggle to make certain meanings stick. (59)

Empathy conjoins the need to make certain that meanings stick with the effort to make particular meanings stick, as particulars—how we engage the site determines what the site can be.

Finally, we may be able to see an ontological side to Berssenbrugge's empathy because it requires such elemental responses to other persons and to the world. Consider the following passage near the end of her poem "Naturalism," which I think sets against socially oriented models of representation a "phenomenological materialism" offering a much more intricate sense of what it means to come to feel one's way into another person's situation:

> The while is long with the speed of time. It is a camera controlled by the
>   participant,
> so the speed and the time control the image, too. The feeling is the afterimage
>   of yourself
> you are always coming to, so I like landscape where coming to the feeling
> is always elemental or hierarchical. Or,
> if camera sounds too harsh or formal for this elusive process, we can just
>   say, we
> grasp an imaginative continuity that corresponds to the landscape,
> creating an emotion greater than what can be accounted for
> by its blue and white plains.
>
> What can be at stake with an emotion is not a location and its occupation,
> but the capacity to move more or less at will. The coast's use of feedback can
>   steady
> and bring into unison several stages of the motion with great elegance. (39–40)

Emotion may have more to do with the quality and relatedness produced by motion and by time than it does with the theaters produced as we try to represent inwardness. First we are told that "feeling is the afterimage of yourself." Then Berssenbrugge's marvelous "Or" makes the force of this afterimage literal by simultaneously extending the self into a range of possibilities and inviting us to read those possibilities back into our understanding of the speaker, from a perspective that the speaker cannot quite control. Intimacy in the present brings versions of the past and the projected future into play, only to gather all those possibilities into two versions of moderate plenitude—the first developed in the expansive sense of landscape, the second in the possibility of correlating what the landscape figures into abstract talk about how emotion is folded into motion.

I cannot be sure that my abstractions quite get Berssenbrugge right or that they can provide a compelling case for trying on this way of envisioning our own possible affective investments. So I want to shift to a more practical mode of thinking about her work by elaborating three distinctive imaginative attitudes that her work helps us both inhabit and appreciate.

The first attitude models possible orientations we can take towards persons with whom we seek intimacy. Critique of the expression and communication models leads Berssenbrugge to envision engaging other people by attuning oneself to those features of a life suppressed by or displaced by efforts at self-representation. A passage towards the end of "Honeymoon," the poem from which I first quoted, brings the anti-representational model of emotion elaborated in the opening stanzas to the core of personal relationships:

> She would wish his wish was to penetrate her behavior by means of referring
>   to what she is feeling,
> in order to reach the same place her reference to herself occupies, that is,
>   before
> she would express the feeling. It is how a particular color would be the
>   knowledge
> that would come of the light of the color, like a source to see whiteness that
>   puffs like clouds,
> or would puff, if she would refer to them, or like a bar of light touching down
>   at the edge of the road. . . .
> She begins to acquire honeymoon as a level of representation, something
>   which we may call
> an application of honey onto a bar of light, or the part of a deep orange
>   moon that is hidden or the part
> that is not hidden by clouds, having a sense of, but no analysis of her seeing,
>   that will explain
> her feeling about an application, how the ambiguity *seems* to alter "how
>   much" is seen. (74)

Here intimacy is beautifully defined as being able to refer to what someone is feeling at the site where the person enters the expressive process rather than at the site produced by the representation. So the need for multiple perspectives now enters time, or enters a sense of the richness and evocativeness of dealing with objects and persons in terms of their ways of being present in what unfolds out of them. And intimacy then can take on the marvelous subtle physical analogues that the poem figures in its treatment of color, light, and the movement of clouds. The visual returns with a vengeance, but as metaphorical extensions of affective states, not as objects compelling our fixed attention.

Among the many aspects of this subtlety that Berrsenbrugge explores, none is more important than this sense of how intimacy modifies our sense of time. Gaining closeness to another person, or to a poem, requires not simply understanding what is said or pictured but recasting the saying and the picturing so as to incorporate protentions and retentions evoking possible futures and impinging pasts. And then a new idea of the sublime enters, based simply on what is involved in opening oneself to how background and foreground fold into each other. Recall that for Kant the sublime consisted in those judgments where the mind finds itself powerless to impose understanding yet finds its thwarted efforts opening into a realm of the supersensible. The sublime would be manifest in quantity as infinite magnitude and in dynamic quality as power that cannot be framed successfully by the understanding. Berssenbrugge wants a sublimity based on empathy, on our awareness of the dynamical power of the small quantities to make large differences by focussing on constant processes of folding and unfolding.

Probably her richest succinct rendering of this sublimity takes place at the center of "The Carmelites," a great poem on the relation between withdrawing into privacy and discovering how that can lead to new visions of connection:

> Experience of it
> is the result of a deepening relation to the light, regressing from conscious
>   recognition
> to a remembered involvement between so many minor cycles of sleep and
>   waking, just as
> your silence begins to look like so many examples of experience. Now, the
>   sublime is the interval
> of the exposure, the way silence once signified but no longer signifies the limits
>   of discourse,
> sabotaging instructive strategies of the film and the garden, in which we are
>   audience or the wall. (35)

"Interval of the exposure" brilliantly correlates time and space: how we adjust exposures establishes the intervals creating the formed silences which reach beyond what had been seen only as limits of discourse. With such a lens we need be neither audience nor wall, figures which analogously no longer signify the limits of intersubjectivity. Once subjectivity is a matter of these intervals, intersubjectivity becomes a process definable primarily by how it establishes substances then reaches beyond them into an awareness of something like pure relational fields.

The second imaginative attitude modifies how we envision art works relating to their audiences. In Berssenbrugge the crucial issue is not whom one addresses but where the address can be envisioned as fully taking place. Questions about identity prove much less important than concerns for being able to shape whatever identities we have to the specific configurations of intimacy that the poems offer. And that in turn alters how we approach intimacy. If one relies on models of communication by self-representation, intimacy takes place as a function of making the self sufficiently visible so that an observer can recognize what the speaker offers. Berssenbrugge is less interested in such recognition than she is in the force that the desire to be known has in composing something like a distinctive site that an observer comes to share. Intimacy is less a matter of coming to know the other better than of learning to enter the space created by the desire to give another access to one's energies as they extend beyond what communication can contain. What intervals produce in time, awareness of the constructive energies of desire composes in space.

Berssenbrugge's "Recitative" makes the bold leap of locating intimacy at the core of opera, since recitative depends so much on the music becoming quiet and the stage itself coming back into focus, so that the bodies there can take on an expressivity that parallels what the orchestra invites when it is fully present:

> Half their conversation is in shadow, so they speak in and out of a diagonal
> wedge of light.
> The possibility of static or a gap on a starry electric night gives the impression
> of her body
> constantly engaged in transition, but she desires to enter a body of material
> by talking.
> . . . .
> One can paint the stars on a black lead background,
> equivocal stars casting carpets of desire here and there in the middle of an
> errand,
> which up to then had proceeded in the state of non-imploring urgency of
> a body in diagonal,
> an image of outreach or hailing. For me, it seemed that love was a spiritual
> exercise in physical form,

and the diagonal was glints off an inferred line of sun lingering, as spring
synchronized with the double space of her desire and her desire for their
    presence
to be hieratic, not wholly expressive, a standard of grace in the corridor of
    a day,
with narcissus. If it is through counting that speech is connected to time,
then crossing an inferred estuary of this conversation is a rest in music. (34)

Theater space modulates into figurative space and space itself becomes the potential for registering how desire takes on material form. Now form extends, by the figure of the eddy, to include rests and sites of grace that keep their place in the larger opera even as they give the plot its human significances. These eddies become sites of grace where diagonals can linger and doubleness be experienced as itself a fully expressive condition.

The third imaginative attitude I want to develop involves Berssenbrugge's distinctive way of dealing with self-consciousness. There are very few poets more concerned with an excruciatingly exact rendering of the modulations of self-consciousness. Yet for Berssenbrugge one major value in so attending to the self is the capacity one finds to gain access there to what has to remain other about the other person. In our standard communication models, self-consciousness seems to destroy the transparency necessary to know the other as other. But for Berssenbrugge the other only comes into focus because of how the self feels itself being modified and led to enter the kind of silences that become rests in music. Feeling is conjectural and not mystical because it is not direct access to object but a mediation through states that the subject attaches to the object? And we have to regress "from conscious recognition" to "remembered involvement" if we are to develop the framing necessary for transforming silence into a sublime interval?

Berssenbrugge's most searching engagement in these issues occurs in the intricate and complex meditation of "Fog." There she seeks to understand how the kinds of luminosity distributed within fog might complement Enlightenment idealizations of the power of daylight to dispel dreams and superstitions. Fog is not darkness or fantasy. Yet it manages to provide a figure insisting upon an irreducible but never specifiable doubleness in our efforts at clarity. We know there are objects in the fog, but we only grasp these objects as pervasively mediated by an element that also creates strange interconnections within a constantly shifting field. Fog is an antithesis to realism: where realism seeks a transparent medium, fog thickens the mediations sustaining the "contradicting ambition of consciousness to acquire impressions and retain strong feelings" (41).

Ultimately fog provides a figure for the pressure of subjectivity on objects of attention—both in its tendencies to displace what realism can render and in its capacity to retain an atmosphere where one feels the framework and the framed intricately suffusing each other, as if both temporal and spatial differences proved indispensable to grasping how one is held by and held within what unifies the particulars of the scene:

The fog of the way we feel our way into this focus, seeking by feeling, lies in the indefiniteness of the concept of continuing focus, or distance and closeness, that is, of our methods of comparing densities between human beings. (48)

A storyline develops based on your moving from one breath to another, and you start to want to continue it, like a span of good health or exceptional beauty. You want to continue it forever, and your memory gets involved, in how you perceive the space around you and the human beings or descendants in the space. (49)

Therefore, we appreciate the fog, as the power to make the space continue beyond the single perception, into raw material or youth of the body, like a body of light.

It dissolves now at the top of her head, now five lights into her heart. Now, it dissolves into her body. Her friends dissolve into light. They dissolve into her family, which seems to dissolve into clouds that were already full of light.
. . . .
It is almost as if the complete dark would be ideal. (50)

Perhaps most impressive in this poem is the way that Berssenbrugge creates a framework for understanding the tensions within her own style. There must be denotation, description, and direct expression because we cannot evade the Enlightenment. Language has to take responsibility for its claims and persons have to try to make visible what they can offer to others. Rhetorical manipulation, on the other hand, separates language from objects and conceals desires while creating for its audience a false confidence in what becomes visible. But resistance to rhetoric need not require Enlightenment fixations on clarity. Lyric poetry can establish this fog-like effect, so that its various luminous tangents quickly lead beyond what can be seen or known. In this kind of poetry we are asked to make frequent leaps of faith enabling us to stay in touch with a mobility of mind always on the verge of dissipating into pure contingency. When the poetry works, it continually regathers those tangents—not into a clear synthetic whole but into the audience's sense that it is beginning to find its way around within a field of loosely related but evocative tiltings of the sense-making process. As we grow more confident within this field we realize that the ultimate aim of the writing is not to convey something we can know but to engage us in processes of attuning which align us with others without providing pictures of either the object known or the knower's confidence. Such work can honor the specificity of its objects, but this specificity is no longer something that can be appreciated solely in cognitive terms. Rather than treat the specific object in terms that characterize its manifest traits, the basic principle of engagement becomes a feeling for how emotional connection can be maintained through fluidly shifting perspectives. In the space conventionally idealized as the site where we come to know what another expresses, there Berssenbrugge wants us to understand relationships as a complex play of shifting and reflecting lights. As Dante might have put it (were he forced to speak post-Enlightenment prose), we enter a field where brightness intensifies because surfaces are constantly active and reflections double back on one another.

There will be times when this fluidity becomes so frustrating that one wants to stress "Fog"'s last line: "It is almost as if the complete dark would be ideal." But complete dark is simply the inverse of complete visibility. It has to ignore the tentativeness, the intricacy, and the seductiveness of all the qualifying utterances in this sentence. It has to ignore everything that makes it virtually impossible to provide a paraphrase adequate to the tones being sounded. In Berssenbrugge's imaginative world the notion of an "ideal" is inseparable from the indecipherable precision of the chain of qualifiers that come to inhabit and to transform the dark—without allowing anyone to think he or she possesses power to flood that place with unequivocal light. Yet in Berssenbrugge's imaginative world that indeterminacy becomes a means, not an end. It provides a vehicle for keeping us aware that there are things we desire from the world and from other persons more important than clarity:

> How you look into the canyon, a relation to lit and unlit complexities of
>   islands on the canyon floor,
> is the complicated question of looking, and the right answer that comes back.
>   The more
> complicated the question, the less light would come back, until no light comes
>   back.
> You would know everything you see in the first place, but the terms of your
>   recognition grow
> increasingly intimate and ecological, like the light of the gold of jewelry on
>   you, which
> while it is still light, is still becoming abstract. (73)

PART II
IN THE MARGINS OF FORM

Towards a New Politics of Representation? Absence and Desire in Denise Chávez's *The Last of the Menu Girls*

AnaLouise Keating

I've been struggling to make sense of Denise Chávez's *The Last of the Menu Girls* for several years; it intrigues me yet resists interpretation. I'm drawn to this puzzling text: I've taught it four times and discussed it briefly in several articles on Latina/Chicana writing. Yet my analyses thus far have been tentative, partial, inadequate . . . somehow lacking. This first-person narrative, consisting of seven stories (or chapters) ranging in length from seven to fifty-one pages, is riddled with enigmatic silences, jarring time shifts, and unexplained temporal gaps. Although narrated primarily from the perspective of Rocío Esquibel, a young New Mexican woman, the chapters are not arranged in chronological order. Even within a single story, Chávez employs abrupt, nonlinear shifts between her protagonist's adolescence, childhood, and young adult life, depicting memories, dreams, brief friendships, and other fragments from Rocío's experiences, experiences which Rocío herself cannot comprehend. These fragments speak to me; I see many similarities between Chávez's narrator/protagonist and myself, yet I lack words to articulate the connections. Like Rocío's childhood memories, which she describes as intangible and temporary—"as elusive as clouds passing"[1] —my attempts to interpret her story have been equally elusive. I cannot make the various fragments cohere; I am left with a jarring kaleidoscope of only partially interconnected scenes, momentary glances into her life, shared "recollections of pain, of loss, with holes to be filled" (49). Rocío's longing is almost palpable, but I can neither explain it nor stop trying to understand.

This elusiveness has shaped my own highly personal, rather experimental ap-

Thanks to Renae Bredin, Marilyn M. Mehaffy, and Jesse Swan for conversations on earlier versions of this essay.

proach in this essay: I will not offer a conventional literary analysis that begins with a tightly woven introduction and proceeds in objective, orderly fashion to illustrate my thesis. Instead, I'll use my unsuccessful attempts to develop this type of thesis-driven argument to explore several issues, including the limitations in multiculturalist efforts to construct ethnic- and gender-specific cultural/literary traditions, the problematic politics of representation these endeavors generally employ, and multiculturalism's potential challenge to standard academic interpretive methods. More specifically, I'll tell you how my inability to interpret *Menu Girls* has altered my understanding of multiculturalism, especially its potential challenge to existing knowledge structures. It's not enough simply to include texts by women, minority men, and other subordinated groups in our syllabi or analyses and declare ourselves multicultural. Rather, the inclusion of previously ignored texts invites us to reexamine and restructure underlying knowledge systems.

Although I return to this challenge in the conclusion, I want to suggest that, in its very elusiveness, Chávez's text opens a space for this epistemological restructuring process. Take, for example, *Menu Girls'* resistance to classification. Scholars have described it as a novel; as a collection of stories so intimately interrelated that it can and should be read as a novel; as a "sequence" of short stories, unified by the protagonist's desire to make sense of her life; as a set of "interlocking stories"; and as neither a novel nor a collection of short stories but rather a short story cycle.[2] Not surprisingly, Chávez herself refuses conventional literary formulations and speculates that *Menu Girls* can—*perhaps*—more usefully be viewed as "scenes" or "vignettes."[3] As these various attempts to label and impose unity on *Menu Girls* indicate, standard literary terms and frameworks are inadequate and far too restrictive.

Similar challenges to boundaries and labels occur within *Menu Girls* as well. Look, for example, at the penultimate chapter, "Space Is A Solid." Even the title invites us to reexamine conventional ways of knowing: What does it mean to describe space as a solid? Like *Menu Girls* itself, this enigmatic title destabilizes rigid boundaries between apparently distinct categories of meaning and defies readers' desire for resolution and clear-cut answers. This challenge, which occurs throughout *Menu Girls*, compels readers—at least some readers, like me—to rethink existing modes of perception. To explore this challenge, I'll retrace my own ambivalent interactions with this text.

> *Latina discourse . . . fills in the omissions,*
> *flourishes between the gaps. . . .*
>   Eliana Ortega and Nancy Sternbach[4]

Originally, I had planned to read *Menu Girls* in the context of Latina/Chicana theory, demonstrating that Chávez constructs a gender-inflected, ethnic-specific model of identity formation that challenges the erasure of marginal groups: After briefly discussing the limited representations of Chicana identity available in literary discourse, I would argue that by depicting the experiences of Rocío Esquibel, Chávez creates new forms of Chicana identity which simultaneously critique and expand existing literary representations of female subjectivity.

However, this approach was far too restrictive. Unlike the Latina writings Ortega and Sternbach describe above, *Menu Girls* does not flourish between the gaps but instead allows the gaps to flourish. Both thematically and structurally *Menu Girls* privileges the omissions. Nor does Chávez's text fit into existing paradigms of Chicana literature. As Tey Diana Rebolledo explains in her groundbreaking overview of Chicana fiction and poetry, a key element in recent writings is the quest for and attainment of increased self-understanding. Interweaving girlhood perspectives "with an adult consciousness that intervenes in the remembering," contemporary Chicana writers redefine the past from their present perspectives, creating new representations of individual and collective identity that speak to their own experiences as Chicanas. As Rebolledo notes, this intervening adult consciousness plays a vital role in constructing these new images of gendered, ethnic-specific identity: "It is often as a result of examining complex situations that the young narrators do not understand . . . that the narrators begin to understand what it means to be a woman, or what it means to be a Chicana."[5]

Like the writers Rebolledo describes, Chávez employs this doubled temporal narrative, interweaving perspectives from childhood and adult life. However, the intervening adult consciousness does not offer additional insights into the meaning of womanhood; nor does she achieve a more adequate comprehension of her identity as a Chicana. Her quest for increased self-understanding is almost entirely unsuccessful. She repeatedly questions conventional meanings of female identity and almost entirely ignores her Mexican-American heritage. Look, for instance, at the second chapter, "Evening in Paris." Set at Christmastime, 1960, this story depicts the young Rocío's unsuccessful attempts to select the perfect Christmas gift for her mother. The present tense narration gives Rocío's childhood experiences a sense of immediacy, reinforcing her urgent desire to please her mother: "The package lays heavily in my hands. I must not drop it. Oh, what a joyful treasure! This is the nicest gift I have ever given Mother. I know she'll like it, I know she will" (70). Yet the child's expectations are not met, and this lovingly selected gift goes unnoticed. Looking back, the adult narrator describes her subsequent feelings of inadequacy, disappointment, and lack: "As usual, I felt unfulfilled, empty, without the right words, gifts, feelings for those whose lives crowded around me and who called themselves my family. How removed I felt, far away as Paris" (74-75). This adult narrative perspective does not provide additional insight into the child's alienation and bewilderment; it simply reconfirms and reinforces the little girl's point of view.

To be sure, I could use the ethnic markers—the Spanish phrases sprinkled throughout *Menu Girls,* the occasional references to tacos, tamales, and compadres—to argue that Rocío draws on her cultural "roots" and creates an ethnic-specific self-image. Yet these markers seem to have little or no impact on Rocío's struggles to achieve some type of satisfactory self-definition. And unlike the comforting, positive atmosphere of "Chicano kitchens . . . filled with abuelitas, mothers, wives, and daughters mixing ingredients and making meals" Rebolledo finds in Chicana literature, the kitchen in *Menu Girls* is most definitely not a "nourishing space."[6] Rocío complains that it smells of burnt food and lemons, and that the refrigerator is filled with green chile and " 'old . . . meat' " (139). Even the tamales she eats in the final scene were not lovingly made by an abuelita or mother; rather, they were purchased at the local tortilla factory. Like the other ethnic-specific markers, these mass-produced tamales are fragments in Rocío's fragmented life.

I could emphasize this fragmentation and argue for a causal relationship between Rocío's detachment from her ethnic "roots" and her only partially spoken desires, but this interpretation relies on a knee-jerk essentialism that I can't accept. It's too easy. I can prove it simply by referring to Rocío's (or Chávez's) Chicana "blood." Such attempts to read *Menu Girls* as an ethnic-specific text rely on what Rey Chow describes as the "myth of consanguinity, *a myth that demands absolute submission because it is empty*" (her italics). As Chow rightly points out, creating literary or political categories based exclusively on biology are far too restrictive: "The submission to consanguinity means the surrender of agency— what is built on work and livelihood rather than blood and race—in the governance of a community."[7] Chávez does *not* create a distinctively Chicana identity. In fact, when I taught *Menu Girls* in a graduate seminar on multicultural US literature, several students insisted that its sensibility seemed distinctively "white"—*especially* in its depiction of Chicana culture.

Yet similar problems arose when I changed my focus and examined *Menu Girls* from a more general feminist perspective. . . .

> *I am a transmitter of the woman's voice, a voice that may or*
> *may not have been heard; in the greater, larger world it has not*
> *been heard.*   Denise Chávez[8]

If, as Chávez suggests in this epigraph, she sees her writerly role as channeling "the woman's voice," then it seemed possible to listen to her words and discover how she was representing previously unexpressed female experiences. Significantly, Chávez does not claim to delineate an ethnic-specific (Chicana) woman's voice but rather implies that she wants to express something universal about women. And so, I decided to read *Menu Girls* in dialogue with more general forms of feminist theory, concentrating specifically on Rocío's efforts to put her experiences into words. Focusing on Rocío's attempts to define herself, I would argue that Chávez develops new representations of nonethnic-specific female subjectivity and desire.

But my attempts to construct this argument have been unsatisfactory. Rocío does *not* embody new representations of female subjectivity. Her voice is exceedingly broken—filled with uncertainty and doubt—and omits vital information. In the title chapter, for instance, Rocío mentions her repressed anger yet explains neither its source nor its impact on her life. She offers a brief reference—"inside, I was always angry"—but no more (34). Although signs of this repressed anger briefly surface in other stories, the anger remains so hidden that Rocío herself never explores it.

At times, Rocío's broken silence can be overwhelming. Consider, for instance, her memory of a childhood event in "Willow Game," when a young boy walked up to her at school and, for no apparent reason, punched her in the stomach. Here is her explanation for why she chose not to report this random act of violence to her teacher: "What could I say to her? To my mother and father? What can I say to you? All has been told. . . . I was filled with immense sadness, the burning snow in a desert land of consistent warmth" (49–50). When I first read this passage I was stunned by Rocío's silence. "No!" I wanted to shout. "All has *not* been told. I don't understand!!!" To be sure, this silence reflects the experiences of many women, including my own. But the intervening adult narrator offers no clues and draws no parallels between her experience and that of others. As in "Evening in Paris," she simply confirms and, by confirming, seems to accept the enormous sadness experienced by her younger self.

This narrative focus on Rocío's inability (or refusal?) to articulate her own experiences and desires receives extended treatment in "Shooting Stars," which depicts her enigmatic, only partially expressed longings for and about women— her "insatiable gleanings and continual speculations into the mysteries of womanhood" (61). Rocío explains that unlike those women who could move "from girlhood to womanhood with ease," she found no models "womanly" enough to enable her to effect the transition (62–63). Significantly, she cannot define the term "womanly;" nor can she articulate what, precisely, becoming a woman entails, and in the opening paragraphs she asks: "What did it mean to be a woman? To be beautiful, complete? Was beauty a physical or a spiritual thing, was it strength of emotion, resolve, a willingness to love? What was it then, that made women lovely?" (53). But Rocío cannot answer these questions. Although she closely observes a series of lovely young women, she cannot explain why she finds them so attractive. Nor can she sustain her admiration: Each of the beautiful girl/women[9] Rocío describes was somehow "lacking," and she concludes this account with an only partially expressed desire that seems to reflect both inner and outer absence: "For most of us, choice is an external sorting of the world, filled with uncertain internal emptiness. Who was I, then, to choose as a model? Eloisa, Diana, Josie, or Barbara? None seemed quite womanly enough. Something seemed to be lacking in each of them. The same thing that was lacking in me, whatever it was" (62). But what is it? What's lacking both in Rocío and in the beautiful young women she observes? Rocío herself never tells us and really doesn't seem to know.

Clearly, Rocío's inability to articulate her experiences and desires made it difficult to argue that Chávez develops new representations of female subjectivity. And so I modified my focus yet again: Exploring these elusive feminine figures of uncertainty and lack, I would argue that *Menu Girls* exposes and critiques the limited representations of female identity available in masculinist discourse.[10] After all, the images of beautiful women appear on the blank wall of the father's study, perhaps indicating the phallocentric context that defines—and, by defining, restricts—female identity. Moreover, Rocío seems to associate womanhood with conventional western images of femininity—Woman as object, Woman as other, Woman as lack. Her intense dissatisfaction with these models, coupled with her only partially expressed, barely recognized desire for alternate representations of womanhood, could illustrate the ineffectiveness of currently existing, male-defined standards.

Yet Chávez's critique of existing representations of womanhood (if that's what it is, and I'm really not really sure) occurs only sporadically, juxtaposed next to what Rosaura Sánchez appropriately describes as Chávez's "conformism," her acceptance of feminine passivity, self-sacrifice, and women's relegation to the private, domestic sphere.[11] Moreover, Rocío does not openly question conventional representations of Woman. Indeed, at times she seems to embrace them, and implies that she wants to become the beautiful female objects she admires— an attractive object of male desire (62–63).

Significantly, however, this desire to *be* the passive object of male desire exists simultaneously with a more ambiguous, only partially expressed desire *for* women. In one of the most enigmatic scenes in the entire book, Rocío dreams of absolving her great aunt Eutilia's bodily decay by performing "a primitive dance, a full moon offering" for this dying woman: "I danced around her bed in my dreams, naked, smiling, jubilant. . . . I danced around Eutilia's bed. I hugged the screen door, my breasts indented in the meshed wire. In the darkness Eutilia moaned, my body wet, her body dry. Steamy we were, and full of prayers" (14–15, her ellipses). This passage illustrates the problematic nature of female expression, sexuality, and desire throughout *Menu Girls*. What is Rocío trying to give to her aunt? What desires do her prayers represent? As Renato Rosaldo observes, this dream-dance has its source in Rocío's "emerging sexuality," and indicates her "bodily, sexual connection with her great aunt."[12] But what, more specifically, do we make of this nascent sexuality? Is it simply the exuberant expression of an adolescent heterosexual girl? Or does this eroticized dream-dance—especially the steamy mingling of wet and dry female bodies—imply some type of same-sex desire and lesbian sexuality?

This partially sexualized desire occurs again in Rocío's brief encounter with Elizabeth Rainey, one of the patients she meets during her summer job at the hospital. Although she suggests that she "fell in love" with this beautiful lonely young woman (26), it's difficult to know what, more precisely, Rocío means when she talks about falling in love. Moreover, these feelings are only partially acknowledged, even by Rocío herself; and the adult narrator asks, "How could I, age seventeen, not knowing love, how could I presume to reach out to this young woman in her sorrow, touch her and say, 'I know, I understand?'" (27). Lacking the self-knowledge to establish a connection with this other woman, she retreats into herself. Yet their brief encounter has permanently marked Rocío, and she tells us that "[a]s long as I live I will carry Elizabeth Rainey's image with me. . . . I would have danced for her, Eutilia, had I but dared" (28).

Does the lasting impression Elizabeth Rainey makes on Rocío, coupled with Rocío's longing to dance both for this woman and for Eutilia, indicate a desire to establish some type of meaningful, but nonsexual, connection with other women? Or, does this oblique allusion to Rocío's highly eroticized woman-centered dream-dance for Eutilia hint at some type of only partially acknowledged same-sex desire? Once again, neither interpretation is satisfactory; neither receives adequate support from the text. As in "Shooting Stars," Rocío experiences an unfulfilled attraction to other women which I cannot fully explain.

At this point in my investigation I decided to change my focus for the fourth time, and to argue that Rocío's vague longings for and about women indicate Chávez's attempt to expose a more specific representational lack: The absence of representations of lesbian sexuality and desire. As a number of theorists have observed, western cultures provide no adequate representations of *lesbian* sexuality. Not surprisingly, given the pervasive heterosexist masculinist bias underlying western sociosymbolic systems, lesbian desire—when it does (almost) appear—is generally coded as masculine.[13] We see this masculinized desire in "Shooting Stars." Rocío uses mythic, religious terms to describe her attraction to Eloisa: "She was Venus. . . . That summer I carried Eloisa around with me—her image a holy card, revered, immutable, an unnamed virgin" (56); she states that "Diana's beauty came out of a certain peacefulness, not her own, but mine" (58); and she praises "the white meat of Josie's pale, lovely breasts" (61). In each instance, Rocío transforms the women she admires into the objects of her own gaze, illustrating de Lauretis' contention that "our cultural imaginary . . . [has] constructed as the visible, what can be seen, . . . the female body displayed as spectacle for the male gaze 'to take it in,' to enter or possess it."[14] In this story female bodies are on display, but the viewer is Rocío herself.

However, this interpretation is really no more valid than the previous interpretations I tried to develop, for it demands that I focus only on part of the text and ignore Rocío's fragmented heterosexual relationships and desires in other stories[15] as well as the acceptance of conventional (and therefore heterosexual) feminine passivity and self-sacrifice I referred to above.

How, then, do I make sense of this puzzling text? How do I explain Rocío's feelings of isolation, emptiness, and despair—feelings which occur throughout *Menu Girls,* whenever Rocío interacts with others or tries to make sense of her life? Although at times she focuses almost obsessively on her own identity, she does not (re)define Chicana, female, or lesbian subjectivities. Her attempts at self-definition—if that's what they are—are intangible and elusive, leading nowhere. Debra Castillo makes a similar point in her discussion of "The Closet": "Rocío enacts a quest for an absolute and absent cause, enacting her first self-inscription in the closed space of the closet which defines both her struggle for self-definition against the darkness and her recognition that it is the darkness itself that most adequately defines her. In that telling of her truths there is little enlightenment."[16]

When I first read this statement, I experienced a shock of surprise: I, too, was searching for an "absolute . . . cause," for theories, for "enlightenment" I could use to explain Rocío's story. But perhaps that's not the point. Perhaps I should apply Castillo's assertion to *Menu Girls* as a whole. Perhaps, throughout *Menu Girls,* Rocío is defined by darkness, absence, and loss. *No wonder my previous attempts to understand this text were so unsatisfactory!* Instead of accepting and focusing on the absence itself, I've tried to fill the narrative lack with theories about ethnic-, gender-, or sexual-specific representations. My lack of success has taught me that recent multiculturalist quests for increasingly accurate images of previously erased groups are inadequate. Let me emphasize: My point is not to deny the importance of developing new, self-affirmative representational tactics. (I know from personal experience that encountering positive self-images can have a powerful effect on readers' identity formation.) Yet, simultaneously, it's vital to recognize the limitations in the representational strategies we employ.

Multiculturalist calls for expanded representational practices rely on a politics of visibility that assumes realistic representational strategies automatically bring about political and cultural change. Instead of developing new forms of identity, this faith in representation simply re-presents already existing categories of meaning. More specifically, the belief that texts can accurately reflect or express the experiences of previously-erased groups relies on forms of thinking which replicate dominant knowledge structures. Representation has its source in Enlightenment modes of thought which rely on and reinforce existing beliefs concerning an objective reality, a unified core self, and rigid boundaries between categories of meaning. As Alice Jardine notes, "[t]he process of representation, the sorting out of identity and difference, is the process of analysis: naming, controlling, remembering, understanding. A process so seemingly natural to us as to be beyond question. Yet . . . it has been diagnosed as being at the very roots of our Western drive to know all, and shown to be inseparable from the imperial speaking subject. . . . [I]t has been denounced as complicitous with a violence as old as Western history itself."[17] This "drive to know all" distorts the people, ideas, and things that it "knows," forcing them into rigid categories: Self/Other, insider/outsider, "black"/"white," male/female, hetero/homosexual. . . . The list seems endless once we begin classifying, labeling, and dividing.

Rather than produce new forms of knowledge and new concepts of identity, multiculturalists' attempts to attain increasingly accurate, authentic representations of the racialized, gendered, or sexualized other inadvertently replicate already-existing standards—beginning with that notorious binary between self and other. Yet the solution is not to forego all representational practices (which would, of course, be impossible) but instead to expand them even further, to encompass the representation of absence itself. Whereas representation generally functions as a way of standing in for lost satisfactions, Chávez foregoes this satisfaction and represents the losses themselves. By so doing, she compels readers to examine our investment in visible representations of the other.

As Peggy Phelan persuasively argues, the politics of visibility underlying conventional representational strategies has its source in our inability to acknowledge our own internal lack, the division that occurs with entry into the Symbolic and the concurrent development of a unified self-identity. Drawing on psychoanalytic theory, she explains that images of the external other supply the sense of psychic wholeness which the observer lacks: "Identity is perceptible only through a relation to an other—which is to say, it is a form of both resisting and claiming the other, declaring the boundary where the self diverges from and merges with the other. In that declaration of identity and identification, there is always loss, the loss of not-being the other and yet remaining dependent on that other for self-seeing, self-being." Because these feelings of loss destabilize our unified sense of self, we try to cover them over by transforming the other into re-presentations of the (Self-)Same. But this transformation enacts a form of violence, negating subjectivity by forcing the other to conform to our own standards and desires. Thus Phelan calls for an acceptance of impotency and loss, opening up "a new relation between the looker and the image of the other [which] requires more attention to communicating nonvisible, rhetorically unmarked aspects of identity and a greater willingness to accept the impotency of the inward gaze." This "unmarked" identity component is itself a type of absence; it "is not spatial; nor is it temporal; it is not metaphorical; nor is it literal. It is a configuration of subjectivity which exceeds, even while informing, both the gaze and language."[18]

Representations of absence in Chávez's text indicate one form these "unmarked aspects of identity" might take. Throughout *Menu Girls* Rocío repeatedly encounters others with whom she cannot fully identify or connect. Significantly, she does not convert the various others in her life into re-presentations of the (Self-)Same. They remain other, and reflect back this otherness to Rocío herself, compelling her to recognize and accept her self *as* other. To return to the example from "Evening in Paris" I offered earlier: After describing the sense of emptiness she feels when the Christmas gift to her mother goes unacknowledged, the intervening adult narrator looks back on her childhood alienation and accepts both the desire for connection or wholeness and the fact that this desire cannot be fulfilled. This acceptance makes possible new models of inter/subjectivity that negotiate between self and other. I employ a diacritical slash between "inter" and "subjectivity" to underscore the always partial nature of our interactions with others, as well as the inevitable self-division that occurs with the development of a unified self-identity.

Representations of absence and loss occur throughout *Menu Girls*, each time Rocío describes or alludes to her fragmented interactions with others and her inability to make sense of her life. These explorations (can) compel readers to recognize our own internal division, thus leading to new forms of inter/subjectivity that acknowledge the split within every apparently unified subject. Refusing to cover over self/other divisions, the textual gaps open new spaces where alternate forms of multicultural consciousness can occur. Absence itself becomes a form of connection, a space of commonality generated by difference. In seeing Rocío's loss, we find a reflection of our own.

If, as a number of theorists suggest, we are "all and always" on the boundary or interface between self and other, we must develop new ways of negotiating this fluid divide. Representations of absence and loss offer one way, among others,[19] to do so.

Beyond the Frame of Whiteness: Harryette Mullen's Revisionary Border Work

Cynthia Hogue

The figure of Woman has become, in the Western tradition that both Edouard Manet's odalisque figure, "Olympia," and lyric poetry exemplify, an overdetermined image—silenced, objectified, at once symbol of lack, truth, inspiration, desire, and bourgeois sign of a man's material success. But it is worth briefly contextualizing Manet's "Olympia" in her historical moment, for although specularized, she is also transgressive, as Christine Stansell has suggested in a review of how nineteenth century painters represented "the woman question" in France. As Stansell observes of the gender dynamics of Manet's Paris:

> Men stared and remarked and observed: women tried to look down and away and sideways. Women were among the sights that flaneurs took in as they slid through the crowds on the streets, but to look boldly in return was to designate oneself a woman of ill repute. The gazes which whizzed about and knocked and glanced against each other in the streets of Paris were an imaginative nexus from which the new painters in their studios fashioned their own stunning ways of seeing and shocking: think of Manet's lounging Olympia and her shameless look.[1]

Olympia is shameless, of course, because she dares to return the male gaze, to enter the always triangulated dynamic of that look (male painter representing, to and for a male audience, the often eroticized, always looked-at woman) as an implicitly active participant.

As Rachel Blau DuPlessis recounts of lyric poetry, recurring triangulations are also paradigmatic of the gendered clusters in its tradition as well. A male "I" speaks to a "postulated, loosely male 'us'" about a beloved "she." DuPlessis contends:

To change any of these pronouns ("I" speaking directly to a "you," . . . ; an "I" who is a "she"; readers claiming to be female) is to jostle, if only slightly, the homosocial triangle of the lyric.

If, as she asserts, "the genre poetry activates notable master plots, ideologies, and moves fundamentally inflected with gender relations,"[2] and I agree that it has, historically, how much more of an Olympian "jostle" is introduced if the "I" who is a "she" is also not white?

That is, in my opening discussion of Manet's "Olympia," I reproduced—in order to underscore—the white blindspot of dominant culture. As Richard Dyer observes in a foundational article on the construction of whiteness in film history, entitled "White":

> Trying to think about the representation of whiteness . . . is difficult, partly because white power secures its dominance by seeming not to be anything in particular. . . . as if it is the natural, inevitable, ordinary way of being human.[3]

If white is what seems "natural" in this ideology of power, black is "unnatural"; if white is "inevitable," black is, paradoxically, at once evident and under erasure (as I may have illustrated in my opening). In dominant culture's art since the nineteenth century, Harryette Mullen observes on the literature of passing, the image of blacks has been pervasively used "to represent repressed elements of what has been constructed ideologically and semiotically as a 'white psyche.'"[4]

And thus, to complete the description of Manet's painting, we have the black woman who stands off to the side and in the background. Apparently a servant, she gazes at the white woman with what Manet portrays as a mixture of reverence and subservience.[5] Although revising the homosocial triangle of Western painting, she is so fully absorbed by her material and schematic function—at once displaying a bouquet and standing in for an absent admirer—that she is quite literally lost in her gaze. As such, she contrasts strikingly with the black cat, which, in arching wide-eyed beside her at the artist beyond the painting's frame, lets the cat (so to speak) out of the bag. The figure of the black woman constitutes an in-frame frame for the white woman, with whom she contrasts. As Mullen has noted, "the white woman's body [is] constructed as beautiful, feminine, seductive, also a little outrageous. The black woman is . . . part of the decor but her presence seems to enhance the qualities that are attributed to the white nude."[6]

If the one woman is aligned, as Manet implies chromatically, with animal nature, the other is human nature. If one is opaque or inscrutable, the other is transparent, open. If one is clothed and desexualized, the other is disrobed and erotically fetishized. The black woman is the background that foregrounds the white nude—the very ground by which an idealized white femininity is constituted as beauty and truth. Although in being in the background, she schematically comprises part of the painting's in-frame frame, she is in actuality completely framed by the whiteness her contrasting presence defines.

Harryette Mullen's first volume, *Tree Tall Woman*, published in 1981,[7] is written beyond that frame of whiteness, which I want to discuss in the essay that follows in order to provide a context for the remarkable trajectory of her work. It explores in part her experience of growing up in a middle class, single-parent, devout home in a "99.9% black neighborhood" in Texas. The volume also builds on the Black Arts movement having already effected the positive revaluation of black culture. Although Mullen now feels that her sense of writing "with a black voice" was very regionally restricted at the time, the space that the Black Arts movement opened up for her gave her the freedom to write about black culture, community, and experience—as she puts it, to write a very black poem—without having to say, "This is a very black [poem]."[8]

The collection spoke to a general audience, but especially to black women, Mullen recalls, because of its adherence to a poetics of accessibility from which she has since moved away. It is full of scenic portraits of black family and community life, as well as extended, playful metaphors, in an expressive language rich in oral and musical qualities. In "The Joy," which I quote in full, the female speaker deliciously tropes on the joy of cooking:

> Here's a bowl of batter
> for your spoon to stir.
> Here's an oven
> to bake your bread in.
> Put some starch
> in your chef's hat, honey,
> and start cookin.
> (*TTW,* 39)

The ways this poem achieves effect—its monologic subjectivity (to be sure, in black dialect); play with extended metaphor; lineation adhering to syntactic unit; sound pattern of mainly percussive plosives, with a sexy, aspirating undertone; location in a poetics of presence reinforced by the repetition of imperative deictics—place it solidly within the formal conventions of Western lyric tradition.

Another poem, "Playing the Invisible Saxophone en el Combo de las Estrellas," opens, "One of these days I'm gonna write a real performance poem." It proceeds conventionally to perform the very act that its opening announces as imagined:

Yeah, gonna have words turning into dance,
bodymoving music,
a get-down poem so kinetically energetic
it sure put disco to shame.
Make it a snazzy jazzy poem extravaganza, with pizzazz.
Poem be going solo,
flying high on improbable improvisational innovation.
Poem be blowing hard!

(*TTW*, 54)

This first collection is admittedly a long way from what Elisabeth Frost has termed the "lyric hybridity" of Mullen's fourth collection.[9] *Muse & Drudge*, with its "Sapphire's lyre styles," makes an extended exploration of "how a border orders disorder."[10] We trace in such early passages, however, the roots of Mullen's mature lexical and poetic concerns.

With their double-entendres, puns, jazzy cadences, and sassy diction, Mullen's early poems playfully reclaim and positively revalue stereotypes of blacks in dominant culture as signs of "illicit sexuality" or "obsequious subservience."[11] She is, moreover, performing a sort of reverse code-switching, since as she has remarked, her first language in childhood was, in fact, a standard English that she learned to switch in and out of, as necessary, in order not to sound like "you are [not] from here" (in other words, not to sound "white").[12] She describes her later style as "multi-voiced" and "mongrel" in a 1996 interview with Calvin Bedient.[13] As Frost notes, it is "an experiment in collective reading and an assertion of the complexities of community, language, and poetic voice"[14]—an assertion, as I have been suggesting, which we can perceive in nascent form in *Tree Tall Woman*. That sense of being in linguistically and racially mongrel community is anticipated in Mullen's code-switching explorations in the early collection.

The pronounced orality of some poems in the collection readily identifies them as spoken in the voice of a black speaker. Other poems, however, written in standard English, explore, as Mullen recounts, "relations among black people, . . . [and] being in the world as a person who has a particular perspective," without continually underscoring that it is written from a black perspective. Mullen speaks in her 1998 interview of enjoying the freedom "to write a poem about a mother braiding her daughter's hair that was a very black poem, but didn't have to say, 'This is a black woman braiding her black child's black hair.'"[15] In a related poem, "Saturday Afternoon When Chores Are Done," the speaker, a single mother of two young girls, says that after she has cleaned the house,

> I oil my hair and brush it soft.
> Then, with the brush in my lap,
> I gather the hair in my hands,
> pull the strands smooth and tight,
> and weave three sections into a fat shiny braid
> that hangs straight down my back.
>
> I remember mama teaching me to plait my hair
> . . . .
> and my braids would fray apart
> no sooner than I'd finished them.
> Mama said, "Just takes practice, is all."
> . . . .
> Between time on the job,
> keeping house, and raising two girls by myself,
> there's never much time like this,
> for thinking and being alone.
> Time to gather life together
> before it unravels like an old jumprope
> and comes apart at the ends.
>
> (*TTW*, 10–11)

The speaker reveals that, because of her life circumstances, she has not had the time to be alone to compose and gather herself in a quiet moment. Then, realizing that her children's noisy play has suddenly grown silent, she looks out the window over the kitchen sink to see that her older daughter is braiding her younger daughter's hair. The mother once had the time to teach her older daughter (implicitly, before the unmentioned father left). Having benefitted from that time, the older daughter is now able to step into the role that her mother no longer is able to fill.

In the closing, the poem shifts to a direct address of this older daughter, which conjures her hearing her mother, in the convention of apostrophe, when she obviously cannot. This figurative and formal shift posits the daughter structurally in the same place as her mother—specifically, in the process of developing the survival skills that she will need as a source of generational strength for younger women, like her younger sister:

Older daughter,
you are learning what I am learning:
to gather the strands together
with strong fingers,
to keep what we do
from coming apart at the ends.

                    (*TTW*, 11)

The enjambed line break in this passage between the penultimate and final lines
of the poem formally enacts the thematic tension in the text between the moth-
er's fantasized desire to protect and preserve her own (to *keep* the fruits of one's
labor, in all senses) and the reality of her experience (the difficulty with which
she struggles simply to *keep it together*).

Braiding the hair becomes, in the course of the poem, a metaphor for the
speaker's fraught capacity to be a model of fortitude for her daughters. That is,
there is an acknowledgment in the poem of the fact that, in order to maintain
the continuity of knowledge in a matrilineal community, roles have had to be
redistributed. Hence, it is the grandmother's voice alone, relegated to the past,
which is represented in black dialect and distinguished from the mother's expe-
rience by the quotation marks.

Thus, while the poem is accessible on many levels to any audience, it has par-
ticular significance to a black female audience, not least because of its resonant
invocation of a strong matrilineality. It is a domestic scene familiar to most
women, but details such as "blackeyed peas" cooking on the stove and the "sweet
potato plant" growing in the garden suggest that the mother is preparing "soul
food" for her daughters, in all senses of the phrase. How we understand the care-
ful description of learning to braid "crooked" braids that "fray apart" and un-
ravel "like an old jumprope," moreover, depends on our perspective, our particu-
lar experience with hair. When Frost observes in her 1997 interview with Mullen
that there "is a lot about hairdos" in *Muse & Drudge*, Mullen responds that not
only are humans "obsessed with hair," but that "if two black women are together
long enough, they will talk about hair."[16] The detail of oiling the hair and brush-
ing it soft quietly resists white assimilation, locating the poem's specificity about
female self-fashioning in a cultural, racial, and gendered history.

What "Saturday Afternoon" achieves through its descriptive details exempli-
fies *Tree Tall Woman*'s signifying reversal of the movement in the literature of
passing from the "not-white margins" to the "white center."[17] Rather, using a
language that almost seamlessly passes (the one seam, the direct quotation, re-
sisting such passing), Mullen marginalizes whiteness and centralizes African
American female experience. Thus, the poem works to undo the pervasive pro-

duction of whiteness and engages productively and specifically in representing aspects of black experience.

Tree Tall Woman is, like Mullen's later work, anti-assimilationalist (the term is Nathaniel Mackey's[18]), albeit with a markedly different aesthetic. In a 1993 lecture entitled "Visionary Literacy: Art, Literature and Indigenous African Writing Systems," Mullen gives us some insight into this striking shift in her poetic development. The lecture takes issue with black literary traditions that privilege orality—a distinguishing "black" diction translated phonetically onto the page:

> This speech-based and racially inflected aesthetic that produces a black poetic diction requires that the writer acknowledge and reproduce in the text a significant difference between the spoken and written language of African Americans and that of other Americans.

As Aldon Nielsen glosses, "Mullen's thesis is that this approach has indeed produced an impoverished and narrowed view of black cultural activities, to some extent because of its questionable assumptions about the construction of African cultural histories."[19] Frost asserts that, rather than allowing issues of racial identity and privilege to lead to "an essentialist politics," Mullen explores in her later work a "poetics that re-charges language and alerts us to the hybridity of its forms."[20]

It would be easy to categorize *Tree Tall Woman* as verging on "an essentialist politics." The overworked, single mother in "Saturday Afternoon," for example, comes close to a widely-circulated cultural stereotype, although the poem's careful attention to the emotional details of lived experience grounds it in ethnographic specificity. Thus, it's more accurate to approach the collection as Mullen has suggested, framed by its regional sense of what constitutes "black culture." Within that framework, we can begin to see her early—at times touching, at times ribald—explorations of the linguistic, racial, gender, and visual border work that created the foundation for her mature poetic project. Speech-based and racially inflected poems like "The Joy" are juxtaposed with experiential, non-vernacular poems like "Saturday Afternoon." Within poems like "Playing the Invisible Saxophone," there is an aurally meaningful but non-visual eruption into a metonymically jazzy, linguistic riff (a "snazzy jazzy poem extravaganza, with pizzazz"), which finally strays into and resolves the poem in Spanish (*en el combo de las estrellas*). The volume as a whole resists any reassimilating tendencies on the part of readers as it begins to explore the "irrevocably composite" nature of American culture, as Albert Murray has argued in *The Omni-Americans*.[21] It is this composite culture that Mullen would investigate in the formal and linguistic innovations of her mature work.

I want to close with an analysis of Mullen's revisionary unsettling of whiteness by looking at her Steinian Olympia-poem in *Trimmings*.[22] This poem could only have been written after Mullen had absorbed the lessons, in graduate school and after, of poststructuralist theory, Gertrude Stein, and Ron Silliman's *The New Sentence*. Having both Manet's "Olympia" and Stein's prose poem, "A Petticoat," in *Tender Buttons*, critically in mind, Mullen signifies on both.[23] Stein's poem in full reads:

> A light white, a disgrace, an ink spot, a rosy charm.[24]

As Frost recounts, following Lisa Ruddick, the white petticoat in this poem is connected to the blank page, the disgraceful blood spot revised into a woman writer's ink, the repressed power of which Stein celebrates as "a rosy charm."[25]

For Mullen, who has speculated that Stein had Manet's "Olympia" in mind, what's overlooked both in Stein's poem and critical readings of it is the repressed dynamics of race (as Frost notes as well). The black woman is thereby erased, written over as *writing* ("an ink spot"), a culturally invisible text. Here is Mullen's prose poem in signifying response, quoted in full:

> A light white disgraceful sugar looks pink, wears an air, pale compared to shadow standing by. To plump recliner, naked truth lies. Behind her shadow wears her color, arms full of flowers. A rosy charm is pink. And she is ink. The mistress wears no petticoat or leaves. The other in shadow, a large, pink dress.
>
> (*T*, 15)

Mullen foregrounds what Stein and Manet relegate to background. As she writes in *Trimmings*' afterword, "Off the Top," she was thinking in the volume as a whole about "language as clothing and clothing as language." The words "pink" and "white" kept recurring in her ruminations through these poems, and as Mullen wryly observes, "As a black woman writing in this language, I suppose I already had an ironic relationship to this pink and white femininity" (*T*, n.p.).

The poem signifies on the Renaissance lyric tradition of the blazon. The conventional blazon could contain, in a poet like John Donne's hands, an attention to the artifice of poetic structures that resists readerly absorption in the material.[26] By analogy, Mullen's poem draws attention to the artificial cultural signs structuring gender and race. At the border between these two iconic figures—the one a punning image of how "naked truth lies," and, in Mullen's resonant invocation of black code-switching, her shadowy other—we find a destabilizing, liminal moment (in Victor Turner's sense of the creative betwixt-and-between of culturally organized categories[27]). The border between the two women is fluid, disordered by its permeability to an exchange of ordering signs. The "mistress," implicitly repositioned in Mullen's poem as supine, "wears an air" (like the Emperor in his new clothes), her whiteness exposed, decentralized, abject. In her pink dress, the black woman, socio-historically and linguistically coded as both "shadow" and "in shadow," actually *overshadows* the other, suggesting that, as a sign of "pink and white" femininity, the dress is arbitrary, literally a put-on.

Mullen graphically mimes this insight in the play between "ink" (the black woman) and "pink" (the white woman), whereby "ink" puts on "pink's" "p."[28] Through the power of a signifying writing, as Mullen's poem suggests, the stable framework of race and gender codes is similarly revealed as artificial, the critically exposed and lexically fluid border between the two women replacing the fixity of familiar ordering structures. The poem destructures the old order without replacing it, the two figures refusing both assimilation and segregation—a disorderingly mongrelized composition, a schematically reframed aggregate. In this terrain of suddenly visible edges and interfaces, we can begin to envision the creative possibility of a transformed and transforming *integration*—what I have termed Mullen's revisionary border work.

Untranslatable Communities, Productive Translation, and Public Transport: Rosmarie Waldrop's *A Key into the Language of America* and Joy Harjo's *The Woman Who Fell from the Sky*

Jonathan Monroe

> To get to the relation to the public—by recognition of absence, of no relation—
> to the other[1]

What counts as an experimental approach to poetry? What characteristic stances toward audience do such approaches imply and what formal strategies do they deploy? What connections can we establish between such strategies and the demands, desires, and needs of particular communities? What kinds of communities do experimental poetries envision and what kinds of poetries do these communities call for in return? How translatable are the intended effects of certain strategies across particular audiences? In the particular ways they address these questions, Rosmarie Waldrop's *A Key into the Language of America* and Harjo's *The Woman Who Fell from the Sky* have a lot to tell us about the range of roles experimental poetry can play in negotiating intersections of language, community, race and ethnicity, gender, nationality, and postcoloniality.

Though both works display a common concern specifically with Native American history and Native American communities, they do so from very different vantage points—Waldrop as a native German-speaking immigrant to the United States after World War II who has long since settled, as she puts it, "in the former territory of the Narragansett Indians" in Providence, Rhode Island (xiii),[2] Harjo as a proud member of the Muscogee tribe. Where Waldrop tends to be associated not only as a poet, but as mentor, editor, and translator (from French and German especially) with Language writing, Harjo's affiliations and recognition have been bound up with the increasing prominence in the past two decades of multicultural poetries. Where Waldrop approaches her complex engagement with the language and culture of the Narragansett Indians in self-consciously mediated fashion through her appropriation of the 1643 book by Roger Williams that gives her book its title, Harjo understands her task as that of a "speaker of the truth" on behalf of her tribe within a late twentieth-century postcolonial frame. A century and a half after Charles Baudelaire's shifting of the terrain of poetic experimentation from verse to prose, "Reconciliation A Prayer,"[3] the opening text of *Woman Who Fell from the Sky*, offers a provocative counter-text to "The Stranger" ("L'étranger"),[4] the emblematic opening prose poem of *Paris Spleen (Le spleen de Paris)*, the collection that more than any other established the force and currency of the prose poem's anti-generic experimentalism.[5] Here, in Louise Varèse's translation, is Baudelaire's seminal text, followed by the first section of Harjo's two-page prose piece:

Tell me, enigmatical man, whom do you love best, your father,
your mother, your sister, or your brother?
I have neither father, nor mother, nor sister, nor brother.
Your friends?
Now you use a word whose meaning I have never known.
Your country?
I do not know in what latitude it lies.
Beauty?
I could indeed love her, Goddess and Immortal.
Gold?
I hate it as you hate God.
Then, what do you love, extraordinary stranger?
I love the clouds . . . the clouds that pass . . . up there . . .
up there . . . the wonderful clouds!   (1)

We gather at the shore of all knowledge as peoples who were put here by a god who wanted relatives.

This god was lonely for touch, and imagined herself as a woman, with children to suckle, to sing with—to continue the web of the terrifyingly beautiful cosmos of her womb.

This god became a father who wished for others to walk beside him in the belly of creation.

This god laughed and cried with us as a sister at the sweet tragedy of our predicament—foolish humans—

Or built a fire, as our brother to keep us warm.

This god who grew to love us became our lover, sharing tables of food enough
for everyone in this whole world.   (xv)

Thoroughly at odds in tone and trajectory, formally as well as thematically
the two texts bear what we may call after Wittgenstein, in this case with no small
irony, a striking family resemblance.[6] Regendering and revisioning the earlier
poem's terms and conclusions, "Reconciliation A Prayer" is, we might say, "The
Stranger's" "sister," if not its "twin."[7] Despite this family resemblance, which
places Harjo's text within a continuum of prose-poetic experimentation—a "tra-
dition of innovation" (an oxymoronic corporate logo if ever there was one) for
which Baudelaire is the pivotal founding figure—with respect to race, gender,
and historical perspective, the two texts represent diametrically opposed per-
spectives. Significantly, the first word to occur in Harjo's opening text, which is
also its first pronoun, is not the second person "you" (*tu*) at the beginning of
"The Stranger," or the first person "I" (*Je*) that quickly follows in response, but
"We," a pronoun that had become entirely suspect from the Baudelairean per-
spective without recourse to irony. Against the tone-setting modernist innova-
tions for which Baudelaire's turn to the prose poem may serve as a programmatic
instance, Harjo's resolutely non-ironic use of the first person plural invites us to
reengage and reexamine, within the present postcolonial or post-postcolonial
context, the aesthetic and political questions and answers these innovations once
implied.

For readers educated into modernist and postmodernist interpretive com-
munities and writerly paradigms that have been shaped by such texts as "The
Stranger" and the whole of *Paris Spleen,* it may be tempting to discount Harjo's
reconciliatory prayer as hopelessly naïve. After Baudelaire, after modernism and
postmodernism, how can a "we" be posited to speak without irony *without* be-
ing naïve? Harjo's answer, historically grounded in her continuing lived relation
to the Muscogee tribe to which she belongs by birth and to which she has re-
mained committed by choice, is that "we"—not just the Muscogees but all of us
on the planet—have reached a point where the alienated stance that prompted
Baudelaire to refer to the poem as itself an "objet de luxe," has become a luxury
the world can scarcely afford. If literary innovation is to amount to more than a
version of aesthetic Fordism or Gatesism after a century in which the cultural
prestige of the "literary" itself has faded and no idea has become so commodified
as the idea of "making it new," "we," Harjo's collection implies, must face up to
the task of reconfiguring what it means to live "in relation," to learn to preserve
what is of value "at the shore(s) of all knowledge," both old and new, as in the
opening words of the fourth and final section of "Reconciliation": "We gather

up these strands broken from the web of life. They shiver with our love, as we call them the names of our relatives and carry them to our home made of the four directions and sing . . . "

As these lines from the closing section of "Reconciliation" suggest, for Harjo the value of innovation cannot be measured in and of itself, but only in terms of the value of what gets preserved and what gets lost in the ever-changing "web" of relations. At this advanced stage on the long march of what Max Horkheimer and Theodor Adorno called the "project of the enlightenment,"[8] with its pervasively demythologizing impulses, Harjo's explicit, unabashed recourse to the language of myth in this regard (as for example in the piece titled "The Myth of Blackbirds") is anything but naïve. Myth figures in her work, rather, as a reminder that the stories we tell ourselves, whether subject to preservation or innovation, have been and will be continually revised and extended to include and displace other stories and the stories of others, stories forgotten and ignored by "relatives" "we" have wanted to claim or not, near or distant, relatives nonetheless, in relation, as related, as listened to, stories told. Blending image and abstraction, references to human characters and animals, objects and historical references, wilderness and urban landscapes, Native American, American, and foreign references, tribal loyalties and extra-tribal affinities, questions of race, ethnicity, and community, familial belonging and gender differences, Harjo's dominant textual mode is one of resolutely non-cynical, imaginative action, a heuristic of community designed not to further divide but to bring together. Innovation resists its own potential fetishization in this landscape, registering as of value to the extent that it serves such ends and the means to achieve them as a permanent condition. That poetry which would involve us in what I have called "productive translation" and "public transport" can do so most effectively, Harjo suggests, by recollecting lost stories that ask to be reclaimed, the human "baggage" figured by the exiled taxi drivers who spark some of the collection's most memorable acts of empathic speculation.

> We fled the drama of lit marble in the capitol for a refuge held up by sweet, everlasting earth. The man from Ghana who wheeled our bags was lonesome for his homeland, but commerce made it necessary to carry someone else's burdens. The stars told me how to find us in the disorder of systems. ("The Myth of Blackbirds," 28)

Although the currency of such speculations may vary from one reading community to the next, their challenge is precisely not to remain satisfied within any one community, however reassuringly homogeneous or like-minded, but to move between and among different communities and divergent writing and reading practices. For however "transporting" a particular community may be, as Harjo reminds us, only the decision to embrace continual movement between and among diverse communities can prevent loyalties to (always changing) cultural scenes and practices from evolving into forms of fetishization, ossification, and self-incarceration.

Harjo's most striking and sustained formal experiment in *Woman Who Fell from the Sky* is her doubling and transvaluation of prose-poetic form to include in each titled piece, with all but a few exceptions, a ghostly italicized after- or post-text:

Stories and songs are like humans who when they laugh are indestructible.

No story or song will translate the full impact of falling, or the inverse power of rising up.

Of rising up.
*

The landscape of the late twentieth century is littered with bodies of our relatives. Native peoples in this country were 100 percent of the population a few hundred years ago. We are now one half of 1 percent. Violence is a prevalent theme in the history of this land. (18–19)

As these closing lines from the pivotal poem, "A Postcolonial Tale," make clear, where the modernist "God" of Baudelaire's "Stranger" is indifferent, absent, hateful, the "god" in Harjo's poem recollects the history of a people who go back long before modernism, who have been displaced by the modern, all but extinguished by it, but who are still here, still capable of affirming the possibility that thinking may yet develop, as Waldrop puts it in *Key*, "out of the negative" (62). In the context of such a history, Baudelairean irony, the alienation of the modern subject, and what Walter Benjamin called the "shock" of modern life appear in a very different light.[9] Faced with the extreme violence and dislocation to which the Muscogee and other Native American tribes have been subjected, Harjo's avowed loyalty to her past, present, and future Native American heritage, and the instantiation of that loyalty throughout the collection, formally as well as thematically, suggest that the impact of "aesthetic" and other innovations can only be understood by moving among multiple cultural locations. What "innovation" transports us *to* is the question, and why, and how. Where does innovation take us, and where has it been? What has been its history and what is its future?

Whose ends does it serve, and how effectively, and for what purposes? It is in the nature of Harjo's project to leave such questions open. The *act* and *practice* of remembering she encourages is in this respect the very ground of innovation, the condition that makes productive translation and public transport possible and justifiable, whether within communities or from one community to another. What is arguably most "experimental" in the current climate about Harjo's response to the destructive consequences of colonialism, and the modernist ethos of experimentation and innovation with which that history is inextricably bound up, is her rejection of the Baudelairean poet's relentlessly ironized, self-ironizing position in favor of a different kind of role that remains, as Harjo's carefully worded formulation at the close of "A Postcolonial Tale" makes clear, radically open-ended:

Their grief is thick with tears that will be soaked up by this beautiful land.

If I am a poet who is charged with speaking the truth (and I believe the word poet is synonymous with truth-teller), what do I have to say about all of this? (19)

Inquiring in her poetry into what language can do for us, Harjo offers a kind of counter-semiotics that affirms language's power to protect, comfort, nourish, heal, and transform. Far from being naïve about questions of context and interpretation, the myths she offers are not so much retellings as purposeful constructions, often mixing the lyrical and narrative language of Native American myth with the language of contemporary science. Sometimes the italicized postscripts (which however are not really "post" at all but integral to the titled text) are longer than the initial, unitalicized part of the text. Usually, they are shorter, offering a combination of personal anecdote and collective history, stories within stories, what might be called (if such terms did not risk obscuring the fact that Native American traditions involved such interweavings long before modernism) a kind of cross-generational "intertextuality" and "interorality."

For Harjo, transportive acts of productive translation involve bearing the burden of what she calls in "A Postcolonial Tale" the "dense unspeakable material" of Native American life, past and present, as of contemporary life generally (18). Well aware of the "constructedness" of texts (as of selves, autobiographies, tribal identifications, etc.), she recounts "myths" that are redeemable as such through the high degree of self-consciousness she brings to what the title of the first of her collection's two sections calls "Tribal Memory," a collective "autobiographical" sense that has less to do with individual identity than with the "web" of shared histories and relations that make up, in her memorable phrase, "the most dynamic point in the structure of [her] family's DNA" (4). Acknowledging the tribal and other myths she recounts and reinvents as both a valued inheritance and a burden ("The Flood," 14), she understands her textual decisions as a complex responsibility. Her myths are both real and not real, language and more than language, historically situated as such. Where Waldrop provides explanatory notes in her introduction to the *Key*, leaving that mode behind thereafter to interweave the four intricate forms that shape each succeeding chapter, Harjo's personal/collective explanations and elaborations unfold gradually across the collection, inviting the reader progressively into a more personal (though not "confessional") relationship to the author and her world.

One result of this procedure is that each italicized section asks for continual rereading of what precedes and succeeds it. The reader is thus drawn into a recursive cycle of reading and rereading, checking myths against personal and impersonal revelations and explanations, and so on. The italicized sections properly read thus do not have the function of shutting down inquiry, but of opening it up still further. As "truth-telling" moments, they might be seen in Brechtian terms as a letting down of the fourth wall, a reminder that the constructedness of the preceding text places the reader in a kind of permanent oscillation between text and commentary, story and understanding, narrative and analysis. Throughout, Harjo's concerns are with intergenerational connections, binding stories, the process of telling and retelling as a never-ending process.

Harjo's postscripts typically involve a certain relaxation of address, a sense of the wise-woman-as-story-teller emerging from behind the curtain, sometimes to amplify or explain the "dense unspeakable material" preceding it:

> *I was in a downtown Chicago hotel room when I called home, as I do every morning and evening when I am away—and was shocked by the story of an Albuquerque taxi driver who was stabbed in the neighborhood I had just moved from a few weeks before. The driver dragged himself to the porch of a home that may have been the house that had been sweet harbor for us, to call for help. He died there. (37)*

Like Waldrop, Harjo frequently interweaves high levels of abstraction with the language of the ordinary, the everyday: "You can manipulate words to turn departure into aperture, but you cannot figure the velocity of love and how it enters every equation" ("Promise," 62); "Perhaps the world will end at the kitchen table, while we are laughing and crying, eating of the last sweet bite" ("Perhaps the World Ends Here," 68). Where Harjo tends to look for what we may have in common despite what apparently separates us, Waldrop tends to prefer, as she acknowledges in the Introduction to *Key*, the "shock" of difference. In contrast to Baudelaire, who experienced the shock of the modern, as Benjamin has argued, as involuntary and unavoidable,[10] Waldrop is shocked on coming to the United States by her "lack of culture shock." "Nothing seemed too different," she writes, "from [her] native Germany—except for the Indian place-names," which "irritated" and "disoriented" her (xiii). As Baudelaire's example reminds us, the birth of modernist poetry and poetics is bound up with the experience not only of shock, but of *ennui,* of shock and boredom as the two corollary states of consciousness that characterize the modern life-world. Although the experience of modern life involves danger—the "horses and vehicles" exploding across the path of the poet-speaker in Baudelaire's "Loss of a Halo" (94), the murdered taxi driver in Harjo's "Letter from the End of the Twentieth Century" —the threat of boredom, as of the generic poetic (re)productions of "some bad poet ... X ... or Z" ("Loss of a Halo," 94) was, as Baudelaire saw, an aesthetic and more than aesthetic problem inviting ever new and experimental poetactics.

The modernist aesthetic of innovation, whether with Baudelaire or Waldrop, is driven not by the prayer for reconciliation that opens Harjo's collection, but by the fear of stagnation, routinization of language use and perspective, the numbing familiarity of the Same. Accordingly, Waldrop's *Key* registers two kinds of shock, one unwelcome, one not—the spirit-deadening shock of a certain cultural homogeneity between Germany and the United States, despite the language difference, on the one hand, and on the other the language-awakening irritation/stimulation of unpronounceable Indian place names. Where Harjo's Muscogee heritage remains crucial to her aesthetic choices, which she understands to be much more than just aesthetically driven, Waldrop's "tribe" is not so much the German family into which she was born, or the white male mainstream culture of her "adopted country" (xxiii), the United States, but the cosmopolitan, transnational tribe of modernist poets whose histories and circumstances open onto a range of aesthetic practices motivated by the desire to negate existing cultural norms. Thus, in "the irritant, the otherness ... the strangeness of ... music" in the Narragansett place names in the surrounding area of her American home of Providence, Rhode Island, Waldrop finds the exotic fascination of signs of a "vanished language and culture" (xxii). Like Harjo, Waldrop reclaims a heritage that might otherwise be lost, but from a very different perspective.

> ... Like Roger Williams, I am ambivalent about my position among the privileged, the 'conquerors.'
>
>   But am I among them? I am white and educated. I am also a poet and a woman. A poet, in our days, is regarded as rather a marginal member of society, whose social usefulness is in doubt. As a woman, I do not figure as conqueror in the shell game of archetypes, but as conquered. A 'war bride.'

> As a woman, I also have no illusions about the Indian societies. They were far from ideal.
>
> I live in Roger Williams' territory. By coincidence and marriage I share his initials. I share his ambivalence. (xx)

Translating her own immigrant experience as an expatriate German in America back through the example of Williams' anthropological treatise, which provides not only the title of her book but a template for the intricate multiform structure of each of its thirty-two sections, Waldrop takes the early American colonist as her point of entry into Narragansett culture. Where Harjo limits her formal innovation, with only a few exceptions, to a sustained alternation within and between titled poems between non-italicized and italicized prose passages, Waldrop's procedure moves from 1) a brief prose section enacting "the clash of Indian and European cultures by a violent collage of phrases with elements from anywhere in [Waldrop's] Western heritage" to 2) word lists that are "not of practical use," like those in Williams' book, but "explore the language context (rather than cultural context) of the chapter titles," to 3) "a narrative section in italics, in the voice of a young woman, ambivalent about her sex and position among the conquerors, to 4) a "final poem" (xxii–xxiii).

Each of the four forms in each of Waldrop's two-page chapters asks to be read in relation not only to the other forms within that chapter, but the same form as it recurs from one chapter to the next. The first, non-italicized prose passage in each case has the primary function of engaging the cultural, historical, political, and economic issues raised by European colonization in ways that attend to the shaping power of language, categorization, rationalization, western science and technology, (mis)understanding and (mis)translation.

> **What paths their swift of foot** have cut in history and philosophy, with distinct genital extensions toward the Great Plains. A feeling of wings in the air will move understanding. So vast, distressed, undone, in search of company to **take tobacco and discourse.** Whirl of environs, exaggerations and limping, lamenting lingua franca.
> (Chapter XI, "Of Travell," 23)

As Waldrop notes in her Introduction, the word lists that follow play off the titles of each chapter in a variety of ways, from "the sound of a title word (e.g. 'fission' in the chapter on fishing)," to its "semantic field ("'interlacing' and 'contagion' in the chapter on 'Relations of Consanguinity')" to "compounds of title words (busy[body], [body]guard, [body]snatcher in Chapter VII) or grammatical elements like suffixes ([season]able, [season]ing in Chapter X)" to the inclusion of "some Narragansett phrases" (xxiii), as in the list in Chapter XVII, "Of Beasts":

Cowsuck.
Gôatsuck.
Pigsuck.
Hógsuck.
(35)

Situated between the historical frame of reference of the first prose passage (what Chapter XIII, "Of the Weather," calls "big masculine history," 28) and the more personal struggles of the female speaker in the italicized prose passage that follows, these passages invite readers to play an active, generative role in remembering, recollecting, restoring, extending, amplifying, and expanding the linguistic and thus cultural possibilities that have resulted from the encounter of colonizer and colonized. The productive translations this strategy entails along with the typically elliptical, oblique, non-sequitorial collisions of sounds, words, phrases, clauses, and whole sentences throughout invite the reader to a kind of shared transport that would not only remember the past but move us—beyond the linguistic and cultural impasses of the postcolonial—"into another language" (Chapter XIV, "Of the Winds," 30).

As important as acts of remembering and productive translation are to both Waldrop and Harjo, Waldrop is clearly the more linguistically experimental writer in her emphasis on working and reworking language at every level, from her attention to "the coining of new words" ("Of Eating and Entertainment," 5), "fragments and English translations" ("Concerning Sleepe and Lodging," 7), "city planning even when applied to lexical items" ("Of the Family and Businesse of the House," 13), and "morphological investigation" and the "Great transport of bodies" ("Of the Sea," 37), to "fine discriminations of the subjunctive mood" ("Of Religion, the Soule," 43), "the deep structure of the marriage bed . . . universally esteemed even in translation" ("Of Marriage," 47), "opaque treaties of which no word can be deciphered" ("Of Debts and Trusting," 53), and "grammatical components . . . nested, multi-branching constructions" ("Of Their Hunting," 55).

With their autobiographical resonances and play of anachronisms between past and present, the italicized prose paragraphs that occupy the third formal position within each chapter develop a sustained narrative of a female speaker wrestling with questions of gender, race, family obligations, and cultural, communal norms that ultimately leave her in an alienated position resembling that of Baudelaire's "Stranger," at "the center of the city . . . deserted, in ruins" ("Of Death and Burial," 66). As the unhappy fates of both the Narragansett tribe and the female character in Waldrop's *Key* suggests, Waldrop's experimental aesthetic is grounded in the destructive legacy of European colonization, the pressure to conform to traditional familial expectations, the confinements of received gender roles ("deducing of identity from missing rib," 35; "*Which might fault me, like any Eve, with expulsion from paradise*," 40; "I distrusted men," 39), and the colonization not only of one people by another, but of daughters by mothers, and of lovers of both genders by each other. Like Harjo, Waldrop distrusts Western civilization's founding myths—myths as unavoidable as Adam and Eve—appropriating them to reinscribe and contest them.

Like Harjo, but in a more demanding, formally experimental mode, Waldrop encourages a kind of public transport that is not limited to instrumental uses of language, but allows instead for multiple ways of knowing. Her understanding of the promise of productive translation and public transport is inseparable from her view of poetry as the place of generative uses of language that allow us to rethink the European colonization of the Americas in ways more reductive, explanatory uses of language do not. As the clarity and accessibility of her introductory material suggest, she does not regard such normative, explanatory uses of language as inherently useless or harmful, only as partial, and perhaps blind to their own partiality. In the case of her Introduction, the explanatory gesture is clearly intended to allow the reader to enter more effectively, which is to say more playfully, into the fundamentally generative textual innovations to come.

Waldrop's textual orientation differs markedly in this sense from that of Harjo, whose collection moves primarily not from accessible explanation to heightened verbal complexity and playfulness, but in reverse, from more or less encrypted myths, parables, anecdotes, and stories, to explanation, amplification of context, the challenges and consolations of shared understanding, ethical reflection, and empathic action. Where Harjo's dominant tendency is toward commonality and the preservation of traditions at risk of vanishing, Waldrop makes the all but vanished language and culture of the Narragansetts her starting point (as mediated by Williams' text) to move more in the direction of linguistic experimentation. As figured in the encrypted, disjunctive narrative of the italicized prose sections and her sense that reconciliation of the kind prayed for in Harjo's opening text remains unavailable, this self-conscious re-orientation is textually motivated in *Key* by the autobiographically-inflected female speaker's dissatisfaction with the dominant culture, a culture she critiques, in contrast to Harjo, from a location Waldrop herself understands to be more "within" than "outside."

*Solitude in heat. I resented my lover turning his back on me for other mournful
realities. Though each crossing of space casually implicates the flesh, attrac-
tion increasing faster than distance diminishes, I found myself alone among
the rubble of love. I had finally reached the center of the city. It was deserted
in ruins, as useless as my birth and as permanent a site of murder.*
(Chapter XXXII, "Of Death and Burial," 66)

Although Waldrop's female speaker finds herself in these italicized passages in a
fundamentally alienated position that recalls Baudelaire's founding modernist
texts, the four-fold multiformity of Waldrop's poetic practice—which both in-
vites and resists narrative recuperation—opens onto a range of discursive, cul-
tural locations, positions, genres, discourses, audiences, and communities in ways
Harjo's innovations also seek to affirm. Motivated by a sense of being "marginal"
to a dominant culture to which she doesn't want to belong, Waldrop cultivates a
range of destabilizing discursive positions, a discursive mobility and fluidity that
holds open the prospect, if not of "reconciliation," then at least of a certain kind
of public transport, a dislocation, irritation, and disorientation of existing com-
munities that opens the door to new possibilities in the face of an unreconciled
postcolonial condition:

> a hitch in time
> then the world changed
> when life could not
> be understood forward
> or backward (66)

The dominant subject position that emerges from Harjo's work is that of an in-
ternal exile (as suggested by her avowed affinities with the figures from Ghana
and Nigeria in "The Myth of Blackbirds" and "Letter from the End of the Twen-
tieth Century") who understands herself as belonging first and foremost to a
particular community, the Muscogee, that remains in crucial respects alienated
from the larger community of the United States to which it both does and does
not belong. In fundamental respects sympathetic to and aligned with Harjo's per-
spective, Waldrop writes also from the (inter)textual location of an "alien" figure,
that of a white European female immigrant steeped in and committed to mod-
ern and postmodern experimental poetic forms, the politics of which resides in
part in what Charles Bernstein has called its "refusal of efficacy," a "complexity
and adversity to conformity" that puts such practices "well outside the stadium
of dominant culture."[11] Though *Woman Who Fell from the Sky* articulates a de-
sire for reconciliation in a more overt mode than *A Key into the Language of*

America, the two texts share a common purpose in responding to the manifestly unreconciled condition of dominant mainstream American culture. The experimental work of both writers models the potential for poetry to explore the generative possibilities of productive translation and public transport, a prospect as unsettling and haunted as it is ecstatic, to move between and among, if not within, to transform communities.

"Nothing, for a Woman, is Worth Trying": A Key into the Rules of Rosmarie Waldrop's Experimentalism

Lynn Keller

Rosmarie Waldrop's early thinking about poetic experimentalism is documented in the doctoral dissertation she wrote in the mid-1960s and published in The Hague (Mouton & Co.) in 1971 with the inquiring title *Against Language?* It is, as the lengthy subtitle announces, a study of *'dissatisfaction with language' as theme and as impulse toward experiments in twentieth century poetry.* Analyzing how twentieth-century poets, mostly from Germany and France, try to change language, this dissertation systematically presents the devices with which western poets break the rules of language use. In the introductory chapter, Waldrop identifies three types of discontent with language, each of which generates particular sorts of experimental techniques.[1] Having established the general technical categories of disruption, negation, and borrowing, and drawing heavily on the structuralist polarities of Roman Jakobson, she devotes the rest of the study to enumerating specific techniques within each of these methods and their subcategories. What I find most striking in *Against Language?* is that it provides such an organized categorization of techniques of linguistic disruption.[2] In doing so, the study reveals a characteristic I see as fundamental to the experimentalist poetics Rosmarie Waldrop would soon begin practicing:[3] a paradoxical attraction at once to system and to deviancy.

In her poetry, this is manifest in continual interplay between a pattern-making tendency to order and arrange on the one hand and an attraction to techniques that foster polyphony, polysemy, disorder, uncertainty, rupture, and indeterminacy on the other. Waldrop herself has acknowledged that she is drawn to rules, and also to their violation, recalling:

It was an important moment for me when I realized consciously that the encounter of a poem-nucleus with an arbitrary pattern (like a rhyme

scheme) would tend to pull the nucleus out of its semantic field in unfore-
seen directions. The tension always generates great energy, not just for
bridging the "gap" between original intention and the pattern, but for
pushing the whole poem farther. . . . I'm spelling out what Ashbery and
others have called the liberating effects of constraints. But what matters
is that *any* constraint, *any* pattern can be generative in this way. . . . [E]x-
treme formalism rarely works to my satisfaction. More often I use a pat-
tern (e.g., the grammatical structure of a given text), but *also* let the words
push and pull in their own directions. Since I make the rules, I also feel
free to break them.[4]

Like much of Waldrop's poetry, her recent volume on which I shall focus, *A Key
into the Language of America,* taps into the liberatory powers of arbitrary pat-
terns. These imposed orders operate in energizing tension with a "semantic nu-
cleus" involving issues of nothingness, emptiness, and erasure. These concerns,
too, are characteristic, as Waldrop signals by taking as epigraph to her extended
autobiographical essay John Cage's statement *"Poetry is having nothing to say and
saying it: we possess nothing."*[5] This, then, is the second trait I see as fundamental
to her experimentalism: a preoccupation with nothingness and emptiness as in
fact substantial, generative realms. In much of her work Waldrop explores the
ways in which negativity and absence—nothingness, emptiness, erasure, loss,
silence, and related conditions such as error, wounding, exile—generate both
meaning and art. The nothingness that proves such a fruitful area of exploration
in *A Key into the Language of America* is strongly linked to the feminine and
to Waldrop's feminist concerns. This feminist perspective, which I posit as the
third element key to her poetics, becomes linked to the others via the stereotype
that associates the female or the feminine with emptiness—woman's supposedly
empty mind, hollow womb, missing penis, etc.—and via Waldrop's sense that
adopting rules and then violating them may help the feminist artist generate so-
cial as well as aesthetic alternative forms.

Feminist thought has for many decades informed Waldrop's writing, though
—in contrast to the poetry commonly recognized as feminist—generally not via
the content or subjects of her work. By the early '70s, she had rejected any focus
on subject matter per se, having concluded that "subject matter is not something
to worry about. Your concerns and obsessions will surface no matter what you
do. This frees you to work on form, which is all one can work on consciously."[6]
She extended this attitude to feminist content: "I don't want to write 'about' any
issues, not even feminist ones, I prefer exploring the forest to hewing a road, even
if the road is in a good direction." But she went on to acknowledge, "my feminist
consciousness inevitably gets in (like my other assumptions)."[7]

The formal structures and imposed experimental patterns of her work have proved to be one important means by which her feminist concerns emerge. For instance, Waldrop has observed that the disruptive technique she favored in the mid-'70s—a technique of syntactic doubling whereby the object of one phrase functions also as the subject of the next—had feminist implications:

> . . . my feminist concerns were surfacing in this very grammar. Who could have more interest in subverting a rigid subject-object relation than women, who have been treated as the object par excellence? Instead, these poems propose a grammar (a society?) in which subject and object functions are not fixed but reversible roles, where there is no hierarchy of main and subordinate clauses, but a fluid and constant alternation.[8]

In her work of the 1990s, both the feminist consciousness itself and the formal techniques in which it becomes manifest are more complex. The recent volume to which I now turn my attention suggests a less utopian vision than Waldrop's early modeling of egalitarian societies in grammatical inversions and fluidities. In part because of the increasing number and variety of procedural rules she simultaneously imposes and resists, the feminist "semantic field" of this recent work becomes more densely accountable to historical complexity—to the history of languages, of particular relationships, of genders, and of nations.

Waldrop is open about the "rules" she imposed on herself in composing *A Key into the Language of America* and about the interests that motivated them. Her prose introduction, titled "A Key into a Key," outlines the multifaceted sense of commonality she felt with Roger Williams, the non-conformist colonist who founded the settlement of Providence, now the city in Rhode Island where she lives. These connections led to her modeling her book on the curiously collaged structure of Williams's dictionary of the Narragansett language first published in 1643, and to her adopting his title as her own.

Waldrop emphasizes that Williams's *A Key into the Language of America* was written not only to provide Christian missionaries with the linguistic and cultural data they would need to convert the Indians, but also—or even more—to teach the colonists about their own failings, since the European settlers often seemed to Williams far less virtuous than those who had only "Nature's teaching." While Williams used the Indians as a "mirror" reflecting back to the English colonists their spiritual shortcomings, Waldrop takes Williams as, in some aspects, a mirror of herself, enabling her to explore her ambivalent relation to colonial conquest and cultural dominance. She explains:

> I live in Roger Williams's territory. I was born in 1935, the year Williams's 300-year banishment officially ended. I was born "on the other side," in Germany. Which was then Nazi Germany. I am not Jewish. I was born on

the side of the (then) winners. I was still a child when World War II ended with the defeat of the Nazis. I immigrated to the US, the country of the winners, as a white, educated European who did not find it too difficult to get jobs, an advanced degree, a university position. I can see myself, to some extent, as a parallel to the European settlers/colonists of Roger Williams's time. . . . Like Roger Williams, I am ambivalent about my position among the privileged, the "conquerors."[9]

Where Williams's extraordinary knowledge of Narragansett culture heightened his ambivalence about colonial culture and the colonists' treatment of the Indians, Waldrop's gender, as well as her being a poet, reinforces her identification with the marginalized and oppressed. She continues in "A Key into a Key":

> But am I among them [the conquerors]? I am white and educated. I am also a poet and a woman. A poet, in our days, is regarded as rather a marginal member of society, whose social usefulness is in doubt. As a woman, I do not figure as conqueror in the shell game of archetypes, but as conquered. A "war bride." As a woman, I also have no illusions about the Indian societies. They were far from ideal. . . . In the shell game of archetypes, the conquered (people or land) is always female. . . . I can identify with both sides of the conflict and am ambivalent about each side. (xix–xx)

In addition to fostering exploration of Waldrop's ambivalence about her ambiguously hegemonic and non-hegemonic position as European immigrant and female poet, Williams's *Key* calls attention to the fertile substance to be found in what the dominant culture takes to be nothing. At several points, Waldrop implies that Williams is to be admired precisely because he sees fullness where others perceive a vacuum: most fundamentally, he "recognized a culture where his compatriots saw only savage otherness" (xiv); additionally, in a tract that the Boston magistrates ordered burned, he argued against the doctrine of *vacuum domicilium*, "the doctrine," Waldrop explains, "that the colonists were entitled to the land because the Indians were not making full use of it" (xvii). Granting that the natives cultivated only a small portion of their land, Williams observed that "they used all of it for hunting and, for this purpose, regularly burned the underbrush" (xvii). He recognized "that the Indians were making rational and full use of the land" (xviii). Those with more power, however, regarding Williams's views as dangerous, denied that same fullness by feminizing it, redefining it as lack. As Waldrop puts it: "The colonization of America put the very 'male' Indian culture in the position of the conquered female, part of the land that was considered there to be 'taken'" (xx). Using Williams's *Key* as her own means to discover the fullness of apparent voids, Rosmarie Waldrop finds in a language "dead" for almost two centuries and in a "vanished" culture abundant material for poetic exploration of very current concerns (xxi, xxii).

In addition to its thematic usefulness, relating to colonialism and cultural conflict as they intersect with language, nothingness, and the feminine, Roger Williams's *Key* also provides the form of Waldrop's *Key into the Language of America.* Her thirty-two chapters follow the sequence of his exactly, each one adopting the title and including some textual material excerpted from his. Moreover, all Waldrop's chapters follow a pattern suggested by the internal composition of Williams's chapters, each of which, Waldrop notes, moves "through three stages: through phrase lists and anthropological observations . . . to a final moralizing poem" (xvi). Waldrop announces her deliberate attempt to generate something analogous: "In parallel to Roger Williams's anthropological passages, the initial prose section of each of my chapters tries to get at the clash of Indian and European cultures by a violent collage of phrases from Williams with elements from anywhere in my Western heritage" (xxii). Thus, for example, the opening of Waldrop's chapter IV, "Of Their Numbers," juxtaposes stock market crashes and the rights asserted in the colonists' "Declaration of Independence" against the Indians' doomed mathematical savvy, seen through Williams's patronizingly appreciative gaze (my brackets identify material taken essentially verbatim from the parallel chapter in Williams):

> Without the help of Wall Street, [how quick they are in casting up] inalienable [numbers]. We do not have them. [With help of] hybrid [corn instead of Europe's pens or] poisons. Edge of ingenuity, between numb and nimble, forest or frigid wave before it crashes. (9)

Like Williams's, moreover, each of Waldrop's chapters contains a word list and a final poem. But in addition to mimicking the three stages of his chapters, Waldrop adds a fourth structural element that emphasizes her feminist interests: "To reinforce the theme of conquest and gender," she explains, "every chapter adds a narrative section in italics, in the voice of a young woman, ambivalent about her sex and position among the conquerors" (xxiii).

Waldrop highlights the formal regulation of her work by making her *Key into the Language of America* more visually regular than Williams's text. While Williams's chapters in modern reprint range from two to thirteen pages, all Waldrop's chapters are two pages long and the two pages are near mirror-images of each other. In every case, the title on the first page is followed by, first, a prose passage containing some bold-faced phrases from Williams, and second, a word list centered between the left and right margins with one word per line and any-where from two to seven words per list.[10] On the verso page, prose again comes first; an italicized prose passage in the voice of a woman whose history in some ways overlaps with Waldrop's is followed by a free verse poem usually a few lines longer than the word list on the preceding page. Compared to, for instance, Susan Howe's experiments with historical documents such as the *Eikon Basilike*, this format is extremely tidy and systematic.

Yet Waldrop's devotion to disruption and disorder is also apparent. The typo-graphic and formal contrasts between parts within the chapters and the white space surrounding each piece in the pattern give the work a richly varied visual texture. Supplementing such rule-determined variety are more arbitrary or rule-breaking irregularities: bold face occurs not just in the opening prose chapter sections as announced in the introduction, but unpredictably in other sections as well. So do Narragansett words with their notably unfamiliar spellings and accent marks. Sometimes word fragments or Narragansett words accompanied by translating phrases substitute for English words in the lists. In one chapter, a numbered series of phrases arranged one per line substitutes for prose in the opening section. The form proves considerably less set than the high degree of regulation presented in the "Key into a Key" might suggest.

Moreover, the language itself—continually shifting in syntactic and interpre-tive density, in cultural and discursive context—renders each section of every chapter thoroughly unpredictable. Syntax is sometimes grammatical, sometimes not; reference may seem consistent for a bit, and then will change or become unclear; dictions shift as formulations move in and out of familiarity. Linguistic instability becomes a principle of composition even for the word lists; these ex-plore widely varying "language contexts" for words in the chapter titles, contexts which may be aural, etymological, semantic, or inaccessible. Sometimes parts of compound words appear, which may themselves function as autonomous terms or only as suggestive fragments, as in the list, "ogue / agent / er," that appears in the chapter titled "Of Travell."

Precisely because the volume is so regular in its structure, such variations are notable and heighten readers' awareness of the multiple strands forming any web of linguistic linkages or of cultural conflict. This complexity does not derive from Williams's *Key;* rather, it distinctively characterizes Waldrop's text. For Wil-liams presents two entirely separate languages, limiting his "language contexts" to those useful for communication between Indians and European settlers; and for him, the cultural clash is mediated by one overriding truth, established by Christianity, according to which the behavior of both cultural groups could be judged. In the complex layerings and violated orderings of Waldrop's text, recti-tude is far less accessible. This is the case in part because of the "nothing" left where the ordering structures of Williams's Christianity had been—a space that in America in the 1990s comes to be ambiguously occupied by language itself.

A passage from one of the last chapters in Waldrop's *Key*, "Of their Paintings," reflexively illuminates some of the complex interactions of rule and disruption, void and pattern, emptiness and fertility that I have been describing. The passage is the chapter's third part, the italicized section in the voice of the young woman:

> *I used iodine to paint my wound, a geometrical design interwoven with collision and conflict. Line securing or towing a boat. A motivation to swell. Or scream in the face of immediate, useless nakedness. In spite of having, without restraint, chosen the wrong role models I have female parts and cultivate outward behavior.* (62)

The initial sentence announcing that the speaker painted a geometrical pattern with an antiseptic fluid suggests that orderly design promotes the healing of wounds. If we take that design to represent the highly regular structure of Waldrop's book, the sentence might suggest that an orderly reworking of the genocidal history to which Williams's *Key* inadvertently contributed and a re-exploration of the language he recorded offer hope for transforming the damage and pain of our nation's history. As Waldrop puts it in her essay "Alarms & Excursions," poetry "can make the culture aware of itself, unveil hidden structures. It questions, resists. Hence it can at least potentially anticipate structures that might lead to social change" (47).

But this intimation of the recuperative powers of art's order is tempered by the geometric design most prominent in Waldrop's *Key*, a visual representation of an act of cultural conquest from the perspective of the conquerors. This bizarrely regular image, which appears cropped on the cover and uncropped on the facing pages between Waldrop's introductory "A Key into A Key" and the text of her *Key*, was created to celebrate a triumph of colonialism (Figure 1). Reproduced from a 1638 publication by a colonial Captain Underhill, it depicts the violent conquest led by him and a Captain Mason of "the Indians' Fort or Palizado in New England." Centered in a stylized orderly landscape of hills and trees are rings of armed Indians and colonists, broken by symmetrical areas of battle on opposite sides of the circular fort. The pointed towers of the fort along with the peaked roofs of the Indian's houses within appear like teeth in a *vagina dentata* at the moment of bold penetration by the British. This geometric drawing may represent, then, the feminization and the wounding of the Narragansett as well as the masculine proving of the colonists—both key to genocidal destruction.

Particularly the cropped version on the cover also suggests an eye, with the ring of soldiers outlining the iris and the Indian fort comprising the pupil. Read

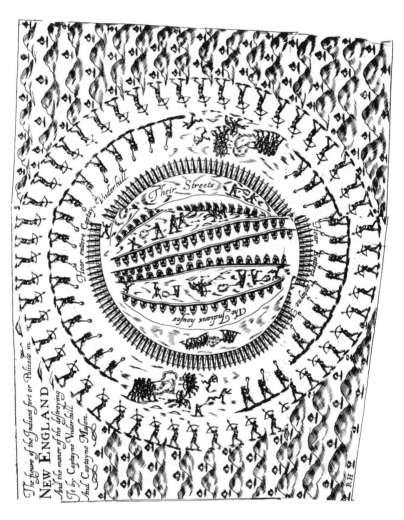

The figure of the Indians fort or Palizado in
NEW ENGLAND
And the maner of the destroying
It by Captayne Underhill
And Captayne Mason.

Their Streets

The Indians houses

Fig. 1
"Indian Fort" (courtesy of the John Carter Brown Library, Brown University)

this way, the image perhaps speaks to the ways in which history and historio-graphic patterns are the products of particular perspectives. History is our invention—in Cage's terms, part of the nothing we possess. *Design* may mean not just an artful ordering but also a plan, particularly a dishonest or selfish one; designs, like deliberate ruptures, may serve admirable or reprehensible ideologies alike. Thus in "Alarms & Excursions" Waldrop notes that despite the changing of the language that was being undertaken by experimental artists in pre-Nazi Germany, "the Nazis had no trouble putting [the German language] to work for their purposes" (47).

In line with this observation, the second sentence in the passage from "Of their Paintings" points to the arbitrariness of humanly imposed meanings. For *painter* can as well signify the line tied to a boat as a person who wields a paint-brush. The word "securing" might indicate that, whether rope or pigment, the painter's line (or perhaps the poet's) provides stability and security. But again in complication, the next clause—"*A motivation to swell*"—recalls the earlier "col-lision and conflict," likely sources of wounds and swellings. The wound, or per-haps the painting of the wound, causes swelling and screaming; which is to say that what is produced at the site of rupture or emptiness is likely to involve suf-fering, even while it may also promote healing.

In abruptly introducing nakedness at this point—*scream in the face of imme-diate, useless nakedness*—Waldrop is silently drawing on the parallel chapter of Williams's *Key*, using it to highlight gender issues. In the sermonizing poem that closes his chapter, Williams introduces nakedness as the antithesis of being painted. Here are the first and last quatrains of Williams's three-stanza poem:

Truth is a Native, naked Beauty; but
Lying Inventions are but Indian Paints;
Dissembling hearts their Beautie's but a Lye.
Truth is the proper Beauty of Gods Saints.

Paints will not bide Christs washing Flames of fire,
Fained Inventions will not bide such stormes:
O that we may prevent him, that betimes,
Repentance Teares may wash of all such Formes.[11]

For Williams, painting symbolizes deceit, a whorish covering of God's naked and enduring truth. But in Waldrop's text, the ugly "fained inventions" seem to be not so much individually willed sins as the conventions of gender roles. The intertext of Williams's lines emphasizes that these roles are inessential and sub-ject to change, preparing for Waldrop's lines that follow, which underscore a person's ability to choose models and modes of behavior (even if one cannot choose the sexed form of one's body). The speaker's "outward behavior" need not be the deceitful feigning Williams deplores; it might be a self-fashioning necessary to the creation of a functioning subject. If so, this painterly application of "color of thought to lacking object" (a line from the first section of this chapter) is a feminist triumph: woman—conventionally defined by her "lack" of, among other things, a penis—gains visibility.

The poem that follows the italicized passage and concludes Waldrop's chapter asserts the possibility of generating change and of constructing something from what is perceived as nothingness. (The notably direct propositional character of the first part of this passage perhaps reflects Waldrop's attraction to regulated order, while the more polysemous and syntactically ambiguous portions, beginning with the open parenthesis, may manifest her tendency to violate the expectations set up by her own procedures.)

> thinking develops
> out of the negative
>
> the vacuum abhorred
> by nature
> is fertile (variables
> perspectives, paper money)
>
> refinanced memory
> washes white (62)

The fertility announced so unequivocally here is, like design, ideologically uncommitted; thus, "paper money," if read as an example of what can develop out of nothing, reminds us that value may be assigned without basis in anything beyond convention. When Williams closes his poem with the hope that "*Repentance Teares may wash of all such forms,*" he presumes the revelation of an *essential* truth. Waldrop, who is no essentialist, posits a different kind of hope and a more ambiguous one in her closing, "refinanced memory / washes white." These lines might indicate that reinventing the forms of our thought can erase received ideas, offer a clean start; but they might also suggest that such reinvention can whitewash past misdeeds, or impose the ideology of the dominant white culture. Starting again from the *tabula rasa* of nothing or from the empty space opened by a wound does not insure progress. Waldrop only goes so far as to indicate that such re-creation *opens possibilities* for changing the coloring of our perceptions;

the designs of our historiographic maps; and our valuing of marginalized gen-
ders, art forms, and ethnic or social groups.[12]

Testing the relation between artistic deviance and social change—particularly
social change involving gender roles and heterosexual interactions—seems to me
a primary undertaking of the sections in which Waldrop uses the italicized voice
of the woman. Again, her intellectual exploration is conducted via an engage-
ment with rules—or rather, with a well established set of literary conventions—
those of the bildungsroman, which traces a process of change in the (usually
male) individual. Waldrop's constant interruption of the girl's biographical nar-
rative by the other sections of her chapters provides an insistent reminder that
any individual's history is thoroughly interwoven with the violence of local, na-
tional, and global history—something few bildungsromans acknowledge. In ad-
dition, by obviously imitating the formulas of the male bildungsroman and then
problematizing them for her female speaker, Waldrop calls attention to the dis-
tinctive difficulties faced in female development within patriarchal societies.
Given that genre conventions are not rigid regulations, revising them for feminist
purposes—a procedure widespread among women writers—needs to be distin-
guished from play with more rule-generated proceduralism.[13] Nonetheless, since
Waldrop directly invokes the most set patterns characterizing this genre in order
to test and challenge its assumptions, her simultaneous use of and rejection of
its patterns deserves attention in the context of Waldrop's relation to ordering
systems.

The italicized section of chapter I ("Salutations") begins as the conventional
first-person life story is supposed to, by locating the protagonist's birth. Here's
the entire passage:

> *I was born in a town on the other side which didn't want me in so many. All
> streets were long and led. In the center, a single person had no house or friends
> to **allay excessive sorrowe**. I, like other girls, forgot my name in the noise of
> traffic, opening my arms more to measure their extension than to offer em-
> brace.* (4)

The speaker, like the typical restless hero of the novel of education, is one for
whom streets and the journeys they symbolize seem to beckon, "*All streets were
long and led.*" This formulation suggests, however, that, just as all roads once led
to Rome, existing streets direct the traveler only to the imperial center or to some
locus of patriarchal power. Moreover, the developmental challenge she faces,
shaped partly by her historical moment of noisy urban culture, is specific to her
feminine gender: "*I, like other girls, forgot my name in the noise of traffic*" (4). The

italicized section of Chapter II is even more explicit in linking the speaker's tale to the formulas of bildungsroman: "*I began my education by walking along the road in search of the heroic*" (6). But the heroic is elusive for her, and in succeeding chapters of Waldrop's *Key*, again and again the unhappy female protagonist seems stuck between two unsatisfactory courses: either trying to pursue this education via the masculine notions of violent heroism that tradition and history legitimize, or remaining within the constraints of approved feminine behavior. "*Sticks and stones and swamps and howling wilderness, or inside a patient garden and ability to behave: intrepid waiting*" (24).

Following the latter course prescribed for the domestic feminine would mean going nowhere. In Chapter 4, the Narragansett term for "one of feminine gender" introduces the speaker's resistance to this deadly order of woman's prescribed passivity, silence, and reliable regularity:

> **Pâwsuck** *with time to dawdle, to cultivate lucidity and metric structure. Yet did not play by numbers. Too many messengers that do not speak. A bowel movement every day and one war every generation. I feared becoming an object too boring for my bones to hold up, however clumsily.* (10)

Clearly, social rules for women must be broken. But not via role-reversal. The solution does not lie in the woman's trying to imitate (European) men, though this is not an easy lesson to learn. Thus, at one point the speaker announces: "*In a mixture of panic and mistaken gender I went West, intending the milky way. Common error*" (28). And again later, "*What was the secret of holsters, nearsighted daring, tools between legs? Who went from coast to coast, but stayed always on top with semicircular canals for balance? My antagonism dissolved into the illusion that I was one of them, consenting to slow harm*" (34). While use of "pâwsuck" here perhaps signals women's oppression within Narragansett society, generally Waldrop's inclusion in her *Key* of material from the eradicated Indian culture foregrounds the harmfulness of masculine patriarchal modes as enacted by Anglo-Europeans. Neither the conventional masculine nor the conventional feminine course is acceptable, and the speaker struggles to locate alternatives.

In the bildungsroman, the hero learns from his errors so as to discover his personal path. If progress is available to Waldrop's female adventurer, it is more qualified and more obviously tied into social institutions and public history. The text provides signals of chronological maturation, but the only clear lesson this woman learns is a bit of Marxist analysis, announced in the chapter "Concerning their Coyne" (XXIV): "*I learned that my face belonged to a covert system of exchange since the mirror showed me a landscape requiring diffidence, and only in nightmares did I find identity or denouement*" (50). As I read the rest of the passage, she tries to call overt attention to woman's commodity function, perhaps by presenting herself as a prostitute, only to find herself more alienated, particularly from other women who are ludicrously blind to their own participation in this economic system: "*At every street corner, I exaggerated my bad character in hopes of being contradicted, but only caused an epidemic of mothers covering their face while exposing private parts*" (50). Similarly, her sexual experiences with men do not generate obvious progress, countering readers' expectations of the bildungsroman's journey toward fulfilled and socially integrated selfhood. The speaker does seem to develop increased acceptance of her sex and sexuality, and greater ability to distinguish her sex from her gender. But she does not gain confidence she can act on this understanding: "*I did not know if my desire to escape cash-and-carry was strong enough to eliminate the platitudes of gender identity or the crowds under my eyelids. I was stuck in a periodicity I supposedly share with Nature, but tired of making concessions to dogs after bones*" (54).

Waldrops's protagonist ends in a situation much like the one in which she began ("single" in the center of a town in Chapter I, "alone" in the center of a city in Chapter XXXII): "*I found myself alone among the rubble of love. I had finally reached the center of the city. It was deserted, in ruins, as useless as my birth and as permanent a site of murder*" (66). Yet I discern some potentially significant gains here. For from her rule-breaking engagement with the rules of the bildungsroman this woman appears to have developed an historical consciousness. In referring to the ruined city as as permanent a site of murder as her birth, the speaker, born "on the other side" (xix, 4), presents herself as, by racial and national heritage, among the privileged invaders who have survived via the socially legitimized murders necessary to war and colonialism. She has also gained access to a possibly generative nothingness in the rubble and ruins now occupying the spaces of collapsed structures—which might include social conventions like those surrounding gender. Whether these ruins will be used to build something of value remains an open question and a looming responsibility for poet and audience alike.

Rules and Restraints in Women's Experimental Writing

Carla Harryman

Constraint

In the article, "Rule and Constraint," from *Oulipo: A Primer of Potential Literature*,[1] Marcel Benabou lambasts those who claim a privileged status for literary inspiration insofar as "inspiration" is taken to be a phenomenon of nature. To Benabou, the devotees of inspiration simply confuse conventional rules with a mistaken notion of natural language. The "inspired" text's properties, he writes, are conventionally thought of as "natural fact;" whereas the use of other "rules," e.g. eccentric, numeric, or unique devices, are from a conventional perspective, "perceived as shameful artifice."

In the context of contemporary women's experimental writing, the use of constraint is not particularly controversial; and in the United States, what might irritate traditionalists more than the use of eccentric devices is the literary author's use of "non-literary" vocabularies drawn from the sciences, philosophy, politics, and sociology. There is sometimes a sense that when such languages enter a literary work, the work is contaminated. In any case, I can assume that the majority of the readers of this essay will not view writers' deliberate use of constraints negatively. Yet, there are also other kinds of rules governing the experimental text. I think of these rules as the ideas that control, motivate, and limit the writer's project.

In *Writing as an Aid to Memory*, Lyn Hejinian employs a numeric constraint based on alphabetization to spatially organize her poem, but Hejinian's interrogation of memory is less dependent on the device than on its thematic concept. In her essay, "Bodies of Work," Kathy Acker discusses the device of repetition in bodybuilding as a metaphor for confrontation with failure, but Acker's use of repetition is contingent on her *a priori* critique of western attitudes toward death. In my play *There Is Nothing Better Than a Theory*, I used a constraint by which each line of the play had to act as either a grammatical, semantic, or rhetorical hinge for the next line, but without its reliance on the a priori concept that language itself is the site of performance, the text would not offer itself as a challenge to the way that plays get made. I would argue then that, in the case of these texts, there are concepts or questions related to pre-existing concepts that motivate the text and create the need for constraint, "a commodious way of passing from language to writing."[2]

In my use of it, the rule is the rule of thought, not of literary convention. This rule of thought is the convention on which the experimental work relies and what the experimental work cannot question without destroying itself. This rule of thought or intellectual position is then what allows the difficult text to come into being at all, and it is what limits its own complexity.

In each of the works under discussion here, the text is directed toward communal knowledge or practice—as it questions conventions of communal practice; the use of writing to aide memory, the use of repetition to create change, the use of text to invent localized as opposed to normative performance. These works also inscribe the regulatory mechanisms and desire of compelling ideas, imply their own limits, create as well as make use of resistance.

The writing that follows is divided into three sections that are meant to variously characterize the "resistant" values of each writer's works. In addition, I take a different approach to my discussion of each writer. I do this to emphasize the difference of concerns among each of us.

The Recalcitrant Text

"Walking Backwards with the Maintains" was a site specific "talk," which I "performed" in the San Francisco live-in loft of Bob Perelman and Francie Shaw in 1977. In the performance, I gave people domestic tasks to do while I read Clark Coolidge's long poem, *The Maintains*, walking backwards. No documentation of the performance remains, although I did videotape the piece for purposes of later discussion with my interdisciplinary art seminar run by movement artist Susanne Helmuth. At the time, the videotaping of the piece was a rather uncomfortable issue for me; I wasn't going to be able to convince many artists to go to a literary event, but I also knew that "the writers" were not going to respond very analytically to the art event. So I did the performance for writers and discussed it with artists. In addition, I felt ambivalent about the trend toward documenting every act of performance art: it went against the grain of my disruptive impulses. I was flirting with a kind of now-you-see-it-now-you-don't aesthetic. I also didn't like the use of the video camera to magnify the self-conscious position of the audience, since it would additionally exploit that position later as the documentation became commodified artifact. This is why I destroyed the tape. It is also why, given that I did choose to use the video camera, I tried to make my use of it obvious. The video camera became an extension of my own tyrannical role in the performance as I commanded others to do my bidding and floated around reading "sacred" text in the wrong direction.

I now think of "Walking Backwards with the Maintains" (1977) as a precursor to "There Is Nothing Better Than a Theory" (1982), a piece for the stage in which theoretical language, abstract language, language derived from domestic situations, and language of public culture are put into play. I suspect that when I performed "Walking Backwards," the wish had been, in part, that *I* had written *The Maintains:* even if it wasn't exactly what I would desire to write. The event was as if a performance of something I would someday, and did, write.

In the performance of "Walking Backwards," I thought of myself as an androgynous figure. I was performing the relationship between abstract art and domesticity: enacting the abstract (male power) work conceptually (backwards) while the audience (subjugated and feminized) did my bidding/my chores. Some of the men later told me that they liked being told what to do and others wouldn't talk to me. The performance, then, was a critique with a lot of twists: nothing was settled precisely in a familiar place. And I was also satirizing the role of the author by enacting a tyrannical (unraveling, whimsical and arbitrary) authority over Coolidge's text and the audience/performers at the same time. This was also a source of discomfort, partly because Coolidge's abstract work was still in the process of being recognized as a "breakthrough" text. Why be so irreverent? These were the questions I imagined, or imagine, the silent unquestioning audience participants would have asked, had they chosen to speak. But I wanted to step into and reverse the man's shoes. This was even to myself somewhat off-putting.

Yet, this performance would disappear, was even intended to disappear while Coolidge's text remained. In the context of the performance, the text was recalcitrant. And even though I performed the text in the wrong way, choosing words in the wrong order, nothing actually changed the text. This concept of a recalcitrant text, within the situation of performance, has been the basis of much if not all of my writing for theater. The text for theater in my *oeuvre* is not meant as an unequivocal medium for performance. The text is meant to perform its own object status as linked to and separate from the live performance of its language.

Perhaps the recalcitrant text, or that of the text that is resistant to easily lending itself to a performed interpretation, restrains one from being able to know it in the way one would know a person. It cannot be transgressed, because the performers will go off and do something else, but, like the indestructible personae in a farce, its words will bounce back up and resume their unruly organization. This fractious order, which is neither opaque nor narrative nor fully definable, resists restagings that bear any relationship to each other. It is highly unlikely that any director or group of collaborators would create even a similar play based on the same text in a restaging of the work. The textual language, because of its freedom from context, suggests to performers open interpretations and open orders, but one pretty much has to reinvent the performance from scratch for every "new" occasion. Such performative writing practice encourages a certain energetic community-based interpretive activity, but it also resists continuity of interpretation: what the text reflects then is an assumed lack of continuity of stable meaning and an assumed loss of continuity within performance community. "There is Nothing Better Than a Theory" speaks for itself, also in this regard:

Oh, theory
Yes
There is nothing better
Than a theory
But confess
What?
We will eating anything.
Anything?
The book
The idea
Or the product
I would prefer that the painting resemble something a little less dry
This has nothing to do with technique
It is all in the sequence
The sequins?
Are on the table
They are not
Looking for a place to stay[3]

The Selected Text

What are the rules, what restrains the text or the reader of the text? A positivist way to think about resistance is through a method of selection. William James, in his *Principles of Psychology*, is interested in the question of selection in thought. If consciousness is a stream, much of it passes by unnoted. When consciousness selects anything or commits itself to any particular thing, it is not choosing many other things. James also questions the normative basis on which selections are made, especially, I think, to defeat moralisms about what passes as legitimate knowledge. Such questions influenced the writings of Gertrude Stein, and certainly they affect the writings of Lyn Hejinian, who has been reading James since 1961. In his essay, "Thought is in Constant Change," James suggests that we use "conventions" of feeling in respect to language consciousness. We gravitate toward particular uses of language related to our subjective feelings for things or our evaluation of what our psychic states are "about." According to James, "So inveterate has our habit become of recognizing the substantive parts alone that language almost refuses to lend itself to any other use."[4] Yet, James suggests, "we ought to say a feeling of *and*, a feeling of *if*, a feeling of *but*, a feeling of *by*, quite as readily as we say a feeling of *cold* or a feeling of *blue*."[5] Like James, Hejinian is interested in the question of the subjective mental fact, not as only that which is defining, definable, or principled but also as an event that is fuzzy, vague, not fully explicable. In a Steinian manner, Hejinian transports James's ideas about the psychological dimension of language to the question of aesthetic practice: why ought poetry to draw from consciousness only that which is easy to objectify, clear, and discernable, when the "subjective stream" offers so many instances of unclarity? Isn't unclarity—even impossibility and unrepresentability —relevant to thought? James writes:

> From the cognitive point of view, all mental facts are intellections. From the subjective point of view all are feelings. Once admit that the passing and evanescent are as real parts of the stream (of consciousness) as the distinct and comparatively abiding; once allow that fringes and halos, inarticulate perceptions, whereof the objects are as yet unnamed, mere nascencies of cognition, premonitions, awarenesses of direction, are thought *sui generis*, as much as articulate imaginings and propositions are; once restore, I say, the *vague* to its psychological rights, and the matter presents no further difficulty. And then we see that the current opposition of Feeling to Knowledge is quite a false issue.[6]

One might describe *Writing as an Aid to Memory* as a work that deals precisely with such mental facts. In some sense, it is as if Hejinian had designed to produce an artwork that would serve as an example of a Jamesian consciousness. Hejinian interestingly, given the debates in the '70s about the splitting of feeling and knowledge in feminist discourse, assumes that the opposition of "feeling to knowledge" is a priori a false issue. What the poet then would want to know is what does the co-presentation of evanescence along with distinctness of language look like? What does it do? *Writing as an Aid to Memory* begins with the following lines:

Apple is shot nod
       ness seen know it around saying
           think for a hundred years
but and perhaps utter errors direct the point to a meadow[7]

The line, "apple is shot nod" could be described as definite, even as its declarative comic metaphor complicates its decodability. The line "ness seen know it around saying" could be described as evanescent. The line "think for a hundred years" is definite, and the fourth line, "but and perhaps utter errors direct the point to a meadows" indicates without precisely identifying them, a relationship between the indefinite, mistakes, and direction. In addition, the use of the word-particle "ness" could be thought to represent a fringe of a word or preceding phrase, while the line "ness seen know it around saying" creates a halo effect through the variations and repetitions of vowel sounds. The poem is certainly as replete as "fits that finally riddle an infinite nature" with what one might call nascencies of cognition such as "purely outward by the time so churches of" or "do edge the so dark." While articulate propositions such as "memory is a trick of coincidence," or "much intention is retrospective/where as much extension is prospective" are everywhere in evidence. Vagueness, then, "new like little with those filling loops," is restored to poetry without overriding other conventional devices of poetic language: rhythm, alliteration, and repetition.

Because of the poem's numeric constraint, and in this work it is an arbitrary device to support temporal fluidity with spatial pattern, I am hyper-aware of Hejinian's method of selecting details from the otherwise unassimilable flow. The fact of the deliberately varied indentations, arranged according to the first letter of a line's place in the alphabet, underscores other features of the writing, including the poet's playing on notions of "selected" memory in her selection of James's work as an influence on her own.

In doing this, Hejinian proposes, I think, a kind of "personness," which is very far from the self-obsessed autobiographical subject but present everywhere in the text. This, this, and this, all of these things were selected by a person. Some of them came from books which are recollected, some of them came from personal recollections of two years, or two minutes. Recollection could be in relationship to anything that the person has selected.

Underpinning Hejinian's poem is the immanently selectable aesthetic category of beauty. Hejinian wanted to make a beautiful poem in order to recuperate, after her move from the country to Berkeley, a relationship to the beauty of rural life;[8] so the stream itself is not natural, it is guided by cultural impulse of the highest order. Yet this categorical beauty is part of the flow, and the poem points to the paradoxes of beauty as a transcendent category. For beauty is a material of consciousness that the poet can select. The poem calls attention to its use of beauty as material as it showcases the command or instruction, "poke beauty," but of course this featuring of beauty's plasticity is again instantly assimilated into the flow.

Yet Hejinian does "poke beauty" by combining erudite pronouncements, vague language and references to unlovely, banal, and domestic events that resist conventional notions of beauty in art. Her "arbitrary" use of constraint also restrains conventional notions of beauty as it constantly calls attention to the temporality and work of making the poem. The way that Hejinian achieves the beauty she aims to make is in the movement of selection that becomes an imitation of the concept of "the stream."

What the poem can't poke at for more than the briefest of pauses is its own positive motion. The writing, which clearly resists dwelling on memory (or memories) produces a language of memory bounded to the process of selection within the domain of the flow. If the writing paused to assess the contexts it depends on to create its own momentum, the motion would stop and its fabric would tear.

Repetition

Both Hejinian and Kathy Acker are interested in the mechanics or physicality of a process of selection. If I am hyper-conscious of Hejinian's hands having done the repetitive work to place the lines of her long poem in their varied positions, I am also hyper-conscious of Acker's presencing of mental effort through the device of repetition—as if the mind is continuously trying to break down the wall of its own limits and the limitations of its culture as represented in others' texts. The mind in Acker is related directly to the social body and the psychosomatic body. The mind is as if viscerally part of the social and physical body. The social body and the physical body are both idea and thing. In her work, Acker consistently searches for ways to dissolve the mind/body split as a means toward individual and social liberation. In writing her novel *Pussy, King of the Pirates,* Acker repeatedly practices masturbating to produce language for the novel. But in this situation, the mind has to struggle to join the ego to the libido, to write and come at the same time. At some point the writing always trails off. The process results in revelation, banality, and impossibility. The text is produced through a retention of this limit of the knowable.

What Hejinian's text resists, the contemplation of its own potential negativity or limits, is exactly what Acker's 1993 essay, "Against Ordinary Language: the Language of the Body," tries to understand. Acker is looking at the "antagonism between the body and verbal language" through the joined practice of body-building and writing. Acker's exploration of negation is paradoxically what allows her to speak of it at all. She locates her understanding of the antagonism in the concept of "failure."

> Having failed time and time again, upon being offered the opportunity to write this essay, I made the following plan: I would attend the gym as usual. Immediately after each workout, I would describe all I had just experienced, thought, and done. Such diary descriptions would provide the raw material.
>
> After each workout, I forgot to write. Repeatedly. I shall begin by analyzing this rejection of ordinary or verbal language.[9]

When Acker recognizes the relationship of repetition to failure, both in writing and bodybuilding, she is able to approach the "speechless language." The speechless language has produced the language of the text through the trope of committed failure: "Bodybuilding," she writes, "can be seen to be about nothing but *failure*." For Acker, bodybuilding connects the literal and the metaphorical significations of writing with the material and spiritual practice of breaking down and reforming the body.

The failure in bodybuilding and in writing brings the body builder/writer to the brink of death and to chaos. At the same time " 'the language of the body' is not arbitrary. When a body builder is counting, he or she is counting her own breath.' " The language of the body is, like a Wittgensteinian language game, "reduced to a minimal, even a closed, set of nouns and to numerical repetition."[10] For Acker, the "language game" is a vehicle to enter, through a route of indirection, a realm of negativity, which seems to both connect her to others and compel her fascination of epistemological possibility and impossibility. A symbol of this "language game" for Acker are Canetti's beggars of Marrakesh who "repeat the name of God."

> In ordinary language, meaning is contextual. Whereas the cry of the beggar means nothing other than what it is; in the city of the beggar, the impossible (as the Wittgenstein of the *Tractatus* and Heidegger see it) occurs in that meaning and breath become one.[11]

Like Hejinian, Acker, who counts her own breath, finally places the value of writing within a construction of consciousness. Yet, unlike that of Hejinian, Acker's construction is not located in the motion of temporal flow, which is in

Hejinian the source of subjectivity, but in an intensity of focus applied through repetitive processes to the body and its architecture. She reduces "verbal language to minimal meaning, to repetition, [to] close the body's outer windows."[12] The trope of bodybuilding then is used as a kind of umbilicus of consciousness that leads Acker in her essay to disclose a labyrinthine structure of references and language games. The interior, "labyrinth," and the exterior, "language game," together "mirror" the unspeakability of the somatic interior and the textual and material reality of the exterior world as symbolized in Canetti's beggars.

In connecting her somatic quest with her writing practice, Acker seems to be casting a spell on the destructive impulses that she identifies in Western systems of dualism: she deploys her own practice of inevitable *failure* against the successful ideology of duality in Western thought. Acker's critique is that the limitations of the body can't really be known, but because it is already defined subjectively and as object, it is subject to and productive of cruelty.

> In our culture, we simultaneously fetishize and disdain the athlete, a worker in the body. For we still live under the sign of Descartes. This sign is also the sign of patriarchy. As long as we continue to regard the body, that which is subject to change, chance, and death, as disgusting and inimical, so long shall we continue to regard our own selves as dangerous others.[13]

And what has motivated me in this writing to say something about the resistances and the limits of "our" works is related to what I see sometimes as a disconnection between the celebration of the woman experimentalist's project and a confrontation with its underlying values. Acker always questioned the underlying values of others' and her own writing.

PART III
THE VISUAL REFERENT/VISUAL PAGE

Im.age … Dis.solve: The Linguistic Image in the Critical Lyric of Norma Cole and Ann Lauterbach

Charles Borkhuis

The latter part of the twentieth century has witnessed a significant shift from its early love affair with photography and film to an increasing suspicion of visual hegemony in a multitude of social and cultural areas. An overwhelming number of recent post-structuralist thinkers in Europe and the United States, profoundly distrustful of the visual, cite its historical association with much that is logocentric in Western metaphysics. A few of the most widely discussed tendencies include the linkage of sight with *eidos,* in its highest form—the Good, the reduction of time to a visual-spatial progression, and the identification of ego construction with an imaginary, ocular unity. Complicated by the production of fetishistic, mass-media advertising and political propaganda, these culturally laden messages have provoked critical theorists and innovative artists alike to question the role of the image in contemporary visual arts and literature, leading, in some cases, to the abandonment of the image entirely. But recent reevaluations of this criticism have noted the limitations of its reductive, binary thinking, recognizing that the image is too ubiquitous and important a source of information to be excluded from contemporary artistic expression.[1] If the growth of the image has greatly overshadowed the other senses, it may be in this dark side of the visual that its hierarchical aspects are most neutralized. Perhaps it is in the shadow of the eye, in the overlooked exchanges of the dispersed senses, in the invisible itself that flashes of visionary insight can still be felt.

The poetry of Norma Cole and Ann Lauterbach, a former painter and an art critic respectively, offers a complex response to the role of the image in innovative contemporary poetry. Each writer has produced a critique of the logocentric reality encoded in the doxa of received cultural images and ideas. Drawing instead upon the shadow presence of a more dispersed sensorium from which textual choices are made, Cole and Lauterbach have helped to introduce a renovated, diacritical image that is both visionary and self reflexive. In avoiding the modernist tendency to interpret the image as a transparent means to eidetic truth, mimetic description, or transcendental *otherness,* Cole and Lauterbach have addressed the image as a material language with its attendant grammatology already in place. But their work has refused to simply reduce the image to the word; each, in her own way, has seen in the *critical image,* a bridge between language and silence, the visible and the invisible, the presentable and the unpresentable. The result, in the poetry of both Cole and Lauterbach, is a paradoxical work of heightened awareness that refuses either to be engulfed by a totalizing unity or divided into a static dualism.

The Labyrinth behind the Looking Glass

what was it you saw in my face?
the light of your own face,
the fire of your own presence?

H.D., "Eurydice"

Like characters in a dream or wanderers on the road, serious readers of Norma Cole's poetry have developed a heightened regard for the travails of the *flâneur.* As with many a radical writer such as Joyce, Kafka, Bataille, or Borges, to whom the image of the labyrinth is a life-metaphor, Cole's intention is not for readers to find Ariadne's thread, but to learn to wander in the dimly lit corridors of uncertainty, which are the metalinguistic, often hallucinogenic passages of the labyrinth itself. Cole's use of syntactical splinterings and infinitely deferred destinations carries the markings of a dispersed, linguistic body stretching from author to reader in a complex network of images and sensual signings.

> Amber in silver. Calculate the strength of the dead. Becoming an
> extension of that pattern in the iron curtain already forgotten, she
> has lost a lot of ink. There are bumps in the air, collisions with
>   obstructions revealed only by the shapes around them, actions
> such as watering or reading, repeating or arriving. "Half my days"
> and then the other half, etc. High water mark, red quartzite, red
> osier, sumac, fire opals seen at dusk. Fear of strange places as
> the fear of not being able to find the way out.[2]

To traverse these passageways is to discover that Cole's sometimes anxiety-producing image-fragments are constructed to evade the reductive security of place, time, and identity in much the same way that her poems elude a totalizing exegesis of their workings. In the poem "Memory Shack," from her book *Moira*, she simply but decisively states, "The image is empty" (*M* 50). Only the surface survives because it is a protean labyrinth that keeps changing and regenerating itself. In another line from "Memory Shack," Cole writes, "Superhero for a day / hot wires run through / wires imitating light / twitch as though attached / and sound scans / the way memory is not local // Shatters the big picture" (*M* 49). Here, we are asked to see the particular paths of the poem crossing at unpredictable junctures due to twists in metonymy or metaphor, which underscore the linguistic movements of the pieces rather than subordinate them to an expressible whole. If we are denied a certain closure in Cole's poetry, it has been replaced by an ever-present intimacy, a nearness and open invitation to walk these paths, to lift these veils, though they will never lead us "home" or reveal a secret code by which they will become clearly decipherable. In the epigram to her most recent book, "Desire & its Double," Cole quotes the film director and critic Raul Ruiz: " . . . travelers should be aware that paths leading nowhere are also part of the trip."[3]

In a sense, Cole's labyrinthine wanderings are spatial evocations punctuated by the falling of images like *tears* into a stream that doubles as a visual screen, where words seen in a moment's plunk recall a *somewhere before*, a space in which language leaks through vision, where memory and the imaginary are entwined in the stir of ripples widening their arcs, while another tear sends new thought-rings spreading and overlapping their orbits, ringing in other meanings in echo-exchange between their parts, and so multiple universes of thought live and accumulate upon the surface of a stream, intersect at certain points, multiply and fade without a center to which their movements can be traced . . . Here, in these spiraling tear-rings, we are reminded of the myth of Echo and Narcissus, for it is in the escape from the Narcissan, self-projecting, ocularcentric gaze that Cole's work can be seen to take a calculated turn.

Narcissus' unrequited love for his own image (misread as a water nymph) causes his tears to fall, breaking his reflection in the motionless pond. But in this myth of mirrored doublings, it is Echo who first suffered rejection by Narcissus, and it is she, ironically, who represents his tears. It is in her name that we recognize the mutable, ringed *echoes* that slowly spread across the pond, and it is in her intersecting ripples that Cole's labyrinth behind the shattered mirror of Narcissus' gaze is suggested.

As a translator of contemporary French poetry and a close reader of the works of Maurice Merleau-Ponty, Emmanuel Levinas, and Gilles Deleuze, among others to whom she has referred, Cole has written a poetry that is in dialogue with much of the philosophical and psychoanalytic tendencies current in French thought. In this context, Cole's poetry shows a striking relationship with one of

the more frequently discussed issues in Jacques Lacan's writings—the develop-
ment of the "mirror stage." In Lacan's view, the child's identification with his
image in the mirror is read as a falsely unified, Narcissus-like viewing of an ear-
lier, more dispersed, multi-sensorial experience. Lacan argued that the persis-
tence in later life of the "mirror stage," with its visually unified ego, indicates a
failure to move beyond the Imaginary to the Symbolic phase, characterized by
the development of a complex, discursive language. But Lacan's privileging of
visual experience, and his linkage of truth with the Idealist tradition of *eidos* in
his Symbolic stage, led Luce Irigaray to view his interpretation as falling into the
blind spot of ocularcentrism itself, a situation Lacan labored hard to avoid. Iri-
garay questioned what might lie behind the "male gaze" implied in Narcissus'
frozen stare. In the introductory chapter of *This Sex That Is Not One*, she tries
to imagine an Alice that moves back and forth through her image in the *flat* mir-
ror but finds instead a double-Alice that will not be reduced to the "one" who
gives a *straight* answer.[4] Readers of Cole's poetic resistance to binary reduction
may find a complementary analog here. For Irigaray, what exists behind the mir-
ror shattered by the tears of Narcissus' Echo is a labyrinth of touching "lips" or
labia, the nexus of an infinitely crossing world of the senses.

Like his forerunners, Nietzsche and Bataille, Jean-François Lyotard has im-
plored readers to recognize that, in their rootless wanderings, neither poetic in-
sight nor philosophical rigor leads to a supra-position or escape route from life's
labyrinth. By now two major trajectories in Cole's poetry can be discussed via
her relationship to the image: 1) evasion from the agents of the "mirror stage"
and 2) evocation of the labyrinth behind the looking glass.

There is no stronger indictment of the controlling "mirror stage" in all of
Cole's books than in her 1994 *Mars*. Dividing the work into six long poems,
Cole distinguishes some of the fine points between lived-experience, and me-
dia representation, seen as contrived political manipulation. But she is also af-
ter the state of institutionalized male-female relations, in which a "nation of
matter" distances itself from the one that doesn't matter. In the poem "Ruth,"
which is footnoted "reading E(mmanuel) L(evinas)," she invents the image of a
"spacer" as a left-over that leaves its mark on the betweens, the *dasein* that stains
the lips.[5] This discarded, worthless, silent observer of tragedy reflects on lan-
guage.

> *anonymous vigilance* is the state of the mother*
> *consciousness*   is the name of the father
> nameless state   vs   stated name
>   what is this
>   relationship?

The state EL describes is the one "known to women". It has never been "enough" for women to speak it. Now the man speaks it, it's *visible.*

The mother-child dyad is paramount paragon paradigm of "being for the other".

* I will call the parents "mother".
(*Ms* 75)

She suggests, later in the same poem, an alternative to the domination of denotative meaning by presenting writing that is "a representation of a / gesture or something / parallel to a gesture / —notions in our genes" (*Ms* 72). Here, she is referring to a movement towards something between the acts, a writing that situates itself in waiting, which is to say a deferred meaning, a "fibrillation of the eyes" that flickers between prose and poetry, escaping the binary by being a double-reading, as Derrida would have it.

In the title poem of this collection, Cole refers to woman as the "other" held hostage to men's wars, linguistically "exiled even in my own words" (*Ms* 9). Levinas' denigration of the visual as a fleeing from the *light* toward the caress that knows not what it seeks, informs much of Cole's reflections on the image, which she reads through a myriad of gender relations. She ends "Mars" with the words "Other. Was it your image. The sun // that absorbs it / protects itself / at the point / it excludes // how they stare in the dark" (*Ms* 28). It is Cole's use of "they" that subtly leads us to the negative image of a plurality of suns in the form of stars that only come out at night. Excluded by the day's rays, they form another, alternative sky. It is this escape route from the logocentric, all-seeing eye of the Narcissan sun that leads Cole towards a night-vision—the means by which the image or the poem itself eschews detection. But this *elusiveness* cannot be read simply as a flight from capture; it is also a generative process, a bursting into flame as images conduct a certain shape, heat, or "ultrasound" vibration that illuminates the invisible for a line or so.

Her most recent collection, *Desire and Its Double,* includes the lines, "along the way I managed to / escape," from an untitled poem for Ruth Singer. Later in a poem entitled "Interpellation" from the same book, she contrasts the stultifying, freeze-framing gaze to the poet's eye that "looks elsewhere. This absence fashions an acute sensation of presence, this vividness you see but do not see."[6] It is not to the retinal, representational, controlling eye that Cole directs her imagery, but to its "double," the generative, elusive, gestural eye that sees with the fluidity, vividness, and desire of a lucid dream. By "Plunging irresistibly into a less visible state,"[7] the hidden eye moves between words and subtle states. Her attention to the invisible often involves introducing the visual indirectly through gesture or sound, which helps to shape it into a compositional metaphor, rather than a visual pointer. Gesture can be thought of here as the *shadow* of an act—not the act itself but a shape cast in darkness behind the object in the light—a blind man's touch at the haptic origins of sight. "Something invisible returns inert and crawling. In this sung desire images rub up against each other."[8] Again and again, she attempts to remove visibility from the image as if this were a way of making the invisible present but not quite seen. "I couldn't make the images empty enough, she said. She / lamented. Renewed and refreshed in the oasis of discontent."[9]

Cole's compositional elements of gesture, sound, and word foreground an imagery that is self-emptying and multidimensional, reminding us of Wallace Stevens' fusion of the aural, material and linguistic within an image. Stevens refuses to let the *bird* simply fly off with the reader but keeps it in mind for a second and third look. Cole writes in *My Bird Book,* "light proofed and green // as it was now / to think in rhythm / in close attendance // concrete / to the mercury // stunned in the way things sourceless / are seen interactive."[10] This cohabitation of sense-as-meaning with the multiplicity of the senses leads to the evocation of a synesthetic, heterogeneous labyrinth, based on word-bridges behind the shattered mirror.

It is in the image as word-bridge that Cole's writings accumulate like "a story traced between two points / beneath which a line was drawn sitting in the place of words . . . "[11] In her serial poem "Paper House," from her first book, *Metamorphopsia,* she writes, "the way bridge is / designation of thought / and thing / cherished, nothing."[12] Here, the image of the bridge functions as an immaterial-material word; it marks the imbrication of thought and thing, which is to say, a *no-thing* or thought-space between things. This overlay of transparencies forms a *bridge of betweens,* to which Cole's work is continually returning. In her most recent full-length book, *Contrafact,* she writes about this bridge across the senses: " . . . a pencil in that *almond shaped space between the hand and the eye, between the eye and the book,* the 'gare intermondiale.' "[13] The hollowed-out image of an "almond shaped" eye is articulated in the space "between her thumb and forefinger." This kind of conceptual, hallucinatory metaphor, found frequently in Cole's work, bridges movement, image, touch, and idea in one gestural composition.

Another poem from *Contrafact,* entitled "Lens," uses the photo of a broken bridge to serve a similar function: " . . . late-twentieth-century photograph / in which women are washing / clothes in the river, clustered / near shattered embankments or blades / and shafts that once had been a bridge."[14] The imagination must reconstruct the missing bridge between the photo and the world, but like "the face of the partial, 'it depends on who's looking.'" Look now and the bridge is in ruins; now, and it has disappeared into the river; now, and it has been restored—all partial descriptions of an imaginative process, analogous to the stages of memory's inventive reconstructions. No one bridge is the true one, but together they form a shifting matrix of truths that appear, dissolve, and re-appear as in a time-lapse film that challenges the primacy of any one time or lived-experience to place its frame over the "bridge" itself. The imaginative memory that dips in and out of these recollections never gets it *right*, but may get it *wrong* in ways that are more poetically truthful to the fluctuations between the visible and invisible. Cole's metonymic bridges lead to an overflowing or overlapping of the senses, each unto the other in a pluralistic economy of exchange.

On the first page of *Desire & Its Double,* entitled "Putting One's Self in a Situation," she makes reference to how this bridging may be approached.

to say explore the experience the very thought of
thought or a unified theory of the senses. Imagine,
you are, going on a trip. At first there was physical
divorce, that is, appearance, that is, acceptance, a
distance. to verify undone, unmade. Taken apart.
the image of an intact yet the materials at hand
like the idea of reason, that the vision was their
faces unmasking   shaking sheets
of metal to simulate thunder putting aside
materials at hand. portraits. secret thoughts. And
I would hear them saying where is all this all this is
the body of the, the body of the body (of the)[15]

Cole is quick to remind us that her attempt to pass behind the Narcissan mirror of an imaginary unity into the synesthetic labyrinth of dynamic flow and exchange does not allow for another unity to slip in through the back door. A constant vigilance is required, a "complicating" of the echoing surfaces of the poem, so that they will always overflow theory and break each new mirror's attempt to confine them. Here we are reminded of Bataille's "dépense," or excess of expenditure, Nietzsche's tears over a beaten, dying horse in the street, or Derrida's mournful lament on sight in which he says, " . . . only man knows how to go beyond seeing and knowing because only he knows how to cry. . . . Only he knows that tears are the essence of the eye—and not sight. . . . "[16] It is the tears of Narcissus' Echo that break the false image of a logocentric, unified gaze and transform it into a plurality of limits, to which poetry inevitably returns.

In the Shadow of the Eye

You must attend to the surface
Stroke or touch, not just to the image, those blooms
Reduced to postcards or the flatness of calendars. . . .
                    —Ann Lauterbach, "Further Thematics," *Clamor*

A highly significant issue raised by the poetry and criticism of Ann Lauterbach, which may be useful in distinguishing certain elements of "Language poetry" from other innovative American poetry, is her defense of the term *beauty* and her use of the linguistic image as an autonomous fragment. In seeing beauty as "part of the solution as well as part of the problem,"[17] Lauterbach opts for a more intricate reworking of the term itself, eschewing the stock categorizations, which tend to hide their biases under a smoke screen of objectivity. Lauterbach's important renovation of beauty and her idea of the "whole fragment" invite a larger discourse on an important strain within avant-garde poetry—the *critical lyric*. In such writing, intelligence is dispersed across the entire sensorium, including the dreaming body, as opposed to residing primarily in the textual mappings of conceptual thought.

In *The Postmodern Condition,* Jean-François Lyotard isolates the aesthetics of the sublime within a tradition that dates back to the third-century Greek philosopher, Longinus, which is picked up in the eighteenth century with Burke and Kant, only to appear again in the twentieth century with Walter Benjamin and Emmanuel Levinas. Understood in this lineage, the sublime refers to an experience that cannot be presented or made visible. It occurs "when the imagination fails to present an object which might, if only in principle, come to match a concept."[18] Thus, the concept "the infinitely powerful" cannot be illustrated by a sensible object. Lyotard echoes Levinas' comparison of the *sublime* with the prohibition against graven images found in Exodus. By contrast, *beauty* is identified with an experience of the presentable and is associated with the usual suspects: classicism, realism, capitalism, transcendental unity, and the totalizing centeredness of the visual. Both modernism and postmodernism end up on the side of the sublime, but modernism is characterized by its nostalgia for lost unity and essence. Postmodernism, on the other hand, "searches for new presentations, not in order to enjoy them but in order to impart a stronger sense of the unpresentable."[19] The *essay* turns out to be postmodern, but the *fragment* can only manage a modernist rating. After blaming the terror of the nineteenth and twentieth centuries on the nostalgia for wholeness or oneness, Lyotard ends *The Postmodern Condition* on a plea: "The answer is: let us wage a war on totality . . . "[20] In the face of such a binary, oppositional mode of discourse, we may become suspicious of the closed categories into which *beauty* and the *sublime* have been so quickly and neatly shuttled.

In a recent conversation with Heather Ramsdell, published in *Murmur 1*, Lauterbach states that she admires Charles Bernstein for "taking irony to the next place which is totally transgressive,"[21] but she suggests that he had to let a lot go, including the idea of beauty, which she is not willing to do. She adds that, for her, this sense of beauty has to do with "the pleasure in the just choice." By invoking the "just choice," Lauterbach is not arguing for an emphasis on the polished manipulation of craft or content—just the opposite. As indicated later in the same conversation, she is attempting to link choice to judgment in a way that implies an ethical concern for the material in its sensual and discursive multiplicity. She emphasizes the construction of the poem as a series of enactments at the local level that are responsive to the reader's passage through an often difficult, dispersed work. The pleasure of the poem comes in response to what beauty has to give, "where pleasure is not entertainment's escape but entailing, engaged, muscular (the erotics of thought inseparable from feeling, for example.) A way of structuring meanings around the site of pleasure."[22]

Lauterbach's concern with rethinking beauty offers a critique of how the term has been misappropriated through its historical association to the True and the Good. In this regard, she is in agreement with Lyotard, Irigaray, Kristeva, and a multitude of others who recognize the totalizing and socially commodifying ends to which beauty has been relegated. However, never happy in a restrictive, either-or dichotomy, Lauterbach prefers to tease out the complications, pointing out that "[Beauty] has an epistemological role not merely a social (constructed) one."[23] She goes on to argue for a "pragmatic beauty," which emphasizes exactitude in the meticulous tracking of "multiple events; layers; not single-point perspective, but moments captured as moments, within a constellation."[24] Her term "pragmatic beauty" is close to Wallace Stevens's notion of "the imagination pressing back against the pressure of reality."[25] But it is the imaginative play of choice between the possible and the actual within the materiality of words on the page that constitutes for Lauterbach the pressures of reality upon the poem. Her focus on the material construction of the image as a layered syntax, concerned with unraveling and decoding meanings rather than encoding them, also distinguishes her work from Mallarmé's exquisite vapor-sensibilities, floating on the folds of a veil. Like Cole, Lauterbach uses the image as a self-reflexive bridge between language and the inexpressible.

The spectacle has been placed in my room.
Can you hear its episode trailing,
pretending to be a thing with variegated wings?

Do you know the name of this thing?
It is a rubbing from an image.
The subject of the image is that which trespasses.[26]

Whereas Lauterbach's early involvement in the visual arts marked her poetry
with a "mutating interior responding voice,"[27] her later, often more dispersed
work, developed out of a need to allow the literal gaps and absences that she was
writing about into the poems. The whole page began to be used to inscribe rather
than describe visible and auditory spacings, and the fragment took on a more
important position in her writings. Although it was not splayed radically across
the page, it subscribed to a wider sense of inclusion, allowing for multiple points
of focus and magnification, as in "In the Museum of the World (Henri Matisse)":

I was shown two rivers, their vistas

> snailfooted/waterskinned abyss
> wheelwinged staring at muck
> weedy, indifferent, purplepronged up
> in avid rays / their comprehensive is
> bearing emblems smaller than time

under the decor
coiled among rocks

I met a woman with odd eyes
she said this is the figure of guilt
hurling a snake boulder
                    wall
ripped from a wall
                         fragment installed,

This country is a
cavern of drunk light / shade rubbed onto day
the corpse is not luminous / vines dangerous / flowers profuse
as in an arbitrary Eden. These
consolations also are damaged / seepage under roofs

thru which the musics
might come.
(*AFE* 96–7)

The "musics," to which Lauterbach refers, appear after a certain "damage /
seepage" has taken place. The "arbitrary Eden" of a received beauty comes with
all the doxa of its cultural baggage intact, but the critically viewed image-frag-
ment, riding on a wind of changing rhythms, helps to disperse and disorient this
picture postcard of reality. It allows for the serious play of another kind of
beauty to emerge. As we have seen, Lyotard regards the fragment as an element
of modernist nostalgia for a lost unity, and there is certainly historical evidence
for such a reading. However, it would be a mistake to assume that the fragment
must necessarily arise from a broken whole. There is nothing inherent in the re-
lationship of whole to fragment that describes a cause and effect chain of events.
The fragment may be considered as a given, that is, part of a distributed field in
duration, which no more needs a whole to complete it than the universe needs
a creator to originate it. Lauterbach agrees with Lyotard's analysis of the mod-
ernist's fragment as a sign of incompletion and yearning for a lost wholeness and
lists Yeats, Pound, Eliot, and even Stevens in this regard. But her reading of post-
modernism makes a distinction between the modernist, nostalgic fragment and
what she terms a "whole fragment." In her essay "How I Think About What I
Write," she says, "Each fragment is in itself a whole, which is why we have a sense
of separation and isolation rather than dissolution."[28] Each word, each letter is
itself and something else; each is a whole and its double, floating in an ocean of
rhythmically changing patterns.

The Principle of Complementarity in quantum physics ascribes to sub-atomic
entities this Janus-faced, dual nature—the capacity to behave as an autonomous
whole particle and, alternatively, as a wave-function in a larger electro-magnetic
or gravitational field. In the last line of Lauterbach's recent poem "ON (Thing),"
she attests to this dual capacity of words and letters to function as parts and
wholes and for each to exist as contextual echoes, participating in and out of the
linear constraints of larger linguistic structures: "voice thread thru stone be-
tween the *s* and the *t* and the *one*."[29] As the "voice" turns the *s* of the *stone* into
sand, the *t* is orphaned as a single letter on its own, while the *one* echoes the
wholeness of the st(one) in its parts.

Many of Lauterbach's longer poems uncover a series of loosely connected
fragments, such as the one above, inside a larger swirl of quasi-narratives. They
do not spin out of each other, in the nomadic nonchalance of Ashbery's sump-
tuous rhythms, so much as change magnifications within parenthetical contexts.
This is not to say that Ashbery is not somewhere present in the movement and

drift of Lauterbach's gesture, but that the conceptual overlay of focus, which places the *imaginary* over the *real* like communicating transparencies, is the legacy of Stevens, as in "For Example (5): Song of the Already Sung":

> Then the real is a convincing show? Of course
> the beam looks real, but is more melancholy
> an inhalation of breath moving across
> to a charged little image.
> It's like looking at a forest
> through the eye of a needle.
> In a shop I found a dirty white vase. I washed it;
> now it is clean.
> There's a form of dreaming in another form
> and there's the sacredness of common objects.
> (*AFE* 59)

Lauterbach's poem invokes a fascinating paradox: she invites us to consider the construction of the real in relation to its presence in thought, but thought leads us inevitably away from the real object. Thinking about the real "beam" in the first part of the poem provokes a melancholic image of its isolation, wherein a Blake-like forest of one suddenly appears. The image of "a dirty white vase" in the second part of the poem is reminiscent of Stevens's celebrated "jar," which "did not give of bird or bush / Like nothing else in Tennessee."[30] Having placed the jar in the wilderness, Stevens also makes us aware that both "jar" and "wilderness" are placed in the poem, providing us with a multi-layered correspondence between word, image, and reality. In Lauterbach's poem, the vase is an ordinary object found in a shop filled with other objects. Here, the shop corresponds to Stevens' wilderness, but the vase does not provoke "dreaming in another form" until it is washed and cleaned and its *otherness* seen. This presence of dream in the meditations on "common objects" places us in the *shadow of the eye,* where the visible floats on the surface of the invisible. Like Stevens, Lauterbach's dreaming "form" or imagination does not obliterate the real object; it is placed over it as a kind of transparency, so that one can be seen through the other. Before their "sacredness" is felt, both the "beam" and the "vase" are imaginatively separated from their surroundings as "common objects" and, like Stevens's "jar," perceived to reverberate within multiple levels of an irreducible paradox.

For Lauterbach, the "just choice" of word selection is a formal judgment that must be flexible enough to change angles of concentration from context to context, but rigorous enough to radically disturb the structure that is emerging. In this regard, the whole is as interesting as the conversation of its parts. Lauterbach's poems often shift rapidly from abstract, minimalist considerations to sensual, lyrical ones as if the next choice depended upon establishing the "whole fragment" at each juncture. In her conversation with Ramsdell, she says,

> And rhetorically it's very hard to try and get work to become minimalist in the art sense, without it becoming excruciating in its aridity—I mean to keep some of the wetness and some of the disturbance and some of the power intact is very hard. . . ."[31]

The poetry of Cole and Lauterbach draws upon an intelligence that is distributed throughout the entire sensorium, including the dream state. By making little use of this option, orthodox "Language" poetry may have backed itself into a conceptual corner. As recent neurochemical research has demonstrated, the older, brain-centered model of intelligence has ceded to a more extended, interdependent system of communicating nodes. This fluid exchange between more localized systems of sensory intelligence may be a primary distinction between the *critical lyric* and "Language" poetry. In this regard, the *critical lyric,* as exemplified by Cole and Lauterbach, allows the recontextualized image to return as an important part of an expanded zone of poetic activity.

The poetry of writers like Cole and Lauterbach, among many others, tangential to but separate from "Language" poetry, gives us clear indications of another significant strain within the American avant-garde. Their subtle reworking of a lyric poetry that foregrounds the question of language has helped to challenge many prevalent, misleading assumptions that have dulled the differences between avant-garde poetries. In helping to express those differences, Cole and Lauterbach have made it more difficult for some mainstream traditionalists to simply lump all experimental poetries into one homogeneous, marginalized camp, and then exclude it from any direct influence upon the ongoing development of American poetry.

Postmodern Romance and the Descriptive Fetish of Vision in Fanny Howe's *The Lives of a Spirit* and Lyn Hejinian's *My Life*

Laura Hinton

Fanny Howe's *The Lives of a Spirit* and Lyn Hejinian's *My Life,* both published in 1987 by Sun & Moon Press,[1] are experimental women's texts that challenge the way in which we chronicle women's lives. I treat these poetic novellas as examples of the romance, a genre that focuses on women's internal experience.[2] As romances, Howe's and Hejinian's works dissociate themselves from the historical mission of realism, which is to generate a picture of external "reality" through a visually represented world. As *postmodern* romances, borrowing that term from Diane Elam, both novellas are richly innovative, questioning not only how we represent reality, but "whether we actually can know the past," "re-membering" the past again and again by re-situating "its temporality," making it "impossible to forget."[3]

Yet by re-membering the past, any romance necessarily courts some form of nostalgia—a nostalgia that relies upon fetishism. Fetishistic nostalgia restages the lost and ruptured past as that which is found and whole, through visual means. *The Lives of a Spirit* and *My Life* are intensely metaphorically visual, flirting with the fetishistic nostalgia normally linked not to the romance but to "realism." They do so, however, in the name of the romance. Romance-inclined, postmodern, these experimental novellas wrestle with the promises and failures of representation, for the sake of imparting women's points of view.

Of course, there are no greater fetishists than the classic realists. These are the artists, the fabulists, who, through the novel of "realism," or classic film's adoption of the novel's suturing techniques, create a seemingly intact picture that denies the subject's Oedipal crisis in perceiving lack: the lack of the phallus upon the mother's image, in Sigmund Freud's reductive account; the lack of the subject's own totality, in Jacques Lacan's more linguistic conceptualization. Fetishism is a method of assuaging the subject's fear of lack through representational excess. It super-adds a symbolic phallus to the mother's body through an object reified or memorialized in various objects of pleasure, like a high-heeled shoe, or a verisimilar description of a high-heeled shoe in a descriptive passage.[4] Since fetishism's representational "re-membered" effects usually take a visual form, critics have viewed fetishism as the providence of "realism," in both its literary and mainstream-cinema forms. But the romance, too, can claim the fetishist's representational touch. By reveling in structural uncertainty and a lack of resolution that the realist text might deny or repress, the romance fascinates its audience by positioning representation at the boundary of the unrepresentable, in other words, in the fetishistic oscillation between the absence and presence of image.[5]

Howe's and Hejinian's experimental romances about women's written lives harness this fetishistic oscillation in order to reveal the crisis of the postmodern female subject. Inhabiting the romance genre to further explore the representational crisis usually associated with masculinity and castration anxiety, the female subjects in both *Lives* and *My Life* impart a difference of viewing position and in the view of representation, in general. These female subjects radically question the fetishistic oscillation between self and other, internal and external, that marks more traditional boundaries within the romance form. Howe's romance—like many romances in the American tradition—is driven by a fetishistic desire to represent the self in rapport with "other," but Howe's "other" is intensely female and enigmatic, metaphorized as the natural universe. Hejinian's *My Life* positions the female subject even more radically on the edge of representation. It engages the self-other dialectic along non-binary channels so as to break the romance sequence of fetishistic oscillation altogether. While Howe's contribution to the romance lies in her challenge to the American romance's particular male lineage—one which begins with the nineteenth-century tradition of Nathaniel Hawthorne and Edgar Allan Poe, and continues into twentieth century meta-fiction with authors like John Barth[6]—Hejinian's contribution rests in the way through which she dodges romance formulas entirely. In *My Life*, Hejinian never fascinates through enigmatic descriptions of the natural world or a castrated self. Rather, visual description in *My Life* is suspended upon a slippery skein of linguistic folds and knots too temporal, too shifting, to commemorate the fetish of vision.

1

The woman romancer's use of the contradictions inherent to the romance form bears special scrutiny, since, in the words of Louise Kaplan, the fetish is like a hysteric, "the epitome of [cultural] femininity . . . as enigmatic and elusive as the female herself."[7] In an essay on George Sand, Naomi Schor asks how a woman writer might employ images of castration, "the wound," an absent presence that, in turn, visually becomes the most beloved part of the female anatomy for the romance fetishist. Schor cites Sand's novel *Valentine,* in which the image of a foot scalded by hot water entices a woman's lover to kiss her foot, causing him to swoon. Schor notes provocatively that only the male figure experiences such passion: "there are no female fetishists . . . female fetishism is . . . an oxymoron."[8] But Schor then suggests a way in which fetishism might offer pleasure for women, through its "oscillation between denial and recognition of castration," which permits women to "effectively counter any move to reduce their bisexuality to a single of its poles." It is a pleasure that operates on both sexual- and textual-visual planes. And it offers women "a *strategy* designed to turn the so-called 'riddle of femininity' to woman's account."[9]

Turning "the so-called 'riddle of femininity' to woman's account" is what Howe's *Lives* achieves. This process has deep roots in a romance tradition once primarily associated with women writers. While early sources of the romance rest in medieval tales of masculine chivalry, later developments in the seventeenth century are attributed to women writers like Madame Scudéry of the French Salon tradition, who used the romance to express female desire, and to seek narrative attainment of women's aspirations in a spiritualized version of love that countered the marriage market conventions of her time.[10] Refuted by that century's male literary establishment as a feminized and frivolous—even dangerous—literature,[11] the romance later attracted early American male novelists, who found in its bastardized form expressions of their own perceived marginality as Americans, as they sought literary roots alternative to those offered in the nineteenth-century British novel and its mimetic tradition.[12] Framing *The Lives of a Spirit* in a genre that historically embraces both this female tradition and an American (albeit male) "marginal" one, Howe aligns herself with disruptive literary practices. A contemporary American *woman* novelist, she transposes a recently masculinized romance genre and all its paradoxes back "to woman's account."

Like Sand, Howe uses the romance to express sentiments and subversions of the female subject. Howe does so in a narrative that further subverts the use of visual description in the process. Howe's text does not embrace "the wound." But through the problems of the visual referent in description, her narrative speaker becomes *like* "the wound"; she becomes a ghostly absent presence felt and occasionally glimpsed through brief, metaphoric images. "There was a bridge from blank to blank, floating," Howe writes in *Lives.*[13] It is as if the writing itself were a suspended bridge, carrying a nearly voiceless, positionless speaker—herself a kind of "blank"—between two fields of "blank," sites of reference that then mysteriously dissolve. Howe's text, indeed, is obsessed with images of "blanks" or "gaps," signifying the presence of something, someone, not quite discernable to the image-making eye. Later in *Lives* we view a female figure moving in and out of the novella, a figure sitting in a valley of rocks. Yet, "When she stood up, as always she sought a gap in the crumbling walls" (50), we are told. The subject of *Lives* is, indeed, always grabbing at "a gap," trying to concretize that which is in the course of an inimitable decay. The "gap" and the "blank" coursing the narrative of *Lives* are figures for "the wound," itself a figure for the female subject—or "spirit," in Howe's conception. It is an ontological space out of which a never fully concretized female speaker-protagonist receives her verbal source.

The first chapter of *Lives* condenses "the wound" metaphor in a profuse series of empty or ruptured images out of which a speaking subject is born. *Lives* begins with tenuous descriptions of a haunted, fragmented natural world fraught with tension and chaos. We are given a description of an icy shoreline, braced by "a hard wind [which] barreled over the sandy soil," and "Rusty war crosses [which] tipped northeast" (9). The war crosses invoke the empty presence of an absent subject, taking form in the unseen spirits seeming to alight "the other side of the cemetery that domiciled on the top of a gnawed cliff" (9). Out of the ghosts of the war-wounded dead, the voice and half-hearted presence of a first-person narrator rises within the text, through which "she"—nameless protagonist "racing aimlessly" along the shore in Paragraph 1—becomes the autobiographical "I" of Paragraph 3. The "aimless" racing of the "I" is reflected in a vacant, yet excessively "fitful" world, in which "A forgotten name moves in such fitful waves, engineered like tumbleweed across the mental floor" (9). Memorialized in the "forgotten name," the absent presence of a narrative subject is a kind of restless ghost, allusive of the New England ghost tales of Howe's romance predecessors, Hawthorne and Poe.

An unsteady mental state ("mental floor") is rendered visually literal in the description of "fitful waves" and moving "tumbleweed." In the next paragraph, such imagery of an external world continues to evoke the subject's excessive, passionate mental state, as "violent crests" of sea "brine" spew "into the air, as if to shuck off excess emotion" (9). But the last thing this image achieves is "to shuck" that "excess emotion" created by the sheer weight of description. Indeed, this image creates *more* "emotion" for this fantastical romance, which oscillates between too much and not enough visual referent. This first chapter introduces us to a fantastical natural landscape as mysterious as it is representational, a world as evocative of what is missing in its description as it is fully described—the partialized visual landscape of romance. In the second paragraph of *Lives,* a sentence, actually a fragment, stands for the dream-like incomprehensibility and irresolution of this fractured romance universe, in the wound-like, abyss-like, female shape of a mouth: "A dream smell of salt and acid, like the inside of a mouth, and I was down in it" (9). We are reminded that the womb and the wound are related female images. And we are reminded that the sexual-sensual excesses of the female body in representational novels and films provide a method both of denying and provoking castration anxiety: the fetish of vision relies upon too much vision, as well as its lack. In an image similarly evocative of the vaginal site of birth in *Lives,* dreamlike landscapes and spatial features give rise not only to an oscillation between excessive presence and absence of visual representation, but a profuse gush of language full of imagistic leaps. We witness terse but lush, romantic, visual descriptions of the "heave of the night sea," the "torn screens" of "Beach houses . . . battened shut" (9).

"Excess," as Elam notes, is a property both of romance and of postmodern fiction. Reveling in "a common excess" that breeds hyperbole and representational obscurity—in the process, dislocating familiar figures and forms—postmodern experimentation has a more-than-coincidental link to romance's historical practices. So, too, in the visual description of violently crashing waves, and through a subject that is violently active and yet radically displaced, Howe's *Lives* reproduces an excess of objects and emotion that we can glimpse and experience—but only temporarily. For excess, by definition, is that which never satiates; it is always compensatory. In classic psychoanalysis, excessive objects and visual descriptions substitute for what the subject cannot envision seeing: the missing phallus, a structural icon of fetishistic sight. But classic psychoanalysis gives but half the story, for castration anxiety is a male subjective phenomenon. In the first chapter of *Lives,* the excess of description and subjectivity swells up and becomes impregnated, seeming to give birth to the other half of the story: a female response. Literally, this response is in the descriptive form of a female infant, lying "with its ankles crossed and its arms spread wide, like one who lives by her feelings" (9–10).

The open-armed baby produced by the conclusion of this first chapter is "a model of something" (10). Of what, we are never told. "Something" is ambiguous and vacant, like the pulsing wound out of which the baby is linguistically spewed. Spawned by a "mother" nature, the "other" of a feminized earth, the infant is uncertain, half-formed: "The baby might have been the least worthy of earth's materials, lacking hardiness as she did" (9). As if out of the intensity of this excessive but also hollow description, the female infant solidifies into language, sense and mass. Her uncertain ontology, at first, is emphasized by the use of the impersonal pronoun "it," and then is superceded by the possessive adjective "her" in a phrase that can only speculate, a phrase which can only vaguely compare the infant to "one who lives by her feelings" (9). These visual descriptions suggest that they can provide, in the romance, the agency of female-associated "feeling." Female agency and emotion is further rendered in a following passage: "The application of her [the baby's] small fist to her lips made her . . . the object of maternal desire" (10). Desire becomes increasingly feminized, sentimentalized and excessive in this chapter of *Lives* when we are given a description of the baby's plush, wound-like mouth: "lips, at the service of gum, tooth, and voice, protruded pink and soft" (10). The baby's "heart," a sentimental image associated with cultural femininity and emotion, is visually described as "a seething fountain of blood" (10). A gushing, bleeding wound, the baby's heart is full of excessive affect and sentiment, an appeal toward stereotypes about women and maternal emotion. The appeal itself is excessive, super-added to something not yet there: "Every part of her seemed extra" (10).

The baby, after all, comes from nowhere. Or, rather, she comes from some metaphoric landscape that can only be visually evoked through romance's fetishistic, fantastical displacements: "They surmised that she had floated from the stars in the navy blue sky. Like rain at sea and no one to see, the coherence of these events and conjectures was never going to be accounted for" (10). The infant symbolizes a verbal-visual beginning for a "spirit" formally inhabiting and directing the course of the *Lives* narrative. Like the baby, this "spirit," however, is a compensatory image. It is tempting to interpret the baby, the "spirit," as a substitute phallus, a Freudian image of provisional maternity expressed by "penis envy"—but viewed not as woman's desire to compensate for lacking the phallus; rather, as a woman's desire for masculine privilege, like imaginative freedom.

In this sense, Howe's infant reflects what Poe called, in his "Marginalia" (1846), "a glimpse of the spirit's outer world." Commenting on Poe's discussion of the romance, Terrence Martin describes what Poe called a "'border-ground,'" which in Martin's words is "a point from which the imagination, unbounded and free from constraint, may journey into the 'supernal.'"[14] Imaginative freedom is an American romance theme. It is no coincidence that Howe ends her description of the infant, and the chapter out of which it emerges, in a reflection upon the status of her subject's ontological freedom: "And will sometimes wonder: Little word, who said me? Am I owned or free?" (10).

In speculating upon the nature of the romance, Henry James once declared that it is the genre that best embodies textual freedom, in an often-quoted passage from his 1908 Preface to *The American:*

> The only *general* attribute of projection romance that I can see . . . is the fact of the kind of experience with which it deals—experience liberated, so to speak; experience disengaged, disembroiled, disencumbered, exempt from the conditions that we usually know to attach to it. . . . [15]

"Disengaged, disembroiled, disencumbered," in an image James goes on to visually shape in the figure of a tethered balloon breaking free, the female subject of

Lives embarks upon a textual journey that at once frees herself from representational restraint but also anchors herself to narrative platforms, like character, descriptive passages conjuring up external space, and time-space continuity. For example, a picture of a young girl opens the second chapter: "She chewed her braid and waited for her mother" (13). This relatively disembodied image nevertheless exists within traditional narrative chronology; we read: "She had eaten as much bread at as many tables as the story of her luck would tell, but she was still feeling empty" (13). "Still feeling empty," this female figure is destined never to be full: "She opened her lunchbox and looked in: a hard lump of bread and jam smeared out of sticky pot, where the red seeds were burned from the sun. Cheap jam" (13). "Cheap jam," the gluing factor, is rejected, as are the narrative connecting devices of conventional plot. Nevertheless, the subject is subject to the fact of her own representation, recognized as a form of slavery. The desire for freedom is juxtaposed against the fact of slavery, in arrestingly visual images, again, of an infant:

> If I weren't a slave walking in shackles, I'd kick like a baby in a bed, and simply delight in this place. After all, what's in that baby's head, rolling down the promenade? Iridescent as a marble, with an organ iris, anything can roll around, *too* illuminated. (70)

Suggesting but then verging away from mimetic representation, the narrative speaker constructs yet another excessive, metaphorical landscape, provoking her to contemplate "the meaning of life," which we might take as "the meaning" of this narrative. "'Spare time,'" responds the figure of a "father," when "the meaning of life" is posed as a question. The "I" who is speaking suggests that she enjoys the fact that "the human being is composed of elements that don't cohere ... give[s] the impression of an intentional mess." She adds: "I think every event is unpredictable" (64). Yet there is an irony in the text to all this romance unpredictability, this romance "mess."

For like other traditional romance speakers and subjects, the postmodern female one of *Lives* quests after a figure that refers both to and beyond the self, a figure imagined as "G-d," with a missing "o." The female wound—the interpolated figure of the missing "o"—is the Father's Law of castration, clung to as fact. "Papa's rules are innate to his landscape," the speaker says; those rules "force you to think twice" (64). Indeed, "Papa's rules" set up a series of oppositional structures throughout *Lives* that leave us gyrating between the promise of presence and the awareness of absence, which focuses us, fetishistically, upon the text's final lack of resolution. In writing about the phallic mother in psychoanalytic discourse, Marcia Ian notes that this fetishistic representation is "the symptom of a compulsion to resolve ambivalence by dissolving it into a specious equiva-lence." [16] So, too, Howe's *Lives* attempts to resolve ambiguity through the con-struction of a self in narration, but ends up making ambiguity the holding pat-tern. Passionate, excessively descriptive romance prose reveals a vision of a female subject willing to ascend into the nothingness and imagined freedom of death:

> How can I scale that wall, never? If the watchtower man has his back turned, can I make a dive into the flume, and crumpled up, get shot? And it's only when you lie down defeated and dream that you experience a love that is frosted with hot lighting and colors, shapes and textures so trans-parent, they are apparitions of perfection. In dreams you see through sol-ids! It's Papa's way of showing you how to know G-d: with all your parts abandoned, cast down, while your spirit is free to move about. (64)

The ascended, transported "spirit" in *The Lives of a Spirit* finally finds in aban-donment the compensation of visual transfiguration.

Blocked by "Papa's rules," this subject aspires to something more, something beyond the veil of language. Like its American romance forebears, Howe's novella brings us closer to the ineffable—but, then, provocatively, stops short of arrival. Freed by this slavery to the veil, present only through the absence of form that allows the fetishistic vision to survive, the female subject of *Lives* lives—but in a bewildered, enchanted, blind state of romance affect. The castrating codes that celebrate a woman's inner "spirit" life also lose the woman of the text in its fe-tishistic ritual, making of her another "blank," a "gap" in discourse.

2

> *In such are we obsessed with our own lives, which lives being now language, the emphasis has moved.*
> —Lyn Hejinian, "If Written Is Writing"

Howe's *Lives* portrays an internal, alternative world of "spirits," a mysterious writerly world akin to what Hawthorne once called "the haunted mind" in an 1835 sketch by that name.[17] Like most romances historically, *The Lives of a Spirit* is a close cousin of the mimetic novel, in its effort seek out a "truer" reality, a more meaningful, if ephemeral, reality "within." In Hejinian's *My Life*, "the em-phasis has moved." It has moved from an inside state of the writer's life onto the language forms through which the writing/written life thrives. There actually is no longer an "inside" or an "outside" to shape the "life." Neither is the mind a haunted space, a "gap" that provocatively offers its own veils to lure the interpreter. Rather, the mind and the "world" are fully encased by language—nevertheless, in that process, made romance-like and "strange."[18]

So Hejinian's *My Life* is both a romance and an anti-romance. "Strangeness" is presented within the tight weave of poetic language from the very first page. "A pause, a rose, something on paper": *My Life's* first section title, often repeated throughout the text, is a gesture toward the visually descriptive, the concrete; and yet it remains embedded within language's strange distillations—the abstracting processes that occur through the mind's use of language.[19] "A rose" emerges as "something on paper," not through "some thing," a concrete visual image, but rather through "a pause," a gap created, not described, in the linguistic sequence. And the "pause" is not perceived as a force of nature in an external world. Instead, any external descriptions remain a function of the linguistic scenery. A "father," for example, "returned home from the war"; and "Somewhere, in the background, rooms share a pattern of small roses" (7). From the beginning, the emerging narrative speaker in *My Life* suggests she will not shape an identity that can be visually rendered and seen through the framework of descriptive images.

Rather, the speaker will reflect upon what a subject does with such images, caught within language and allusions to prior texts. "Pretty is as pretty does," we are told, following the sentence about the pattern of roses. This limerick line both borders on the nonsensical, reminiscent of Edward Lear, and alludes to the shipmaster-at-arm's sly jesting of Billy Budd, Herman Melville's "handsome sailor." The comment in Melville's romance novella comes when Billy, the hero, awkwardly spills his soup across the ship deck: "'Handsomely done, my lad! And handsome is as handsome did it, too!'"[20] In the novella that bears the "handsome sailor's" name, Melville suggests that the story of Billy is not just another "romance," such as that which aggrandizing sailors like to tell.[21] For Billy himself is a less-than-ideal representation, a figure who not only spills soup but who also reveals what Melville wryly calls an "organic hesitancy": a stutter.[22] A tendency to "pause" in speech, a language of supposed directness, becomes, for Hejinian, both a warning and a delight in *My Life*. Following the allusion to *Billy Budd*, Hejinian turns her focus toward the given "hesitancy" (to borrow Melville's term) within writing: "The better things were gathered in a pen" (*My Life* 7).

We are not to unknit those "things," such a statement suggests. Indeed, Hejinian never does interpret the meaning of a "pattern of . . . roses." And there are no external "truths" to be divorced from the language of description that structures them. From the beginning of *My Life*, to tell one's story, to describe "things" of the past, are acts steadily disciplined through a poetics that locates every vision, all objects under scrutiny and within memory, inside writing as an ongoing material practice. Therefore, in *My Life*, the subject that emerges does so only through the physicality of words on the page. There is no fetishized separation between self and object, writing and "things" written about. In this sense, *My Life* reconfigures the very basis of romance and its related genre of autobiography, in which a self-as-personality is constructed through condensations of "past" representational scenes, and in which a narrative persona seems to exist as if behind a gauzy veil, a persona the reader always wishes to see, know and penetrate.[23]

I focus on the early pages of *My Life* because they continually refer to what this novella will not do, and what it will. That it will slyly refer to the fetishistic, interpretative veil is suggested in a sentence that teases the reader with an allusion to the domestic novel, a genre also related to the romance,[24] and which typically features women as subjects. Such an allusion is made in *My Life* in a visual scene of literal domestic confinement: "The windows were narrowed by white gauze curtains which were never loosened" (7). If the reader is tempted to interpret "never loosened" as an image, say, of domestic propriety or proper Victorian female sexuality, the reader is abruptly severed from that thought, spun into a new mode of recognition, in the following sentence: "Here I refer to irrelevance, that rigidity which never intrudes" (7). "Rigidity," that which is "never loosened," is "irrelevance," and knowledge based upon traditional logical sequences of descriptive-object interpretation creates but a mirage of understanding. Instead, *My Life* insists in this passage that knowledge comes but playfully, in a kind of mimicry of traditional forms of knowledge, through word banter and association. In that banter and play is the refusal to rigidify the boundaries of self versus "the world," or to fetishize the subject of romance as a set of objects that become its reified emblems.

For Hejinian's insistently language-invented speaker is among those who love to astonish, as well as " 'love to be astonished,' " a line which echoes like a refrain throughout *My Life*. The speaker is one rooted in language perceptions; therefore, "she" never yearns for freedom from social structures mired in language. In this sense, again, *My Life* is an anti-romance, or a romance in which a romance counter-critique is formulated. In *My Life*, any momentary reflection upon the self or characterization external to this wall of words is immediately absorbed back into a wordplay that curiously marks the postmodern romance as a form. In using the term "absorb," I borrow from Charles Bernstein's concept of experimental poetics in his verse essay, "Artifice of Absorption," in which he writes that "a 'poem' may be understood as/writing specifically designed to absorb, or inflate/with, proactive—rather than reactive—styles of/reading."[25] Different than James's balloon, rising untethered to the sky, Bernstein's concept of "absorption" refers to a "proactive" engagement with linguistic arrangements, and a poem or poetic narrative that self-referentially connects with the grounds upon which language socially-historically rests. "Poetry" is, by definition, for Bernstein, that which seeks out and takes in its own "artifice," defined as "a measure of a poem's/intractability to being read as the sum of its/devices & subject matters," which contradicts the tradition of

"realism," with
its insistence on presenting an unmediated
("immediate") experience of facts, either of the
"external" world of nature or the "internal" world
of the mind; for example, naturalistic
representation or phenomenological consciousness
mapping.[26]

It is precisely this "intractability" that *My Life* celebrates in its poetics of astonishment: the recreation of every event, every moment of the past, as an astonishing *linguistic* activity, words-as-event reemerging, beginning, "again and again," to borrow that phrase from Gertrude Stein, a writer to whom Hejinian's work owes a great debt.[27] To repeat, to reconstruct, words-as-event is not to ignore a "mapping" of "phenomenological consciousness" that ties Hejinian's *My Life* to the romance. Rather, to repeat, to reconstruct, is to de-naturalize—and de-fetishize—the excess of words endemic to the romance project. "Life is but in the way life is conducted and that authentically speaking is composition," writes Stein.[28] "The plush must be worn away," declares the speaker of *My Life* (7). And so any representational excess, any residue of a vision that is aimed outside the text, is rubbed and frayed until it is absorbed by its own verbal profusion.

We are offered nature images within these exemplary first chapters: "An occasional sunset is reflected on the windows. A little puddle is overcast" (7). But following lines will remind the reader that "Long time lines trail behind every idea, object, person, pet, vehicle, and event" (7), and that no visual referent is safe from its language-presence in history: "Thicker, she agreed" (7). This narrative speaker does not capitulate to the seductions of a nostalgic reliance on the past, or a fetishistic disavowal that what she sees is not what she knows. Rather, the speaker is engaged in an on-going effort to make sense out of the *non*sense of signs, and, in the process, is continually "astonished" by her "life," which exists because of wordplay itself. This speaker is "self" and self-reflection at once.

The following passage might symbolize the narcissistic, almost infantile, romance fascination the speaker has with her reflection that is language: "and now she bobbed like my toy plastic bird on the edge of its glass, dipping into and recoiling from the water" (7–8). The next sentence warns, as if to Narcissus before taking the plunge, "But a word is a bottomless pit" (8). "Bottomless," astonishing, and narcissistic, perhaps, but never mysterious and enigmatic. The *My Life* speaker suggests that words "became magically pregnant and one day split open (8), a Lacanian allusion to the emergence of child speech. The speaker continues to allude to language's emergence through a combination of fantastical, improbable images that invoke both Imaginary and Symbolic processes: "When daylight moves, we delight in distance" (8).

Yet language is no nostalgic representation of lost unifications. Rather, language is a formal celebration of "distance," and marks what the *My Life* speaker calls the "incoherent border" of sleep. This is not Hawthorne's "haunted mind," a mental category that describes a period between wakefulness and sleep. Rather, the "incoherent border" is a dark side to the categorical potential in descriptive language, a dark side equally romancing and questioning of romance when the vigilant subject resists, and yet relies upon, the fetishistic re-envisioning of events through the storytelling function:

> The resistance on sleeping to being asleep . . . "Everything is a question of sleep," says Cocteau, but he forgets the shark, which does not. Anxiety is vigilant . . . restlessness is already conventional, establishing *the incoherent border which will later separate events from experience.* Find a drawer that's not filled up. That we sleep plunges our work into the dark. (8—emphasis added)

Into the dark, into the shifting shakiness of words-on-view, as if placed in a "drawer . . . not filled up," *we* view the castrating Father of Lacan's law—but not as a stern taskmaster, rather as a figure like every other: a figure of darkness and delight, since he, too, takes his source in language's astonishing configurations. "The incoherent border" that separates, and also conjoins, "events from experience" may be a fetishistic vision of the "magically pregnant" text. But it is a vision within and of a text that fosters both linguistic separations and gatherings "with a pen," and which contains within this vision all of the genetic imprints of a fully socialized and yet purely personal language.

My Life romances the romance, by establishing a continually "astonished" and female-romance sensibility, which exists not *beyond* but *within* the history of personal language. Sometimes there are frightening consequences to absorbing all of one's "life" into the forms and shadows of the verbal-visual romance terrain: "There are strings in the terrible distance . . . The trees are continually receiving their own shadows" (13). But, in *My Life*, the shadows are part of the incandescence of the woman writer's life-as-text. The "life" is a fantasy linguistically staged, in which event and experience are forever—and never—complete.

"Drawings with Words": Susan Howe's Visual Poetics

Alan Golding

In the last few years, the burgeoning number of commentators on Susan Howe has started to pay increased attention to the material, visual dimension of her poetry—page layout, deployment of white space, her many forms of palimpsestic text or over-writing. If one can agree broadly with Howe's complaint that critics "very rarely" "consider poetry as a physical act . . . [or] look at the print on the page, at the shapes of words, at the surface—the space of the paper itself" (*BM*, 157),[1] the generalization no longer applies to her own readers. In this essay I want to examine the visual aspects of Howe's poetry via some questions that, while sometimes addressed in these readings, still warrant further treatment: how do page and typographical design connect to Howe's particular brand of feminist poetics? And relatedly, how do the multiple possibilities for reading created by Howe's visually exploded page and use of space relate to her examining and decentering of a frequently patriarchal authority? To see Howe's use of page space solely or too persistently in gender terms would be to narrow her work, to impose on her a version of her own (admittedly arguable) complaint that "women who take a theoretical position are allowed to take a theoretical position only as long as it's a feminist theoretical position, and to me that's an isolation" (*I*, 21). At the same time, as Rachel Blau DuPlessis argues, gender questions in Howe (which are nearly always historiographical questions at the same time) do frequently take the form of "line breaks, page canvas, the use of space/silence/ silencing the piercing of whiteness,"[2] and to this extent Howe's visual page invites a gendered reading.

Howe's beginnings as a painter are well known, and critics have proposed various terms that are applicable to discussing her use of the page as a kind of canvas. In an essay on Anne-Marie Albiach that is directly relevant to Howe's work, DuPlessis writes of the "visual text or page poem"—"a concerted, intended, and forthright use of the white space of the page, not as neutral, unnoticed, and uncritically accepted, but as a deliberate ground for the text's typography and placement." And this "page poem has a transgressive aim." Nathaniel Mackey's term for the foregrounding of the visual, material aspects of the poetic text is "graphicity." For Mackey, as for DuPlessis, the graphic impulse suggests "a principle of tolerance . . . for its disruptive, de-formalist thrust, often outright celebration of it." Finally, Michael Davidson's notion of the "palimtext" captures usefully both the material forms of Howe's layered intertextuality and their ideological implications: "As its name implies, the palimtext retains vestiges of prior inscriptions out of which it emerges. Or, more accurately, it is the still-visible record of its responses to those earlier writings." When this mode makes marginal(ized) and so-called authoritative texts collide, as it does in Howe's hands, "the poem as palimtext becomes a window onto forces of stabilization in the culture at large."[3]

Before advancing to my main argument about graphicity in Howe, about her palimtextual "page poems" or "visual pages," it's worth contextualizing this aspect of Howe's work. Craig Dworkin summarizes usefully what Howe's page poems are *not*. They are not Olsonian scores for performance; they are not sites for experimentation with the materials of printing—ink, type, font, and so forth; they are not shape, picture or pattern poems; they are not concrete poetry.[4] While her pages are indeed not designed as keys to breath or performance, Howe's poetry remains much more in the line of Olson than in that of the international avant-garde traditions of visual poetry traced by Willard Bohn and Johanna Drucker.[5] More significantly, for Howe, page space is directly connected with the feminine in Olson: "the feminine is very much in his poems. . . . It has to do with the presence of absence. With articulation of sound forms. The fractured syntax, the gaps, the silences are equal to the sounds in *Maximus*. That's what [George] Butterick saw so clearly. He printed Olson's Space" (*BM*, 180).[6] Along similar lines, Kathleen Fraser has proposed Olson's importance more generally—even given his notoriously unsympathetic gender politics—for contemporary female practitioners of a visual poetics. She argues that women writers investigating "the visual potential of the page" "would have lacked such a clear concept of PAGE as canvas or screen on which to project flux, without the major invitation Olson provided . . . this, in spite of his inclusive/exclusive boy-talk." These writers, then, have claimed Olson's experiments "for entirely different uses and meanings—notations mapped directly out of the very lives Olson tended to discredit by his act of non-address."[7]

Fraser's argument and the perhaps surprising juxtaposition of space and the feminine in Howe's reading of Olson helps address the risk of essentializing "space" in approaching Howe's page poems. The issue is how space on the page is deployed and populated—not in what the space "is," then, but in how it is used. The differences between and within male and female uses of space (with Olson, Howe, and Albiach representing three points on that spectrum) mean that we cannot mark page space as intrinsically gendered; the question is what space means in Howe, not what it means, period. DuPlessis points out that in Albiach's *Mezza Voce* the blank page is gendered male: "*the donné[e] of this work is that the male figure is the page on which the woman is attempting to write,*" with whiteness as the possibility of male erasure of the female word.[8] In Howe, however, as DuPlessis argues elsewhere, white space functions in an implicitly gender-based way "as a trope for an anti-authoritarian practice. The foregrounding of otherness. The critique of centers, hierarchies, authorities. The apprehension of power."[9]

Not surprisingly, Howe connects her design of page space to her painterly beginnings. As she moved from painting (in which she worked in collage forms) to mixing pictures, paintings, and lists of words in artist's books, she "always left a lot of white space on the page" (*I*, 5), and in fact she has remarked that if she could paint her writing, "it would be blank. It would be a white canvas. White."[10] However, the word on that page/canvas is itself always visual too: "words, even single letters, are images. The look of a word is part of its meaning" (*I*, 6). (As Howe writes in a 1988 symposium on the poetic line, "First I was a painter, so for me, words shimmer. Each one has an aura.")[11] She stresses that the visual design of her work is intended to register what she calls a "meaning connection" among its overlapping parts: "The getting it right has to do with how it's structured on the page as well as how it sounds—this is the meaning" (*I*, 8). Given that the structure of Howe's page is integral to its meaning, as readers we need to consider how that is so, and to do so in a way that goes beyond, without necessarily neglecting, notions of imitative form.

Introducing her 1994 interview with Howe, Lynn Keller notes that "[Howe's] writing embodies absence . . . in its dramatic use of space on the page."[12] This is a useful formulation, not least in its paradoxical notion of embodying absence. The question then becomes, whose absence is thus embodied, and how? That question moves us toward the connection between Howe's use of the visual and her distinctive feminism, toward understanding how her page space and design reflects forms of and responses to the erasure and silencing of female historical presence(s). Typically in Howe the female runs as a visible thread (one of her recurrent images, as it has been for many women writers) through the work, appearing and receding. No sooner does the figure of Mary Magdalene enter "The Nonconformist's Memorial," and theological history, via a quotation from St. John's Gospel, than "the act of Uniformity // ejected her" (*NM*, 5), in appropriately evenly spaced, left-justified, uniform lines. Over the next few pages, however, Mary returns as a sub-script to disrupt this uniformity, as an echoing, mar-

ginal presence in upside-down lines. Use of reversed text (*NM*, 6; Figure 1), Howe
says, "conveys [Mary's] erasure" from canonical accounts of the Resurrection,
but also her continuing repressed presence: "I was trying to illustrate the process
of her interruption and erasure, and that she's continuing through these narra-
tives" (*I*, 11). Woman is the reversed underside of this sequence; or to put it an-
other way, subversion (literally, "overturning from underneath") within the text
is gendered female: "Pronoun *I* or her name // Or break its boundaries" appears
upside down to complicate the "intractable ethical paradox // Vindicated by up-
rightness" (*NM*, 20; Figure 2)—including the uprightness of the page itself. "She"
appears, that is, typed semi-legibly under and within the "upright" male text, as
"Undertype Shadow Sacrifice," "Waiting for a restoration / and righteousness"
(*NM*, 26).

Rendering the female, textual or historical (in Howe these three are often in-
tertwined) "Undertype Shadow" visible requires Howe to reconstruct the page.
In her preface to "A Bibliography of the King's Book or, Eikon Basilike," Howe
reiterates, using Pierre Macherey, the familiar position that any discourse is
"'coiled about an absent centre which it can neither conceal nor reveal'" (*NM*,
50)—an "absent centre" that suggests the instability of authorship, the untrace-
ability of origins, the textuality of history. It seems that from the first Howe saw
these issues taking visual form:

> I wanted to write something filled with gaps and words tossed, and words
> touching, words crowding each other, letters mixing and falling away from
> each other, commands and dreams, verticals and circles. If it was impos-
> sible to print, that didn't matter. Because it's about impossibility anyway.
> About the impossibility of putting in print what the mind really sees and
> the impossibility of finding the original in a bibliography (*BM*, 175).

Given these remarks on writing the "Eikon Basilike," it is appropriate that, after
Howe's customary prose preface, the sequence begins in instant breakdown. The
first poem (Figure 3) is a canvas of erasures ("nfortunate," "un ust"), erratic
spacings, archaic-seeming nonce words ("Futnre") and actual archaic spellings
("comand," "woule"), Latin and French ("OMne," "envions"), typographical
slippage ("Mans"), jammed-together double meanings (the weaving term "beer-
ing" and the notion of royal "bearing"), a whole range of "obwructions trans-
posed" (*NM*, 51)—this latter phrase printed upside down, fittingly enough—into
a poem. Unpacking a poem like this parallels the uncertain twists and turns of
the historiographical and bibliographical process generally, and more specifically
Howe's own process of researching the *Eikon Basilike*. Like Howe herself, we find
ourselves confronting a text with no center, offering multiple possible directions
for reading. "Singularities of space," as Howe says, create "possibilities of choice"

1.

nether John and John harbinger

In Peter she is nameless
Actual world nothing ideal

headstrong anarchy thoughts
A single thread of narrative

She was coming to anoint him
As if all history were a progress

Fig. 1

Excerpt #1 from "The Nonconformist's Memorial" by Susan Howe (© 1993 by Susan Howe and reprinted by permission of New Directions Publishing Corp.)

Intractable ethical paradox

Or break its boundaries
Vindicated by uprightness

Pronoun I or her name
utter immensities whisper

Fig. 2

Excerpt #2 from "The Nonconformist's Memorial" by Susan Howe (© 1993 by Susan Howe and reprinted by permission of New Directions Publishing Corp.)

(*BM*, 181). This is what it is like—for writer and reader—to try and catch the "Horrifying drift errancy" (*NM*, 66) of history.

At one level, the "absent center" of this sequence is the ghostly king Charles I (the absent center of patriarchal power) who may or may not have written the book, the *Eikon Basilike*, whose provenance and history Howe is investigating. But in "Eikon Basilike" as elsewhere Howe also renders the persistently sought absence in visual terms and genders it female: "She is the blank page / writing ghost writing" (68). Along with its other subjects, Howe's poem concerns not just

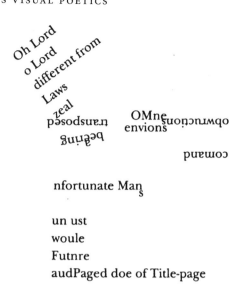

Fig. 3

Excerpt #1 from "Eikon Basilike" by Susan Howe (© 1993 by Susan Howe and reprinted by permission of New Directions Publishing Corp.)

the "fanatical swift moving authority" (72) of the Puritan regicides, but how the grammatical and judicial "Sentences" of "Judges and ghostly fathers" constitute the "Opening words of *Patriarcha*" (71), and how, in such a history, the female is only a trace. A thread left by those ancient workers in thread, "Archaic Arachne Ariadne," a longstanding but tenuous mythic presence, "She is gone she sends her memory" (69). Yet that memory floats visibly through the text, for instance in the broken summary of the Ariadne myth. "Trace weft" (79), Howe instructs herself, and we realize that this female weft can be traced back to the "beering," a dividing of the warp, of the sequence's first poem (51). This "weft" or "Thread," this "Thought" of the "daughter" (and daughter of the King, Minos) is to be traced through the "*Centuries*" tangled on Howe's page (79; Figure 4).

Both in this sequence and in a larger patriarchal history, this female face has been gotten rid of, hidden, swaddled, clothed ("SWADLIER Centuries I No rhid Face CLOATHE" [79]). But Howe's page makes "dominant ideologies drift" (80), and the thread of the female, of Ariadne drifts through the history and texts that would obscure it. She appears as the "fictive Pamela" (49) of Sir Philip Sidney's *Arcadia* whose presence John Milton uses to argue the *Eikon*'s inauthenticity, and reappears later as the same "heathen woman / out of heathen legend" (67); she appears as an unnamed sister figure, and as the wife of Bishop John Gauden, the cleric who claimed authorship of the *Eikon Basilike*. In the last poem of the sequence (Figure 5), her name may be unstable—"Arachne" or "Ariagne"; it may

utmost

light

mote

Sp$^{ir e}$

Therfrom
evry
edge

all

                                               Illimited

Ariadne   led Theseus

let down   in every

                                perceptive

Minos'   from

  daughter   Thread   Sphere

                          pierced

                           Light symbolism

Thought   Trace
               weft

daughter
SWADLIER Centom Centuries I No
                     rhid

Fire   To her   Face

          fate   CLOATHE

distant

        the lay

Island place
         deathless

Place they stood on
      Stars

away who remember
    Flood   Crown

         she wore
    and the sea

Eyes   up

        to   -
        Fire

Fig. 4

Excerpt #2 from "Eikon Basilike" by Susan Howe (© 1993 by Susan Howe and reprinted by permission of New Directions Publishing Corp.)

still be inverted and thus made harder to read, in the interstices of another text; but it enjoys a central place on the page, capitalized next to the male SUN as his equal, companion, and inversion. Like Arachne, Howe has been subtly "winding wool" through the "Eikon Basilike" sequence, "trace" and "weft" bending and stretching on this page but holding, her female "thread" on the righthand side running through the male military "shield"—a shield from the partial erasure of which emerges female potential, "she'll" echoing in "shiel." And so we conclude with "soft thread," but soft thread with "a twist," in a way that calls up Ariadne, an apocryphal Shelley poem cited in the OED entry for "weft," and the first poem of the sequence. "Weft" threads cross from side to side at right angles to the warp threads with which they are interlaced, the ends of which are divided into the beers referred to in the sequence's beginning. A weft-way thread is *twisted* to the right in spinning. But "weft" can also mean a streak of cloud, as in "To the Queen of my Heart," once thought to be written by Shelley: "And thy beauty more bright / Than the stars' *soft* light, / Shall seem as a weft from the sky."[13]

Like much French feminist theory, and particularly that of Julia Kristeva, Howe's poetics associates the feminine with rupture, gaps, erasure, absence—visually, with various forms of fragmented text or "empty" space.[14] "She must be traced through many dark paths"—isolated at the bottom of the page after a lot of space, almost like a footnote, in the original edition of "The Liberties," and on her own page in the Sun and Moon reprint, but either way "to be read by guesswork through obliteration" (*ET*, 162, 163).[15] Howe comments explicitly on her association of space with the suppressed feminine when she says: "If you are a woman, archives hold perpetual ironies. Because the gaps and silences are where you find yourself" (*BM*, 158). Or rather, we might say, where you don't find yourself, the spaces where you would find yourself if you were there. If "the real plot [is] invisible," (*ET*, 169), as Howe puts it in "The Liberties," then it is to invisibility we must look for the real plot.

In the section of "The Liberties" called "Formation of a Separatist, I," both the formation of a female self and the lifting of Jonathan Swift's lover Hester Johnson out of historical invisibility are accomplished visually. In contrast to the section's beginning in full predication with a male warrior who "swung his sword / said he would slash and slay" (204), the historical female self is re-con-structed out of single words arranged in a porous block on the page. Amid that construction (set up on the previous page by a buried narrative of building in white stone like the white of the page) "Stella" (Swift's name for Johnson) is freed from the closed parentheses of history to become a part of the primary text:

stirring   inlaid   (   )   enclosure
                         stellar

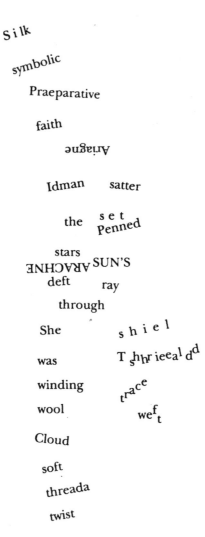

Fig. 5
Excerpt #3 from "Eikon Basilike" by Susan Howe (© 1993 by Susan Howe and reprinted by permission of New Directions Publishing Corp.)

—the parenthesis not quite wide enough to contain her (204). "The Liberties" had begun by connecting the materiality of print and female silence: "page in her coffin . . . / Do those dots mean that the speaker lapsed / into silence?" (158). Finally, however, visuality and materiality help produce an emergent self: "print pen dot i still / hole yew skip 1" (206). Print and pen dot (or complete) the "i," which is emerging tentatively as widely spaced fragments of text, unsure if it is whole or "hole" and with its relationships guardedly encoded in pun ("yew" and "i"). "I" in these pages is simultaneously Stella, *King Lear*'s Cordelia, and Howe, who is "formed" in a complex combination of visual compression, erasure, and displacement. Her name enters as a riddle complete with an (unnecessary) key that resembles a key*board* and that contains elements of textual mystery ("enigma," "crypto,"), the male ("mastif"), and the female ("femiated"): "e n i g m a s t i f e m i a t e d c r y p t o a t h." Place becomes writing ("graphy," with the "geo-" dropped), and Howe's "I" emerges out of Ireland only by being displaced to the next line ("reland / I") (209).

Countermanding the power represented in "The Liberties" by Swift, Lear, and the slashing warrior, Howe insistently uses visual design in her work—as I have already suggested with regard to "Eikon Basilike"—to render suspect notions of authority and centrality. She drafts poems and keeps notes in blank notebooks, on a page where "there is no up or down, backwards or forwards. You impose a direction by beginning" (*I*, 6)—a description that could apply equally well to the reading of her own more visually hyperactive pages. Those pages radically destabilize our typical reading processes, collapsing the very categories of the vertical and the horizontal. Howe often constructs a page so that it is hard to know either where to begin or in what direction to proceed.[16] Indeed she resists the idea of an authoritative or "right" reading even of her own pages: "The way they look profoundly affects the reading, for me, anyway. I can't speak for anyone else" (13). Through their layout, the poems deny the possibility both of an authoritative point-of-view within the text or an authoritative movement through it. In Howe's page poems, what cannot be read from one point-of-view can be read from another. No one position is central.

"He / said you know print settles it" (*NM*, 150)—according to this unnamed male authority, print stabilizes a manuscript (such as Emily Dickinson's) and appears to resolve unanswered questions it might raise. This is the view that Howe takes of the editing of Dickinson's manuscripts, a view that has had some influence in recent Dickinson studies. Especially relevant here is the relation that Howe lays out, in commenting on Dickinson's editorial history, between visually normalizing print conventions and questions of patriarchal authority, tradition, custom, and propriety. Howe reads Thomas Johnson's editing of Dickinson's handwritten manuscripts as the exercise of male editorial control over an innovative female writer's visual disruptiveness, over the marks of her excess.[17] For Dickinson's editors and the institution (Harvard) that they represent, "the conventions of print require humilities of caution. Obedience to tradition. Dress up dissonance. Customary usage." In practice this means that, for instance, "lines will be brought into line," "subdivided in conformity with propriety" (*BM*, 140). As a result of such editing, Howe argues, "provoking visual fragmentation will

be banished from the body of the 'poem proper'" and "the production of mean-
ing will be brought under the control of social authority" (140), even as the
"polyphonic visual complexity" (141) of Dickinson's manuscripts resist that con-
trol in the interest of a visual "scattering" of meaning, "indirection," "uncer-
tainty," "indecipherable variation" (148)—meaning as excess, not access.

The element of self-description and self-justification in Howe's account of
Dickinson's manuscripts should be clear. "Lines trail off interrupting sense.
Margins perish into edges tipped by crosses and calligraphic slashes"—com-
ments like this describe a Dickinson manuscript page and many Howe pages
equally. In the case of Dickinson, editing such pages has involved the exercise of
a royal, almost divinely ordained male power: Dickinson's editor, Thomas H.
Johnson, "has chosen a sovereign system for her line endings—his preappointed
Plan." [18] Howe uses the space of her page actively to destabilize such relations
between margin and center. She creates "a page space that is a canvas of mar-
gins," [19] perhaps nowhere more bluntly than in two pages of "Melville's Margi-
nalia" (NM, 96–97; Figures 6 and 7). The first page quotes that canonical defense
of centralizing literary institutions, Matthew Arnold's "The Literary Influence
of Academies," while a vertical line firmly marginalizes from that text, at an op-
posing angle, the word "NONCOMPATIBLES," a class that the obscure and ec-
centric nineteenth-century poet James Clarence Mangan (and perhaps Howe
herself) would surely fit. The opposite page has been emptied of its authoritative,
evaluative discourse, however; "SIMPLETONS," visually connecting with "NON-
COMPATIBLES," is similarly marginal, but the center has been emptied and the
margins are shaky—uncertain (two non-parallel lines on the left), broken on the
right, and on both sides no longer confidently vertical. And though not explicitly
so in these two poems, these margin-center relations are typically gendered for
Howe. In "Melville's Marginalia," Elizabeth Melville and Mary Shelley are writ-
ers in the margins of Promethean male texts, and, as elsewhere in Howe, the un-
packing of margins that she announces as her project yields female presences, in
a nice phonetic parody of canonical male bonding: "I will dismember marginalia
/ 'l' for 'i' and 'i' for 'l' / Ophelia Juliet Cordelia" (146).

A longer discussion would be able to treat numerous other examples of the
intersection of visual design and a gender-based social critique in Howe's work:
the groping investigation of a father-daughter relationship and of the idea of the
hero via the partial marks and sounds on an open page in *Secret History of the
Dividing Line*; the visual regulation of the female-named Hope Atherton's dis-
cursive wanderings in controlled square forms and the mythic or pre-historical
female presence searched for throughout "Articulation of Sound Forms in
Time"; in "Thorow," the comparable search for "she, the Strange, excluded from
formalism," whose "forms of wildness . . . become desire and multiply" (S, 41)

NONCOMPATIBLES So baneful
He could not storm the alphabet of art
bête   x[Bestial ?]
and social weakness
A style so bent on effect and the expense of soul
so far from classic truth and grace
must surely be said to have the note of .
PROVINCIALITY

Fig. 6
Excerpt #1 from "Melville's Marginalia" by Susan Howe (© 1993 by Susan Howe and reprinted by permission of New Directions Publishing Corp.)

Fig. 7
Excerpt #2 from "Melville's Marginalia" by Susan Howe (© 1993 by Susan Howe and reprinted by permission of New Directions Publishing Corp.)

in the shattered pages and floating word fragments that conclude that sequence. In these sequences, as well as in those I have touched on here, we can see some of the ways in which Howe visually, as well as thematically and stylistically, answers her own question: "How do I, choosing messages from the code of others in order to participate in the universal theme of Language, pull SHE from all the myriad symbols and sightings of HE" (*MED*, 17–18).

This "pulling" calls for work with margins, space, thread, invisibility—visual figures of the feminine, from Emily Dickinson (at least that far back) to Howe. And to Rae Armantrout, writing (I think) about Dickinson but in a way equally applicable to Howe. This stanza from Armantrout's "Getting Warm" provides a fitting conclusion to a discussion of Howe's visual poetics:

> She is in the dark,
> sewing, stringing holes together
> with invisible thread.
> That's a feminine accomplishment:
> a feat of memory, a managed
> repletion or resplendence.[20]

Armantrout's lines, which ironize her central image in the act of claiming it, may allude to R. P. Blackmur's notorious description of Dickinson as "a private poet who wrote indefatigably as some women cook or knit. Her gift for words and the cultural predicament of her time drove her to poetry instead of antimacassars."[21] Howe herself responds to the overdetermined nature of such imagery when she objects with energetic skepticism to Sandra Gilbert and Susan Gubar's depiction of Emily Dickinson as "spider artist" engaged in "artful stitching": "Who is this Spider-Artist? Not *my* Emily Dickinson. This is poetry not life, and certainly not sewing" (*MED*, 14). Certainly not; and like Armantrout's quixotic anti-seamstress, Howe constructs her "feminine [and femin*ist*] accomplishment" in and out of far-from-empty space.

"Bodies Written Off": Economies of Race and Gender in the Visual/Verbal Collaborative Clash of Erica Hunt's and Alison Saar's *Arcade*

Linda A. Kinnahan

This essay will look at the verbal and visual collaboration of *Arcade,* by Erica Hunt (verbal texts) and Alison Saar (woodcuts), exploring how this collaboration poses questions about the social organization of the body. This collection focuses, both through its artwork and its poetry, upon representations and codes of race and gender as they interact within a modern commodity culture. As a part of this project, the formal disjunctions, ellipses, and paratactical qualities of Hunt's poetry investigate discursive mediations of experience, calling into question the "experience" of race or gender as a pure or pre-cultural (pre-signified) category. Simultaneously, creating interesting tensions, Saar's woodcuts make use of signifying elements that are customarily attached to racial and gender identities within an economy asserting the primacy of the specular, a primacy marking the operations of consumer capitalism. Consequently, the text performs a continual interplay between the visual and the verbal that speculates upon the production of the visual body to signify identity within capitalist economy and the processes by which language both sustains and disrupts such representational systems.

Developing an analysis within the framework of what Robyn Wiegman calls "the economy of race," this essay seeks to suggest the relations between visual and discursive productions of the raced / sexed body and the economic arrangements of capitalism.[1] In particular, through variously evoking the body's movement through social space and the organization and textualization of that body, *Arcade* considers the implications of a culture privileging the visual as a mode of organizing, containing, locating, and shaping the body; additionally, the text considers the public realm as spectacle that, within a commodity culture, absorbs, recirculates, and co-opts oppositional models of identity. Part of the task of this essay will be to pursue the commentary upon identity politics, based upon visual markers of race and identity, that *Arcade* performs, in many ways upsetting the status of the visual (through making use of the visual) in signifying identity and in attaching meaning to the raced / sexed body.

As a collaborative volume, *Arcade* enacts a hybrid process of composition described by Hunt and Saar as "two years of exchange, short, long, short lengths of sun, strips of fog, show and tell leads to drafts and drafts jiggle pictures, pictures snap back, flames curl figures of speech, shapes recall shadows, shadows box."[2] Saar, a sculptor, printmaker, and installation artist who has exhibited work at the Hirshhorn Museum, the Oakland Museum, the Cleveland Center for Contemporary Art, and the Whitney, combines images of men and women with simple but potent symbols (hearts, flames, ropes, etc.) in woodcuts that signify in multiple directions within each composition and in relation to the verbal passages produced by Hunt. Noting that Saar's work "fuses traditional academic study of art" with her "own aesthetic experience of folk art traditions," bell hooks highlights the artist's treatment throughout her work of the "black female body" in relation/resistance to its depiction within "sexist and racist iconography."[3] Within *Arcade*, Saar's figures—most often female but at times male—call up this iconography to interrogate its systemic power, an oppositional project borne out of the conjunctions of image and word in the text. Hunt, whose first volume, *Local History*, reconfigures genre boundaries in its "reworking of prose," joins Saar in *Arcade* to resituate language's relationship to the social through reworkings of the visual and verbal that extend beyond the text to involve the organization of the social body.[4]

Encouraging a reading practice attentive to relations between the visual and the verbal, particularly as they relate to race, social experience, and language, the volume actively interrogates what bell hooks terms foundationalist or "essentialist assumptions about black identity," an interrogation that engages "in an act of decolonization that empowers and liberates."[5] Hunt's earlier essay, "Notes for an Oppositional Poetics," similarly questions the efficacy of oppositional politics/poetics based upon naturalized difference while acknowledging their historical necessity. Claiming that in "communities of color, oppositional frames of reference are the borders critical to survival," and that "treatment as an undifferentiated mass of other by the dominant class fosters collective identity," Hunt goes on to complicate this identity construction through arguing its paradoxical dependence upon "the external definition by the dominant group . . . [which] shapes the bonds of opposition." In effect, a "quasidependent quality" permeates the relation of a claimed collective identity and the "hostility" of the dominant group, so that "we get stuck with the old codes even as we try to negate them."[6] This concern with codes and opposition to them occupies the collaborative interchange of Hunt and Saar in *Arcade*, emerging from the textual practice of contiguity, a "reading and writing practice . . . [that] suggests new synthes[e]s that move out of the sphere of a monoculture of denial" of the "codes of containment" simultaneously containing and carried by us.[7] Encouraging "insights based on language as a mediation of consciousness" through engaging contiguous systems of visual and verbal representations, Hunt and Saar's hybrid text strives to help fill the "void in which visionary culture confronts power."[8]

Arcade opens, after the table of contents listing the poems, to a full-page image of a mature female figure (the sex identified by the breast), curled in a fetal position within a red sphere. The womb image, accomplished in red and brown woodcut on white translucent paper, situates the visual as a register of textual beginning, and the idea of beginning is echoed on the next page by the initial poem's title, "First Words." While the womb can be read as introducing us to a feminine space before the "first words" (the visual / feminine as pre-lingual), such a relation of visual and verbal is immediately complicated by the physical manipulation of the materials of the page. The translucent paper allows the words of the poem that follows it on the next page to seep through in partial visibility; indeed, the clearest words are those of the poem's title, occupying the upper left corner of the visual image with "First Words." Bits of the poem can be read, particularly through the areas of white in the woodcut; the body, language, and the visual are immediately held in relationship as the text begins, dissuading a customary reading of the visuals as subsidiary illustrations of the (more important) verbal texts, or as separate entities. As one turns the page to the poem, the back side of the image shows through the translucent paper now facing the poem, the colors subdued as if the image is veiled by gauze. Now the figure curves in toward the poem, the faded womb-image balancing (or counterpointing?) the facing page of words.

As the image and the title of the poem imply, the question of origins is taken up by the poem's rearticulation of the Genesis text by an "I" who claims, "I stray from my lines" in awakening "nude" into language: "Awake nude to match reality / where words fill the future / with mental muscle / and facts ripen into the clauses / waiting for them —" (Hunt 10). The poem's initial focus on the "I am" who awakes, transfigures into a focus on "the words"; consequently, the embodied "I" as the origin of meaning gives over to a nuanced sense of the body marked by and produced within language, "the words in bones / stand for what they are part of" (Hunt 11). The natural body is rendered suspect as a category of identification or originary meaning, yet remains crucial to the process by which language produces meaning; in a sense, the female body within the womb, clutching her own knees, is overwritten by the text's physical and conceptual interplay of visual and verbal which points toward the text's continuing investigation of the body and "the words that give nothing / beyond the marks carried in ourselves" (Hunt 11).

As the first image uses a sphere shape to enclose a female body, the image following "First Words" repeats while lengthening the womb-like sphere, holding within its oval shape the upside-down figure of a woman, hung by her ankles. She holds her breast with one hand and covers her pubic area with the other (Figure 1). This body, unlike the first which signifies itself in terms of gender only, begins to register itself visually within a category of features Robyn Wiegman calls the "visible economy of race," the corporeal signs that, within "the logic of race" in U.S. culture, "anchors whiteness in the visible epistemology of black skin."[9] Although the face moves toward a stylized identification as African, it remains ambiguous within an economy equating identity with visible signs; in short, the figure's seeming ambiguity frustrates the visual logic of a binary system of race, particularly in the figure's placement within a context of referents to the impact of that system on the body marked as raced. The ambiguously marked body of the woodcut exists within quite specific specular references to American experiences of race and gender; most obviously, the hanging rope echoes a history of lynching in which the spectacle of the body becomes a vehicle for disciplining a population and cohering "white" identity. Moreover, for black men this disciplining often included physical castration, a genital mutilation resignifying black men to the white community as feminized, as not-men. The woodcut's insertion of the female body into this scenario allows a double vision of the feminization of the black male body attending post-Reconstruction America along with the marking of the black female body in terms of historical violence. The hands that hold the breast and genitals call our attention to the particular "visual regimes" defining black women in American history: nineteenth-century science and its interest in the genitals of African-descended women to prove their hypersexuality and their closeness to animals; slavery's use of the black female body as a breeding site in support of the economy; longstanding intersections of race and maternity; past and present modes of policing black female sexuality.[10]

Indeed, the prose piece that follows and faces this hanging image, "Coronary Artist (1)," ponders the relation between "our most visible selves" and the naturalizing of the self through cultural customs and scripts. In this poem, an awakening again takes place, but this time located within the ordinary and everyday as a woman awakens to her household roles within the family. Struggling "To promote sunshine to my daughter while surviving my own ferocious will to sleep," the speaker thinks of domestic details: "the dirty clothes are crying and want to be washed. Piles of clothes begin to mount from the sky down." Later, after awakening, she muses, "Custom has it that a woman gets up first to solve the dilemma of the burning moment" (Hunt 13). There are scripts to be followed, as "One becomes an adult without knowing the details of how it is to be done,

Fig. 1
Woodcut by Alison Saar, untitled (from *Arcade,* by Erica Hunt and Alison Saar, © 1996
by Kelsey Street Press; used by permission)

only knowing which team you're on, which hat corresponds to your glands."
These "sexual politics" (enforced by an unnamed "they") forbid "passion outside
the parentheses," and yet moments of recognition of "the sources of our hunger"
can occur "in the center of our most visible selves" (Hunt 14). This sense of being
within a physical set of glands and bodies that result in identity assignments
nonetheless raises the question, at the end, of how the "visible" self can appro-
priate the system's mechanisms to satisfy its hungers; moreover, an understand-
ing of how the "visible selves" are constructed offers potential for reapprehend-
ing the self and its experiences.

Experience, like the visible self, has been constructed in white, western cul-
tures as a naturalized arena, an unmediated source of self-knowledge. "Coronary
Artist (2)," the next piece in the sequence, places the "I" in relation to discursive

classifications that produce or frame experience and, implicitly, a subject ideologically shaped by the disciplining of the "managed impulse," the body organized for economic, industrial efficiency. This is the body that has "lived through the glory of numbers" and watched "fate bleed uncontrollably through a vast chain of explanatory footnotes"; who has "peered through a keyhole into that narrow room, history, where it is happening to someone else upstairs overhead." The role of science, history, mathematics—of constructs of modern knowledge based upon notions of objectivity and observation—colludes with language to enforce a "path of managed impulse," and the speaker yearns "to become an alien" in her own language, "for a moment to lose the feeling of being both separated and crowded" by her "own experience" (Hunt 15). The self splits in the ensuing fantasy, one self running off and the other remaining in her "body armor," resisting the "urge to reconfigure paradise with perfect weather and regular elections." Instead of reinscribing the "managing impulse" over experience, the speaker ends with an ambiguously embodied, ambiguously voiced claim: "Where I stand now, I shout out of my body armor. I whisper parts of the roar" (Hunt 16).

What is the "I," and what is the "body armor" in which she stands, and what is the "experience" that language both crowds her with and separates her from? Facing the page ending the poem is the third woodcut, again on translucent paper but this time the page is covered with more color so that the words behind the page are less readable. The image is of a kneeling woman, her head bent to her right side, her hair cascading from the top of her head in a semi-circle that continues under her knees. The hair is held on the other side of the body by her left hand, the left arm a straight line from the shoulder. The linkage of curved neck, head, hair, hand, arm, and shoulder meeting the neck echoes the circular motif of the first two woodcuts, the womb now hair in a transfiguration of images that the text continues (hair later becomes like a rope, for example). The woman's face, more so than in the earlier images, incorporates corporeal signifiers of race in American culture, particularly through a widened nose. This image, calling attention to the gendered body through curved breasts and nipples that show through a short dress, also takes part in a tradition of representing the female body, especially the black female body, in so-called "primitive" positions. The angles of the legs and feet, the flatfooted bare feet, recall a visual history that both sought to contain and mark black women while also providing them with a visual mode to be appropriated in asserting control over negative stereotypes, as in the instance of the dancer Josephine Baker.[11] Such a speaking through "the body's armor" necessitates a rejection of the body as naturalized and a negotiation of forces mediating the body.

The prose piece that follows the image (and faces its reverse on the translucent page) ends the "Coronary" sequence. "Coronary Artist (3)," plunges us into the process by which the body's parts are organized within collusions of capitalist and racist pressures. This piece, broken into verse lines, links the production of the raced body to the production of the commodified body necessary for capitalist systems. Structured upon complicated layers of racial history rendered through the visual, the poem iterates the role of the visual in organizing western concepts of race. The poem in full follows.

In a dream I go to a room of spare parts.
We apply porcelain to our hair.
There are special scholars who study temples.
Someone sweeps shoulder-length tresses across the floor.
Arms in varieties of salute beckon, bent and dimpled.
I have one leg up.
I'm not fast enough and they take the other.
They hand me costume lips.
My ears are festooned.
What remains after my waist is whittled is little more
      than a functioning crease.
I bat my eyes to practice fascination.
But of particular concern is my hair, my hair, my hair.
So dry it crackles, as it is french-twisted and lacquered bright vermillion.
With this hair I stop traffic, eliminate the inconvenience of passageways,
duration between significant events, for something is always happening,
I travel through mirrors, I'm on the subway platform and the train comes,
an IND. I get on. (Hunt 17)

The organization of the body as "spare parts" underlies the disciplinary demands of industrialization, which Jonathan Crary discusses in terms of early nineteenth-century physiology and the rise of human sciences. Striving, for example, to understand the eye and nerve structure, science worked in concert with industrial aims of mass production and consumption through breaking down the body to better understand how its component parts could most efficiently be coordinated and worked.[12] The "body," reorganized as a compendium of mechanized parts, itself becomes an expendable commodity. At the same time, the rise of biology and its classifying systems begin to postulate race as stable and primary, and various pseudo-scientific discourses arise to offer body "parts" as proof of racial difference that is both "evolutionary and hierarchical."[13] Hunt's poem locates the raced body within what Weigman identifies as the "historical production of race" developing out of the "economy of the visual that attends modernity" and transforms "western knowledge regimes."[14] For example, in the poem, the rhetoric of nineteenth-century phrenology and craniology (the "special scholars who study temples" who theorized lower intelligence for women and blacks based upon skull size) interweaves with contemporaneous discourses of black female sexuality. The "one leg up" and the other spread by a "they," the "costume lips," the "festooned" ears, the "whittled" waist all reference an "economy of parts that enables the viewer to ascertain the subject's rightful place in a racial chain of being," citing the "body as the inevitable locus of 'being,'" an economy shaping the cultural, scientific, and social terrain of the nineteenth century in ways that remain foundational to thinking about race. The particular body parts mentioned in the poem suggest a raced and gendered body produced through discourses signifying the black female body in ways exemplified by nineteenth-century science's interest in viewing and measuring body parts, particularly the genitalia and buttocks of African-descended women, to pursue a construction of the hypersexualized primitive. The case of Saartjie Baartmann (Sarah Bartmann), who was exhibited through Europe from 1810–1815 as the "Hottentot Venus," demonstrates the visual emphasis upon body parts to characterize "for scientific and public communities alike the voluptuousness and lasciviousness of the black female" whose sexual organs were deemed hyperdeveloped. Alleging a "mutilation of body parts" underlying this racialized sexualization, bell hooks links this process to the fictive construction of "black female sexuality . . . in popular rap and R & B songs solely as commodity—sexual service for money and power, pleasure is secondary."[15] The web of meanings attached to the black female body on the basis of the visual extends, quite obviously, to the material body of the female slave, which "became the commodified technology of the slave economy's reproduction."[16]

In the first half of the poem, the body is acted upon; however, after the speaker relates that "what remains" of her waist is "little more than a functioning crease," the "I" returns as agent, *performing* the gendered, raced body: "I bat my eyes to practice concentration," she says prior to turning attention to "my hair, my hair, my hair." The hair becomes part of a self-conscious spectacle of the body, perhaps mockingly appropriating the hair of "whiteness" and the practice of "passing" while asserting them within a different configuration of the body: "french-twisted and lacquered bright vermillion," the hair allows the "I" a degree of control, mobility, and agency: "With this hair I stop traffic . . . I travel through mirrors . . . I get on." What I find interesting in this poem's final lines is not only the suggestive recalling of a kind of trickster / passing / mask derived from a long tradition of African-American writing, collapsed into a more contemporary feel (vermillion hair), but also the way in which the identity asserted at the end resists the naturalizing impulse of an identity politics that, as both Wiegman and hooks, among others, have argued, can be easily reabsorbed into contemporary capitalism's increasingly diversified forms of consumption. Instead, a politics of identity is performed in the poem through a textual layering of historical mappings of the body, negotiated by the poem rather than "reinscribing the logic of the system it hopes to defeat," the system that spread the legs of black women to view the "proof" of their culturally assigned status within a white-privileged hierarchy, that spread their legs to economically sustain such hierarchy through producing slave bodies.[17]

The poem, drawing upon a range of scientific and historical rhetoric on race in American culture, engages race as a "discursive construction with real effects."[18] Moreover, in specifying the primacy of the specular in this construction, the poem joins other parts of *Arcade*, both visual and verbal, in considering the relation between mappings of the body and the importance of the "seen," while identifying the operative role of the "unseen" in a visual regime. In a Foucaultian scheme, the "modern panoptic regime" relies "on a visual production that exceeds the limited boundaries of the eye"; within an application of this framework to race, the body regulates itself in relation to a "racial script that precedes and instantiates the subject in a relation of subjection."[19] The power of this script to shape both experience and knowledge registers as a systemic mechanism of careful codes and deliberate elisions in "Magritte's Black Flag" and "Starting With A." Both poems, following immediately upon "Coronary Artist (3)," deal explicitly with the exchange or movement of information in public spaces and how this information affects social bodies. "Magritte's Black Flag," a compilation of instructional prose detailing commuter train routes, delays, and alternate routes, reads as a neutral, precise set of directions to commuters awaiting morning trains, although as train routes and lines are displaced by other routes and lines, the precise categories of labeling ("the Number 6," "the LL trains," etc.) prove disorienting in their displacement:

> Passengers are advised to take alternate routes to their destination, such as the N or R lines. The N & R lines have been switched to the LL tracks to make room for additional 5 & 6 trains making all BMT stops.

> The LL trains have been moved to the Number 1 line. The Number 1 is on the 2 and the 2 is on the Three. (Hunt 18)

Although the precise and quantifiable transmission of information suggests that a careful listener will avoid getting lost, the very precision of the information is confusing without a fuller knowledge of why and how such decisions are made. In other words, the logic of context is removed, and an overall structure of knowledge is concealed from the listener, who is left dependent upon pieces of information. Moreover, this process of filtering information abruptly halts in the final lines: "Passengers wishing to continue to Long Island City are advised that there are buses at the 59th Street Bridge. Bus schedules have not yet been made public" (Hunt 18). Suddenly, movement and access seem threatened by a with-holding of public information, an inaccessibility to the organization of knowl-edge clearly controlled—as all the route changes suggest—by authorities who guide bodies through social spaces but need not explain why particular routes are chosen or banned, or where alternatives might take us. The implicit com-muter, the body moving through public space, is faced with a choice to move only as knowledge is available to her, or through uncharted, bewildering routes where nothing is as it seems: the Number 2 train is not the Number 2, and all lines have been switched to the point that a guiding structure is hidden from view.

Learning the names, codes, and systems, then, facilitates the body's move-ment, although this movement is without knowledge and at a cost to experiences not recognized by the given code. "Starting With A" ponders the "routes" "ap-proximately marked" for racial interaction, offering a glimpse of stepping off the route, of abandoning the representational alphabet that "give[s] to every ter-ror a soothing name." An unnamed girl walks down a street as the piece begins, and "She passes through pockets of warm air in a cold season, assailed by night noises, sounds in a correspondence based more on bravura than the contents of this failing world." This movement through public space puts into play codes of behavior based upon visual signifiers of race, and, indeed, her movement and speech become a "correspondence based . . . on bravura" as she comes upon and greets a white boy, refusing the self-effacement and silence expected in this ra-cialized encounter. According to the code making up the "contents of this failing world," her act is equated with death: "Death is a white boy backing out a lawn-mower from the garage, staring down the black girl's hello, silently re-entering the cool shell of his house." Going against the scripts of race and gender with her hello, "she is working without quotes, never looking down" in a submissive gesture. In this night walk, "the shortest moments rustle in their chains; the in-visible blends in," an image suggesting America's racial history and its varied manifestations of chains; significantly, as emphasized in these final words, the "correspondence" based on visible signs (of race and gender) between death and inappropriate (code-defying) behavior, depends as much upon the *invisible* or *unseen* forms of (self) regulation enacted within and furthered by the white boy's response and the black girl's infringement (Hunt 19).

The next of Saar's woodcut images calls our attention to the relations of self, seen, and unseen. As viewers, we see a blackened figure's shoulders and head from behind while we gaze with the figure into the mirror held in front of the face and reflecting a "white" face with "black" features. Perhaps a trick of the woodcut—its design necessitating the contrast of the white face within the blackened mirror—this reflected image nevertheless registers as starkly white. Does the figure wish to be white? Is the coalescing of "black" features and "white face" a deliberate suggestion of racial identity as a category of ambivalence? of performance? Certainly, the poem facing this image, "Motion Sickness," concerns itself with relations of identity, race, and language, alerting us in the first stanza to the "brain /arranged to fit / the stories plus / new slogans" (21). The poem's movement is word-generated, as sound and rhyme give rise to word sequences without sequential logic: "tune / tin tongue / ritual / spoon / spin spun / pinned on / words" (Hunt 21). A cacophony of sounds, repeated words and phrases accumulate down the poem's quick listing of short lines and, as though acknowledging the permeating effect of (seemingly) random-flung but (actually) systematically constructed verbal arrangements, the speaker finally confesses, "can't help it, / can't help listening / as in incriminating / myself / can't help this" (23). This blur between what one hears and how one perceives oneself evokes the process through which discourse ideologically produces the social subject to self-regulate her position within the social order. However, this process provocatively interrogates identity politics as the poem progresses:

ray charles instead of
face to face talk
erase talk
race talk
erases race
chases thought
down disowned
alleys of envied
sports figures (24)

Such a spare but suggestive movement of words offers multiple possibilities for reading, but the claim that "race talk / erases race" seems intent on locating the dynamics of racial construction along lines other than a naturalized identity politics. Like Saar's preceding woodcut, identity formulations based on the visual remain problematic here, in danger of producing bodies as commodities. The "sports figure" as emblem of black identity suggests the complex mechanisms of late consumer capitalism to appropriate identity formations and to re-produce them as bodies performing a commodified function within a free market system.[20] Elsewhere, Hunt defines the danger of "cooptation" as "the reinscription by dominant discourse on conceptual advances made by oppositional groups into the terms, values and structures of dominant ideology."[21] The poem ends by presenting an alternative model, "out of control" because unbound by what another poem calls "the reasonable grip of stock behavior"; in effect, this alternative to naturalized identity politics rejects models of self-regulation that accommodate "the sense of purse" and thus sustain a commodity culture:[22]

> the corridor awaits
> leading out of control
> over the bridge made of
> common sense, the
> figure in the words. (24)

The "figure in the words" flees the "bridge" of "common sense" to unravel the discursive layers of identity, complicating the "seen" with the "unseen" to disempower the realm of the specular.

This realm forcefully reasserts its power to assign categories of racial identity within the woodcut following "Motion Sickness." One of the few masculine images, Saar's three-color woodcut foregrounds a pin-striped male with a hand-tilted fedora, his eyes obscured by the hatbrim's shadow, and his nose and lips widened, full. In the upper left-hand corner of the composition, behind his shoulder, hangs the body of a nude woman by her wrists, her body the white of the paper except for the darkened pubic triangle and circular shadows beneath the breasts. Behind his other shoulder arise red, flame-like shapes that accentuate the red of his lower lip and suit tie. Rich with references to the circulation of images and roles layered upon black masculinity, the visual image recalls a range of social myths and taboos regarding race and sex in this country, while also raising the specter of intra-racial misogyny through "lynching" the woman (whose "race" is finally indistinguishable) as background context for this construction / composition of visual references to the black male. In other words, the woodcut suggestively holds in relationship the denuded, hanging female body with the male figure, as though questioning how the foregrounded construction of masculinity depends upon the backgrounded and bound feminine. Further registers of the visual are enacted through the image of the hanging figure, recalling the feminization of the black man through lynching and the regulatory role of such spectacle. As the subsequent poem, "Squeeze Play," states, "The culture beats the brow with equal parts spectacle and punishment," depending upon reciprocal powers of the seen and the unseen to shape the social subject (Hunt 25).

A few pages later, Hunt writes in "Science of the Concrete" that "the unseen

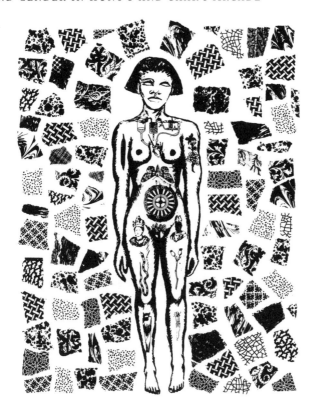

Fig. 2
Woodcut by Alison Saar, untitled (from *Arcade,* by Erica Hunt and Alison Saar, © 1996
by Kelsey Street Press; used by permission)

part / is a controlling force / over bodies written off / as repetition of the already
seen" (30). The intertwining of the specular (what is "already seen," such as
lynchings, minstrel shows, the Hottentot Venus) with the "unseen" to regulate
the body and the subject is rendered visually by Saar's woodcut adorning the
cover of *Arcade.* This image recurs in the text within a sequence of poems par-
ticularly attentive to the uses, organizations, and inscriptions of the body within
systems of exchange alternatively inflected by bodily pleasure and capitalist ide-
ology (Figure 2). While a treatment of this movement between pleasure (the
"body" as a site for touch, merging) and commodification (the "body" as regu-
lated) cannot be accomplished here and remains part of a larger project, a final
look at Saar's image ties together much of this essay's concern with the visual
while pointing to the many more complicated issues at hand.

A full-length portrayal of a woman whose hair, wide lips and nostrils not only signify visual markers of "race" within American culture, this image maps the body through other visual signifiers of historical discourses, practices, and systems that have shaped the production of race and gender while also drawing upon forms of racism and sexism within particular historical contexts. As though revealing the "unseen" within the body, a motivation of nineteenth-century science, the image implicates the representation of the "unseen" with forces and discourses affecting the material black female body: here is science—a set of tubes and flasks overlays the clavicle area, emptying into (or drawing from?) the heart; here is nature—the exotic butterfly, flowers, the seductive poppy, the African okra all over the body; here is labor—the saw making up the calf bone; here is sexuality—the mistletoe over the pubic area, promising passion and poison; here is empire—the white British queen on one thigh contrasted by a dark African noble on the other; here is the conflation of logic and accident—the roulette wheel in the mid-section that reads eerily as a bulls-eye. The body's interior, the unseen, is the "already seen," topped by the figure's head, stylized like an African mask. The logic of the mask in African-American tradition—to resist the seen by appropriating its markers, to manipulate the scripts of the unseen—melds with the ritual power of the mask to "body forth" meaning. As in this image, the relations between the seen and unseen, visual and verbal, multiply as an "arcade" of meanings attached to bodies. The gesture of the text, I like to think, is encapsulated not so much in the line from which my title comes, "bodies written off," but in a line in the final poem, "Variations." Imagining "raising bodies from the text" (Hunt 50) this final poem suggests a process of reconsidering "identity" much like the one the entire volume has enacted, in which re-presented signifiers of "race" unveil the "production of significations attached to the body," the body raced and the body gendered within the eye of the western world.[23]

PART IV
PERFORMATIVE BODIES

"In Another Tongue": Body, Image, Text in Theresa Hak Kyung Cha's *Dictée*

Elisabeth A. Frost

Theresa Hak Kyung Cha's *Dictée* begins with a blurred photograph from whose black and white surface emerge lines of characters. Shelley Sunn Wong translates from the Korean: "Mother / I miss you / I am hungry / I want to go home." As Wong explains, the words are attributed to a Korean exile and are scratched into the wall of a Japanese coal mine, evoking the exile's visceral desire for home.[1] Rendered in the language outlawed by Korea's colonizer, the message is inescapably clear, at least to those who can recognize the signs: loss of one's native land evinces a pain as sharp, as physical, as bodily hunger. The inscription, and Cha's reproduction of it on the space of the page, assert the material presence of a language so powerful, so enduring, that it is literally etched in stone. A few pages later the urgent, material word that converts sign to flesh is invoked in a passage attributed to Sappho (bringing to bear the Greek motif hybridized with Korean history throughout *Dictée*): "May I write words more naked than flesh, / stronger than bone, more resilient than / sinew, sensitive than nerve."[2]

As this opening suggests, Cha, like a number of contemporary women conceptual artists and avant-garde poets, provokes through verbal and visual means an inquiry into the nature of cultural identity and corporeality. Throughout *Dictée* Cha combines divergent modes of representation: visual images (photographs and diagrams) alternate with passages of English, French, Latin, and Chinese. Hand-written passages and calligraphic ideograms large enough to fill a page blur the lines between the discursive and the imagistic. Cha evokes multiple discourses and their accompanying conventions: lyric and epic poetry, parable, translation, correspondence, catechism, historical narrative, cinematic prose. *Dictée*

Thanks to Jin Lee and Yuki Terazawa for research assistance and Cynthia Hogue for editorial guidance.

embodies diaspora—the hybridity that epitomizes the post-colonial dispersal of self across national, racial, and linguistic lines; Cha's nine sections, named for the Greek muses, constitute an appropriated mythology for subjects marred by unspeakable loss—silence, exile, or death.

Given that Cha sets the reader adrift in an often violent textual terrain, how are the images and texts in *Dictée* to be read? To what extent is the writer's "dictation," notes from the muses rendered in an obscure tongue, legible at all? The frontispiece reveals the difficulty of such questions. Even one conversant with Hangul (Korean script) would find the inscription puzzling without knowledge of the historical contexts Cha evokes; any other reader would find in the signs at the start of *Dictée* merely glyphs that render this opening, imbued with the history of colonialism and cultural imperialism, unintelligible. *Dictée*'s pages are crowded with such instances of language that impedes signification, images whose figural content belies their hermeticism. Such impasses reveal the degree to which image and text in *Dictée* function as unreadable signifiers. Further, that Cha underlines the materiality of visual and verbal signs suggests that, despite its presence in *Dictée,* the material body remains elusive as well, subject to the same contingency that governs the acts of reading and translating. Image and text in *Dictée* hold out hope for a means of reading the body. Yet such heightened awareness goes unrealized.

Dictée is replete with verbal and visual signs of the body: Western and Chinese medical diagrams; accounts of political acts of bodily self-sacrifice; narratives of physical illness and healing; and detailed examples of the materiality of speech and writing. This recourse to the corporeal suggests that text and image are tools to render the body intelligible—legible. Divergent traditions testify to this effort. On the one hand, Cha's disjunctions subvert linguistic boundaries to connote a postmodern fractured state of being—a view reinforced by the presence of multiple voices, time-frames, and generic conventions in the text. Collage composition in *Dictée* parallels the tradition of what Johanna Drucker calls the "material word" in avant-garde poetics. Cha understands that "writing's visual forms possess an irresolvably dual identity in their material existence as images and their function as elements of language." Composing a text of both "material words" and discursive images, Cha—like other recent feminist experimentalists—mixes signifying systems and modes of representation.[3] In this poststructuralist approach, the signifier takes on increasing materiality, even as the body becomes less material—a Foucaultian product of discourse. Yet Cha also evokes a literary tradition that articulates social critique in and through a fundamentally empirical body. Cha's "words more naked than flesh, / stronger than bone" bring to mind the call to corporeality of Western feminists and black liberation poets, whose "poems / like fists" attempted a violent signifying.[4]

Dictée thus presents ambivalent intersections of the symbolic and the material. The presence of medical discourse provides an index to Cha's fascination with a human body whose materiality is ignored at our peril even as its cultural construction is inevitable. Charlotte Furth describes the search for a similar middle ground between the vanishing point of social construction and the literalism of a positivist approach. "On the one hand," she argues, "the body cannot be considered an object. . . . On the other hand, basic bodily functions—menstruation, conception, childbirth, lactation—cannot be treated just as the products of the languages through which they become culturally known. [Such functions] stand across cultures as stable, materially grounded forms of human embodiment." [5] *Dictée* partakes of this ambivalence. Cha's acts of translation, between languages and cultures, seek an understanding of "human embodiment." But rather than illuminating the body, image and word in *Dictée*—highlighted as culturally specific, material objects—provoke awareness of the body as a stubbornly unreadable text.

Drawing on a long tradition of resistance in Korea, Cha evokes a political discourse that seeks to "put the body on the line." As Elaine Kim explains, *Dictée* alludes to the body as the material of sacrifice: in "negotiating the tensions between self and the world, . . . the body and language," Cha evokes a Korean belief in "the reciprocal relationships between spirit and flesh," as well as allusions to martyrdom. Kim points to a history of movements in which protest is powerfully effected by "workers and students who immolate themselves or plunge to their deaths from rooftops"; she notes the examples of such heroes as Lee Joon, who in 1907 stabbed himself to death to protest European betrayal of Korean self-determination at the Second Hague Peace Conference. [6] In *Dictée* such examples reveal the extent to which the body becomes the material of resistance; struggle for autonomy of the "body politic" is figured through a corporeal text whose meaning is inescapable and whose immanence is its strength.

Yu Guan Soon (1903-1920) supplies Cha with a fierce example of such material signification. In "Clio / History," Cha assembles a collage of text around the narrative of this female martyr to the cause of Korean independence from Japanese colonization during the March 1 Movement of 1919. The visceral sense of oppression felt by Koreans paradoxically transforms the "Enemy nation" from the concrete to the abstract ("The enemy becomes abstract. The relationship becomes abstract"). In its cultural imperialism (the Korean language was banned, replaced with Japanese), "Japan has become the sign. The alphabet. The vocabulary" (32). Yet the problem of knowledge is corporeal; Korea is abandoned by "other nations who are not witnesses," who "cannot know," because their exposure is *not* of the body, and as a result they cannot ever fully comprehend the signs that present themselves: "Unfathomable the words, the terminology: enemy, atrocities, conquest, betrayal, invasion, destruction. . . . Not physical enough. Not to the very flesh and bone, to the core, to the mark, to the point where it is necessary to intervene" (32). Into this breach Yu Guan Soon ("Child revolutionary child patriot woman soldier deliverer of nation") imposes her body: she "is arrested as a leader of the revolution. . . . She is stabbed in the chest, and subjected to questioning to which she reveals no names" (37); her physicality redeems from abstraction the plight of Koreans under colonial domination, and she controls her self-expression, substituting her body's sacrifice for the names she refuses to speak. The final image in this section is a photograph of an execution (39). Three blindfolded figures, arms extended outward suggesting crucifixion, face several others who presumably control their fate. This discursive image with its horrific implied narrative attests, like the story of Yu Guan Soon, to the sacrifice of the body as a tool of political agency—the ultimate form of signification.

Almost all the sections of *Dictée* are framed, like this one, by photographs that are for the most part more descriptive than disruptive. As Shu-mei Shih argues, such representational photographs in *Dictée* tend to oppose "concrete, material, physical, and above all bloody reality" with the "mere words" of an inadequate historiography.[7] Two photographs frame the section about Cha's mother, for example. Complementing the largely representational language included in this part of *Dictée*, these figural images lend poignancy to her story and offer pictorial verification, making the (part autobiographical and part mythic) mother figure "real." The images provide a point of reference and signify both the concrete effects of time's passage and a historical frame. By contrast, other visual images in *Dictée* subvert the discursive functions of journalistic photographs or diagrams, pushing the text (rather than the referents) of *Dictée* toward materiality, as in the desert scenes that recur (the cover photo shows a lifeless terrain of sand and boulders, identified by Shih as an Egyptian ruin, while another image shows mummy-like statues poised in a desert [166]), or the suggestive image of a hand print on stone (134).

Whether figural or not, images in *Dictée* assume a sense of materiality that contrasts with the transparency of much "protest" writing, which often takes for granted an empirical reality beyond its textual confines. Hence the "blood writing" (*hyulso*) used by Korean dissidents to symbolize their loyalty to the nationalist cause,[8] or the troping of the body as a site of political struggle in feminist and other Western activist poetry, whose aesthetics of accessibility is an element of its politics. By contrast Cha, like other avant-garde writers, investigates what Judith Butler identifies as "the constraints by which bodies are materialized" in a "violent circumscription of cultural intelligibility"; the focus is not stable forms but "*a process of materialization that stabilizes over time to produce the effect of*

boundary, fixity, and surface we call matter." Accordingly, Cha points to the sig-
nifying powers of the body by emphasizing her medium, particularly the corpo-
real origins of speech. From its very opening—the exile's inscription in the stone
of a Japanese mine—*Dictée* makes speech material. The "Diseuse," literally a fe-
male speaker (the term can also denote a theatrical performer), evokes the cor-
poreality of the speech she struggles to release.[9] The "Bared noise, groan, bits torn
from words" that emerge come from deep within a body: "From the back of her
neck she releases her shoulders free. She swallows once more. (Once more. One
more time would do.) In preparation" (3). The disruption of transparency—as in
other passages in *Dictée*—reveals Cha's elevation of her medium from the status
of "vessel." Yet however concrete a work, *Dictée* reveals a dissonance among repre-
sentational systems concerning the body, rendering it (in text and image alike)
"illegible": suggesting not empirical certainty but ineluctable indeterminacy.

Two diagrams frame the "Urania / Astronomy" section—efforts toward an
empirical approach that would render the body legible. The first diagram shows
front and rear views of the human form, covered with parallel lines like those on
a topographical map and surrounded by Chinese characters (Figure 1). Scattered
points appear in clusters in each view, particularly dense in the front-facing
figure, suggesting paths of fluid movement. The schematic of the human shape
is universal. But the mapping of these forms—not to mention the textual glosses
—shows the need for cultural literacy in order to read the iconography; its very
language subverts the legibility of the image. Even the term "body" is problematic:

The word [body] is a shorthand, a product of limitations of English that do
not hobble the Chinese *shen* . . . sometimes translated "body/person". . . .
Such a body encompasses psyche and emotions, blurring the mind-body
dualism that makes our English-language "body" the object of our own
gaze; it also privileges process over structures, effacing the anatomical foun-
dations of the biomedical body we think of as the norm today.[10]

Affirming this approach to the biological, psychological, and emotional, Judith
Farquhar interprets a 1977 textbook, *Foundations of Chinese Medicine:* "reduc-
tionist definitions are not aimed at," "Anatomy is missing entirely," and the body
itself "is not an extramedical given, especially when we consider the dynamic and
transformative character of the 'internal interconnections' that constitute it."
The fact that the entire form, front and back, appears in the instructional dia-
gram Cha reproduces is suggestive, for in Chinese medicine, "no one system is
more determinative of healthful functioning than the others."[11] Rather, the en-
tirety of inter-related parts, and the dynamic currents that transverse it, consti-
tute *shen*, or body/self.

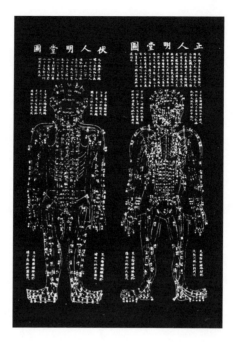

Fig. 1

From *Dictée*, by Theresa Hak Kyung Cha (© 1995 The Regents of the University of California; used by permission)

Significantly, this page is printed in negative: white-on-black. That formal choice is fitting for the first image in the "Astronomy" section; its white points on a black background bring to mind the night sky and stars. But there is historical resonance as well: during the Han dynasty in China, a fundamental connection arose between cosmology and medicine. *The Yellow Emperor's Inner Canon*, the foundational text of the medical practice of acupuncture, employed "cosmology—*qi*, yin yang and Five Phase theory—to explain health and disease, firmly establishing correlative relationships between the cosmos and the microcosm of the body." The same force—*qi*—that governs the universe also infuses the human body: "In the cosmos, *qi* named the fundamental energy at life's source, the unitary One prior to all differentiations. A tiny bit of this Heavenly *qi* . . . maintains life and growth, supports generative vitality and declines with age. Its exhaustion means death."[12] Cha's image-text thus represents a map of the body in the specific tradition of classical Chinese medicine, and its subtle reversal of the norm of black type on white surface alludes to an ideology that connects all things, in which a fundamental materiality is shared alike by human body and heavenly matter.

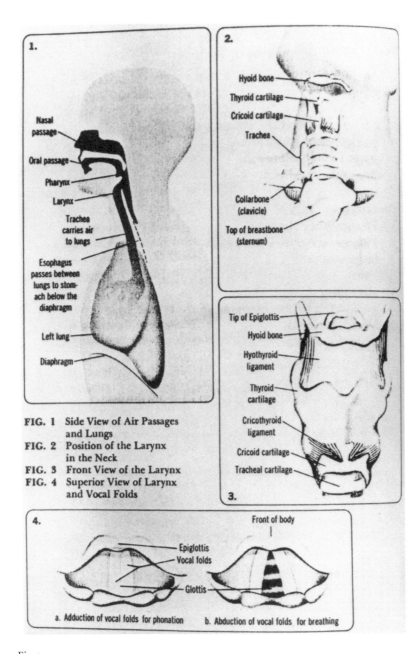

FIG. 1 Side View of Air Passages and Lungs

FIG. 2 Position of the Larynx in the Neck

FIG. 3 Front View of the Larynx

FIG. 4 Superior View of Larynx and Vocal Folds

Fig. 2

From *Dictée*, by Theresa Hak Kyung Cha (© 1995 The Regents of the University of California; used by permission)

The contrast with this section's closing image—a Western diagram of anatomy —is striking (Figure 2). As mentioned above, Furth points out that the concept of anatomy is foreign to classical Chinese medicine; the piecemeal approach to the body in Cha's later image reveals an emphasis on structure over process. Four numbered figures show views of the organs used for breathing and speech: air passages, lungs, larynx, vocal folds, diaphragm, and so on. The largest view, placed in the upper-left corner of the page, is a profile that ranges from head to abdomen. There is no complete body imaged here; rather, the various diagrams represent a series of parts without reference to the whole. Cha's text on the facing page "anatomizes" sound and speech: "One by one. / The sounds. The sounds that move at a time / stops. Starts again. Exceptions / stops and starts again" (75). The percussive rhythm and irregular gestures—"Stop. Start. Starts."—contrast with the fluidity evoked in the Chinese image of acupuncture points throughout the body; if we are meant to infer a direct relation between the diagram and Cha's text, the result of this analytical exercise is breakage—an inability to speak: "Contractions. Noise. Semblance of noise. / Broken speech. One to one. At a time. / Cracked tongue. Broken tongue. / Pidgeon. Semblance of speech." Figure 4 on the left-hand page facing Cha's text provides a "Superior View of Larynx and Vocal Folds," with captions labeled "a." and "b.": "Adduction of vocal folds for phonation," and "Abduction of vocal folds for breathing." It is as though breath and speech were incompatible, body and text irreconcilable.

These divergent interpretative systems reveal the obstacles to rendering the body legible. A Western reader would be unlikely to recognize the lines on the Chinese diagram as paths of *qi* through the body's acupuncture points. A Chinese- (or Korean-) American reader, whose cultural knowledge is hybrid, would be more likely to comprehend *both* this body-chart *and* the Western rendering of anatomy featuring throat, larynx, and vocal cords. As Juliana Spahr points out, *Dictée* defies "one of the major assumptions of reading": that the text will be available to a reader "without recourse to other systems of knowledge."[13] What degree of specialized knowledge is required in this case? To what extent does "body" diverge from or connote "self" (*shen*) in these depictions? The dissonance between representational systems reveals that the body's materiality is contingent on a process of cultural imaging whose accessibility cannot be taken for granted.

The passages of text couched between the two framing images in the "Astronomy" section provide an analogue to such inaccessibility: translation. In contrast to the images of bodies that focus our attention on corporeality as a metaphor for cultural identity, translation passages throughout *Dictée* highlight the material impasses within the symbolic itself. While Cha's choice of the word "dictée" as title clearly refers to a figurative "dictation" taken from the muses, the word denotes as well an oral translation exercise: "Mass every First Friday. Dictée first. Every Friday" (18). The routine act of dictée represents the effort to master another tongue, achieved with a limited success evident in recurring errors: "Vous l'avez dit Votre Promesse . . . nos espoir notre bonheure (or was it votre) dans la tendresse . . . (or was it ma tendresse) / les enfants de Mon Sacre Coeur" (18–19, Cha's ellipses). As in other such passages, this one omits a needed accent, makes more than one error of agreement in gender and case, and (parenthetically) reveals the writer's uncertainty. As Spahr points out, *Dictée* voices "the revisions, the gaps that second language speakers utilize." Yet rather than serving as "a paradigm for the cultural mixing that defines any reader's encounters with a work," such passages reveal what *can't* successfully be hybridized. As Walter Benjamin puts it, "A real translation is transparent; it does not cover the original, does not block its light." But this ideal is unattainable: "all translation is only a somewhat provisional way of coming to terms with the foreignness of languages." In an observation of uncanny relevance to Cha's polyglot text, Benjamin notes wryly that "There is no muse of philosophy, nor is there one of translation."[14] Cha finds her muses where she may—she appropriates the nine Greek deities to name the sections of *Dictée*. Yet she shares with Benjamin the ironic awareness that if translation—the art that underlies the project of *Dictée*—benefits from no muse's inspiration, it must indeed be a futile endeavor. Language, then, is both material and finally irreducible.

In "Astronomy," phrases that represent the body's formation of speech appear in French on the left-hand page and English on the right. The inexactitude of the task of translation paradoxically reveals both its necessity and its futility. The phrase "To bite the tongue," for example, inevitably suggests the more idiomatic charge, "Bite your tongue!"; the French "Mordre la langue" is both unidiomatic and far more anatomical. Similarly, Cha's emphasis on the materiality of signification ("Commas, periods, the / pauses") subverts the possibility of transparent communication in either language (68–69, 72–73). Sound, so crucial to the experience of the poetic text, is similarly inaccessible in translation: a French homophone contains a pun that cannot be rendered with the same effect in English: "J'écoutais les cygnes" ("I heard the swans") later becomes "J'écoutais les signes" ("I heard the signs") (66–67, 68–69).

Despite such impasses, *Dictée* raises the possibility of a "bothness" of word and flesh that might negotiate between the empirical body and the constructed body, transparency and opacity, original and translation. The tongue becomes a figure for such a border zone: forger of words, organ at the boundary of the body and the symbolic, the tongue retains a stubborn corporeality (more pronounced, for example, than that of eyes, figured as transcendent "soul"). Among other sites, Cha locates such liminality in the sacrament of Holy Communion, through

which the religious subject is formed: "Kneel down on the marble the cold be-
neath rising through the bent knees. Close eyes and as the lids flutter, push out
the tongue." Receiving "The Host Wafer (His Body. His Blood)" is a corporeal
act, re-enacting that of incarnation: "Dissolving in the mouth to the liquid
tongue saliva (Wine to Blood. Bread to Flesh.) His." Elsewhere in *Dictée* words
similarly materialize, returned to their origins in the body: "Particles bits of
sound and noise gathered pick up lint, dust. They might scatter and become in-
visible. Speech morsels. Broken chips of stones"; "Secrete saliva the words / Saliva
secrete the words / Secretion of words flow liquid form / Salivate the words" (13,
56, 130). In such ritual fusions of immanence and transcendence, is the body
finally legible, obviating the symbolic? Hinting at such a possibility, Cha follows
a passage in "Astronomy" on giving blood with a meditation on "*the near-black
liquid ink*" (Cha's emphasis) that spills from inside out, crossing borders:

> Something of the ink that resembles the stain from the interior emptied
> onto emptied into emptied upon this boundary this surface. More. Others.
> When possible ever possible to puncture to scratch to imprint. Expel. Ne
> te cache pas. Révèle toi. Sang. Encre. (65)

The border zone is the space of abjection, where "the jettisoned object" veers
"toward the place where meaning collapses," failing to "respect borders, posi-
tions, rules."[15] This liminal site is also the sublime point from which the body
signifies. Cha's writing here is opaque, self-conscious; it includes not just a list of
prepositions, with their distinctions of location (onto, into, upon), but also an-
other recourse to French, with a bilingual pun on "Sang" as blood, ink, and
"song." If astronomy is the art of navigating heavenly bodies, this terrestrial
body is still mapped by the rigors of the symbolic, trapped even as it is "emp-
tied."

However seductive the notion of a signifying body, Cha's corporeal texts insist
on illegibility. In the process they dramatize the subject's lack of location in any
single terrain or discourse. The phrase "In another tongue" evokes the displace-
ment evident in such acts of translation, particularly for the post-colonial sub-
ject: "In another tongue. Same word. Slight mutation of the same. Undefinable.
Shift. Shift slightly" (157). In exile in Japanese-occupied Manchuria, the mother
in "Calliope / Epic Poetry" lives this experience of disruption. In public she is
forced to deny her native tongue and with it both self and "home":

> you speak the tongue the mandatory language like the others. It is not your
> own. Even if it is not you know you must. You are Bi-lingual. You are Tri-
> lingual. The tongue that is forbidden is your own mother tongue. You

speak in the dark. In the secret. The one that is yours. . . . Mother tongue
is your refuge. It is being home. (45–46)

Like the exile's exhortation—"Mother / I miss you / I am hungry / I want to go
home"—this secret exercise of the mother tongue only reinforces the body's ab-
jection. Compelled to speak not merely in secret but in *the* secret, the "you" is
positioned in an impossible space, in which physical location has dissolved and
the shattered subject struggles to keep the body whole.

It is perhaps unexpected, then, that the final narrative in *Dictée* begins by em-
phasizing not materiality but transparency. A child implores, "Lift me up mom
to the window" whose opening is "too high above her view the glass between
some image a blur now darks and greys mere shadows lingering." Earlier in *Dic-
tée* window-glass also appeared, with the stress on opacity:

> Finally. View. This view. What is it finally.
> Finally. Seen. All. Seen. Finally. Again.
> . . . .
> One is deceived. One was deceived of the view
> outside inside stain glass. Opaque. Reflects
> never. (126)

By contrast, now a distant wall reflects the light: "Walls hives of stone . . . harbor
the gold and reflect the white of the rays." But if the glass does not obstruct vi-
sion—suggesting access to an empirical "beyond"—what is seeable is never ap-
parent, for the passage (and *Dictée* as a whole) closes with neither body nor im-
age-text but with pure sound: "the bells fall peal follow the sound of ropes
holding weight scraping on wood to break stillness bells fall a peal to sky" (179).
These words leave unresolved the longing to break the barrier glass. But they do
suggest a different kind of material, non-verbal "speech," produced by "ropes
holding weight scraping on wood." The bells, with their anthropomorphic
"tongues," release both a body of sound ("a peal") and a symbolic communica-
tion (an "a[p]peal to sky").

The bells, then, hold out once again the promise of a legible body. Their
sounding is evocative. It suggests Cha's ambivalence toward the embodiment she
evokes, for if in *Dictée* Cha negotiates modes of signification—image and text as
figures for *shen* or body/self—she also seeks to recuperate the corporeal in the
face of constant re- and de-constructions. The abundance of differing modes of
representation in *Dictée* suggests the urgency of Cha's attempts to render the
body legible, even as the text repeatedly thwarts efforts to decode its material
signs. The inability to read the traces of Cha's visual and verbal figures implies

a paradox: resistant in its very corporeality, the body is nonetheless radically contingent. The bells' tone resonates within the body of the hearer as meaningful, if unintelligible, sound. In the end we are left with another unreadable "text," one that suggests both the power of materiality and the elusive status of the human bodies *Dictée* seeks again and again to render legible—the ambiguous products of our own, as well as another's, tongue.

Painful Bodies: Kathy Acker's Last Texts[1]

Nicole Cooley

Janey, the central figure in Kathy Acker's early novel *Blood and Guts in High School,* observes that "politics don't disappear but take place inside my body."[2] Throughout Acker's work, the body is explicitly political. For Acker, writing practices are bodily practices, and the body is always a text, the text at every moment a body. Yet, toward the end of her career, before her death from breast cancer in late November 1997, Acker pursues questions about the intersection of body, text and politics with a particular and poignant urgency. The suffering body is, now, very real: it is Acker's own as she battles disease. And, significantly, the practice through which she writes the body is autobiography.

In this essay, I read two of Acker's last and most personal works, "Eurydice in the Underworld," part of a novel-in-progress she was working on when she died, and her essay "The Gift of Disease," published on the Internet. Both narratives describe breast cancer and its treatment. Formally, however, the two are quite dissimilar. "Eurydice" plays with language, voice and structure, whereas "The Gift of Disease" offers a more apparently conventional "story." Yet when read together, these texts reveal Acker's autobiographical poetics as well as her politics and allow us to fully understand her contribution to the field of innovative women's writing at the end of the century. My reading of these autobiographical narratives focuses on how the link between text and body is formulated in terms of the reader/writer relationship. Both "Eurydice in the Underworld" and "The Gift of Disease" explore the performances of the autobiographical body, and, by doing so, interrogate and challenge the relation between the reader and writer of these last texts. While everywhere in Acker's work, text and body have been connected, even coterminous, here, as Acker writes, literally, against her own impending death, she negotiates the relationship between text, body and politics within a new context: the body in pain.[3]

But, throughout her career, Acker's relation to autobiography as a mode of writing has always been complicated. In all of her narratives, interviews, and essays, Acker turns us back on her biography again and again, forcing us to ask: who is Kathy Acker? Her portrait appears in close-up on the covers of her Grove Press editions. With an expression of defiance, she stares back at us, tattoos and piercings revealed. Any reader of Acker's work must contend with her visible body, pierced, decorated, and exposed. In interviews, she often explains that she had a career in the sex industry simultaneous with her early writing experiments, referring frequently to the period of time she spent working in a live-sex show on New York's 42nd Street. She likes to assert, playfully, that "the body's more text." [4] If her body is an extension of her texts, how do we read her writing? How do we reconcile Acker's own performances with the performances of her texts? The question of how to position Acker's own physical body in relation to her textual body is nowhere more vexed and vexing than in "Eurydice in the Under-world" and "The Gift of Disease." While Acker's writing continually insists that the body is constructed, textual, a discursive entity, in these last texts her physical body reminds her—and us, as readers—of its stark and undeniable material presence, and of the fact that she is dying.

The Body in the Underworld

As a mode of life writing, autobiography foregrounds the relation of subjectivity to representation and seems to highlight the naturalized voice; it appears to construct that voice in terms of an authentic, truthful narrative. Paul Smith observes that "autobiography itself cannot be underestimated as a privileged form of ideological text wherein the demand that we should consist as coherent and recognizable 'subjects' in relation to a particular knowledge appears to be rationalized." [5] However, Acker challenges the traditional link between ideology and knowledge and the notion of the "coherent subject" everywhere in her work. Although her narrators are sometimes named Kathy—as in the novel *Kathy Goes to Haiti*—she never gives us a narrator whose subjectivity is not refracted, split and unstable.

In fact, Acker speaks overtly about her interest in splitting the autobiographical subject, discussing her earliest interest in autobiography in terms of schizophrenia: "I wanted to explore the use of the word 'I,' that's the only thing I wanted to do. So I placed very direct autobiography, just diary material, right next to fake diary material . . . I was experimenting about identity in terms of language." [6] In this passage, Acker's phrasing is double-edged and very suggestive. On the one hand, she asserts that her literary experiments are focused on how autobiography works in terms of language. Yet at the same time, she experiments with the self or the subject through language. Here, language *produces* the subject. And, thus, when Acker claims that "it's texts that create the identity,"[7] she offers insight into her autobiographical practice: Acker's autobiography doesn't simply represent subjectivity but rather constructs the autobiographical subject.

"Eurydice in the Underworld" is Acker's revision of the Orpheus/Eurydice myth. She planned to write the revision as a novel; it is now available as the title story in a collection of short pieces published in England by Arcadia Books. For centuries, writers have appropriated and re-worked this myth, but its literary and cultural politics are crucial to remember. Indeed, as Melissa Zieger suggests, the Orpheus and Eurydice narrative is "an episode that has shaped critical thinking about elegy and even about language in general."[8] While the gendered paradigm the myth installs—male archetypal poet as subject, dead beloved woman as object—is central to Acker's reinvention, its relationship to language is no less important. Thus, Acker interrogates gender, the body and the relationship of both to language as she reinvents this myth. In Acker's version, Orpheus and Eurydice are relocated in Algiers, but the new setting is not the most surprising transformation here. The most significant change in the narrative involves illness.

Acker reformulates the narrative around the diagnosis and treatment of Eurydice's breast cancer. In the course of the narrative, Eurydice undergoes a mastectomy and is told by her doctor that her lymph nodes show cancer. The text moves from the underworld to the "overworld" and includes a long section titled "Diary Written by Eurydice When She's Dead." While the myth as it circulates in our culture foregrounds Orpheus' tragic mistake (his look backward) and the subsequent loss of his wife, in Acker's text the pain and loss belong to Eurydice. Now subject rather than object, Eurydice is the central figure of Acker's text. The narrative trauma revolves around Eurydice's illness, medical interventions and fear of death. And the violence that will be inflicted on Eurydice's body by doctors and by disease echoes Acker's own experience with breast cancer and treatment.

Yet, despite the "truth"—the fact of Kathy Acker's real-life illness—that underlies this text, "Eurydice in the Underworld" nevertheless begins without reference to realist authenticity. Instead, notably, it opens with the dramatic: most of the narrative is structured like a play, with set descriptions and stage directions. Immediately, then, Acker underscores the fact that this text is a performance:

> This apartment and this girl can be found in Algiers:
> Perching high up, this room overlooks the world. Huge windows surround the head of its bed. Through the glass, there are hills covered by houses and trees. Until there are only trees rising upon trees . . .
> A number of stuffed animals sit on the red bed.

EURYDICE (or YOU) wears a blue-and-green striped shirt.
YOU (sinking back into the pillows): Oh.[9]

The naming of the central figure of this text is very significant for Acker's re-
negotiations of the conventions of autobiography. Naming Eurydice "YOU," I
want to suggest, reformulates and even challenges the relationship between
writer and reader of the autobiographical text. Here, Acker subverts a conven-
tional autobiographical definition of the autobiographical subject as the writer.
Through her re-naming, *the reader* ("YOU") is instead positioned as the auto-
biographical subject. Acker is playing with the notion of reader identification.
Thus, in a slippage that is crucial to our experience of this text, Eurydice's suf-
ferings become not simply her own, and not simply Acker's, but also ours. In
addition, she names Orpheus "OR." This name underscores identity's provision-
ality and the destabilized binary that runs underneath the surface of this text,
never allowing us any reassurance about Eurydice's future.

Our first introduction to Eurydice or "YOU" shows her alone, at home, after
her mastectomy. Her first action is parodic: she sinks back on the pillows in bed,
"Her hand on her head like Camille . . . " By referencing the famous Greta Garbo
film, this simile invokes the long-standing trope of the beautiful, dying woman.
In fact, when OR enters the room, he "looks at this girl as if he's looking at a
picture." Acker challenges this gendered subject and object relation as soon as
she invokes it; two lines later, when OR bends to kiss YOU, she vomits. Her status
as a mythic icon is subverted by the reality of her suffering body. The stage di-
rections tell us that YOU "[w]ants to scratch her head; swallows instead. She
hates, more than anything else, the smell of vomit. Doesn't smell like her own
cunt."[10] Acker often uses the language of pornography throughout her work. Yet,
here, she turns that discourse back on itself by employing it in a clearly non-sex-
ual way—by linking the sexualized body with the medicalized body, with illness.

Post surgery, when YOU returns to see the doctor, she is told that six of the
eight lymph nodes he removed reveal cancer. The doctor, who resembles a "movie
star" patronizes YOU by telling her, "Some of us are going to die in twenty years,
some in five." Here, although the doctor appears to be consoling YOU by includ-
ing himself ("some of us"), he depersonalizes her individual experience when he
enlarges the frame of reference. Later he commiserates with Orpheus: "Not
many men would do this . . . Remain with a woman in her condition. I admire
you."[11] While OR is more of a man for staying with her during her cancer treat-
ment, the same treatment is rendering YOU less and less of a person and more
and more of a patient. This new identity is predicated upon her being an object
rather than a subject. The most moving section of the text describes the morning
of her surgery:

NURSE 2: We just have to . . . (Not too carefully, she winds scotch tape around YOU's earrings and the skin to which they're attached, around the motorcycle bracelet on YOU's wrist and adjacent skin, over the piercing in YOU's bellybutton.) We don't want anything that an electrical wire could touch. Is there anywhere else?

YOU sticks out her tongue. It's pierced. The NURSE tries to tape up the tongue and fails. She scurries away.

The same or another NURSE approaches. She puts a green plastic shower cap, similar to the one all the ambiguous humans wear, over YOU's head. It's so large, it covers almost all of YOU's face. No longer able to see, she looks up at OR, who's looking down at her, as best she can.

NURSE: Stick out your tongue.

The thing under the cap sticks out its tongue.[12]

The transformation involves a subject becoming an object. To be an ill patient is to be dehumanized, an object, a "thing." The conflict focuses on ownership; YOU no longer possesses the body she has defined and marked with her own piercings. Instead, it is a text to be inscribed by medicine's technological and violent interventions. Paradoxically, she is all body yet she is nobody. YOU's dehumanization is complete at the end of this chilling passage when she names herself "the thing under the cap." As she goes under the anesthetic, Orpheus wanders on the hospital grounds, calling, "Can anyone tell me: Oh, where is Eurydice?"[13] But his plea serves to remind us of Acker's transformation of the myth: we know where Eurydice is. We know she is in the netherworld of anesthesia, cast under surgery's required oblivion where no one can reach her. Acker undercuts Orpheus' symbolic loss from the myth with her own narrative of Eurydice's loss of health and bodily integrity.

A large part of the narrative takes place in the underworld, presumably after YOU's death. Yet she narrates her experience from this position. When Eurydice moves through the underworld, she writes in a diary, describing her experience of illness and treatment. For Acker, the diary is an autobiographical signature; at many points in her novels, female figures detail their private experience in a diary that interrupts the text of the larger narrative. Yet, significantly, Acker has also called the diary one of her favorite forms of "fake autobiography."[14] As such, the diary works to challenge the codes of autobiography and the notion of private writing. In her diary, Eurydice describes traveling through the underworld with several other "girls." Significantly, in many of Acker's narratives, the female "narrator" travels with groups of "girls." Frequently, she invokes the trope of piracy, and the girls work as a pirate gang. (In the novel *Pussy, King of the Pirates,* she plays directly with this trope.) Yet the pirate girl gang is also a figure of power and freedom. In "Eurydice in the Underworld," however, the terms of the trope are different: these pirate girls are dead, "murdered" by a male figure who is an analogue for the surgeon. Rather than the girl gang signifying liberation, it is associated with bodily trauma and death. And, notably, in a move Acker will support and extend in "The Gift of Disease," medical intervention is figured as the cause of the patient's death; conventional Western medicine, rather than the disease, becomes the enemy.

Eurydice's diary of the underworld also includes a hand-drawn map of her surroundings. In many of her books, Acker utilizes maps to depict dream landscapes and to show, visually, the trajectory of a quest. Mapping also functions as a statement of Acker's textual practice: a map is explicitly anti-narrative (synchronic rather than diachronic) and it charts an already existing landscape in a new fashion. However, in "Eurydice," the map takes on a particularly poignant resonance. Titled "A Picture of the Underworld," the map reveals such structures as "the courtroom of the world," "the lonely complex of buildings," and, most deeply unsettling, "the bed of sleep or of death."[15] The notion of "dream" deployed by the maps in Acker's other books has been refigured in this narrative to stand for death.

"Eurydice in the Underworld" concludes with an exchange of letters between Orpheus and Eurydice. First, Acker includes a short section titled "letter found from Orpheus after his death" which is then followed by "E's Reply." In his letter, Orpheus tells YOU, "I've decided you're not the girl I want." In "E's Reply," Acker describes Eurydice's need for Orpheus during her illness while he pulled away. Yet this section concludes: "This is just one of the poems the dead girls can write to each other in memory of the life above."[16] The narrative ground shifts radically: Eurydice's reply to Orpheus is thus a poem written by one dead girl to another. OR becomes one of the dead girls. The gender categories on which the myth depends continue to be subverted in the narrative's final section when Orpheus states, "All the worry about U-turn dying made me physically sick . . . Actually I'm a woman. U-turn never understood this."[17]

Yet the most significant subject position in flux is, finally, that of the reader in "Eurydice in the Underworld." In the end, as both the autobiographical subject and the reader, YOU unsettles all binaries. Again, we return to OR as a trope which undermines any dichotomy. According to the terms of this textual instability, the reader is YOU or YOU is Kathy Acker. But naming Eurydice "U-turn" directs the reader to turn from the autobiographical subject at the end of the text, as she approaches her death. There is a sense in which, by turning from YOU, the reader enacts the violence inflicted upon YOU's body throughout the narrative, and, consequently, the reader is aligned with the medical interventions that have failed. Thus, the act of reading the text becomes coterminous with the act of treating YOU's disease. Yet, in another respect, the reader is, in the last moments of this narrative, also inextricably linked with YOU. The reader is left in a contradictory position in terms of the writer and the autobiographical subject: the reader is her and yet at the same time turns from her. And yet despite the textual instability that is everywhere in this narrative, it is at the same time grounded in a very real suffering body.

The School of the Body

I would like to suggest, ultimately, that when YOU in "Eurydice in the Underworld" narrates from the underworld after her death, she is enacting a fantasy of agency. As Acker writes against her own death, she re-negotiates questions about textuality and the body. Her essay "The Gift of Disease" operates in a similar way, according to such a structure of fantasy. This essay also documents Acker's breast cancer diagnosis and treatment and, like "Eurydice in the Underworld," it reconceives the reader/writer relationship through the female body. Significantly, this essay recasts the act of reading from its very premise: "The Gift of Disease" is only available on the Internet.[18] Thus, the private self of autobiography becomes a widely dispersed textual play, available to anyone. And, significantly, the reader requires a technological intervention in order to experience the text. Thus, the act of reading here is mediated and denaturalized.

"The Gift of Disease" opens by declaring itself to be different from Acker's other writings: "I am going to tell this story as I know it. Even now, it is strange to me. I have no idea why I am telling it. I have never been sentimental. Perhaps just to say that it happened." When she says she will tell the story as she "knows" it, Acker immediately invokes the relationship between the autobiographical subject and knowledge noted earlier by Paul Smith. This relationship would seem uncomplicated when, a few sentences later, Acker declares realism as her narrative mode: "I want to describe as exactly as possible what it is like to experience conventional cancer medicine. However, I am omitting the more horrific details."[19] Acker's work is infamous for its unflinching refusal to turn away from horror. Why does she turn away from describing her own suffering?

Yet, as in "Eurydice in the Underworld," I would like to suggest that the realism of this text is being performed. A crucial point of connection between these two last texts is Acker's use of dramatic convention. Acker states, "What next happened I remember as if it were a play."[20] As in "Eurydice in the Underworld," the experience of the suffering body can only be experienced by the autobiographical subject as a performance, a series of gestures or acts that the body takes on. Furthermore, another aspect of Acker's performance of realist autobiography is revealed by her use of the appropriation of other texts. Throughout her work,

Acker constantly invokes texts stolen from other writers and sources, the act of writing she calls "plagiarism." From High Modernist fiction to popular pornography, other texts structure Acker's work, and at the same time always disrupt its surface. Thus, Acker contests literary authority, originality and context, challenging all of the assumptions on which art-making is traditionally based.[21]

However, in "The Gift of Disease," plagiarism functions quite differently than it has in her other works. Kathy Acker is plagiarizing Kathy Acker; she appropriates text from herself, pulling the more fictional "Eurydice in the Underworld" and the explicitly autobiographical "The Gift of Disease" together. The pieces of text that Acker has chosen to repeat mark the most troubling moments in the larger narrative of her illness and treatment. For instance, in Acker's opera titled "Requiem," included in *Eurydice in the Underworld* and performed in spring 1998, these same passages describing the cancer diagnosis and treatment are also utilized. Thus, plagiarism underscores the violence done to the body by repeated medical interventions. This exceeds one single text, and echoes instead across multiple texts. Sadly, such suffering and pain simply cannot be contained within language, though, paradoxically, language mediates the experience.[22]

Notably, Acker uses the same dialogue from the scene with the surgeon here, including the surgeon's patronizing and insensitive comment, "All of us are going to die. Some of us are going to die in twenty years, some in five. . . . " And she repeats the dehumanizing pre-surgery moment: " . . . a green shower-cap-like thing similar to what all the figures were wearing was put on my head. It fell over my eyes: I could no longer see. Scotch tape was wound round what jewelry couldn't be removed and the adjacent skin. I was being reduced to what I couldn't recognize." [23] She is being "reduced," the marks that define her as a subject taped and hidden. As a dying patient, she is a text not according to her own terms but one for the medical establishment to control and inscribe. How does the suffering body make its meanings? How does a patient experience suffering as a subject rather than as an object? As I noted earlier, Acker's insistence that the body is text has always been part of her poetics; now, in these last autobiographical works, she must resist this formulation, refusing to be a surface on which medical intervention inscribes its treatments.

And, here, we might recall Janey's comment from *Blood and Guts in High School* that politics occur within her body. Discussing cancer treatment, Acker calls breast cancer "big business."[24] This business "reduces" the body "to a body that was only material . . . The reduction of all that one is to materiality is a necessary part of the practice of conventional western medicine . . . *To live was to stay alive and to not be reduced to materiality.*"[25] I want to unpack this language and look closely at its ambivalences, which reveal the ways in which Acker renegotiates her writing practices in the face of suffering and death. First, I want to emphasize her choice of the word "materiality." Acker cannot deny the materiality of her suffering body; the illness has denied her that luxury, as if modern medicine forecloses the symbolic. Yet, at the same time, she refuses any "reduction" of bodily meaning in favor of a play of significations. The subject is split; the self is all range, flux and movement. This apparent contradiction demands attention because it points toward Acker's desire to make the body a site of resistance. Her choice to refuse chemotherapy is part of this refusal of passivity and desire for bodily agency.

Increasingly, she identifies conventional western medicine's interventions with conservative politics and social beliefs: "to walk away from conventional medicine is to walk away from normal society." In her search for a resistance to such treatments, Acker consults a nutritionist, a psychic surgeon, an herbalist, a cranial therapist, and Greg Shelkun, a practitioner of alternative medicine who "signaled my entry into school. A school in which I, who had done things like bodybuild for most of my adult life, began to learn about my body." With this metaphor, the body is denaturalized (it is something to be "learned" about) and, crucially, it is linked inextricably to language.[26] Once again, the body is a text, and the text is a body. Yet, here, physical suffering has politicized this connection.

Finally, in "The Gift of Disease," the connection between language and the body and the ways in which the body is a discursive entity become the narrative's focus:

> When I walked out of the surgeon's office and didn't know where to go, I asked myself what I could know. Did I have anything in myself, in my life that could help me know and so, deal with cancer?
>
> My answer was: It takes strength to know. Where, then, is my strength? Answer: in my work, my writing.
>
> What are the tools of my writing? Imagination and will.[27]

Rather than the U-turn of "Eurydice in the Underworld" in which Orpheus (and the reader) turns away, the gesture here is decidedly confrontational. The turn here is one that moves inward and toward writing. In other words, Acker turns to her texts to heal her body, yet she recognizes the separation of the symbolic and material realms and hopes to reconcile one with the other. Somehow we know this act will fail, a knowledge which makes this passage, I believe, all the more moving. Throughout her work, Acker has linked language with the body, emphasizing that the body is constituted by language. However, here, the autobiography of the body is its own language, a vocabulary. Acker wants to insist that her body is inextricably linked to her writing, that the self is a discursive entity constituted by writing. Here, Acker wants to believe that writing can make the body a site of resistance, that writing can save the body.

Last Performances

Sadly, Kathy Acker's cancer recurred and she died in late November, 1997. In these two last texts, Acker seeks to produce the body's meanings through writing. Specifically, she wants to heal herself, as if she might write a textual body that could become her material body. Textual play has become a matter of life and death. As she writes against her own death, she tests her theories about the nexus of connections between body, text, and politics in a new way. While the three have always had a close link in Acker's work, her last texts re-negotiate the connection with great strength, poignancy and determination.

In March 1997, several months before her death, I had the chance to read with Kathy Acker at the Hollins College Literary Festival. (Acker had been writer-in-residence at Hollins during the spring semester.) Her performance was nothing short of riveting. On stage, in the dark, dressed in white, Acker read from "Eurydice in the Underworld." Her voice was low, her body completely still, the audience enthralled. As she read her descriptions of her encounters with medical treatment and her refusal to give in to her illness, the conjunction of text, body and politics she makes in her work was startlingly visible and real in her presence. There is a sense in which the depiction of self in "Eurydice in the Underworld" and "The Gift of Disease" is Acker's last wished performance. If her body of work reveals an awareness of autobiography's role in the creation of identity, we read these last texts as a performance of health, a wish for triumph over the illness that is devastating her body. Kathy Acker's last autobiographical performances leave us with a body of work that explores the work of the body.

"Eyes in All Heads": Anne Waldman's Performance of Bigendered Imagination in *IOVIS I*

Heather Thomas

Anne Waldman's mythopoetic epic *IOVIS I* recasts the hero as a feminist, shamanist bard who performs epic's historical and cultural inquiry through a "body poetics" of bigendered imagination. In Book I of this work, now in two volumes, Waldman reproposes poetry as an unabashedly heroic act, and the poet herself as heroic figure, by engendering a revision of the 'heroic' itself. No simple reversal to produce fe-machismo, an anti-heroic everywoman or picaresque bad girl happens here, but the enactment of woman as "open system," strong and vulnerable, capable of herself and others, matter and phenomena, history and myth.[1]

This open system evolves from Waldman's synthesis of innovative poetics, feminist attitude, and Buddhist thought. A nonhierarchical perspective framed through the book's multiple subjectivities combines the quest for Buddhist "emptiness" with Gertrude Stein's injunction to "act so that there is no use in a centre."[2] Waldman effectively recasts the bardic voice in the spirit of many-headed Tibetan deities with wise, third eyes. She broadens epic's scope and possibility so that the poem goes in "all ten directions," identified as poetry's ability to travel "in many directions simultaneously . . . sacred and secular," and the poet's ability to be "compassionate, aware, awake, available in 'myriad directions.'"[3] Indeed, Book I's 336 pages are Waldman's attempt to "catch the vibration, or patterned energy, of one woman on this planet as she collides with all apparent and non-apparent phenomena."[4]

Instead of directly feminizing the epic hero, as Alice Notley does in *The Descent of Alette*, Waldman does so indirectly by dismantling essential constructs of gender and approaching gender as the play of masculine and feminine forces within an individual, a community, and culture. Finally, she realigns these forces into a new, bigendered imagination, a subjectivity at once personal and political. Her purpose, boldly self-implicating and culturally subversive, is to target excess masculine aggression—a force Waldman admits in herself before critiquing its pernicious operation in history, politics, and culture. *IOVIS I* enacts a cunning self-inquiry, weaves the shifting threads of its argument beyond the personal into spheres historical, spiritual, and mythic, and demonstrates regard and compassion for many male figures, real and mythic. The title, translated from the Latin, suggests that all is made from Jove, or Jupiter, the Roman god and patriarch. Yet he has become an exhausted figure in an entropic world, as seen by one of Waldman's personae, the Hag, whose own holy powers were erased by Christian patriarchal myth.

As I will argue, *IOVIS I* seeks an alternative to violence, on the one hand, and to entropy, on the other: a transfiguration of the bard's own subjectivity that also constructs a utopian vision of bigendered imagination and agency consistent with a transcendent American poetic vision of "sublime democracy." Waldman undertakes this transfiguration through a performative poetics that ritualizes self-inquiry and launches epic's investigation of history and culture. Rather than the singular "I" of conventional ego and poetry, her concept of bigendered imagination suggests male-female siblings, the multiple subjectivity of experimental poetics, and the dispersed ego of Buddhism, all of which the poet practices as cures for the cultural diagnosis of aggression-overload. Her weapons are voice and language: "I had a lung / I sang him down / what need his guns?" she chants.[5]

The book's inclusive anthology of genres, inventive poetic forms and modes reinforces the nonhierarchical perspective, questing spirit, and performativity. No single form predominates, solves the compositional problem, or promotes a teleological resolution. However, as a magnet draws dispersed fragments together, the bardic voice and the work's dramatic script-like quality serve to unify the text through the one element it lacks: Waldman's actual performance. Indeed, the compositional process presumes performance as an extension of words off the page into a ritual vocalization that lifts the "I" into many eyes, many heads and minds in a reciprocal exchange of energy.

If Waldman's own scattered energies prefigure the chaos of *IOVIS I*'s radically shifting and dispersed textual forms, the patterns that provide coherence are comparable to those posited in chaos and systems theory. Waldman has made this connection in proposing her poetics of "dissipative structures" as influenced by Ilya Prigogine's theories of subatomic physics.[6] Waldman considers herself "a dissipative structure—a flowing apparent wholeness, highly organized but always in process."[7] Prigogine sees an ongoing process of becoming reflected in nature's dynamic patterns of order, evident in systems ranging from insect colonies to human memory. Waldman's phrase "open systems" derives from Prigogine's theory of a "continual exchange of energy with the environment." Within the fluctuating subjectivity, or system, that constitutes the bard herself, change hinges on "ironic instability": "The dissipation of energy creates the potential for sudden reordering," which may be spontaneous and is precisely the power and usefulness of poetry and performance. Thus, performance extends "the written word off the page into a ritual vocalization and event, so that 'I' is no longer a personal 'I'" (*FSW* 128).

Further, this theory suggests Waldman's ties to Charles Olson's projective verse and to Buddhist principles. Waldman is indebted to Olson's idea that the poem manifests voice and body as a "high energy-construct" and "field" entered by the voice and body. However, Olson's view of the poem as an "energy discharge" from poet to reader becomes, crucially for Waldman, an ongoing reciprocity of energy.[8] She rejects the one-way paradigm that allows agency only to the poet and renders the reader a receiver—classic hegemonic male-female model. In this way, Waldman's desire for reciprocity among poet, poem, and reader reflects *IOVIS I*'s nonhegemonic and feminist perspectives. These perspectives are framed within Buddhism, which is also based on concepts of reciprocity, such as karma. Waldman appropriates Olson's image of "eyes in all heads," but shifts the inference to suggest the multiplication of individual subjectivity as well as community vision, and the dissolution of inside-outside boundaries consistent with Buddhist philosophy.[9]

Trafficking among masks, Waldman crosses with numerous female personae, real and mythic or sacred figures drawn from East, West, and Oceanic cultures, from prehistoric, ancient and civilized eras, and conjured as forms of empowerment and healing. The bard identifies with the Hag, or crone, as a channel for "everywoman's cri de coeur" and "to transcend" vanity, recalling Pound's injunction in *The Cantos,* changed here into the burden of social conditioning that inscribes the "feminine" in terms of physical appearance.[10] But she crosses the Hag with the spirit of the beautiful Egyptian goddess Isis, who steals the secret word, or the power of names, from the sun god Ra. Refusing to reveal this word, the Hag chants, "What do words do?" (*I* 147).

In a spirit epic, ludic, and didactic, the poem's quotidian persona—that of the insomniac poet inscribing her myth and psyche onto a sleepless night—encodes, in Alice Notley's words, a "search for harmless and healing ways to be grand, . . . for ways to free one from the quotidian, as we are expected to live it in a society grown away from myth and religion."[11] Waldman's raids on other cultures for female myths and on her own experience for autobiographical material demonstrate that history and myth are constructed from individual experience amassing into both the collective conscious and unconscious. The protest against war, weapons culture, and male culpability in such "crimes" is framed with compassionate references to Waldman's father, a World War II veteran. As his daughter, raised in the military-industrial culture, she also implicates herself in war culture. In conveying a sense of history, personal materials here compel a context no less significant than that derived from historical records; furthermore, these materials are dispersed in larger contexts as elements of dissipative structure—of the ego and its dissolve—a key element of Waldman's epic revision.

Waldman's wry pronouncement of herself as epic bard—"I'm the total they add to, and you have to have arms / for the woman, you know"—parodies the first line of Virgil's Aeneid, "Arms and the man I sing" (*I* 162). The "total" is part suburban mother in Boulder, Colorado, piloting an orange Volvo near the Rocky Flats nuclear weapons plant with her son, Ambrose, in the passenger seat chanting his spontaneous "ode for the guardianship of plutonium." Daughter, sister, lover, teacher, she is a politicized kitchen witch bent on cleaning up the world, signing her businesslike protest letters "Anne-Who-Grasps-The-Broom-Tightly." Ignited by fires of passion and purification, she is Anne-Who-Burns in correspondence with male deities. She inhabits the mythic Navajo Spider Woman and the Gaelic Hag of Beare, Shiva's wife Shakti from Hindu myth, and others. She becomes the boy, soldier, and king, transforming in the all-inclusive terms of her intention: both male and female; the declaiming, devouring goddess and creative force for rebirth; the frenzied poet and the mere trace of her words.

The overarching persona, however, is that of the traveler spinning threads in the multiple, weblike directions of a pre-Aztec Amazonian fate spinner. This movement goes in "all ten directions" at once, a Buddhist concept suggesting for Waldman the "mind grammar & psycho-physical rhythmic patterns of the poet-mind." [12] The number ten refers to stages on the path to enlightenment and to the ten powers of a buddha. The spiritual practice involves a process of trans-formation reflected in the poem's own formal and linguistic jump-cuts from cluster to block to string of words in whatever guise and form occupy the mo-ment. The polymorphous shapeshifting across personae enables the epic motif of travel, death, and renewal to occur. This process reaches a climax in section XI, "Shiva Ratri," which I will discuss as exemplary of the female bard's trans-figuration and of Waldman's revision of the epic hero's conflict with demonic forces on the path toward renewal.

In "Shiva Ratri," poet and son travel to Bali, represented as an "other" world imbued with spiritual values and the power of ritual, unlike the materialistic United States. This is a place for study and healing, where the bard will enact a ritual of transfiguration, death, and rebirth in multiple dimensions of mythic and quotidian time and space. Poetry is choreographed in relation to a "Hindu code of body movement which enacts a spiritual narrative." She takes on the persona of Kali, or Shakti, female correspondence to Shiva, the oldest god of the Hindu Vedic male trinity: Brahma-Vishnu-Shiva (*I* 154). As Kali, the Hindu triple goddess of creation, preservation, and destruction in the forms of virgin, mother, and crone, the bard performs a kinetic ritual of destruction and rebirth that reinforces one of *IOVIS I*'s key image patterns, the spiral, and themes, karmic recurrence. The bard-as-spirit-dancer, however, never strays too far from Waldman's quotidian persona as the uneasy rider of a rental motorbike tearing about the island sightseeing, buying cheap mangosteens in a smelly, fly-infested market, and acquiring a talismanic fetish of green cloth, the color of this verdant place, of heart-energy in the Hindu chakras, and, in western culture, the symbolic color of jealousy.

Having arrived with a broken heart, she invokes the masculine force to come out—as muse, lover and tormentor. She will, of course, pursue him. Recalling again the Egyptian Isis' longing for the secret power of names—or poetry—she implores the muse to "take my tongue and inscribe on it all / the magic syllables." Circumstances implying marital difficulty are contextualized within the poet's search for renewed artistic powers and embedded within the larger frame of patriarchal history and myth that encloses and infuriates her: "she lives inside him, she / lives in the corner of his eye, she writes as / woman-who-had-stretched-to-this-point . . . / wasted old widow, prostitute & eater of infants, she comes to spread / death & / plague on the land" (*I* 158).

At the heart of "Shiva Ratri," the bard enacts a ritual transformation into a "gigantic supernatural being with thousands of heads & and arms brandishing weapons" of speech and beauty (*I* 154). This creature synthesizes the overpowering forces of male aggression integrated into her own hermaphroditic consciousness with a grotesque version of many-headed eastern deities and a nightmarish vision of multiplied female subjectivity. Ritual drama, mythic metamorphosis, operatic pitch, and dark wit are in full play. Goddesses are invoked, including Mother Uma, Kali's Destroyer or Crone aspect most commonly recognizable as Mother of Death.[13] The monster sallies forth with tusks, fangs, fiery tongue and Tiresian pendulous dugs until, entranced, men rise, stab themselves, and drop into comas. Prayers, chants, invocations, and stories bring on a cleansing rain, for the bard burns with unextinguishable fire. The lines leap frenetically across the page, then concentrate in text blocks, a wrenching dance of symbolic death and rebirth that leads to the opening split or space within, where male and female commingle and co-originate:

You walk through the split in your life
you are half male, half female
you are never too late to meet yourself halfway
each step brings you closer to the split that forced you here
arriving in a red car, a white car
into the inner temple of your mind

look . . .
it's simple.
I'm no fool.
(*I* 172–3)

The bard, whose ritual drama enacts a search for poetic authority as much as anything else, burns into a new awareness. This includes the Lacanian construct of the unconscious as a language: "every syllable is conscious / & the unconscious, too, structured like a language / . . . moving us up and down" unavoidably in a gender struggle for dominance (*I* 171). This consciousness can conceive a new universe, as the Hindu Brahma did by envisioning a tree with its roots in heaven: " . . . one branch /goes into "god" itself, the branches are sentences, the / leaves are like words / language a living system in the zone of convergence." The metaphor for external world becomes apt for the internal "rhythm, pace, sonic blast, parapraxes / inherent in my nervous system /a patterning to live for" (*I* 171). As the cycle of death and rebirth brings male and female energies into balance, the bard's perspective remains female, with "eyes in every pore of her body cervix is the window of her world" (*I* 165). It's a feminist response to Charles Olson's "eyes in all heads" phrase, for the body and the cervical door to birth become the site and seat of female vision.

This work recasts the inscription of the archetypal hero in two crucial ways. First, the conventional narrative trajectory of departure, conquest, fulfillment, and return (rooted within patriarchal paradigms of linearity and rising/falling action), is refigured as a process that reproposes those elements differently: Waldman's chaos, or dissipative structure, achieves a patterning that is contingent on her performative approach to language and poetic process. This emphasis on performative language provides *IOVIS I* with a force and power that otherwise might arise from an epic's narrative trajectory. Second, Waldman's bard refigures the epic hero through a compositional alchemy that reproposes gender. The bard transforms in order to conquer forces within herself, not an external monster; however, the monster within, as it recalls excessive male aggression, implies destructive force in the outer world. The space in which this self-transformation occurs is chaotic, and the process involves a quest for becoming that demonstrates the workings of Waldman's "open system" in *IOVIS I.*

In performing her transformation, the bard enacts a ritual that also dramatizes the possibility for change within those who read her, accompany her imaginatively, or witness her in action; such reciprocity sets in motion the energy transfer or emotional charge of Waldman's performative process. Long an unabashed missionary for poetry, she hopes to engage readers through her poetic performance in a quest for change within themselves. The epic tradition, with its convention of moral instruction, permits *IOVIS I*'s enactment of Waldman's "sublime democracy," a utopian vision of release from the limitations of gender and ego-identity which, in creating difference, also foster imbalance. This vision also releases one into the astonishing emptiness beyond identity, which may recall the regressive, undifferentiated, primal chaos of the pre-linguistic, semiotic realm. But *IOVIS I* also models the confrontation and overcoming of elemental chaos in order to transcend into a different emptiness, a sense of community or a connection with the universal, the nirvana beyond names.

Let me briefly elaborate the gender issue before concluding with a discussion of the performative. To an extent, Waldman recasts the classic notion of "split" identity, a familiar theme for women poets struggling with the political, psychosocial, and historical issues of gender, identity, and vocation.[14] Her "split" is a place half-male, half-female, which must be entered by the questing bard. Traditionally, a woman poet deals with a role conflict here, or the question, how can she be both "woman" and "poet," given the restrictive social and historical codes of each, particularly the encoding of "poet" as "male"? Waldman updates this inquiry by locating both gender energies with an individual, female or male. Although she identifies aggression, for instance, as male, it is contained within the female as well. She avoids essentializing gender, positing instead various kinds of gendered energy that may be situated within any/body or subjectivity. The concept of gender, therefore, can shift and reconstruct within any/one, thus making the split a space of possibility, discovery, and meaning within an individual. Imagined in larger terms, this space of striving and transformation raises the prospect of altered social and political relations. A vision of sublime democracy? The quest is performed as the central yet recurrent action of the text. It is the ritual enactment at the heart of the poem through which the bard "sacrifices" herself and resurrects as a sacramental, yet self-deprecating figure, the Buddha within.

Because this transformation necessitates pain, struggle and a figurative death, Waldman's "split" suggests also the rim of a wound, making *IOVIS I* an effort to heal a wound that never really closes. Such are the conditions for the strange, invented qualities of an artist's work, according to Federico García Lorca's theory of the duende, which helps to illuminate Waldman's experimental and performative poetics. As García Lorca says, the search for duende is a search for "the bitter root" of human existence, "the pain which has no explanation," and this is the source of great art.[15] Indeed, the bard's battle with the demon in "Shiva Ratri" models the artist's relationship to the spirit of duende, which is one of struggle enacted as ritual performance. Protruding tusks, fangs, and pendulous breasts mark the emerging monster as a demonic earth spirit that mocks the limits of the bard's intelligence; the monster, as well, projects her own imagined monstrosity/death wish. The bard confronts death in a shamanic performance that enacts one of art's elemental, recurring quests—the overcoming of destructive forces in order to stage a rebirth of the life force.

Cognizant of her own voice as instrument on and off the page—and as a force for creating community—Waldman created *IOVIS* as a text of performative utterance as well as a composition for performance. She initiates a collaboration between the page and the voice that extends the poem's "voice"; some sections recall compositional notes for music (XXII, "Pieces of an Hour") or dance (XIV, "Primum Mobile"). This rich textual modulation is embodied in actual vocal performances of the poem. Waldman has worked this way since her 1970s chant-like pieces such as "Fast Speaking Woman" and "Skin Meat BONES," seeking to create performative texts enacting a range of emotional and psychological possibility.

In *IOVIS*, chants are only one manifestation of duende as the power of performative utterance through which the shamanic bard becomes a channel for earthy, irrational energies signifying forces both creative and destructive. Performative utterance in *IOVIS I* manifests a new relation of the performative to history, an issue which has been theorized by Shoshana Felman. If we consider that the epic poem, as Pound defined it, is a poem containing history, the speech acts of performative utterance comprise, in part, the material of history in a post-Einsteinian and post-Marxist world, according to Felman. In this world, matter itself has ceased to be a thing but is a "materialism of the speaking body."[16] Felman's theory makes a useful conjunction with Waldman's body poetics of performative utterance. In *IOVIS*, the urgency of the body fuses with a shamanist and protest poetics to create a fiery spiritual and political call to act.

IOVIS enacts a performative poetics rooted in Waldman's fascination with the power of language as it comes through her body and subjectivity to alter her own consciousness, to establish her artistic authority, and to affect her audience. When she declares that she enacts "language ritual as open-ended survival," Waldman claims performative utterance as instrument in the struggle to survive and thrive as a woman poet (*FSW* 128). This survival does not presume another's defeat, but rather, as I have argued, a process of reciprocity. As a performative text both on and off the page, Waldman's words scatter the 'I' into a ritual event that dissipates the self to effect exchange with the audience, and to catalyze change.

The range, quality and tone of her performative utterance, a larger subject than present space allows, shifts and mutates through myriad forms and relationships between the speaker, who assumes various personae, and the addressee, who may be one or many others, as well as herself. She per/forms the text as letter, incantation, mantra, prayer, dialogue, rant, argument, charm, spell, and finally, instruction. One instance of invocation of the epic muse may briefly exemplify Waldman's performative utterance. Its imperatives command attention, its recurrent phrases summon power and cast a spell, and its foreign words reinforce and complicate that power. While all of the words have a talismanic or ritual function, they are used with a self-parodying wit and deployed with self-deprecating negation "not to escape the comedy of burning, / the miracle of burning / nor not be witness / to me, newly charged with power coming out of the dangerous cave / . . . come out! / come out now! / you can come out now

> Take my tongue and inscribe on it all
> the magic syllables
> > ANG UNG MANG
> make my voice sweet with the inscriptions
> of honey
> Make my epic, my song of male sakti, sing!
> (*I* 158–59)

The recurrent references to burning and the pleading-then-commanding tone of the call to "come out" create immediacy and intensity as the speaker leaps into prayer; the prayer itself is expressed through imperatives ("Take my tongue . . .") yet the offer of self-sacrifice also implores as it commands. The capitalized foreign phrases (such as "ang ung mang"—a Balinese mantra, or invocation of body, speech, mind) move the utterance to the edge of the unknown, where words become totemic or highly charged sounds, magical or mystical. This performative language complements the poem's mutating form, which spirals in a snail-like, labyrinthine manner as well as constantly transforming, like a snake shedding its skin.

Finally, Waldman performs to instruct her readers/students. This gesture concludes Book I with fulfillment of the epic's conventional didactic function, altered, as was invocation of the muse, through performative utterance. The instruction is foreshadowed as "the gnostic dream within the dream and the human potential for resurrection," lines through which Waldman signals her desire for an utterance both performative and holy: "I speak a new doctrine to an old form" (*I* 5). Unrolling a kind of dream spiral, she articulates, among others, the dream of bigendered imagination "where the twins / rule / the / cosmos / & take an artist as their queen" (*I* 333). The advice to the tribe invokes the potential female twin within the male, or those female energies that he may contain, as she herself contains the male. This suggests "hermaphrodite as the ultimate mental state," although not necessarily a state of grace (*I* 34).

Waldman's quest is for connection between male and female, integrated action of heart, mind, and speech. Her feminism, experimentalism and performativity advocate increased agency and social activism in the world, beginning with awareness of individual agency as the fabric of politics, history, and ultimately, myth. *IOVIS I* accomplishes the redefinition of history and myth as they are central to epic practice, thus offering an alternative system of nonhegemonic, nonhierarchical values. In this reproposition of the poetic "heroic," Waldman's revised female hero, like the notion of the Buddha within, offers the same possibility for others that she imagines for herself.

"Sonic Revolutionaries": Voice and Experiment in the Spoken Word Poetry of Tracie Morris

Kathleen Crown

> *Swing the shoutout.*
> *Soundwaves loud.*
> *Pushing the envelope*
> *while moving through the crowd.*
>
> Tracie Morris, *Intermission*[1]

In an August 1999 café performance at the Brooklyn Academy of Music in Fort Greene, Brooklyn, a district that is something of a mecca for black cultural life, the poet Tracie Morris improvised her way through several experimental "sound poems." Almost two hundred people filled the café's intimate, red-brick space, listening intently to Morris's performative lyrics as she blurred the boundary between verbal and nonverbal expression. In these poems or "sonic improvisations," Morris breaks, riffs, scats, rushes, bops, and glides her way through a brief "found" text—for example, the following familiar line taken from a Sam Cooke song:

That's the sound of the man working on the chain gang.

Through extreme manipulations of her voice as a kind of musical instrument, Morris takes these recognizable words and disarticulates them into traumatized fragments, so that the hard "ch" and "g" sounds of "chain gang," for example, evoke the physical sounds of clanking chains and the grunts and heavy-breathing rhythms of physical labor. In a prolonged and visceral "working" of the line, Morris then allows the fragmented syllables to rearticulate themselves, improvisationally, as ecstatic, multivocal, and healing utterances, so that we hear emerging from the English words the reconstituted Yoruba words "Agun" and

"Ogun," the names of West African deities. In this performance of trauma, political protest, and healing, the responsibility for the process of rearticulation falls somewhere between the improvising poet and the participatory audience—both collaborate in the recomposition of meaning as it is voiced or heard, but neither is in full control of how the inarticulate, improvised sounds become reconstituted or finally heard and understood.

Morris's jarring yet lyrical sound poems represent a radical departure from her popular spoken word poems, several of which she also performed at the BAM Café, along with several jazz-poems accompanied by music. Tracie Morris is a poet whose origins are thoroughly embedded in the spoken word movement, and most of her poems are meant for public performance, whether as monologues or dialogues to be delivered in theatrical settings or as "lyrics," a term unconventionally defined by Morris as "words accompanied by music but *not* sung." [2] As a spoken word poet, Morris has held championship titles in the Nuyorican Grand Slam and the National Haiku Slam, and her work has appeared alongside other slam poetry in *ALOUD: Voices from the NuYorican Poets Cafe*, edited by Miguel Algarín and Bob Holman (cofounders of the café) and in *The United States of Poetry*, a book, film, and compact disc project produced by Bob Holman. [3]

We can get a sense of Morris's diverse influences through her jazz-poem tribute to those black poets, orators, and musicians that she calls "the messengers":

From: the right reverend amiri/seer sonia/sister sandra maria/the wizard wonder/uncle etheridge/cleric rakim/minister morrison/savior sekou/baba john/deacon diva lisa/empress erykah/rector victor cruz/zoastrian zora hurston/trixster darius/freemason mosley/fundamentalist yusef/priestess pat landrum/hierophant hettie gosset/holy roller nona hendrix/ecumenical ethelbert/monkess jayne cortez/guru babs gonzalez/preacher quincy/his funkness formerly known as/deacon steve cannon/and sunday teacher ted joans/ they let me lay my burden low. they are the runway from which I go! [4]

As this list of influences demonstrates, Morris's poetry draws on what Geneva Smitherman, in *Talkin and Testifyin: The Language of Black America*, has identified as the four traditions of "Black Semantics": West African language; servitude and oppression; music and "cool talk"; and the traditional black church ("testifyin," "gittin the spirit," and "talking in tongue"). [5] Morris works within the oral, musical tradition of African American writing, continuing its emphasis on politically motivated protest against racial and social injustice. Only recently has Morris departed from this oral tradition to take her poems fully from stage to page, with the publication of the 1998 volume *Intermission* (New York: Soft Skull Press). As the "print debut" of the performer's "live style," *Intermission* self-consciously locates itself "between acts," as the poet shifts her focus toward newer and riskier "page work," which Morris says provides her with "a forum for another voice."[6] In page-oriented poems like "Overview" and "Writer's Delight," Morris turns toward a more visual sensibility, emphasizing the page as an attempt to "score with words" the "[a]ctivist verbiage rounds" and "primordial sounds."[7] In this newer work, Morris surrenders the univocal lyric I and replaces the narrative-driven poem with multiple, public, and disjunctive voices. Here is a representative quatrain:

Fade black smack dab
in history.
Mysterious backdraft
liquid consistency.[8]

This dense and minimalist "page-oriented voice," as Morris terms it, exists alongside a range of performance poetry, from the more accessible spoken word poetry to the sound poems that Morris calls her "most experimental performance work."[9]

My focus in this essay will be on the pronounced shift in the social and performative functions of poetic voice across a range of Morris's work—from spoken word to sound improvisation to page work. In her performance poetry, I will argue, Morris uses the fully embodied, performative voice with the activist, feminist goal of developing, affirming, and mobilizing a social collective. However, I will show that "voice" functions in very different ways in Morris's work, and that exploring these variations in voice can force us to reconsider contemporary critical ideas about what constitutes poetic experimentation and poetic activism. If Morris's activist poetics centers around organizing and affirming members of her own disenfranchised, working-class community, how can such fragmented sonic improvisations be "revolutionary," as Morris suggests they should be (in her evocative phrase "sonic / revolutionaries")?[10] To what extent does Morris's poetry activism—the "mission" embedded in her book's title, which aims to develop, affirm, and mobilize a specific urban community—also participate in a new and emerging culture of experimentalism? In an interview the day after the Brooklyn performance, Morris addressed the frustration on the part of some of her audience that her work was becoming too "experimental" and, therefore, less politically effective. "There are a lot of ways to be politically active," Morris pointed out in the interview:

Yeah, my stuff is becoming more experimental. But the validity of experimentation is a part of the tradition of black America, of black people. Innovation. Our entire experience here is predicated on innovation. . . . To

separate that from ourselves, to me, is a political attack. That is as plain as
I can make it.

I. Performance Poetry, Feminism, and the Politics of "Voice"

The recent groundswell of poetry in public locations—spoken word, under-
ground, and performative—testifies to a popular demand for a return to "voice"
and "presence" as fundamental principles of lyric poetry. In new venues such
as cafés, bookstores, churches, and community centers, poetry is inextricably
bound up with *bodies*—not just the body of the speaker but that of the audi-
ence—and thus with *voice,* which belongs to the body and is produced by it. Po-
etic voice in these locations is public, exoteric, material, explosive, confronta-
tional, human, and fully embodied. By focusing on the persona of the poet who
takes the stage, spoken word poetry seems at times to exalt the authoritative *pres-
ence* of the poet's body and the esoteric *aura* of the poem's voiced body prior to
any technology of reproduction (whether the printed page or a tape recording).

Yet this resurgence of spoken word poetry over the past two decades has
emerged alongside an experimentalist poetic impulse that views these poetic ide-
als of voice and presence as irredeemably contaminated by humanist ideals of
self-presence, sincerity, spontaneity, and authenticity. Of these critical categories,
perhaps the most problematic for strenuous advocates of poetic experimental-
ism—those loosely affiliated with "language writing" or "linguistically innova-
tive poetics"—is that of voice.[11] Many avant-garde poets and critics dismiss the
contemporary lyric or "voice poem," in part because it offers the reader the il-
lusion of a natural voice or self-presence. In combating mainstream poetry's em-
phasis on voice, the avant-garde has tended to value language over lyricism and
written experimentation over vocal expression.

This rejection of poetic voice inaugurates a new relation with the poem's au-
dience. Whereas the oral roots of the lyric tradition require the poet to conjure
the "voice" or "presence" of an authentic and representative self with which the
reader can identify, even to the point of total, or absorptive, identification, lan-
guage writing actively disrupts and complicates this identification between audi-
ence and speaker, deflecting the reader into language and away from the poet. In
this way, language-based writing avoids the naïve assertion of "natural speech"
as truth, recognizing how such speech has been coopted by the very commodity
culture it aims to critique. Yet the decentered "I" and active "non-sense" found
in language-based poetries can be too fragmented to connect readers and build
a community and insufficiently representative to bear poetic witness and thereby
to effect social change.

A further problem arises when this category of "voice poem"—originally referring to the inner-directed utterance and sedate epiphanies that dominate the conversational workshop lyric—is commandeered by avant-garde critics to denigrate an identity-based poetry or "representative verse"[12] in which the poet chooses to speak to, for, or from a particular community or identity. This dismissal of the voice poem as irredeemably mired in the devitalized language of consumer culture is especially problematic as a response to work derived from African American and other poetic traditions that have been understood primarily in terms of orality and performance. At the same time, African American writers whose work is concerned with the techniques and instruments of literacy or with the visual practices of reading and writing might feel held "hostage," as poet and critic Harryette Mullen does, by the community's demand for a representative and transparent voice—and thereby forced into "silence, invisibility, or self-effacement." [13] My question here is whether and how poetic "voice" might be detached from its baggage of transparency, presence, authenticity, and identitarian claims to representativeness *without* losing its ability to invoke communal participation and meaningful political response.

The problem takes on special urgency when viewed through the lens of a feminist and performative poetics. Feminist poets and critics are understandably wary of bracketing questions of the poet's body and voice in order to advocate a text- or language-based subjectivity or an abstract "author-function" (to borrow Foucault's term). As feminist thinking has always told us, we need both/and, not either/or. We need both the body-centered and the technophilic, both vocal expression and textual experiment. Who speaks, and the materiality of the speaking body (its race, gender, sexuality), *matters.* The making of meaning is always an embodied process, and emphasizing the performative aspect of poetry avails us of its provisional, contingent, revisionary, and recreative possibilities. It is performance poets who most fully attempt to "embody" or "speak" the lyric, and they do so within an emerging and linguistically experimental culture. Dedicated to what Roland Barthes calls *"the encounter between a language and a voice,"*[14] performance poets draw on the lyric tradition's oral and musical components, while at the same time experimenting with those components to push them toward a public, activist, and community oriented poetics. In performance poetry, voice—which gives "body" to and "engenders" language—is made conspicuous. As Maria Damon points out in a description of Morris's performances, her voice is "fully embodied," "in the house," and answers the audience's call to "stand up and be counted."[15] But the performance poet's insistence on a bodily, auratic voice, often free from acoustical and reproductive technologies, does not mean that voice is unmanipulated, unmediated by apparatus, or a mere expression of a personal, earnest, and stable sensibility. "Long, long before acoustical technologies," writes Adalaide Morris in the introduction to *Sound States: Innovative Po-*

etics and Acoustical Technology, "poets were wired for sound."[16] Or as Jed Rasula puts it, in a discussion of poetic voice as structured by displacement, "Poetic voice is not strictly human. . . . Poetry may not be humanizing, but dehumanizing."[17]

It is true, however, that "voice" in many of Morris's early spoken word poems operates as a coherent, transpersonal structure that connects speaker and listener through a kind of identity politics. In this poetry, the speaker represents, affirms, and calls into a collectivity a particular group with which some members of the audience can identify. Take, for example, the affirmative, rousing conclusion to "Project Princess," an epic catalogue and feminist ode to the young black women who live in the Brooklyn housing projects where Morris herself grew up:

> She's the one. Give her some. Under fire.
> Smoking gun. Of which songs are sung,
> raps are spun, bells are rung, rocked, pistols
> cocked, unwanted advances blocked,
> well-stacked she's jock. It's all
> about you girl. You go on.
> Don't you dare stop.[18]

"Project Princess" was one of the poems that propelled Morris to the status of "spoken word diva."[19] As the national grand slam titles attest, Morris's spoken word poems are audience pleasers—she's been called the reigning "queen of hip-hop poetry"[20]—and her slam-oriented poems often rely on a compelling, single-voiced speaking "I," a straightforward narrative premise, and a political, activist stance that is oriented toward a specific audience. The goal of slam poetry is to engage a bodily response from the audience in the house; the topics are current and often political; the methods, as in "Project Princess," include loud, in-your-face rhymes and insistent sound repetitions inspired by the sophisticated play of assonance and consonance in hip-hop. While "voice" in these poems is not the expression of a personal, interior consciousness, it is often a transparent medium for social commentary. Moreover, in many of these spoken word poems, such as the popular "Ten Men" (a list of former boyfriends and their fatal flaws) and "queens" (a humorous account of a confrontation between "homegirl strangers" on the subway),[21] the poetic speaker is nearly indistinguishable from the performing poet's body on stage, as it is marked by such categories as gender, race, and class (in Morris's case, the body on stage is identifiably black, female, young, and urban). Despite the sonic flux and intensity of these spoken word poems, which are deeply inflected by the language-expanding influences of hip-hop and rap, the poetic voice develops mostly through the natural rhythms of speech and popular culture and through rhyming riffs on outworn phrases ("smoking gun" and "you can't touch this").

What is innovative and disruptive about this poetry, however, is its status as *performance:* the poem-texts are basically scores from which Morris works out a live performance whose "verbal pyrotechnics," as Maria Damon puts it, "defamiliarizes not only normative American English but her own already highly vernacular written text."[22] The performative aspect of "Project Princess" as a poem —its relentless rhymes, unrepentant clichés, and vivid vernacular—is suggested by the outrageousness of the project princess's wardrobe—her "multidimensional shrimp earrings," "clinking rings" and "dragon fingers." The power of both of these performances—that of the poem and the princess—lies in their uncontrollable excess and in the pure pleasure of theatricality as it refuses to constrain itself to fit the demands of mainstream culture.

Morris developed her large and enthusiastic following through slam performances in such venues as the NuYorican Poets Café and the Brooklyn Moon Café, and many among this loyal audience view the poet's newer sound poems as "more experimental," "riskier," and "less accessible" than her earlier work. Although vestiges of natural speech rhythms remain in the sound poems, the poet's "voice" is far more densely allusive, syntactically disjunctive, and depersonalized (so that natural speech rhythms, for example, are disrupted rather than imitated). The impulse to create "identification" between poet and listener is replaced by a desire to recover previously unheard voices and experiences through an "ecstatic" method that is open to contingency, chance, and seemingly alien influences. In avant-garde circles, performance poetry has often been understood as conflating "voice" with "body," and thus failing to differentiate the "speaker" from the "poet." The ecstatic dimension of Morris's work, in which the poet seems possessed by "outside" voices and alien sounds, and seems to cultivate multiple voices, defies this conventional understanding of performance poetry and forces a more nuanced reading of the relation of performance poetry to avant-garde sound experimentation.

II. Ecstasy, Technology, Experiment: The Performative Voice as "Medium"

As Morris has moved in the direction of a more experimental sound poetry, she has increasingly emphasized the disruptive sonic elements of her work. Most of these sound poems testify to trauma—to oppressive racial and gender practices —and do so through an ecstatic poetic method in which "voice" is not the possession of a speaking subject but something that is *in possession of* the speaker. The audience experiences a voice that is wounded, dismembered, cut up and fragmented. At one level, Morris's sound performances enact the repetition of trauma, in which the poetic subject's possession by language takes the form of stuttering sounds, autonomic vocalizations, and enraptured speakings. In these sound poems, Morris conceives of "voice" as repressed and tries to free it—even at the cost of greater violence. Repressed voices are brought forward more or less violently by the poet, in order that they may undergo a collective hearing and verification. The performance poet is pure catalyst—she permits or conjures what manifests in the unrepeatable performative moment, but she does not command or control its presence. To understand this kind of ecstatic poetics as an ethical response to traumatic events, we need a view of poetic "voice" that goes beyond voice as the seat of personal expression of sincere emotion and individual will. Morris's poetry asks us to understand voice, instead, as a *medium:* a medium of being, a medium of history, and a medium through which language and personhood occurs.

An example of a sound poem that seeks to bear witness to a local community's grief, loss, and trauma is Morris's poem of tribute to the memory of Anthony Baez.[23] The performance is an elegy for a young man killed in 1994 by a New York City police officer, under circumstances that provoked charges of police brutality. As Nick Yasinski points out in a reading of this performance, Morris "does not recount the flimsiness of the shooting's justification or even the pervasiveness and endurance of police racism."[24] Instead, the poem consists solely of two words—the young man's first and last names—which Morris repeats over a long period, expressively shifting pitch, tempo, and tone. The live performance is profoundly moving, as the name "Baez," through the stuttering repetition, disintegration, and reintegration endemic to traumatic experience, comes to suggest an entirely other vocabulary, most notably the resonant word "bias" (meaning prejudice).

In other sound poems, Morris works through a "given" phrase—the line from Sam Cooke's song, for example, "that's the sound of the man working on the chain gang"—by dismantling it into components of phoneme, syllable, letter, stutter, and sigh. She then rearranges the sounds to transfigure enslaved and exploited black Americans into Yoruba divinities or ancestors. In another sound poem, which Morris introduces by saying "this is about spousal abuse" and by describing the poem's inspiration by Doris Day movies, she riffs on familiar song lyrics:

I'm in heaven,
I'm in heaven
And my heart beats
so that I
can hardly speak.[25]

In the performance, Morris beats out time on her chest and throat, with increasing violence to the sound. The audience, meanwhile, becomes more and more uncomfortable listening to the prolonged stress to which the poet subjects her body and vocal cords. Finally, the word "speak" is squeaked out in a painful whisper that, in some versions of the performance, ends the poem. "[M]y voice takes a beating with those poems," says Morris in an interview, going on to emphasize her volatile poetic practice as one of allowing sounds to emerge and speak for themselves:

> Stuff comes out that I am not prepared to utter. I have to let go and completely accept that this is what needs to be done, that whatever is coming out will also take care of my throat. . . . There's a lot of stuff that is not conscious, and lot of it has nothing to do with me. I just want to be honest about that. The harnessing involves a lot of breaking down and building up. Because the work is improvisational, I don't always know what the ending is going to be. . . . Almost all the time, sounds come up that never have presented themselves before.

The unpredictability of the material context of the performance—stage, microphone, body, and café audience—is intimately involved in Morris's poetic and spiritual strategy of "harnessing" external sounds and voices.

Although the poet surrenders partial control of the performance to these outside forces, she does not relinquish meaning or rationality to become an entirely passive medium. In "Las Brujitas," a kind of *ars poetica*, Morris connects her poetic method of "reworking the kinetics" with the rhythmic playground games of her girlhood and their "left-turn, right-turn / over-hand aesthetics":

> Significadence
> ain't random
> We clasp our hands
> in tandem.[26]

The poem suggests that if the signifying work and poetic "cadences" are not fully under the poet's control, neither are they arbitrary or random—their force derives from a "tandem" or collaborative relationship, including that between speaker and audience. As performance theorist Elin Diamond puts it, "performance is never only a voluntaristic or intentional act of making and communicating, but also, and simultaneously, an engagement with what constrains, limits, extends and distorts such acts."[27] For Morris, these limiting and extending factors include outside forces—not just the bodies of the audience as they give response and feedback, but also the surprising body of language itself:

A lot of it has to do with the energy that I'm getting from the audience. And a lot of it has to do with whatever it is that's manifesting and has very little to do with me . . . there's a spiritual dimension, with the sound poems in particular, but also with the text poems, that I just submit to, and I don't always know what's going to happen.

Morris suggests that it is the unpredictability and contingency of the performative moment that allows her to bear witness to inarticulate voices—whether enslaved African Americans or women trapped in abusive relationships. She views this witnessing function of poetry as a "duty, because those voices were not allowed to be heard. They were completely cut off. The choking, the rushing of sounds to finally be articulated—I'm a descendant of that. That's my job." Morris's insistence that poets need to articulate previously unregistered experiences that were "not allowed to be heard" asks us to read the disintegrating language of Morris's sound poems not as pathological reenactments of trauma but as acts of *critical memory* and *history making*.

This understanding of disarticulated language as a means of access to cultural memory and recovery participates in an African diasporic tradition. As the poet and critic Harryette Mullen suggests, much innovative African American poetry draws on "the African diaspora's aesthetic and therapeutic use of disarticulation for the evocation of spiritual and emotional states of being."[28] Rather than degenerating into the uncommunicative babble or glossolalia of the alienated speaker, disarticulation in Morris's work is an ethical poetic method capable of rearticulating lost connections and building a collective sensibility—especially given the performative/stage context in which the poem is heard or witnessed collectively. Mullen's argument about disarticulation draws on anthropological accounts of individuals possessed by Afro-Haitian spirits, in which possessed speakers are shown actually to heighten a sense of communal and collective possibilities for action. Such possessed speakers, Mullen suggests, "may produce inarticulate sounds that nevertheless are subject to interpretation by other participants. The very openness of signification that such enigmatic expressions allow serves to generate the creative interpretive energies of the collectivity."[29] In Morris's poetry, these collective energies are mobilized at the intersections of spirituality, voice and sound technologies, and experimental play.

The convergence of these elements is evident in the "chain gang" poem that Morris derives from the Sam Cooke lyrics. Morris wrote this poem as a political protest against the recent reintroduction of chain gangs in the United States. In an interview, she used the language of shock and trauma to describe the news that propelled her to write the poem, and she suggests that sound poems provide a means of coping with and communicating that trauma:

It was like a physical blow. Looking at my people working for free, with chains on in public. It's just mindblowing. I was deeply offended, and I went into a bit of shock. One of the things about the sound poems is that sometimes . . . there are things that I can't really bear to articulate in detail. To delineate each aspect might be a little too much.

The entire poem consists of repetitions and distortions of the song lyrics, along with a range of sounds (replicating grunts and clanking chains) that slip in and out of words taken from the Yoruba language. In composing this poem, Morris says that she was asking, "What is the sound that's going to physically work here?"

A lot of times that's not in English. Each language has its own relationship to the ear and to the body. The body is full of these cavities that reverberate sounds. Sounds are physical things. They are just invisible waves, but they certainly have physical applications, right? Sometimes Yoruba words are the words that are the correct physical construct for the time, but they also happen to have a lot of very strong vowel sounds that are very bottom heavy, as musicians would say. They have a lot of bass, a lot of bottom.

In turning to Yoruba words, Morris was seeking not merely to recover a lost African spiritual tradition, but also to recover the sense of physical movement and dynamics that the sounds of the Yoruba language could provide. She develops a verbal-musical performative voice that allows us to listen to sound rather than sense. The tinny, upper-register sounds of chains, for example, are balanced by the bass of words like "Agun" and "Ogun," to give the sense of people moving and working, and the expiration of breath coming from the lower diaphragm. Not only are the physical aspects of the words important, but their meanings are consistent with the piece, evoking the tradition of ancestor worship and the Yoruba god of ironwork and metallurgy:

So in this delineation, you have a god of metallurgy in chains, and here you are, wrapped in chains, working. You're in his house, but out of his house. So the irony of that (the *iron* of that!), of the chain gang, isn't that the Agun, isn't that the Ogun, working on the *sshhkk*—these are people with an ancestral tradition, with a tradition of metallurgy, dealing with the fact that they are manipulating chains and ironwork. . . . There are physical connections between those words, a deliberate physical connec-

tion, and there are aesthetic considerations, and then there are the literal
meanings. There are different things working at the same time.

For Morris, harnessing the knowledge that sounds possess is a kind of his-
torical witnessing, which she views as a kind of "standing-beside-yourself work"
that has an ecstatic, spiritual, and *political* dimension:

> African-based spirituality has always been something that has been
> threatening. Let me just be blunt—threatening . . . What freaks people
> out—particularly academics—is that you can't control that, you cannot
> presume authority over people saying they are representing their ancestors
> and they're coming through. . . . So there is a very strong political applica-
> tion to this kind of standing beside yourself work. Our situation here as
> black people and as women is that we have to articulate and give voice to
> whatever is required for us to give voice to, because not only do we have
> the overarching racial dynamic, but also as the cultural retainers, bearers,
> and primary conveyors of information, it's our responsibility to deal and
> convey that information.

Morris seeks to reconnect her audience with lost sources of spiritual power, and
she does so in part by refiguring poetic voice so that it is no longer expressive of
a deep, interior consciousness, or of a unique, personal, or original sensibility.
Instead, voice is a go-between, a migrant, a transmitter, an intermediary—mov-
ing between body and language but situated finally in neither. As Régis Durand
theorizes in "The Disposition of the Voice," it is voice that "affirms that ecstasy
is possible, can be attained through discourse":

> The voices that thrill us allow us to apprehend their power of dissocia-
> tion. They themselves are not concerned with diction, expressive effect.
> They let something through which has to do with origin and loss, and the
> determination of a space where ecstasy is possible.[30]

Morris's ecstatic method offers a poetic voice that is less concerned with self-
expression than it is with re-memory and cultural re-integration after traumatic
historical events.

III. Pleasing the Audience? Critical Distance and Identification

Not all of Morris's sound poems take off from traumatic material or ecstatic
occasions. The delightfully comical poem "Pick Up Line" consists entirely of a

series of male and female throat clearings that communicate a range of sexually fraught encounters that words themselves would be hard pressed to characterize. Yet Morris suggests that it is in dealing with traumatic experience that her sound experiments have the most force and value. Although the sound poems—with their breakdown of language into fragments and vocal gestures—might seem difficult to grasp and less "accessible" to a general audience, Morris finds that they make the most immediate and forceful impact on the audience:

> People have said things to me in connection to sound poems that they have never said to me when I was doing page stuff that was considered accessible. It's been beyond humbling. Sort of devastating. Because I have such little control. I'm harnessing. I'm not really determinist in what comes up, comes out, in a lot of those poems. People would walk up to me and say, "I was sexually abused, my husband used to beat me, I know what you're talking about."

What is remarkable about Morris's sound performances is the audience's experience of being in a room with a voice that has opened itself up to the risk of contingency. The audience that watches Morris choking—beating her hand against her throat to simulate the silencing effects of domestic abuse—cannot escape into an intellectualizing, abstract contemplation of the poem's words or language. Instead, they are caught up in a visceral event whose final outcome is unpredictable.

Despite the experimental, disjunctive, and sometimes violating quality of Morris's sound poems, they remain accessible and meaningful to a general audience. In fact, Morris claims that it is "*too* accessible, in some cases":

> Because you can't run away from that. When you hear somebody choking, talking about spousal abuse, and how real that is, you can't brace yourself, you have to experience, you have to live in the moment with that person.

The discomfort and violence of Morris's sound poems demonstrates that while Morris remains interested in shaping and building an audience for work, she has become *less* concerned with pleasing the listener. She is less interested in making her poetry consumable—or at least less so than one might expect from a poet whose performance will be immediately judged according to an Olympics-style, number-based ratings form. In an article in *Ms.* magazine, Morris insists "I don't want people to pressure me to compromise my aesthetic just to get over. They like the sassy black woman vibe, and that's just one aspect of my personality."[31]

Yet in a more recent interview Morris also makes a point of her deep respect for the audience, for "the fact that people come and pay to see my face on stage. I don't want to disrespect that or take that for granted. But there's something else that's more important than pleasing them. It's not even pleasing *me*." Without completely renouncing audience pleasure as a goal of her performance poetry, Morris challenges the idea of any easy or passive pleasure to be obtained from her work. The poems seek less audience approval than the kind of pleasure that comes from active participation. As performance theorist Anne Ubersfeld argues, the spectator of a performance finds that "the pleasure of understanding is always the pleasure not only of receiving but of doing. . . . Since the pleasure of critical distance counterbalances the pleasure of identification, the spectator, once more, moves back and forth between the two."[32]

It is this new relation with the audience—one that shuttles uncomfortably between critical distance and ecstatic identification with otherness—that will be the test of Morris's sonic improvisations. In poetry's current situation, poets who experiment with sound distortions and sonic revolutions walk a dangerous tightrope. On the one hand is a condition of epistemological failure, in which a fragmented poetry or a poetry of commercialized language merely mirrors the debris condition of postmodern culture. The result is a failure to mobilize a social collective toward goals of political action and change. On the other hand, poets are turning to disarticulation as the grounds for establishing a new epistemology —a new way of making knowledge—in which the poet can recover or "recycle" disfigured and nearly lost languages. By working at this boundary, and marking out a new epistemological space, Morris's performance poetry points the way toward a new postmodern poetry that is at once "noise" *and* "voice," disjunctive *and* lyrical. More importantly, perhaps, it suggests the outlines of a new relation between audience and poet—one that is critical yet intimate, and capable of drawing fully on the constructive, collaborative, and contingent nature of poetic performance.

Capillary Currents: Jayne Cortez

Aldon Lynn Nielsen

> *at that moment of no compromise*
> *his poetry became poetry unique to poetry*
>
> Jayne Cortez

The music is already there. By the time that the ear falls prey to the groove, the music is already multiplying, leveling monuments to expectation and erecting newer castles in the air; a layering with open work areas dangerously unguarded. This is not at all unusual these days, and never was. Still, each generation hears ellipses. Still, Jayne Cortez is already listening, present tense, as she begins "I See Chano Pozo." The band is already at play. The seven minutes and thirty-one seconds of the poem's second site in Cortez's 1982 recording, *There It Is* (which, without a "whoop," intriguingly prefigures the doubled variant versions of the next decade's rap hit, "Whoop, There It Is"), open with percussive punctuation. Elliptical hand patterns on bongo and conga look ahead to what we will hear of Chano Pozo in the poem, while adverting to the backward glance at the poem's title. As the other instruments intervene, a harmolodic whirl ensues. There is a discernible tonal reference point, but we seem to be free of strict key. Bass and guitar refuse to fall into the usual gestures of accompaniment. Rather, each independently carves in air series of serious notes, selected with an ear to what the other is doing but never settling into the prefabricated chord that an audience might intuit. The "It" of *There It Is* is, in Cortez's explanation, an "example of what a poet does with music and what musicians do with poetry."[1] It is, then, a sample, and as is true of all samples, it thus refuses coincidence with itself. The poem takes its place at the nexus of prefigured and post-produced poetic history, and it displaces it.

Only after the musicians have begun to chart out the paths by which they will defamiliarize the territory does the human voice intrude in the mix. Familiarity is in the nature of song, but familiarity is not identity. Male voices in the recorded version of the poem commence a titular chant, but it is not until the poem's second stanza that listeners hear how the poem's very name is harmolodically deflected. The chanting musicians sing a long, North American, "a" in the initial syllable of Pozo's proper name, "I see Chano Pozo." When Cortez follows, pronouncing the name in her own voice, she gives it a more properly Spanish inflection, "Chano Pozo," and the distance between the two accentual naming patterns names the distance traveled from the call of Pozo's Cubana Bop to the harmolodic discrepencies of Ornette Coleman's response, and that of his Prime Time band members, who form the nucleus of the recording unit for *There It Is.* As Cortez intones the poem's first line, "A very fine conga of sweat,"[2] it is apparent that we have been dropped *in medias res,* into the propulsive power point of a synaesthetic difference engine. As the differing pronunciations of Chano Pozo's name might indicate, we are not so much in the middle of some most particular thing in progress as we are in the middle of progress itself, in the middle of the Middle Passage.

In the version of the poem that Cortez performs in the same year for the film *Poetry in Motion,*[3] there are no chanting counterpoints to the poet's pronunciation. Nonetheless, because her own voice, speaking in an interview, overlaps the performance's opening bars, leaving behind the image of poet as interview subject and leading us to the image of the poet surrounded by already performing musicians, the text of what we presume to be her poem spread on a stand before her, the same effects of difference within familiarity, figured differently, again obtain. The interviewed poet is speaking of the tradition of call and response as the film editor thrusts us into the already-in-progress jazz poem. Is the paper in front of the poet a visible sign of the difference between prose speech and jazzed poem or, more likely, a moving prop against which rest all such ultimately unanswerable questions. The performance is a response to the poem, an example of what musicians do with poetry. The poem is a prior response to jazz, an example of what a poet does with music. The interview statement is in response to a question, an example of what an audience does with jazz poems. And there it is, the core of possibility in jazz text. All calls participate in a rhetorical logic by which they incorporate in advance the anticipation of an answer. All response is response to something, and thus shapes itself to its calling while transposing it. All performances of "I See Chano Pozo," on page or staged, partake of this same shifting logic, harmolodic transposition of a calling in anticipatory response.

"A very fine conga of sweat" (*C* 65). The drum is already in play, someone sweating over it. Cortez calls us to attend to a long history of *Cubanismo* in North American discourse, a *Cubanismo* long embargoed by an aggressively consumerist politics that would prefer to have its antecedents and eat them too. As I write, near century's end, North America is again celebrating one of its periodic seizures of love for Cuban music. Compay Segundo, Ibrahím Ferrer, Rubén González and other members of that ad hoc social construction known as the Buena Vista Social Club are circulating successfully through North American venues on a seemingly endless tour whose energetic performances belie the superannuated birth certificates of the musicians. Los Van Van, one of Cuba's most popular bands, are playing to standing-room only houses across the country, even in Miami, where anti-Castro exile activists, culturally depraved by our long dark embargo of the soul, attempted to shut down their countrymen's concerts. The way was made smoother for this most recent eruption of Cubanaphilia not only by Ry Cooder's yeoman service as cultural ambassador, but by the earlier tours of virtuoso pianist Gonzalo Rubalcaba. Charlie Haden, the bassist who was at Ornette Coleman's side during the invention of harmolodics, took the Cooder role in that earlier episode, arranging recording dates and concert appearances with the astonishing young pianist. For his earliest U.S. appearances, though, Rubalcaba was forced to philanthropy by our State Department. Not permitted to play for pay, the Cuban artist played two major concert benefits on the coasts of the United States as a means of building audiences for his recordings, though his first releases (widely available in the States) had to be released through his American label's Japanese division in order to meet, however circuitously, the demands of the embargo. That American officials went to such lengths to keep Cuban arts out of the United States, while presumably keeping their arms wide open in welcome to any Cubans willing permanently to separate themselves from their island, is testimony to their knowledge of both the powers of Cuban cultural innovation and the willingness of an unembargoed American mind to lend an ear.

The ironies of these most recent Cuban sorties of course follow after Cortez's poem. But there had been a similar phenomenon shortly prior to her release of *There It Is*. In 1979, Irakere, among the most spectacular concentrations of Cuban music talent, had released its first Anglo album, following close on the heels of a triumphant tour of international jazz festivals. This was the first time that most American music fans were able to hear Paquito D'Rivera, Chucho Valdes and Arturo Sandoval, names that have continued to claim the attention of serious music lovers in the years since. The 1979 American label album was the direct result of a visit of American jazz artists to Havana in 1977. In the same way that Charlie Haden and Ry Cooder have been able to introduce North Americans to art their representative government did not want them to know in the nineties, American jazz greats constituted themselves as an advance guard for Irakere's storming of the jazz festivals at Montreaux and Newport two decades earlier.

And here we come to a more direct intersection with Cortez's poem, for the American artists most responsible for bringing the good news of Irakere north were Stan Getz, who had visited Cuba in the fifties, and Dizzy Gillespie, who was visiting Cuba for the first time despite the fact that he had been, more than any other, the man responsible for the explosion of Afro-Cuban music within the Bop revolution of the forties. His collaborator in that fecund syncretic concoction was Chano Pozo, who Jayne Cortez saw perform with Gillespie in 1948, just months after the historic recording sessions that produced "Cubana Be" and "Cubana Bop." Cortez was witness when Pozo and Gillespie appeared at Wrigley Field in Los Angeles, the same venue memorialized by Jay Wright in his book *The Homecoming Singer*.[4]

In his liner notes to the 1979 Irakere album, Leonardo Acosta remarks as one of the group's contributions to the expansive vocabulary of Latin jazz their bringing into the popular music of Cuba the "intricate and vigorous Yoruba and Carabalí rhythms which have been well known in Cuba but which had not been 'integrated' into the mainstream"[5] of the music, a cultural syncretism that is matched in Cortez's poem. Acosta also makes an intriguing suggestion regarding the long history of Latin infusions into American jazz idioms. "Their affinity comes from before the existence of jazz as such," he asserts. "We all know the history of the beginnings of jazz, but we don't always associate it with the ending of slavery in Cuba, between 1880 and 1889, and the massive immigration of black Cubans, free but jobless, to places like New Orleans." Jelly Roll Morton, he reports, once listed Cuba among the sites of origin for jazz. If Acosta is at all right in his genealogies of jazz, this means that not just Irakere's interventions in American music but Chano Pozo's initial forays as well might be marked out as a return as much as an immigration. Afro-Cuban rhythms, the subsequent additions of Yoruban and Carabalí timings to those of Congo and Dahomey, might be a reappearance within the modernity of jazz.

The BeBop innovations of Parker and Gillespie revolutionized jazz, that music most intimately identified with North American modernity. Their rewritings of the rule books of harmony against the backdrop of a reinvigorated pulse within the rhythm section were radical wrinkles within the already modern. In this context, Gillespie's work with Chano Pozo, identified by Cortez in her liner notes to *There It Is* as "the first conga player to play with a jazz band," must be heard as a return of an African-Caribbean anterior already echoed in the structures of jazz. Similarly, the post-Bop renovations orchestrated by Ornette Coleman, given Coleman's experiences playing Rhythm and Blues in his circuit-riding youth, are a return with a difference. Bop reoriented the solo line's relationship within harmony. Coleman's jazz stripped away the usual chordal structural supports of harmony, leading through his early Free Jazz stage to his later harmolodics, while at the same time moving from Bop-oriented rhythms to a further funk. All of these differential returnings are audible in the harmolodic music of Cortez's musical associates, both on *There It Is* and in the somewhat smaller-scale performance caught by *Poetry In Motion*. And this syncretic mode of renewal is heard again in Cortez's poetics.

In her *Poetry In Motion* interview, Cortez says, "It's about sound; the sound of the music against the sound of the poetry." This is as true of the printed poem on the page as it is in any of its performance variants. Speaking to Sascha Feinstein about her more recent work, Cortez remarks the deadliness that can attach to an artist whose signature song is demanded by all audiences, about how "repeating something exactly as it had been recorded . . . is no longer a release."[6] One way to avoid such staleness is to vary the piece with each release, while maintaining the recognizable script of the signature itself. This is what Cortez has done with her multiple performances of "I See Chano Pozo," but it is also what she has already done in the poem's composition. The lyric's refrain alters with each reappearance, and within the semantic registers of the sounds she has elected to carry her chorus we can reread the perpetual postmodernizings of Latin Jazz's renewed incursions. Cortez's unpunctuated rhetorical question, "Is there anyone finer today" (inside of which I hear a Bop-styled pop refrain from an earlier era: "Nothing could be finer . . . "), finds its respondent chorus chanting:

> olé   okay
> Oye   I say
> I see Chano Pozo
>   (*C* 65)

Here the Spanish cheer is answered with a peculiarly American idiom. Both "olé" and "okay" pick up the internal rhyme with "today" from earlier in the line, troping the rhetorical question with the rhetoric of the idiomatic. The origins of the American "okay" are shrouded in philological controversy. This prototypical Americanism has frequently been given a West African etymological source and has also been traced to American Indian ancestry. It was without doubt widely popularized as a result of its use in early American partisan politics. In any event, the appearance of its close linguistic cousin "Okeh" as the name of one of the most popular race records labels earlier in the twentieth century solidified its shadow racial connotations. The next line repeats this alternation of Spanish and English, this time following the command "Oye" with the declarative, "I say," all the while punching percussively at that rhyme with "today." Finally, speech turns to sight, matched by a phonic modulation from "a" to "e," as the declaration completes itself, or finds its answer, in "I see." The grammatical ambiguity proceeds

from the absence of graphic punctuation, leaving us unable ultimately to deter-
mine whether the poet is saying that she sees Chano Pozo, or if she is saying and
seeing him, saying *as* seeing, an uncertainty that acts as analogue to the unre-
solved tonalities of the harmolodic music in the recorded versions. As it hap-
pens, that uncertainty has its audible rhyme in the contending pronunciations
of Pozo's first name in the version heard on *There It Is.* The musicians pronounce
"Chano" so that its initial syllable rhymes with Cortez's "olé," "okay," "oye" and
"I say," but Cortez herself, marking a sort of harmolodic distinction, does not.
In her reading of it, the first syllable of the name rhymes with the first syllable
in "Havana," the place name that immediately follows Pozo's in the poem, citing
his home.

Such differences make a circle of signifying, as Pozo is lauded within the
poem as "The one who made Obonu into / a circle of signifying snakes." That
circle of Dickinsonian sibilance sews Pozo's name through the circuit of stanzas,
reminding us of its echoes in the name "Cortez," plaiting a sonic signature
within the onomastic weave of the praise poem. This is an occasional poem, after
all, first composed by Cortez for the Chano Pozo Music Festival held at Dart-
mouth in 1980. In her interview years later with Sascha Feinstein, speaking of
her poem "Flying Home," Cortez distinguishes between the signature tune with
which an artist might saddle herself for life and "depth or art or spontaneity."
But she leaves an enticing opening in another remark she makes on that occasion:
"A signature is a signal before an intermission . . . ."[7] Her literal referent is that
commonly brief stretch of readily identifiable melody or theme with which mu-
sicians signal that they are about to take a break. For over two decades the melody
Miles Davis used in this way was titled simply "Theme." Miles, though, never
signed his theme the same way twice. One need only audition the versions heard
in his mid-sixties live recordings and compare them to the torqued and retooled
electric versions heard just a few years later at venues like the Fillmore auditori-
ums to see just how far a signature can be stretched without snapping out of
legibility. Cortez's poem is her way of signing a certain history in music and let-
ters, but she has incorporated the signatures of others as well, gathering them
into a sheaf of allusion.

For "I See Chano Pozo" asserts a second genealogy alongside the melody line
that follows the *Cubanismo* of Jazz from its beginnings in New Orleans, through
its reappearance with the advent of Chano Pozo in Bop, and into the more recent
figurings of Irakere and the Buena Vista Social Club. That second genealogy is
literary, Afro-Spanish and again attached to the music. North Americans now
are listening again to the *sonedores* of Cuba. In doing so they retrace the listen-
ings of an earlier mode of modernism, one that found in Afro-Cuban musical
forms a way to revivify the legacy of *modernismo* left by Rubén Darío. By the

time of Darío's death in 1916, the aesthetics of the *modernismo* that he had championed were waning throughout Latin America. *Modernismo* lingered in a somewhat attenuated fashion in Cuba, where it had been wedded to the techniques left to that national literature by José Martí and Julián del Casal. By the time of the earliest poems of Nicolás Guillén, *modernismo* was increasingly overshadowed by the poetics of those newer artists collectively known in Cuba as *Los nuevos.*[8]

As international modernism seized upon the imaginations of artists, the fascination with the Africanesque on display in the works of Picasso, Bracques and others found its way increasingly to places where African culture was considerably more immediate than any museum piece, awaiting ready, if tardy, reappropriation and redirection. In the Spanish-speaking New World this led to the *Negrista* poetics of such white writers as Luis Palés Matos and José Zacarías Tallet. Afro-Cubano writers, though, were early on seeking out other models and they found them, as did the Negritude poets of the Francophone Caribbean, in the arts of the Harlem Renaissance. This brought into being a circle of signifying cross-influences that overlaps the musical history memorialized in "I See Chano Pozo." Poets like Césaire, Damas, and Cuba's Nicolás Guillén came to read the English language poets of the Harlem Renaissance, among whom the Caribbean influence was already powerfully apparent. In turn, as Langston Hughes's endless travels brought him frequently through the Caribbean region, he made a point of meeting with these poets, subsequently assisting in their works' appearance in English translations in North America. Along with Mercer Cook's translations of the Negritude poets he had met in his trips to France, translations that he shared with generations of students at Howard University, this marked the first recycling through North American audiences of an Afro-Caribbean, avant garde aesthetics with its accompanying radical politics, resonant with the lingering echoes of earlier Caribbean contacts within the poetics of African-American culture.

Caribbean movements emphasizing the indigenous in the arts came increasingly to revalue the African elements in their cultures, and this revaluation inevitably brought about a political reconfiguration. While Guillén never developed as far-reaching a philosophical critique of European culture and ideology as did the Negritude of Césaire and Senghor, his version of *Negrismo,* in contrast to the works of his white predecessors (which might be seen as having more in common with Van Vechten than with Césaire), increasingly took aim at the presumptions and neocolonial aspirations of his giant neighbor to the North. Thus the romanticism of Guillén's earliest poems, published in *Camagüey Gráfico,* is soon given greater edge by the political ironies of his collections *Sones para turistas* and *West Indies, LTD.* But it is the diasporic Africanity found in the forms

and language of Guillén's poetry of the thirties and forties that signs itself in
the poetry of Jayne Cortez decades later.

North Americans fill concert halls today listening raptly to the *sones* sung by
Ibrahím Ferrer. It is an old music new to many Yankee Boomer ears. One of the
ways in which Nicolás Guillén rewrote the *modernismo* of Darío more than sixty
years ago was to embrace the Afro-Cuban *son* as a form in which to realign his
poetic language with the languages of African America that he heard in the air
all around him. In a series of early books including *Motivos de son, Songoro
cosongo* and *El son entero,* Guillén accomplished a breakthrough in Cuban letters
parallel to what Langston Hughes and Sterling Brown did by basing a literary art
in the form of the blues. Guillén's intention was, as he put it, "to incorporate into
Cuban literature—not simply as a musical motif but rather as an element of true
poetry—what might be called the poem-*son*."[9] Turning from the tortured dialect
of earlier popular Africanist verse, Guillén increasingly drew upon the inventive
potential of his polyglot culture. Spanish is spoken differently in the Americas,
in part thanks to its forced marriage with the idioms of Yoruba and Dahomey.
Guillén used a novel word, *jitanjáforas,* to describe the coinage of terms in every-
day Afro-Spanish, words that suggest a meztiso linguistic history and that tunnel
under the fortifications erected in the Spanish of the Conquistadors. The title of
his book *Songoro cosongo* is itself a *jitanjáfora,* an Africanesque neologism cre-
ating a syncretic metaphor wedded to the meters of the *son.* In his introduction
to his 1931 collection, *Motivos de son,* Guillén speaks of the injection of Africa
into Cuba so deep that "many capillary currents cross and interweave in our
well-irrigated social hydrography."[10] Because of this deep capillary network, "the
two races that emerge on the surface of the island, though apparently distant,
are linked subterraneously to each other, like those underwater bridges which
secretly join two continents." It is just this deep capillary network that Cortez
brings to the surface in "I See Chano Pozo," the same capillary network join-
ing this woman poet to the musicians surrounding her in her performances of
the poem.

Guillén's use of *jitanjáforas* conjoins him to a lineage of modernist and post-
modernist linguistic experimentation that, when discussed in most contempo-
rary criticism, generally elides Cuba, the Caribbean, the Spanish language and
all things Yoruban. Such a critical oversight would likely not have been made by
William Carlos Williams, for despite his many and overt prejudices he liked to
draw attention to the Caribbean hydrography of his own familial and intellectual
past. Guillén's turn to the quotidian idioms of Cuban speech links him again to
the modernisms of Williams and of Hughes. Most importantly, for Guillén there
is no inherent political opposition between the novel, perhaps partially opaque,
construction of the *jitanjáfora* and the deceptive seeming-transparence of every-

day language. What Guillén, Hughes and Williams recognized was that "the people" experiment with language every day of their lives. This was the sort of "populist modernism" that Amiri Baraka was to make a rallying cry for the first generation of postmodernists, the generation of Jayne Cortez.

In his "*Son número 6,*" Guillén writes:

> *Yoruba soy,*
> *cantando voy,*
> *llorando estoy,*
> *y cuando no soy yoruba,*
> *soy congo, mandinga, carabalí.*
> *Atiendan, amigos, mi son, que empieza así*[11]

Guillén is the post-*modernismo sonero* who commands the reader's attention to the opening out of his *son*. His *son* commences mid-poem, *in medias res,* calling out from the middle passage of song, that subterranean capillary network that conjoins continents and epochs. This is the call Cortez hears in the drumming of Chano Pozo: "Chano," she calls him, "connector of two worlds" (*C* 66). Guillén's drumbeat reads the roll of diasporic languages: "*soy congo, mandinga, carabalí.*" It is a roll Cortez continues upon her return from "the cemetery of drums":

Lucumi	Abakwá	Lucumi	Abakwá

Olé   okay
(*C* 67)

Earlier, Cortez asked a question that might well have been addressed to that mode of Anglo-American modernism that sealed itself off from all this, embargoed itself, all the while reserving unto itself the right to vacation in the spiritual Cuba of Wallace Stevens's florid mundo. In the poem "Do You Think," Cortez asked, "Do you think time speaks english" (*C* 13)? In the rooms that open beneath the foundations of modernity (rooms marked "Conquest," "Middle Passage," and "Slavery"), those rooms that connect continents in time, English is one of many idioms from which America's *jitanjáforas* might emerge. In "I See Chano Pozo," Cortez wonders aloud, "what made your technology of thumps so new" (*C* 66). What Cortez calls to in her poetry is a modernity that constantly makes itself new by attending to the accents that speak its conditions of possibility. For decades the post-Bop, post-Free Jazz Art Ensemble of Chicago has had as their slogan, "Great Black Music: Ancient to the Future." The late Lester Bowie

knew exactly the technologies of newness that link Nicolás Guillén to Langston
Hughes and William Carlos Williams, that bring Chano Pozo together with
Dizzy Gillespie, that Charlie Haden hears in Gonzalo Rubalcaba. It is the tech-
nology of thumps (school of hard knocks?) that Billy Higgins hears echoing
from out the Congo as he propels a harmolodic Ornette Coleman. It is the con-
gress of *jitanjáforas* that Roscoe Mitchell, Lester Bowie, Joseph Jarman, Famadou
Don Moye and Malachi Favors Magoustous heard bubbling from beneath the
Chicago streets and shouted out to the world, what sets the Urban Bushwomen
singing. It is what Jayne Cortez heard flowing from the fingertips of Chano Pozo
one night in 1948 and refigured thirty-two years later as black American contem-
poraneity, a capillary action drawing up ancient centuries into our anaphoric
future:

> A very fine tree stump of drones
> a very fine shuffle of shrines
> a very fine turn of the head
> a very fine tissue of skin
> a very fine smack of the lips
> a very fine pulse
> a very fine *encuentro*
> (*C* 67)

Afterword
Draft 48: Being Astonished

Rachel Blau DuPlessis

> "My voice does not exist outside of amazement."
> —Rochelle Owens

1.
"I used the floor.
I used the flexed foot.
I showed effort.
My foot was bare."

"I was outside the realm of women."

2.
"Women" waft, drift, attracted to
red, what things color luxury sale, all names, heard, seen   "Womanliness . . .
markdown, entire stock at discount
their faces given to stripes,
mirror's retinal tain silvery behind
eyes in struggle with the face;
some save 40 years of scraps
in the closet, *Family Circle;* early Marilyn   could be worn as a mask
as shepherdess, holding a sheep
by the neck, piled   to hide"
in the "home" as fretted space
given to things vulnerable and wonderful, the distraction "she   intellection
got" "I want" masking "he got" "what do I want"   called (astonishingly)

whether these are thoughts   masculinity
they are what   happened once
love/l'oeuf
eat please/ ee   puppet   to avert
    pl p
    pulp   reprisals
    polyp   a diminished 7th
                revelatory

3.
The poem of Herman Boyard (blatant pseudonym)   "Ignore Gender.
was playful enough but lacked some impetus;
turns out the task was serious. I was a woman,   You Might As Well.
generally. Even in my mask.
Externally.
Also, often internally.   No One Else
Where not?
Well, there were rivulets of leak.   Will."
I felt break, beak and boyishness. Independent dependence.
Little girl bug saying "I never noticed" (the whole apparatus)
(of gender). Her-man-boy had no questions to ask.
"But they were so nice to me at the Playboy mansion!"
deep the corners of forgetfulness
What, then, and where, was the task?

4.
Belated
beknighted, acquiesce,
poetess, you have little leverage
despite some qualified success.
Tess
in your tress
confess. You are depressed. You are grotesque.
Just look at the rhyme skim of this poem; what a mess.
You women are / you are so conscious of your address
so cultured. So cultureless
so artful. So artless
you(r) dear natural song "like a nightingale" "like a lark" "like a cuckoo"
has the briefest access, attributable to flesh, more or less.

9

9

Cheap looking dress, you are upset: under stress.
I can't follow the way you digress
you bring me overflowing handfuls of bountiful distress
Cress

5.
Ah lovely one,
after considering wells and towers
up and down, inside and out—
this folk tale and that, long hair, rampant need for greens,
stuck in the finger for *fingere* means making,
after mimicking the pellucid brushstrokes of the Renaissance
and the exacting matte colors in a muted palette of azzurro and carnelian
you have found, in actuality, a courtyard, a real place
where, at the bottom of the well,
someone once upon a time constructed a room.
"Now there's a thing!
it's a long cylindrical stone shaft
with a large stone square chamber at the base!"

6.
flaccid praxis. eggs. milk.
no time. no time for the cow mouse pad.
tuneless piano. coolish room
the lamb caught, stroked softly
"nakee" "nakee baby"
take-out, everything smells, a grand
fever, all-red ears,
kiss her face
licking kitten

7.
The letter condensed black holding ink. writing overflowed itself.
It held the untranscendent overprinted stain dampening pages
It was an "A" spelled with pennies, an "E"
with staves, laddered for three octaves of new chunk music.
It was "R" so flat without its leg it looked like "Q"
for quim or quote or queer.   "transcend gender"
Build of the human confrontation with its space

its politics, alphabets   "be androgynous"
longings and losses   versus
a looming tack and a quickening
the deep flung crevasses   "name woman; say woman; speak
of your female-historical shapes
that embody the imprint of intricate substance.
                                            what you call 'woman.'"
Arms up!
Cradles and alerts your desire for powers.
Arms and all we are to sing, O daughters inside the covenant,
break with with female circumspection, grasp
the smallest chancy bit, the bit and build: but given our excess of care and
    hedging
what is it to open the book?

It's deposition time.
Take down the full ghost.

8.
Speaking midrash in a mid-rush   traces
Her revulsion to the book the obverse   on the wunderblock
of her attachment to the Book   of all the poems ever read
in the textual traditions on which she draws   look for the "women"
And revulsion to poetry—want to speak of that?

"Will no one tell me what she sings?"

9. (cut-off sonnet)

Should she shave? shouldn't she just shave
her moustache? I mean in this culture.
Maybe not in some other.
It looks so disgusting.

That was such a big spider
its forefoot and its ragged claw
I killed on my light yellow wall
with my dark yellow *Differences*

"Trouble in the archives" threw it?
or did "the phallus issue" do it?

10.
there is no here or there in the dream
in the dream there is no now or then
no pointing to an other space from this
male and female are hypersaturated   "I write beyond
multiple steps and disarticulated
in the dream, no he or she all part of me and
staged so I am many   the range of my identity"
vaginies, penies and other binaries
with sensations, all sorts hither and yon them and you
but nowhere, in b&w,
in sepia, and in living color there are intersections in the dream
visual ectoplasms slide and change
swollen clitties wander cities
shadow and conventions from
the whole of photography   "cupidity and the pencil of light"
from longer pregnancy are there;
hear music and voices in the dream
pale, irremediable, unmemorable
see the dead, cut like crazy, suture meister
and tinny, and sweet,
come in a dream, lobby labia
along with cars, chutes, climbs, tidal waves
onrush, stone terror, paralysis and missed births
malformed fetal stuff—felt, flat and legless,
switched track, trains trestled,
and can't run at all, lead legs sucking gravely back

so what's the point?
I can't show you anything
(it's my dream)
except a vast history of radiant practices
and dark cunnings
penises et al. redistributed
potluck for phalluck and rend her
into a variety of sites, places, and suctions:

altogether "people" shim and sheen—
So where is the dreamer's gender in the dream?

11.
"Beauty Supplies. Hardware. Human Hair. Discount."
"Fundamental Observation. Anatomical Detail. Error in Diagnosis. Other."
Poetry is the space of the fold—s/he can fold over he/s, transgender and inside it:
now there's a banquet!
Too bad poetry has barely done this yet since nothing
but almost the whole poetic tradition
stops it.

O "danger to Poetry
as it should exist
of the poetess
turned feminist"!

12.
She hectors me in the car.
She andromaches me in the car.
She penelopes me in the car.
She nestors me in the car.
I drive, she sd what she sd,
head on, looking for the road loop.
We go back a long ways.

I ode her in the car.
I goad her in the car.
I lyre her in the car.
I tire her in the car.
Drive, she sd. Drive, I replied.
This car needs gas. This car is low.
Back a long ways is where we go.

13.
She said it doesn't matter, "woman."   "to assert a gendered self
I could go for that.
She said, I write what I want, and it
comes up "the mother."

Better than trying to,   and to escape a gendered self"
it's there, and rises, rose-gigantic attar.
Whatever. That is, the Mother.
Puns in *Hamlet* about "matter."

She said it didn't matter, gender.   these be
Of course she *is* a woman.
It hadn't really struck her?
It didn't matter the way some people

claimed ("too loud"?) it mattered?   the simultaneous
The revolution frozen as conventional writing.
So quick the insight went into natter
she said, so refused "predictable, ritualistic"

"rules" of theme and tone ("too flat"?)   the contradictory
affirmation, closure, transcendence and release
the must say this or must say that—
obligation (she said) and ennuis.

Hung out to dry (I thought I *was* subtle)   the impossible
in this argument, I am touched (really)
by imagining (astonished) that being a woman
in literary life doesn't matter (no irony)

the way it seems to—like historical marginality.
Of course, at other times she
will insist it does matter. Forget gender neutrality.
There too I know just what she means.

Who wants to have it (being "a" "woman") matter
in any stagy, rigid ways that close down   goals.
investigation and capacity for invention that
might just (of course) have gotten compromised   goads.

because of gender. But could it possibly matter
always the same ways?
So does it, or does it not in this case?
Neither one of us wants this "theory" flatter.

14.
A cow ripe place, a cool air, a fine spoon, a fun stone
a barn stein, an amber sweet, a pert sweat, a putt putt. Fail us. Don't fail us.
Feel us
nod rope peel. Pal us. Pale us, lip
stick, trip pack; chap stuck, hemistich. Something unfolds back. Stoked you.
Awning, all in. Grounded charge. He-arpe, strung. Harp heap. Heart sleep.
Bug stung. Red on a red day. Red on a bed day. Read on a bad day. Deed
globe. Water cry. A flat store, but very there. A veg. A charm. Rounded spurge.
Tanager. Orange no rhyme; orange. Orage thunder. Osage orange. Bois
d'arc. Ark en cell. Bodark. Bend her bow, bow. Boy. Wow. Daily cream.
Plate cheeser. Charger. Three joined roller-wheel wagon. A veegee. A veggie.
Answer prints. Feed that cow, girl, feed her
an icy tear.
a pink clear. Feed her   fattie fattie two step buckle   forage in her deep meat
Hero. Her row in, her bonnie bow.
here to there
heretofore.

15.
"Cut with a Kitchen Knife." "We called this photomontage because it
reflected our aversion to claiming to be artists. We regarded ourselves as
engineers; we maintained that we were building things; we said we put
our works together like fitters."

We called this writing because it reflected our aversion to claiming to be
poets. Poetry had a place for us. Poetry staged us *there,* not a leg to stand
on. Pretty in pink; plenty up. Poetry made us poettes. The show before
the show. Kick, girls, you've got great legs. But we wanted all that—poet,
poette, makir, shaker—on our terms, in your face, on everyone's territory.
The way we had to struggle to get it; struggle with our peers; struggle
with our friends; struggle with our selves, with our constricted throat,
and with the apparent history of poetry. But we regarded ourselves as
constructors; we maintained that we were building things; we said we put
our works together from some materials, the materials of every day and
rearranging. The whole dictionary glossalalia-ed, tip tongue, agitations
of syntax, extra-sequence, multilingual sententia, language clots, big
prostheses and assessments. We cut with our fine-tuned scissors photos
of generals, brand name products, sand from the playground, under-
ripe peaches, trash on the exit ramp. Mucilage—the musty juice. Pasted.
We stick. We keep Journals of Ordinary Thought. We had hard times,

money sour, fake promises (forget resources), coffee breaks, "liked your 'performance'?"—huh?—unmatched black fabrics, dead people's nightgowns in the thrift store, overcast (stitch? weather?) this—This is where. This was the claim, this was the site of the lives we were in, this was our sex and our place and our caste, this was our race and this was our slap, this was our color, and our matter; this was the baby, the adolescent, and the father; this was the hot dance, the cold tap, the implacable fact, the urges that we wanted urgently to Make From. We made it matter. "To Investigate." "To Layer." "To Disclose." "To Activate." "To Cut with" "A" "Kitchen Knife."

16.

Quack diddley o so quack-quack-quack.	Wherever
Say san y'rico y'rico-rico-ri-ko.	Lacan
Velour. Velour.	wrote *phallus*
Velour-velour-velour.	substitute
VE	
LOUR	the word *dildo.*

one   2   three   4

17.

The large glass cracks trucked over the Brooklyn Bridge. Harp hurt. Pink screen with mesh capillaries. UNSTRUNG string, dud sound. Snap. Rules said what she needed. CARE. what Broke. All back of what. She made from events. SEE Green. Canvas Bag distributed to each TASK FORCE member. Touch, before you open that door, Aquamarine. Ghosts. Fax rattle. HELLO, watch out. I hear voices whispering; no filter; all the messages pile stereophonic. CLEAN your MESSAGE MACHINE. McCARTHY called me on his telephone. Get you Get you. Fussing for coins, Find the BREAD. webbings of wirest closets of electricalness. Closest Dead Basin story. Sit up and pee. It is like ploughing. DEFEAT OF THE ERA, JUNE 3, 1982. Never wanted to be poisoned with dread, but AM That way. Get you get you. Fucking commie. Need C. NEED C, and D and A. Enclosed is a brochure describing a unique career. The INSTRUCTOR has a fuzzy mind. With the Clandestine Service in the Directorate of Operations. Fucking lezzie. For liberal arts students. Espionage. Covert Action. Counter-Intelligence. Get you. She made from events. THIS WAS THE DAY THIS WEEK. She cited them from newspapers. saw a peregrine falcon on the 10th

floor. saw a flicker break its neck, fall to its death. Like Matthiessen. saw
hundreds of little dead birds on the plaza between the WORLD TRADE
CENTER buildings. Bright glass snap. Simone de Beauvoir died. I recording
shatter shitty scratched among impinging million of needle events.

18.
Feigning passivity, the chartreuse free-form, ten-inch
ashtray of the very early 50s,
speckled by imbedded arts of glitter dotting,
lies low, lurking on the Swedish
modern palette shaped coffee table
veneer over veneer.
Stubs of butts, aching with lipstick,
smelled up the place, stuffed up the sinuses
with green pus smoke-corpses
even before "cancer" was the
foregone conclusion.

10 years after she died, I began talking a little
to my mother's handkerchief
basically telling it what I was doing
to keep in touch
with whomever,
to offer the one tied in knots
remembrance, rueful undirected bits
of lost time, bleeding one-breast,
scar tissue and dust clots.

A wall, freshly painted, should be free
"of drips, spatters, overspray,
of foreign materials,
of lumps, skins, runs, sags,
holidays, misses, strike-throughs
or insufficient coverage."

That's literary history for you!

19.
Look at it—I was such a cute girl they didn't know. They claim it did / did
not affect her— she rose her darknight spangle silver star veil and took it out.

Effect her. She took the point guard out. The ball hooked in. I was so sexy,
I did what I wanted. I knew beyond it; but they just saw my face. I drank,
yelled back. I was what I was, but no one knew I was more. Open the sealed,
hermetic adventurer. Dear(est) A, deer ist B, dear alphabet in the middle
of my hart, are you a twirler, a wholeness, a wildness, a wilderness, a void, an
open mouth. Are you a swirling set of scarfs, are you arouser, wear trouser?
a mourner? in a corner? are you eater. Sweeter. I was called out. I was chosen.
I worked. I did 20 chapbooks. I published magazine. I learned layout.
Does the language have to be ripped apart syllable and phoneme? does it
get layered in the bereft intricacies of absolute syntax? Rearrange arrange-
ment. "What do you do when you are there and don't have a name for
it?" vocab. diction selection possibility; choked up, a long long binding.
"Don't be too wry, your thing's impossible." What interior space. spangle. You
surely don't believe that stuff about "feminine language"! When women
look in a mirror, people applaud. Toss that golden hair. Toss that currly
red, gurrl. Flap and guise those belladonna eyes, glistening with concealment.
When women reflect on their own silvery shining, what. Refracted viewing
leverage. Bang on the direct cart as you become the great gamelan elder. Sliver
the mirror. Reflect on the reflection. When they reflect, reflect on the
reflection, with inflection, convection, conviction—people have been known
not to applaud those women's depth and charged perception
but to deny
it ever, ever happened.

20.
children sold
to coke and pepsi
it's so different
it's so sexy

go by any high
school, prom time
all that aerosol in the ditch
what do you think that's about,
bitch.

21.
Tall well-dressed woman chatting with friends
swings out of the bookstore, heading for a latte
trips a voice, wherefrom,

loud, WATCH
OUT speaks the invisible pale sick
puffed face half
sunk wool hat hunched down crooked old bag
lady

22.
Restrained, elegant, and solid,
handsome and laughing,
the man who, in that colloquium,
said women writers
should write worshipping maleness, males as holy and numinous—
and they should do this for
about 200 years.
Whereupon men and women writers
will be more equal (he addresses me, pointedly)
and things can then proceed as if normal.
He said it would take 200 years, meaning from now,
it's 1992, for women
to be (real) poets, an observation (even playful and ironic)
that protects people of his generation and later
already satisfactorily and recognizably poets
from direct confrontation
with existing histories of work, with the splay of choices,
with the working conditions, the mighty and even
moderate works and days of a considerable human population.
But talk of problems! I become astonished.
Where was my 200 years? I was alive now,
defined as "woman" irrevocably,
symptomatically enraged, *senza mesura,*
and about to undergo erasure
just by virtue of living when I was born.

Was the task worship? was the task writing? Don't ask.
It didn't matter. I had failed at the task.
This was a simple fact derived from how I happened
to occur in time, not maturing 170 years from now.
Hence what H. said made me paralytically contumacious
some newfangled return
of the icy hot. I shake with stubbornness.
I freeze and I burn.

23.
excisions of letters by unknown hands, scraps tossed
typed material cut and pasted, the other side of the page blurred, lost
cut out names alter some pronouns
loss of, blame for, shame on, underscore,
undo dating, misassign linkages,
take colleagueship and make it influence
make equality into hierarchy
take collateral damage and lighten it;
forget whole eras of her poetry, the nonconformist time,
stabilize and tame poetic texts, and finally, for the rest,
take the dead woman's life's-work in journals, and all her papers,
and burn them

at her own request.

24.
Ladies, here's some Helpful Advice for your Writing Career!
Want To Publish a well-received and Celebrity Book Today?
Quote, Well, If you wanted To
Repudiate the Women's Movement,
we'd be Rather Interested, Unquote.
This being a true story.

25.
"Laid off? Perhaps you could start selling those crafts you make for fun."

26.
"Well, the gender question. The 'sputter plot.'
It's about work. It's about having to go out
and get a job. I think really that is about gender,
because of this constant negotiation with all these different variables . . .
How women have to keep bouncing
all these different narratives. Juggle these things literally.
Keep things going.
And the aesthetics of that.
It seems to me it's very much a fractal life."

27.
Stanza about sexism. Stanza.
What is sexism. Why was that term, at first, a bonanza?

What is critical reception.
How did you work from your career's inception
how many "positions" can you "take up" in your poetry
what is the source of your authority?   "If I am not
tell us your cultural autobiography.
where have you put your agency   who you
and how is it deployed, what it has meant?
what is judgment, what is unction   say I am,
how do they function
how many writers have you seen ploughed under
you've really got to wonder

what did she think she was doing
apologizing for "want of women's wit"
and why can she now be republished after centuries forgotten?
"Now" (whenever that is) we have her in the *Norton*
here we go again, don't have this be   then you are not
another story about silence.
Or Collateral Wreckage, the women speaking   who
about how they are not so sentimental as that other woman.
Besides—Woman—no one wants this to be a crude idea   you think you are."
crudely enforced. Nor to be synonymous
with anonymity and loss.

28.
She talked of the "extra act" of the woman writer
she said one always had to define
some relation to "gender identity"—to embrace it
deny it
hide it
articulate it

an act invested, not neutral,
and this "extra act" changes and has changed
(has changed her, she changes it)
over time.

29.
Made of oil drums, struck by twin mallets.

As you increase the amplitude of the area that you're exciting

you get a lot of vibrations,

and the charm of heart music, skilled touch of the player

from something that looks

like a garbage can.

As the drummer pounds harder on a particular note

the vibration spreads

until almost the entire drum reverberates

and radiates sound, wheel spoke speaking,

first by sounding a note alone

then the double lobes of a repeat

vibrating in sympathy

so that harmonics form, even before the other players begin

their twinning, a sound spectrum rich in the intended

and the fortuitous

until the whole is alive with its own couplings and overtones

stirring vibrations

from the area excited

creating sounds, charged with their own

full-blown astonishment.

30.

Identify the story.

Tell the story.

Tell the story again. And again. Good audience.

Modernize the story, diction, or setting. Bring it Up-to-date. change the surface of the characters. Dress them today.

Alter the helpers. Have dogs speak.

Mo says, Good story!

Revise the story. Make it end differently. Bring some odd part up from the wilderness into the picture. More.

Look at unspoken matters in the story.

Look at unspoken characters in the story.

Speak out of the standpoint of the silent ones, the suppressed. The wanderers, the inarticulate. Write about what's hardly been written about before. Childbirth is an example.

Give voice to the voiceless.

Think about the word "give" and what you are claiming, who you are in speaking; can you "give" and what work does this rhetorical word really accomplish?

Note how odd the story seems from what you have now called the "other side" of "the story."

Try to figure out how many facets something called the "other side" might have, if one said

"sides." See whether two sides are, in practice, enough. Forget "sides." Enter. Identify the qualities and textures of silence, the materials involved in silencing, the slight

rustling or traces of the silent.

Set them down in syntax and fragment.

Identify the story. Discuss the politics of point of view. Be cogent.

Talk about the "the" in this phrase: "the story."

Why might one story be exemplary ("the") and another be forgotten (no story there)?

Observe the power over you and the staginess of the mechanisms of identification: "I" speak in "her" voice. "I" speak for her? What makes the power of making memorable story? What lets stories stay remembered? What is the story of no story? Can you

tell it? Is "a story" a gaze? Or many gazes? Are there materials in the story for its own undoing? Who is looking? How many ways is it possible to hear and look. Where do you stop? Where did this story come from? Where is no story? Where is power?

How does the writer speak in the story? Does she lecture, structure, repeat,
or abide?
Are there frozen powers made into sweeties in this story? Do you eat them
like candy?
Is it a story when you can't or won't end it?
Does it have to be consistent?
Does the story bind you down? Is that your joy?
Learn to respect stories. Again and again.
Was any story compelling? Does it remain so?
What is "a story"? How is one made? Can I make one?
If I were to make one, who would hear me?
Is what I make not really any story?

Now what about poems.

31.
I want this section damp and black with ink I want it wet
blue indigo pages, azurite paint and a blue-black surface never to dry
I want the letters overprinted and confused, I want the much-maligned slither
bopping hither, a writing whose condition is lubricated over writing
resisting poetry, the whole contestable site. I want what I can't write
so contrarian it turns consciousness inside out with a burst of post-talmudic
    literate light;
I want to write in gold and silver ink even the most ordinary thought, I want
    it all
dissolved in coal thick mix poetry as critical,
poetry as critique, manifests of resistance and unrest. Belle rebel ring on clarity
and opacity, I want gliss, twanging acres of microtones, with the release.
Get secular, get mixed, get everything you know,
and what you don't know, down, and don't shun nothing neither: allow.
    Get smart.
For today they have discovered, at some odd e-site auction,
the second known, if still debatable, photograph of Emily D.
Today therefore is a good day to start.
Exfoliate rupture genderation by genderation.
How many changes will it take to change powetry?

October 1999, May 2000
to the equally astonished

Draft 48: Being Astonished. The various she's, her's, you's, he's and we's are to be imagined as specific composites and splittings of positions, arguments, and possibilities explored by a variety of people in this fecund period of women's experimental poetry.

Notes (by section): Title: Lyn Hejinian, with thanks. Epigraph: Rochelle Owens, *W. C. Fields in French Light.* 1. Martha Graham, *Blood Memory.* 2. Sidebar. Joan Rivière, "Womanliness as Masquerade." 3. Quip by Joel Lewis 5. Letter from Sarah Bradpiece. 8. William Wordsworth, "To a Solitary Reaper." 10. Sidebars: Modified from Harryette Mullen and from Margaret Cameron. 11. Main citation modified from Linda A. Kinnahan. 13. Some words from Joan Rettalack on Sylvia Plath in *Aerial* magazine. Sidebar: Heather Thomas on Alice Notley. 15. Hannah Höch's collage; she is also the source of the citation about photomontage. Allusion to work by Barbara Cole. 18. List from Dave Harden Paint and Paperhanging contract. 26. Tina Darragh (in interview with Joan Rettalack, *Aerial* magazine, 1989). 27. Aemelia Layner. Sidebar: Ralph Ellison. 28. Johanna Drucker. 29. Section developed from a *New York Times* article by William J. Broad on the steel drum or "pan" from the Caribbean: "the most important new acoustical musical instrument developed in the 20th century" (July 9, 1996), with citations from musicologists Thomas Tossing and Uwe Hansen.

Notes

Introduction: Oppositions and Astonishing Contiguities

1. Marjorie Perloff, *Radical Artifice: Writing Poetry in the Age of Media* (Chicago: University of Chicago Press, 1991), 27–28.

2. Although even the most tradition-bound poets today, such as the New Formalists, argue that they, too, are exploring these aspects of the medium, albeit from a very different aesthetic. See, for example, Dana Gioia, "Notes toward a New Bohemia," *Poetry Flash* 248 (1993): 7–14; and Annie Finch (ed.), *After New Formalism: Poets on Form, Narrative, and Tradition* (Ashland, OR: Story Line Press, 1999).

3. Marianne DeKoven, "Gertrude's Granddaughters," *The Women's Review of Books* 4, 2(1986):13; quoted in Linda Kinnahan, *Poetics of the Feminine: Authority and Literary Tradition in William Carlos Williams, Mina Loy, Denise Levertov, and Kathleen Fraser* (New York: Cambridge University Press, 1994), 227. See also Marianne DeKoven, "Male Signature, Female Aesthetic: The Gender Politics of Experimental Writing," *Breaking the Sequence: Women's Experimental Fiction,* eds. Ellen G. Friedman and Miriam Fuchs (Princeton: Princeton University Press, 1989), 72–81.

4. Erica Hunt, "Notes for an Oppositional Poetics," *Moving Borders: Three Decades of Innovative Writing by Women,* ed. Mary Margaret Sloan (Jersey City, N.J.: Talisman House, 1998), 687.

5. On audience and community, see, for example, Allison Cummings, "Public Subjects: Ideas of Audience in the Poetry of Brooks, Hunt, and Mullen" (paper presented at conference on lyric and language poetries, Barnard College, New York, NY, April 1999). On artistic and intellectual communities being institutionalized (and thus often depoliticized) as creative writing programs in the academy, see Charles Bernstein, Ann Lauterbach, Jonathan Monroe, and Bob Perelman, "Poetry, Community, Movement: A Conversation," *diacritics* 26, 4 (Fall-Winter, 1996): 196–210. For a Habermasian analysis of the possibility of poetry contributing to social change by entering the public sphere, or creating a counter-public sphere, see Jamie Owen Daniel,

"Does 'Poetry Make Nothing Happen'?: The Case for Public Poetry as a Counter-Public Sphere" (paper presented at conference, "Poetry and the Public Sphere," Rutgers University, April 1997; text available electronically at www.rci.rutgers.edu/~engweb/poetry.html). A number of literary journals have made concerted efforts to create community: for example, Ed Foster's *Talisman*, Rebecca Wolff's *Fence*, Gillian Conoley's *Volt*, Nathaniel Mackey's *Hambone*, Stephen-Paul Martin's and Eve Ensler's *Central Park*. See Juliana Spahr, "Spiderwasp *or* Literary Criticism," *Fence* 3, 1 (Spring-Summer, 2000): 130–47, for a discussion of a poetics of "joining" apparent among emerging writers: that is, "the tendency to violate the aesthetic separations of various schools" (133); and Spahr, *Everybody's Autonomy: Connective Readings and Collective Identity* (Tuscaloosa: University of Alabama Press, 2000).

6. Fanny Howe, "Bewilderment," *HOW(ever)2* 1.1 (1999). Electronic journal archives at http://scc01.rutgers.edu/however/v1__1__1999/fhbewild.html.

7. For useful overviews of the historical and current debates about formal issues in post-World War II poetries, see, for example, Christopher Beach, *Poetic Culture: Contemporary American Poetry between Community and Institution* (Evanston, IL: Northwestern University Press, 1999); Alan Golding, *From Outlaw to Classic: Canons in American Poetry* (Madison, WI: University of Wisconsin Press, 1995); Bob Perelman, *The Marginalization of Poetry* (Princeton, NJ: Princeton University Press, 1997); and Hank Lazer, *Opposing Poetries*, vol. 1 (Evanston, IL: Northwestern University Press, 1996). As Beach contends, to demand a consensus "in today's literary culture . . . is to reject as 'inappropriate, irrelevant [or] extrinsic' to the 'true nature' of poetry all forms of poetic expression which depart from one's own expectations and desires for the genre in question" (13).

8. Charles Altieri, "What Is Living and What Is Dead in American Postmodernism: Establishing the Contemporaneity of Some American Poetry," *Critical Inquiry* 22, 4 (Summer 1996): 767, 768. See also Altieri, "Some Problems About Agency in the Theories of Radical Poetries," *Contemporary Literature* 33, 2 (1996): 207–36.

9. For other discussions of representational art and politics, see also Charles Bernstein, *A Poetics* (Cambridge, MA, 1992); and "The Politics of the Signifier: A Conversation on the Whitney Biennial," *October* 66 (Fall 1993): 3–27.

10. Sloan, *Moving Borders*, 3.

11. Issues of space have prohibited treatment of other significant innovative women writers—Leslie Scalapino, Hannah Weiner, Sonia Sanchez, and Rachel Blau DuPlessis among some obvious absences, but also Alicia Ostriker's neo-midrashic experiments, Alice Fulton's "fractal poetics," Brenda Hillman's "langpo" trajectory, or Ntosake Shangé performance poems come to mind.

12. See Rachel Blau DuPlessis, "Manifests," *diacritics* 26, 3–4 (Fall-Winter, 1996): 31–53.

13. See, for example, Donald Allen's groundbreaking anthology about the Beat, Black Mountain, and New York poets, *The New American Poets* (1960); Andrei Codrescu, *American Poetry Since 1970: Up Late* (1987); and Jerome Rothenberg and Pierre Joris (eds.), *Poems for the Millennium: The University of California Book of*

Modern and Postmodern Poetry (1995), in all of which women writers are under-represented. On such oversights, see Alan Golding, "*Poems for the Millennium* and Rothenberg as Editor" (paper presented at conference on lyric and language poetries, Barnard College, New York, NY, April 1999). For a useful discussion noting the over-sight of writers of color in Douglas Messerli (ed.), *"Language" Poetries: An Anthology* (1987) and Ron Silliman (ed.), *In the American Tree: Language, Realism, and Poetry* (1986), see Hank Lazer, *Opposing Poetries* (vol. 1), 37–46. For another corrective, see Sharon Bryan (ed.), *Where We Stand: Women Poets on Literary Tradition* (New York: Norton, 1993).

14. Linda Kinnahan is quoted from "Forum," *HOW(ever)*2 1 (Spring 1999); http://scco1.rutgers.edu/however/v1__1__1999/fhbewild.html.

15. See, for example, Antony Easthope and John Thompson (eds.), *Contemporary Poetry Meets Modern Theory* (Toronto: Toronto University Press, 1991); and Rachel Blau DuPlessis and Peter Quartermain (eds.), *The Objectivist Nexus: Essays in Cultural Poetics* (Tuscaloosa: University of Alabama Press, 1999). For recent anthologies that juxtapose criticism on women writers of both traditional and innovative poetry, see Lynn Keller and Cristanne Miller (eds.), *Feminist Measures: Soundings in Poetry and Theory* (University of Michigan Press, 1994); and Jacqueline V. Brogan and Cordelia Candelaria (eds.), *Women Poets of the Americas* (University of Notre Dame Press, 1999). For the first major study of women's epic poetry in this conceptual vein, see Lynn Keller's *Forms of Expansion: Recent Long Poems by Women* (Chicago: University of Chicago Press, 1997). For crucial studies of innovative poets of color, see Maria Damon, *At the Dark End of the Street: Margins in American Poetry Vanguards* (Minneapolis: University of Minnesota Press, 1993); and Aldon Lynn Nielsen, *Black Chant: Languages of African-American Postmodernism* (New York: Cambridge University Press, 1997). For critical studies on the tradition of innovative writing, see Marjorie Perloff, *Poetic License: Essays on Modernist and Postmodernist Lyric* (Evanston: Northwestern University Press, 1990); Stephen-Paul Martin, *Open Form and the Feminine Imagination: The Politics of Reading in Twentieth-Century Innovative Writing* (Washington, D.C.: Maisonneuve Press, 1988); Christopher Beach (ed.), *Artifice and Indeterminacy: An Anthology of New Poetics* (Tuscaloosa: University of Alabama Press, 1998).

16. The 1999 conferences include "The Page Mothers Conference," held in San Diego in March and featuring women writers who have also edited publications; "Where Lyric Tradition Meets Language Poetry: Innovation in Contemporary American Poetry," held at Barnard College in New York City in April. The organizers of the latter conference, Claudia Rankine and Allison Cummings, are both editing important collections of essays (from Wesleyan University Press and the University of California Press, respectively). For the texts of featured poets' and organizers' statements from this conference, see *Fence* 3, 1 (Spring-Summer, 2000): 87–127. But as Frances Richard observes in her foreword, it is "interesting" that the uptown Barnard Conference on women's poetry was "pitted against" the downtown People's Poetry Festival, which celebrated another historically marginalized group: "the people" (87).

"A Poetics of Emerging Evidence": Experiment in Kathleen Fraser's Poetry

1. "The Tradition of Marginality" (1989), in *Translating the Unspeakable: Poetry and the Innovative Necessity* (Tuscaloosa and London: University of Alabama Press, 2000), 27. Subsequent references to this collection of essays will be given in parentheses in the text.

2. "Introduction: Taking It On," in *Feminist Poetics*, ed. Kathleen Fraser (San Francisco: San Francisco State University, 1984), 7.

3. *il cuore : the heart* (Hanover and London: Wesleyan University Press, 1997). Subsequent references to *il cuore* will be given in parentheses in the text.

4. Critics have placed Fraser's work specifically in the context of modernist experimentation. Linda Kinnahan discusses her poetic project in relation to Williams, in *Poetics of the Feminine: Authority and Literary Tradition in William Carlos Williams, Mina Loy, Denise Levertov, and Kathleen Fraser* (Cambridge: Cambridge University Press, 1994), 218–236. Marianne DeKoven recovers Stein as Fraser's predecessor, in "Gertrude's Granddaughters," *Women's Review of Books* 4, no. 2 (1986): 13–14. Cynthia Hogue, following the poet's own lead, discusses Fraser in relation to H.D. See Fraser's essay, "The Blank Page: H.D.'s Invitation to Trust and Mistrust Language" (1997), in *Translating*, 53–62. See also by Cynthia Hogue, "'I am not of that feather': Kathleen Fraser's Postmodernist Poetics," in *H.D. and Poets After*, ed. Donna Hollenberg (Iowa City: University of Iowa Press, 2000); "'To Go Back to the Idea of Process': Form, Feminism, and Kathleen Fraser's Poetry," presented at the conference "Poetry and the Public Sphere," Rutgers University, April 1997 (available at http://english.rutgers.edu/fraser.htm); and "Infectious Ecstasy: On the Poetics of Performative Transformation," in *Women Poets of the Americas: Symposium of Critical Essays*, ed. Jacqueline Vaught Brogan and Cordelia Candelaria (Notre Dame: University of Notre Dame Press, 1999). Fraser herself acknowledges these predecessors, but more immediately writers of later generations—Lorine Niedecker, Charles Olson, George Oppen, Frank O'Hara, and Barbara Guest.

5. "Continuum and Instability" (rev. of Charles Alexander, *arc of light/dark matter*), *Talisman* (Spring 1994).

6. Interview with Cynthia Hogue, *Contemporary Literature* 39 (1998): 19.

7. This phrase comes from Fraser's comment concerning Barbara Guest's poem "Parachutes, My Love, Could Carry Us Higher": "The poet is not interested in one-dimensional revelation but in capturing this particular structure of difficulty" (*Translating* 128).

8. See Kinnahan's chapter on Fraser.

9. *Notes Preceding Trust* (Santa Monica, San Francisco: Lapis Press, 1987), 11, 16.

10. "Soft Pages," *Common Knowledge* 7, no. 2 (Fall 1998): 76.

11. Interview with Jack Foley, KPFA Radio, Berkeley, California, February 1998.

12. Interview with Hogue, 23.

13. "Thought, Split Inward" (rev. of *il cuore : the heart*), *Poetry Flash: A Poetry Review & Literary Calendar for the West*, no. 277 (June-July 1998): 17.

14. Fraser, *Translating*, 144; and Hogue, "'To Go Back to the Idea of Process.'"

15. Interview with Hogue, 15; see also Hogue's comments on "Etruscan Pages" in "'I am not of that feather,'" and in "'To Go Back to the Idea of Process.'"

16. *il cuore*, 118, 151, 185, 186, 188.

17. H.D., "The Walls Do Not Fall," in *Collected Poems, 1912–1944*, ed. Louis L. Martz (New York: New Directions, 1983), 509–10.

18. Hogue's very insightful comments on Fraser's literary relation to H.D., especially in "Etruscan Pages," emphasize her technical experimentation in constructing a feminist poetics. See note 15.

19. The phrase is an epigram to "frammenti romani," in *when new time folds up* (Minneapolis: Chad Press, 1993), 35.

20. Ibid., 64.

21. Hogue, "To Go Back to the Idea of Process."

22. "The Disappeared" was published in *Chelsea* 57 (1994).

23. Fraser's father was trained as an architect, and in an early poem ("La Reproduction Interdite") she speaks of claiming his tools after his sudden death, "each a potential source of precision and invention, given a hand to hold it" (*il cuore* 20). One can't help but imagine that the poem in some oblique way pays homage to this figure of craft and this point of loss.

24. I am indebted to Hogue's discussion of "WING" in "'I am not of that feather'"; see also Fraser's remarks in her interview with Hogue on "when new time" (21–22) and "WING" (24–26).

25. Interview with Hogue, 21.

26. Ibid.

27. Ibid., 24–26.

Asterisk: Separation at the Threshold of Meaning in the Poetry of Rae Armantrout

1. The most famous cases of poets slowing down their pace of publication may be Frank O'Hara and Ted Berrigan who, between them, wrote less than a dozen pages in the last few years of their lives. Steve Benson, Armantrout's contemporary, has published just two of his eight books since 1985, nothing in the 1990s.

2. Armantrout's work to date could be printed in a single 250-page volume without even resorting to Sun & Moon's undersized typography.

3. *The Collected Poems of Wallace Stevens* (New York: Vintage, 1982), 83. Ellipsis in the original.

4. Rae Armantrout, *Extremities* (Berkeley: The Figures, 1978), 15.

5. Imagine how much more complex this poem would become if it had been written in an era in which the interpretation of a lesbian wedding ceremony could be entertained.

6. At another level, Armantrout's title can be read as a verb, shifting its point of entry into the poem from "years" to the creation of the now-absent trail, very nearly a self-consuming artifact. Neither reading cancels the other out.

7. Rae Armantrout, *Made to Seem* (Los Angeles: Sun & Moon, 1995), 21–22.

8. Silence can exist only within sound—indeed, it is sound's "special case"—but sound is nothing more than a series of waves registering in time. Even if you could identify a specific point on the wavelength (a theoretical if not practical possibility), you could not "hear" it.

9. Roman Jakobson, "The Newest Russian Poetry: Velimir Xlebnikov [Excerpts]," in *My Futurist Years,* ed. Bengt Jangfeld, trans. Edward J. Brown (New York: Marsilio, 1997), 173–208. See especially pages 193 to the end.

10. It is part of the inherent logic of carrying the consonants forward that radically dissimilar words sound as if they were parts of a single root's conjugations.

11. Consider, for example, the famous ad slogan that Welch wrote for his "day job" in marketing: "Raid Kills Bugs Dead."

12. Try it. Alternate orderings don't just lead to a "different" poem, but to the unraveling of the text altogether.

13. Rae Armantrout, *Necromance* (Los Angeles: Sun & Moon, 1991), 27–28.

14. E-mail to the author, August 13, 1998.

15. One way to get a sense of how such bracketing works in general is to consider the poems of any poet with whose writing you have been long familiar once these works are jammed together into a collected edition that aggregates more than one piece to a page. It is not as though the writing of any given author isn't of a whole (not even Hank Lazer's programmatically schizoid *Doublespace*), but the margin about the poem, regardless of its size, is itself always already a part of the work. I find more than a few of these collected editions unreadable precisely because, in violating the space about the text, they leave a portion of the writing out, in much the same way as the omission of Catullus' Latin from its facing-page relation to Zukofsky's homophonic translations mars the Johns Hopkins edition of the *Complete Short Poetry.*

16. Rae Armantrout, *Precedence* (Providence: Burning Deck, 1985), 29–31. The second word in the title is deliberately lower case (as are the first letters of both the first and last sections) in order to heighten the contrast with the lines that appear entirely in caps.

17. Thus sections 32 and 33 of "Of Being Numerous" can be read as a single sentence. George Oppen, *Collected Poems* (New York: New Directions, 1975), 173.

Alice Notley's Experimental Epic: "An Ecstasy of Finding Another Way of Being"

1. Alice Notley, *The Descent of Alette* (New York: Penguin Books, 1996). All subsequent references to *Descent* will be given parenthetically in the text.

2. Susan Stanford Friedman, "Craving Stories," in *Feminist Measures* (Ann Arbor: University of Michigan Press, 1994), 20.

3. Friedman, "Craving Stories," 19.

4. H.D., "Eurydice," in *The Collected Poems: 1912–1944* (New York: New Directions, 1983), 55.

5. H.D., *Helen in Egypt* (New York: New Directions, 1961), 256.

6. Judith Butler, *Bodies That Matter: On the Discursive Limits of "Sex"* (New York: Routledge, 1993), 39.

7. Butler, *Bodies That Matter,* 40.

8. Teresa de Lauretis, *Alice Doesn't: Feminism, Semiotics, Cinema* (Bloomington: Indiana University Press, 1984), 109.

9. De Lauretis, *Alice Doesn't,* 112.

10. De Lauretis, *Alice Doesn't,* 118–19.

11. H.D., "Eurydice," 55.

12. Page duBois, *Sappho Is Burning* (Chicago: The University of Chicago Press, 1995), 117.

13. Tom Tykwer, *Run Lola Run* (Germany: Bavaria Film International, 1999).

14. Elizabeth Grosz, *Volatile Bodies: Toward a Corporeal Feminism* (Bloomington: Indiana University Press, 1994), 5.

15. DuBois, *Sappho Is Burning,* 84.

16. Hélène Cixous, "Castration or Decapitation?," *Signs* 43, no. 7 (1981): 41–55.

17. Alice Notley, "Epic and Women Poets," in *Disembodied Poetics,* ed. Anne Waldman and Andrew Schelling (Albuquerque: University of New Mexico Press, 1994), 106.

18. William Carlos Williams, "Spring & All," in *Imaginations* (1938), 101.

Intimacy and Experiment in Mei-Mei Berssenbrugge's *Empathy*

1. Theory on the emotions is obviously in a more complicated situation than I indicate. But even those still influenced by Michel Foucault like their emotions to be based on narrative scenarios because that makes them easier to deal with as social constructs deeply woven into prevailing ideologies. So for now it will have to suffice to say that we can distinguish two basic stances in philosophy that dominate the field, and which have more in common than either would like to admit. The approach with the greatest staying power has been what philosophers and psychologists call cognitivism. Its focus is on how emotions involve conceptual projections, which help us adapt to states of satisfaction and dissatisfaction and which provide necessary sorting principles facilitating our making practical judgments. Emotions provide reasons for action and make reason attentive to complex particulars, which, in turn, provide the elements for the plots that we use to interpret what the emotion is. Here the now-classic work is by Ronald de Sousa, *The Rationality of Emotion* (Cambridge: MIT Press, 1987). But there are many important refinements in books like Keith Oatley, *Best Laid Schemes* (Cambridge: Cambridge University Press, 1999), and in historical treatments of the emotions like Martha Nussbaum, *The Therapy of Desire* (Princeton: Princeton University Press, 1994).

The second basic contemporary perspective is "expressivist." Most expressivist theory is hermeneutic, focusing on what is involved in making emotions articulate and in determining how we can best engage such articulation. Some of the best work in this field is fundamentally psychoanalytic—notably John Deigh, "Cognitivism in the Theory of the Emotions," *Ethics* (1994): 824–54; and Richard Wollheim, *On the Emotions* (New Haven and London: Yale University Press, 1999). Sue Campbell, in *Interpreting the Personal: Expression and the Formation of Feelings* (Ithaca: Cornell University Press, 1997) develops a second hermeneutic perspective more consistent with the expressivist tradition stemming from Croce but put elegantly in relation to feminist political concerns. Her version of expressivism is less concerned with how we understand our emotions than with how our manner of enacting our affective concerns defines who we are and establishes possible lines of relation with other people. In my theoretical work I am trying to develop this "adverbial" approach by bringing to expressivist theory the arguments from Richard Moran's brilliant essay, "The Expression of Feeling in Imagination," *The Philosophical Review* 103 (1994): 75–106. Berssenbrugge matters for this project because hers is decidedly an adverbial approach to the rendering and understanding of affect.

2. I have seen one so far unpublished essay by Rob Kaufman from the book he is writing on this topic and I have engaged him in conversation about this book.

3. Mei-Mei Berssenbrugge, *Empathy* (New York: Station Hill Press, 1989), 68. Future references will be cited in parentheses within the text.

Towards a New Politics of Representation? Absence and Desire in Denise Chávez's *The Last of the Menu Girls*

1. Denise Chávez, *The Last of the Menu Girls* (Houston: Arte Público, 1990), 57. Further references cited in the text.

2. Both Annie O. Eysturoy, in *Daughters of Self-Creation: The Contemporary Chicana Novel* (Albuquerque: University of New Mexico Press, 1996), and Alma Quintana, in *Home Girls: Chicana Literary Voices* (Philadelphia: Temple University Press, 1996), describe *Menu Girls* as a novel. Rudolfo Anaya, in "Preface, to *Last of the Menu Girls*," n.p., and Bonnie TuSmith, in *All My Relatives: Community in Contemporary Ethnic American Literatures,* (Ann Arbor: University of Michigan Press, 1994), 176, argue that although the text is a collection of stories, the stories are so intimately interrelated that *Menu Girls* can and should be read as a novel. Debra Castillo, in *Talking Back: Toward a Latin American Feminist Literary Criticism* (Ithaca: Cornell University Press, 1992), 266, describes *Menu Girls* as a "sequence" of short stories. Douglas Anderson, in "Displaced Abjection and States of Grace: Denise Chávez's *The Last of the Menu Girls*," from *American Women Short Story Writers: A Collection of Critical Essays,* ed. Julie Brown (New York: Garland, 1995), 236, views it as a set of "interlocking stories." Renato Rosaldo, in *Criticism in the Borderlands: Studies in Chicano Literature, Culture, and Ideology,* eds. Héctor Calderón and Jose David Saldívar (Durham: Duke University Press, 1991), 93, describes *Menu Girls* as a short story cycle.

3. Denise Chávez, qtd. in Annie O. Eysturoy, "Denise Chávez," in *This Is About*

Vision: Interviews with Southwestern Writers, eds. John F. Crawford, William Balassi, and Annie O. Eysturoy (Albuquerque: University of New Mexico Press, 1990), 167.

4. Eliana Ortega and Nancy Saporta Sternbach, "At the Threshold of the Unnamed: Latina Literary Discourse in the Eighties," in *Breaking Boundaries: Latina Writing and Critical Readings,* ed. Asunción Horno-Delgado, Eliana Ortega, Nina M. Scott, and Nancy Saporta Sternbach (Amherst: University of Massachusetts Press, 1989), 13.

5. Tey Diana Rebolledo, *Women Singing in the Snow: A Cultural Analysis of Chicana Literature* (Tucson: University of Arizona Press, 1995), 108. Significantly, but not surprisingly, although Rebolledo cites *Menu Girls* in her bibliography of Chicana-authored texts, she does not mention it in *Women Singing in the Snow. Menu Girls* appears neither in her discussion of growing-up narratives nor elsewhere in her extensive survey of Chicana literature.

6. Rebolledo, *Women Singing,* 130.

7. Rey Chow, *Writing Diaspora: Tactics of Intervention in Contemporary Cultural Studies* (Bloomington: Indiana University Press, 1993), 24 (her emphasis).

8. Quoted in Annie O. Eysturoy, "Denise Chávez," 165.

9. I describe these characters as "girl/women" because they seem to exist in a liminal stage, on the cusp between childhood and adult life.

10. For discussions of the limited representations of female subjectivity available in masculinist discourse systems, see Teresa de Lauretis, "Sexual Indifference and Lesbian Representation," *Theatre Journal* 40 (1988): 155–77; Luce Irigaray, *Speculum of the Other Woman,* trans. Gillian C. Gill (Ithaca: Cornell University Press, 1985); and Linda Singer, "True Confessions: Cixous and Foucault on Sexuality and Power," *The Thinking Muse: Feminism and Modern French Philosophy,* eds. Jeffner Allen and Iris Marion Young (Bloomington: Indiana University Press, 1989), 136–55.

11. Rosaura Sánchez, "Reconstructing Chicana Gender Identity," *American Literary History* 9 (1997), 354. For another discussion of Chávez's conservatism, see Quintana, *Home Girls,* 105–7.

12. Rosaldo, "Fables of the Fallen Guy," 90.

13. For discussions of the heterosexist masculinist bias underlying western socio-symbolic systems, see Teresa de Lauretis, "Sexual Indifference and Lesbian Representation," and Marilyn R. Farwell, *Heterosexual Plots and Lesbian Narratives* (New York: New York University Press, 1996).

14. Teresa de Lauretis, "Film and the Visible," in *How Do I Look? Queer Film and Video,* ed. Bad Object-Choices (Seattle: Bay Press, 1991), 255.

15. See, for instance, "Last of the Menu Girls" and "Space Is a Solid."

16. Castillo, *Talking Back,* 268.

17. Alice Jardine, *Gynesis: Configurations of Woman and Modernity* (Ithaca: Cornell University Press, 1985), 118–19.

18. Peggy Phelan, *Unmarked: The Politics of Performance* (New York: Routledge, 1993), 13, 26, 27.

19. The pun is intentional.

Beyond the Frame of Whiteness: Harryette Mullen's Revisionary Border Work

1. Christine Stansell, "The Misogynists Got It Right," review of *Representing Women,* by Linda Nochlins, *London Review of Books,* 1 July 1999, 11.

2. Rachel Blau DuPlessis, "'Corpses of Poesy': Some Modern Poets and Some Gender Ideologies of Lyric," *Feminist Measures: Soundings in Poetry and Theory,* ed. Lynn Keller and Cristanne Miller (Ann Arbor: University of Michigan, 1994), 71.

3. Richard Dyer, "White," *Screen: the Journal of the Society for Education in Film and Television* 29 (1988): 44.

4. Harryette Mullen, "Optic White: Blackness and the Production of Whiteness," *Diacritics: A Review of Contemporary Criticism* 24, nos.2–3 (Summer-Fall 1994): 83.

5. Let me note here, however, that one of my first-year students picks up on the white woman's "shameless look," and suggests that the black woman "seems the more respectable and innocent, looking at the [white] woman with a questioning expression as if disgusted by her promiscuity and self-assuredness. This innocence is further brought across by the bouquet of flowers in her arms." Jennifer Silbert, journal entry 5 April 1999; quoted with permission.

6. Harryette Mullen, "Interview with Harryette Mullen," interview by Cynthia Hogue, *Postmodern Culture : An Electronic Journal of Interdisciplinary Criticism* 9, no. 1 (1999): 20; available at http://jefferson.village.virginia.edu/pmc/contents.all.html.

7. Harryette Mullen, *Tree Tall Woman* (Galveston, Texas: Earth Energy Communications, 1981); hereafter cited parenthetically in text, abbreviated as *TTW,* followed by page number.

8. Mullen, "Interview with Harryette Mullen," interview by Hogue, 3, 10.

9. Elizabeth A. Frost, "'Ruses of the lunatic muse': Harryette Mullen and Lyric Hybridity," *Women's Studies* 27 (1998): 465.

10. Harryette Mullen, *Muse & Drudge* (Philadelphia: Singing Horse Press, 1995), 1, 10.

11. Mullen, "Optic White," 88.

12. Mullen, "Interview with Harryette Mullen," interview by Hogue, 3.

13. Harryette Mullen, "The Solo Mysterioso Blues: An Interview with Harryette Mullen," interview by Calvin Bedient, *Callaloo* 19, no. 3 (1996): 652.

14. Frost, "Ruses," 466.

15. Mullen, "Interview with Harryette Mullen," interview by Hogue, 10.

16. Elizabeth Frost, "Interview with Harryette Mullen," *Contemporary Literature* 41, no. 3 (Fall 2000): 397–421. I take this opportunity to thank Elizabeth Frost for generously sharing this interview with me in manuscript.

17. Mullen, "Optic White," 74.

18. See Frost, "Ruses," 475.

19. Harryette Mullen, "Visionary Literacy: Art, Literature and Indigenous African Writing Systems" (lecture delivered at Intersection for the Arts, San Francisco, CA, May 24, 1993); quoted in Aldon Lynn Nielsen, *Black Chant: Languages of African-American Postmodernism* (New York: Cambridge University Press, 1997), 35.

20. Frost, "Ruses," 475.

21. Albert Murray, *The Omni-Americans: New Perspectives on Black Experience and American Culture* (New York: Outerbridge & Dienstfrey, 1970), 22 (Murray's italics); quoted in Frost, ibid., 479 n. 20.

22. Harryette Mullen, *Trimmings* (New York: Tender Buttons Press, 1991); hereafter cited parenthetically in text, abbreviated to a *T*, followed by page number.

23. See Elizabeth Frost, "Signifyin(g) on Stein: The Revisionist Poetics of Harryette Mullen and Leslie Scalapino." *Postmodern Culture: An Electronic Journal of Interdisciplinary Criticism* 5, no. 3 (May 1995); available at: http://jefferson.village.virginia.edu/pmc/contents.all.html. Although our readings of the Mullen poem differ, I am indebted to Frost's thorough discussion and direct readers to it. As Frost contends of Mullen's poem in *Trimmings*, her "play on Stein's famous 'rosy charm' is perhaps the most striking instance of her recasting of *Tender Buttons* so as to explore questions of race that Stein didn't take on in her poetry but made all too clear in 'Melanctha' " (20).

24. Gertrude Stein, *Tender Buttons*, ed. Carl Van Vechten (New York: Random House, 1962), 471; quoted in Frost, ibid.

25. See Lisa Ruddick, "A Rosy Charm: Gertrude Stein and the Repressed Feminine," in *Critical Essays on Gertrude Stein*, ed. Michael J. Hoffman (Boston: G. K. Hall, 1986), 225–40; discussed in Frost, ibid.

26. For an analysis of this dynamic in Donne, see Barbara L. Estrin, *Laura: Uncovering Gender and Genre in Wyatt, Donne, and Marvell* (Durham: Duke University Press, 1994), 149–226. For a foundational essay on readerly absorption, see Charles Bernstein, *A Poetics* (Cambridge, MA: Harvard University Press, 1992), 9–89.

27. See, for example, Victor Turner, "Betwixt and Between: The Liminal Period in *Rites de Passage*," *The Forest of Symbols* (Ithaca: Cornell University Press, 1994), 93–111.

28. Cf. Frost, "Signifyin(g)": "This passage uses the same technique of multiple meanings [as Stein's 'rosy charm' passage in *Tender Buttons*] and the connotation of innocence conjured by the color pink to point out the disturbing 'naked truth': 'pink' is 'a rosy charm' in the white world only when it's worn by someone 'pale,' 'white,' and 'sugary.' The one whose skin is 'ink' remains in shadow. She is, literally, incomplete: the word 'pink' minus the 'p' gives us 'ink.' And yet, she still has the power to signify— after all, writing is produced with 'ink' " (21).

Untranslatable Communities, Productive Translation, and Public Transport: Rosmarie Waldrop's *A Key into the Language of America* and Joy Harjo's *The Woman Who Fell from the Sky*

1. Leslie Scalapino, *The Public World / Syntactically Impermanence* (Hanover and London: Wesleyan University Press, 1999), 53.

2. Rosmarie Waldrop, *A Key into the Language of America* (New York: New Directions, 1994).

3. Joy Harjo, *The Woman Who Fell from the Sky* (New York: Norton, 1994).

4. Charles Baudelaire, *Paris Spleen*, trans. Louise Varèse, 1947 reprint (New York: New Directions, 1970), 1; *Oeuvres complètes*, ed. Claude Pichois, 2 vols. (Paris: Gallimard, Editions Pléiade, 1975), 277. The original reads as follows:

L'étranger

—*Qui aimes-tu le mieux, homme énigmatique, dis? Ton père, ta mère, ta soeur ou ton frère?*

—*Je n'ai ni père, ni mère, ni soeur, ni frère.*

—*Amis?*

—*Vous vous servez là d'une parole dont le sens m'est resté jusqu'à ce jour inconnu.*

—*Ta patrie?*

—*J'ignore sous quelle latitude elle est située.*

—*La beauté?*

—*Je l'aimerais volontiers, déesse et immortelle.*

—*L'or?*

—*Je le hais comme vous haïssez Dieu.*

—*Eh! Qu'aimes-tu donc, extraordinaire étranger?*

—*J'aime les nuages . . . les nuages qui passent . . . là-bas . . . là-bas . . . les merveilleux nuages!*

5. Jonathan Monroe, "Introduction: The Prose Poem as a Dialogical Genre," in *A Poverty of Objects: the Prose Poem and the Politics of Genre* (Ithaca: Cornell University Press, 1987), 15–42.

6. Ludwig Wittgenstein, *Philosophical Investigations,* trans. G. E. M. Anscombe (Oxford: Basil Blackwell, 1963).

7. I refer of course to the famous closing line of "To the Reader" ("Au lecteur")—counterpart of "The Stranger" as the opening poem of *The Flowers of Evil (Les fleurs du mal)*—which in the original reads: "Hypocrite lecteur, mon semblable, mon frère."

8. Max Horkheimer and Theodor Adorno, *Dialectic of Enlightenment,* trans. John Cumming (New York: Continuum, 1991).

9. Walter Benjamin, "Some Motifs in Baudelaire," *Charles Baudelaire: A Lyric Poet in the Era of High Capitalism,* trans. Harry Zohn (London: Verso, 1985), 107–54.

10. Ibid.

11. Charles Bernstein, "Revenge of the Poet-Critic," *My Way: Speeches and Poems* (Chicago and London: University of Chicago Press, 1999), 4.

"Nothing, for a Woman, is Worth Trying": A Key into the Rules of Rosmarie Waldrop's Experimentalism

1. The first cause of discontent, a consciousness that the absolute, ineffable, and transcendent are not in language and may be hidden by it, leads to techniques of disruption that explore the borders of silence. The second cause, the sense that pure

matter or energy, of which the human unconscious is part, defies formulation, leads to experiments that reject logic and, as in automatic writing, approach the conditions of pure flux. The third cause, a dramatically increased preoccupation with the world of physical things, which in their self-sufficiency are found to elude language, leads to techniques that foreground the strangeness of things and the materiality of the word as thing.

2. Waldrop's 1995 lecture "Form and Discontent" provides a recent example of a similarly systematized categorization of "wild" forms (*Diacritics* 26.3–4 [1996]: 54–62).

3. The first section of Waldrop's first volume, *The Aggressive Ways of the Casual Stranger* (New York: Random House, 1972), suggests that her own poetry in the 1960s was not experimental. It contains personally expressive lyrics concerning the domestic issues confronting a young wife, with titles like "And how do you see yourself, Mrs. Waldrop?" "Cleaning," "Menstruation," and "Insomnia."

4. *Ecstatic Occasions, Expedient Forms: 65 Leading Contemporary Poets Select and Comment on Their Poems,* ed. David Lehman (New York: Macmillan, 1987), 197.

5. "Rosmarie Waldrop," *Contemporary Authors Autobiographical Series,* Volume 30 (Detroit: Gale Research, 1998), 297.

6. Rosmarie Waldrop, "Thinking of Follows," *Moving Borders: Three Decades of Innovative Writing by Women,* ed. Mary Margaret Sloan (Jersey City, New Jersey: Talisman House, 1998), 615.

7. "Alarms & Excursions," *The Politics of Poetic Form: Poetry and Public Policy,* ed. Charles Bernstein (New York: ROOF, 1990), 65.

8. "Rosmarie Waldrop," *Contemporary Authors,* 308.

9. Rosmarie Waldrop, *A Key into the Language of America* (New York: New Directions, 1994), xix. Page numbers for subsequent references to this book will appear parenthetically in the text.

10. Comparison with Williams's book reveals that the phrases in bold are often slight modifications, not exact quotations from his text, and that most chapters contain additional material taken directly from Williams but not signaled in bold.

11. Roger Williams, *A Key into the Language of America,* ed. John J. Teunissen and Evelyn J. Hinz (Detroit: Wayne State University Press, 1973), 241.

12. Waldrop's sense of art's powers and limitations here, as well as the figure of the wound painted in red that figures them, is closely related to the work of Edmond Jabes, which she has translated for many years. An epigraph in *The Book of Questions* reads "Mark the first page of the book with a red marker. For, in the beginning, the wound is invisible" (*From the Book to the Book: An Edmond Jabes Reader,* trans. Rosmarie Waldrop [Hanover, NH: Wesleyan University Press, 1991], 31). Jabes is Jewish and his preoccupation with the wound has partly to do with Jewish history. He writes, "There is nothing at the threshold of the open page, it seems, but this wound of a race born of the book, whose order and disorder are roads of suffering. Nothing but this pain, whose past and whose permanence is also that of writing" (34). Translating the wound into writing, as the iodine painter does in Waldrop's *Key,* "is an act

of silence that makes it legible to us in its entirety" (Jabes quoted by Waldrop in "Silence, the Devil, and Jabes," *The Art of Translation,* ed. Rosmarie Waldrop [Boston: Northeastern University Press, 1989]), 230.

13. In *Unending Design: The Forms of Postmodern Poetry* (Ithaca: Cornell University Press, 1991), Joseph M. Conte usefully classifies postmodern extended poetic forms as either serial or procedural. A procedural form follows a system of arbitrary constraints which functions as a generative device.

Rules and Restraints in Women's Experimental Writing

1. Marcel Benabou, "Rule and Constraint," *Oulipo: A Primer of Potential Literature,* trans. and ed. Warren F. Motte Jr. (Nebraska, 1986), 40–41.

2. Ibid., 41.

3. Carla Harryman, "There Is Nothing Better Than a Theory," in *Animal Instincts* (Berkeley, CA: This Press, 1989), 94–95.

4. William James, "The Principals of Psychology," *William James: the Essential Writings,* ed. Bruce W. Wilshire (New York, 1984), 57.

5. Ibid., 57.

6. Ibid., 117.

7. Lyn Hejinian, *Writing As an Aid to Memory* (Berkeley, CA: The Figures, 1989), n.p.

8. Lyn Hejinian, personal correspondence with author, August 1999.

9. Kathy Acker, "Against Ordinary Language: The Language of the Body," *Kathy Acker: Bodies of Work* (London, England: Serpent's Tail Press, 1997), 150.

10. Acker writes in a footnote, "Here and throughout the rest of this article, whenever I use the phrase 'language game,' I am referring to Ludwig Wittgenstein's discussion of language games in *The Brown Book* (151). Acker's references to Wittgenstein are of interest to me both in respect to a larger consideration of her work as systems of "simpler language[s] than ours" (Wittgenstein, *The Brown Book)* and in respect to Wittgenstein's obvious considerations of the writings of William James, which would bear on further consideration of Acker's and Hejinian's projects.

11. Ibid., 148.

12. Ibid., 150.

13. Ibid., 150.

Im.age . . . Dis.solve: The Linguistic Image in the Critical Lyric of Norma Cole and Ann Lauterbach

1. For a highly informative study of French visual-cultural theory, see Martin Jay, *Downcast Eyes, The Denigration of Vision in 20th-Century French Thought* (Berkeley, CA: University of California Press, 1994). For an additional survey of critical-cultural theory in the visual arts, see Chris Jenks (ed.), *Visual Culture* (London: Routledge

Press, 1995). For a helpful source on the culture of advertising, see Robert Goldman and Stephan Papson, *Sign Wars* (New York: Guilford, 1996).

2. Norma Cole, "He Dreams of Me," *Moira* (Oakland, CA: O Books, 1995), 80; hereafter cited parenthetically in text, abbreviated as *M,* followed by page number.

3. Raul Ruiz, "Poetics of Cinema," quoted in Cole's *Desire & Its Double* (Saratoga, CA: Instress Press, 1998), n.p.

4. Luce Irigaray, *This Sex That Is Not One,* trans. Catherine Porter (New York: Cornell University Press, 1985), 9–22.

5. Cole, "Ruth," *Mars* (Berkeley, CA: Listening Chamber Press, 1994), 94; hereafter cited parenthetically in text as *Ms,* followed by page number.

6. Cole, "Interpellation," *Desire & Its Double,* n.p.

7. Cole, "The Provinces," *Metamorphopsia* (Elmwood, CT: Potes & Poets Press, 1988), 74.

8. Cole, "Aurora," *My Bird Book* (Los Angeles, CA: Littoral Press, 1991), 72.

9. Cole, "Destitution: A Tale," *My Bird Book,* 102.

10. Cole, "Starling," *My Bird Book,* 15.

11. Cole, "Method," Contrafact (Elmwood, CT: Potes & Poets Press, 1996), xlv.

12. Cole, "Paper House," *Metamorphopsia,* 34.

13. Cole, "The Coming of Sugar," *Contrafact,* xvi.

14. Cole, "Lens," *Contrafact,* xliii.

15. Cole, "Putting One's Self in a Situation," *Desire & Its Double,* n.p.

16. Jacques Derrida, "Memoires d'aveugle: L'autoportrait et autres ruines," in catalogue of exhibition at the Louvre's Napoleon Hall, October 26, 1990–January 21, 1991 (Paris, 1991), 2.

17. Ann Lauterbach, "Pragmatic Examples: The Nonce," *Moving Borders,* ed. Mary Margaret Sloan (Jersey City, NJ: Talisman House Press, 1998), 600.

18. Jean-François Lyotard, *The Postmodern Condition: A Report on Knowledge,* trans. Geoff Bennington and Brian Massumi (Minneapolis, MN: University of Minnesota Press, 1984), 78.

19. Ibid., 81.

20. Ibid., 82.

21. Lauterbach and Heather Ramsdell, "Conversations," *Murmur I* (New York: Duck Rabbit Press, 1998), 59.

22. Lauterbach, "Pragmatic Examples: The Nonce," *Moving Borders,* 600–601.

23. Ibid., 600.

24. Ibid., 600.

25. Wallace Stevens, "The Noble Rider and the Sound of Words," *The Necessary Angel* (New York: Random House, 1942), 36.

26. Lauterbach, "Eclipse with Object," *And for Example* (New York: Penguin, 1994), 3; hereafter cited parenthetically in text as *AFE,* followed by the page number.

27. Lauterbach, "How I Think About What I Write," *New American Writing 14,* ed. Paul Hoover and Maxine Chernoff (Mill Valley, CA: OINK! Press, 1996).

28. Ibid.

29. Lauterbach, "On (Thing)," *On a Stair* (New York: Penguin, 1996), 51.

30. Stevens, "Anecdote of the Jar," *The Collected Poems of Wallace Stevens* (New York: Random House, 1982), 76.

31. Lauterbach and Ramsdell, "Conversation," *Murmur I*, 59–60.

Postmodern Romance and the Descriptive Fetish of Vision in Fanny Howe's *The Lives of a Spirit* and Lyn Hejinian's *My Life*

1. An earlier version of Lyn Hejinian's *My Life* was published in 1980 by Burning Deck Press.

2. While little scholarship has been written about Fanny Howe's *The Lives of a Spirit*, much has been written on Hejinian's *My Life*, although never as a romance. For treatment of *My Life* as autobiography, see, for example, Hilary Clark, "The Mnemonics of Autobiography: Lyn Hejinian's *My Life*," *Biography* 14, no. 4 (Fall 1991): 315–35; and Juliana Spahr, "Resignifying Autobiography: Lyn Hejinian's *My Life*," *American Literature* 68, no. 1 (1996): 11–37. On the way in which *My Life* works as an experimental text, see David R. Jarraway, "*My Life* through the Eighties: The Exemplary L=A=N=G=U=A=G=E of Lyn Hejinian," *Contemporary Literature* 33, no. 2 (Summer 1992): 319–36; and Craig Douglas Dworkin, *Contemporary Literature* 36, no. 1 (Spring 1995): 58–81. For a study of Lyn Hejinian's writings, in general, as both experimental "Language" poetry and socially conscious feminism, see Megan Simpson, *Poetic Epistemologies: Gender and Knowing in Women's Language-Oriented Writing* (Albany, NY: SUNY Press, 2000); also see my own earlier article on the feminist aspects of Hejinian's writings, "Women, Narrative, Postmodernism: An Introduction to the Writings of Lyn Hejinian and Leslie Scalapino," *Private Arts* 10 (1996): 47–57.

3. Diane Elam, *Romancing the Postmodern* (New York: Routledge, 1992), 15.

4. This is classically exemplified by Gustave Flaubert in his description of "a pretty high-heeled shoe adorned with a black rose," in his short story, "Mémoires d'un fou," in *Oeuvres complètes*, vol. 1 (Paris: Seuil 1964), 230. Naomi Schor cites this description as an example of a "primal . . . scene of fetishism in Flaubert," in which the fetish of the shoe serves as a "screen object destined both to screen off and to gesture toward the unrepresentable memory of the actual sighting of the mother's genitals" (for which Schor suggests the "black rose" stands). See Schor's discussion of this Flaubert passage in "Fetishism and Its Ironies," *Fetishism as Cultural Discourse*, ed. Emily Apter and William Pietz (Ithaca, NY: Cornell University Press), 95–96.

5. The subject of fetishism, in the past decade, has moved beyond the more narrow subject of perverse pleasure and has been studied adroitly as a powerful source of literary representation. Feminist literary and cultural critics, in particular, have written on the icon of the female fetish as that which concretizes and symbolizes enigma, contradiction, and ambiguity. Several helpful articles on this topic include the essays in the Apter-Pietz volume, as well as Louise Kaplan, "Fits and Misfits: The Body of a Woman," *American Imago* 50, no. 4 (1993): 457–80; Marcia Ian, *Remember-*

ing the Phallic Mother: Psychoanalysis, Modernism and the Fetish (Ithaca, NY: Cornell University Press, 1993); and Anne McClintock, "Screwing the System: Sexwork, Race, and the Law," *Feminism and Postmodernism,* ed. Margaret Ferguson and Jennifer Wicke (Durham, NC: Duke University Press, 1994), 103–28.

6. For a discussion of the relationship of romance to metafiction, focusing on the romance techniques of John Barth, see Daniel Green, "Metafiction and Romance," *Studies in American Fiction* 19, no. 2 (1991): 229–42.

7. Kaplan links the model of female hysteria, as studied by early psychoanalysis, to fetishism in her article "Fits and Misfits: The Body of a Woman," 459.

8. See Schor, "Female Fetishism: The Case of George Sand," *Poetics Today* 6, no. 1–2 (1985): 303.

9. Ibid., 306–7 (Schor's emphasis).

10. Deborah Ross, in *The Excellence of Falsehood: Romance, Realism, and Women's Contribution to the Novel* (University of Kentucky Press, 1991), speculates that literate women of class privilege during the seventeenth century might have been drawn to the romance because its narratives of desire, which end in romantic fulfillment, "provided an imaginative escape from what for most of them, in a time of arranged marriages, must have been an emotionally dreary life" (3).

11. The romance was attacked as trivial and "feminine," writes Ross; its detractors during the seventeenth century were "linked in serious critical condemnations" of the form (1). Critics like Nicolas Boileau condemned French romances for creating "falsehoods" about "both the past and the present" (Ross 2). Later critics like Samuel Johnson "blamed his boyhood habit of reading romances"—here Ross quotes Johnson's biographer James Boswell—"for 'that unsettled turn of mind which prevented his ever fixing in any profession'" (Ross 3).

12. Richard Chase, in *The American Novel and Its Tradition* (Baltimore: Johns Hopkins University Press, 1957), first established the importance of the romance genre to nineteenth-century American developments of the novel. Chase suggests that authors like Hawthorne, Herman Melville, and Henry James preferred the romance because it offered them a "freer" and "more daring" fictional mode than "the solid moral inclusiveness and massive equability of the English novel" (viii).

13. Fanny Howe, *The Lives of a Spirit* (Los Angeles: Sun & Moon Press, 1987), 13. All other references are parenthetically cited.

14. Terrence Martin, "The Romance," *The Columbia History of the American Novel,* ed. Emory Elliot et al. (New York: Columbia University Press, 1991), 78.

15. Henry James, 1908 Preface, *The American* (New York: Norton).

16. Ian, 6.

17. Nathaniel Hawthorne, "The Haunted Mind," quoted in Martin (76). Martin describes this "world" as a state of mind reached in "an hour of the night when one wakes suddenly into a world of scattered dreams . . . when yesterday has vanished and tomorrow has not yet emerged, a 'neutral ground,' according to Hawthorne, or 'intermediate space where the business of life does not intrude'" (Martin 76).

18. Hejinian uses this term when meditating on the effect of description in her

essay, "Strangeness," *Artifice and Indeterminacy: An Anthology of New Poetics,* ed. Christopher Beach (University of Alabama Press, 1998), 140–54.

19. Lyn Hejinian, *My Life* (Los Angeles: Sun & Moon Press, 1987), 1. All other references are parenthetically cited.

20. "Billy Budd, Sailor," *Forms of the Novella: Ten Short Novels,* ed. David H. Richter (New York: Knopf, 1981), 88.

21. Ibid., 83.

22. Ibid., 721. Melville adds: "The avowal of such an imperfection in the Handsome Sailor should be evidence not alone that he is not presented as a conventional hero, but also that the story in which he is the main figure is no romance."

23. For a commentary on *My Life*'s challenge to the autobiography genre, "where the conventions of representation are narrative, where text 'uncovers' a visible and essentially legible self," see Spahr, "Resignifying Autobiography," (139). Clark, too, in "The Mnemonics of Autobiography," focuses upon the way in which *My Life* resists the chronological development that autobiography traditionally assumes, an act that is important for the woman writer: "Hejinian specifically shows us the ways by which a woman writer remembers when she challenges dominant discursive practices. . . . " (Clark 316).

24. Sometimes a novel can be both a romance and a domestic novel, as might be argued is the case in Jane Austen's works.

25. Charles Bernstein, "Artifice of Absorption," *A Poetics* (Cambridge, MA: Harvard University Press, 1992), 9.

26. Ibid.

27. Gertrude Stein, "Composition as Explanation," *Selected Writings of Gertrude Stein,* ed. Carl Van Vechten (New York: Vintage, 1972), 518.

28. Ibid., 517.

"Drawings with Words": Susan Howe's Visual Poetics

1. Works by Susan Howe are cited parenthetically in the text using the following abbreviations: *BM—The Birth-mark: Unsettling the Wilderness in American Literary History* (Hanover, N.H.: University Press of New England, 1993); *ET—The Europe of Trusts* (Los Angeles: Sun and Moon Press, 1990); *I—*"An Interview with Susan Howe" (by Lynn Keller), *Contemporary Literature* 36, no. 1 (1995): 1–34; *MED—My Emily Dickinson* (Berkeley: North Atlantic Books, 1985); *NM—The Nonconformist's Memorial* (Hanover, N.H.: University Press of New England, 1993); *S—Singularities* (Hanover, N.H.: University Press of New England, 1990).

2. Rachel Blau DuPlessis, *The Pink Guitar: Writing as Feminist Practice* (New York: Routledge, 1990), 132.

3. DuPlessis, " 'A White Fiction': A Woman and a Page," *Temblor,* no. 10 (1989), 168, 170; Nathaniel Mackey, *Discrepant Engagements: Dissonance, Cross-Culturality, and Experimental Writing* (New York: Cambridge University Press, 1993), 123; Michael Davidson, *Ghostlier Demarcations: Modern Poetry and the Material Word* (Berkeley: University of California Press, 1997), 68, 92. For a companion essay to DuPlessis', see

Cole Swensen, "Against the Limits of Language: The Geometries of Anne-Marie Al-biach and Susan Howe," in *Moving Borders: Three Decades of Innovative Writing by Women*, ed. Mary Margaret Sloan (Jersey City, N.J.: Talisman House, 1998), 630–41.

4. Craig Douglas Dworkin, "'Waging political babble': Susan Howe's Visual Prosody and the Politics of Noise," *Word & Image* 12, no. 4 (1996), 391–93.

5. Willard Bohn, *The Aesthetics of Visual Poetry 1914–1928* (New York: Cambridge University Press, 1986); Johanna Drucker, *The Visible Word: Experimental Typography and Modern Art, 1909–1923* (Chicago: University of Chicago Press, 1994).

6. George Butterick was the editor of numerous Olson texts, most relevantly *The Maximus Poems* and *The Collected Poems of Charles Olson* (Berkeley: University of California Press, 1983 and 1987 respectively).

7. Kathleen Fraser, *Translating the Unspeakable: Poetry and the Innovative Necessity* (Tuscaloosa: University of Alabama Press, 2000), 176, 177. The quotations are drawn from the essay "Translating the Unspeakable: Visual Poetics, As Projected through Olson's 'Field' into Current Female Practice"; for a related essay on women's visual poetics, see Fraser's "Line. On the Line. Lining up. Lined with. Between the Lines. Bottom line," *Translating the Unspeakable*, 141–60.

8. DuPlessis, "'A White Fiction,'" 170.

9. DuPlessis, *Pink Guitar*, 133.

10. Howe, "Speaking with Susan Howe," *The Difficulties* 3, no. 2 (1989), 42.

11. Howe, untitled contribution to *The Line in Postmodern Poetry*, ed. Robert Frank and Henry Sayre (Urbana: University of Illinois Press, 1988), 209. For an extended meditation on the incandescent materiality of words and letters, relevant to Howe's comment that words "shimmer," see Michel Leiris' 1948 "Alphabet," in *Scratches*, trans. Lydia Davis (Baltimore: Johns Hopkins University Press, 1991), 31–63.

12. Keller, introduction to "Interview with Susan Howe," 1.

13. All uncited quotations in this paragraph are from *NM*, 82. "To the Queen of my Heart" can be found in *The Complete Poetical Works of Percy Bysshe Shelley*, ed. Edward Dowden (New York: Thomas Y. Crowell, 1900), 674, with the following editorial note: "Printed as Shelley's by Medwin; reprinted by Mrs. Shelley, first edition of 1839, but subsequently withdrawn as of doubtful genuineness." Thus Howe ends the "Eikon Basilike" with an allusion to yet another obscure inauthentic text. My thanks to Jerome McGann for his help in tracking down the "Shelley" poem.

14. For one apposite example of this widely proposed applicability of Kristevan theory to contemporary avant-garde poetics, see Fraser, "Translating the Unspeakable," 175, who connects visual experimentation in contemporary women poets with "the very female subjectivity proposed by Julia Kristeva as linking cyclical and monumental time." See also, more ambivalently, DuPlessis, *Pink Guitar*, 84–88. Contrast, however, Peter Middleton's argument that Kristeva offers "a theory whose definitions of language and rationality are far too narrow" to account for Howe's work, "On Ice: Julia Kristeva, Susan Howe and Avant Garde Poetics," in *Contemporary Poetry Meets Modern Theory*, ed. Antony Easthope and John O. Thompson (Toronto: University of Toronto Press, 1991), 81–95.

15. The first of these quotations appears in the poem's original edition, *Defenes-*

tration of Prague (New York: Kulchur Foundation, 1983), 75, at the bottom right corner of a large (ten-by seven-inch) page, disconnected from all other text on the page.

16. Cf. McGann, *Black Riders,* 102, for whom Howe specifically breaks down "the law of the margin (left to right reading) and the law of headers and footers (top to bottom reading)."

17. For a book-length extrapolation of Howe's arguments about visual materiality in Dickinson's manuscripts, see Marta L. Werner, *Emily Dickinson's Open Folios: Scenes of Reading, Surfaces of Writing* (Ann Arbor: University of Michigan Press, 1995). McGann, *Black Riders,* 38, shares Howe's position that Dickinson's manuscripts should be seen as "potentially significant *at the aesthetic or expressive level.*"

18. Howe, "Women and Their Effect in the Distance," *Ironwood* 14, no. 2 (1986), 79.

19. DuPlessis, *Pink Guitar,* 136.

20. Rae Armantrout, *Necromance* (Los Angeles: Sun and Moon Press, 1991), 43.

21. R. P. Blackmur, *Language as Gesture: Essays in Poetry* (New York: Columbia University Press, 1981), 49.

"Bodies Written Off": Economies of Race and Gender in the Visual/Verbal Collaborative Clash of Erica Hunt's and Alison Saar's *Arcade*

1. Robyn Wiegman, *American Anatomies: Theorizing Race and Gender* (Durham: Duke University Press, 1995), 21.

2. "Collaborative Statement," Erica Hunt and Alison Saar, *Arcade* (Berkeley: Kelsey St. Press, 1996), 53. All quotes from Hunt's work and visual images by Saar will be taken from this volume, unless otherwise noted. Page numbers will be indicated parenthetically.

3. "The Poetics of Soul: Art for Everyone," in bell hooks, *Art on My Mind: Visual Politics* (New York: The New Press, 1995), 13, 16–17. See also in the same volume her interview with Saar, "Talking Art With Alison Saar," 22–34.

4. *Local History* (New York: Roof Books, 1993). The quote in reference to Hunt's first book is by Charles Bernstein, found on the back cover of *Local History.*

5. "The Poetics of Soul: Art for Everyone," 11. hooks focuses upon Saar as an example of such decolonizing practice.

6. Hunt, "Notes for an Oppositional Poetics," *The Politics of Poetic Form: Poetry and Public Policy,* ed. Charles Bernstein (New York: Roof, 1990), 200.

7. Hunt, "Notes for an Oppositional Poetics," 205, 200. Hunt theorizes *contiguity* as "textual and social practice," referring to the relationship of oppositional groups and textual practices.

8. Ibid., 198.

9. Wiegman, 22.

10. For example, see Hazel Carby's "Policing the Black Woman's Body in an Ur-

ban Context" (in *Identities*, eds. Kwame Anthony Appiah and Henry Louis Gates [Chicago: University of Chicago Press, 1995], 115–32) for a discussion of urbanization and the "discourse of black female sexuality" attending the migration of black, working-class women to American cities (124). Carby's essay, focusing upon the twenties, nonetheless carries forward important implications for the "major discursive elements" continuing to define black female urban behavior as pathological in the public mind and policy decisions (117).

11. See hooks, p. 117, for discussion of this point. Also, my thanks to Cara Cilano for alerting me to the context of Josephine Baker in relation to representations of the raced and gendered body, and for splendid discussions of these issues with our students.

12. Jonathan Crary, *Techniques of the Observer: On Vision and Modernity in the Nineteenth Century* (Cambridge, MA, and London: MIT Press, 1990), 352; quoted in Wiegman, 36.

13. Wiegman, 32.

14. Ibid., 10.

15. bell hooks, "Selling Hot Pussy: Representations of Black Female Sexuality in the Cultural Marketplace," in *The Politics of Women's Bodies: Sexuality, Appearance, and Behavior*, ed. Rose Weitz (New York: Oxford University Press, 1998), 117.

16. Wiegman, 12.

17. Ibid., 6.

18. Donald Lowe, *The Body in Late-Capitalist USA* (Durham: Duke University Press, 1995), 103.

19. Wiegman, 41.

20. See hooks, "Selling Hot Pussy."

21. Hunt, "Notes on an Oppositional Poetics," 201.

22. Hunt, "After Baudelaire's 'The Muse for Hire,'" 41.

23. Wiegman, 4.

"In Another Tongue": Body, Image, Text in Theresa Hak Kyung Cha's Dicteé

1. Shelley Sunn Wong, "Unnaming the Same: Theresa Hak Kyung Cha's *DIC-TEE*," in *Feminist Measures: Soundings in Poetry and Theory*, ed. Lynn Keller and Cristanne Miller (Ann Arbor: University of Michigan Press, 1994), 46.

2. Theresa Hak Kyung Cha, *Dictée* (Berkeley: Third Woman Press, 1995), n.p. Subsequent references cited parenthetically. Elaine H. Kim notes that the lines are apocryphal ("Poised on the In-between: A Korean American's Reflections on Theresa Hak Kyung Cha's *Dictée*," in *Writing Self Writing Nation: A Collection of Essays on DICTEE by Theresa Hak Kyung Cha*, ed. Elaine H. Kim and Norma Alarcón [Berkeley: Third Woman Press, 1994], n. 3, 66).

3. Johanna Drucker, *Figuring the Word: Essays on Books, Writing, and Visual Poetics* (New York: Granary Books, 1998), 57. Other feminist writers experimenting with

text and image include Drucker, Hannah Weiner, Erica Hunt, Leslie Scalapino, and others.

4. The phrase is from LeRoi Jones' "Black Art." See Michael Bibby, *Hearts and Minds: Bodies, Poetry, and Resistance in the Vietnam Era* (New Brunswick: Rutgers University Press, 1996), 29ff, for a discussion of this poem and corporeality in black liberation poetry.

5. Charlotte Furth, *A Flourishing Yin: Gender in China's Medical History, 960–1665* (Los Angeles: University of California Press, 1999), 13–14.

6. Kim, 14, 15.

7. Shu-mei Shih, "Nationalism and Korean American Women's Writing: Theresa Hak Kyung Cha's *Dictee*," in *Speaking the Other Self: American Women Writers*, ed. Jeanne Campbell Reesman (Athens: University of Georgia Press, 1997), 150.

8. Shih, 154. Cha's evocations of such bodily sacrifice suggest parallels with resistance literature in the West, as shown by Bibby and by Kim Whitehead in *The Feminist Poetry Movement* (Jackson: University Press of Mississippi, 1996): "Just as Black Liberationists essentialized race as corporeal, many feminists essentialized gender so that Women's Liberation was construed as a movement organized against the oppression that all women were subjected to principally on the basis of their sexual anatomy" (Bibby, 92). Whitehead discusses the politics of transparency in the work of such poets as Judy Grahn, June Jordan, and Minnie Bruce Pratt. Concerning avant-garde poetry and women writers of color, see my "'Ruses of the Lunatic Muse': Harryette Mullen and Lyric Hybridity," *Women's Studies* 27 (1998): 465–81.

9. Judith Butler, *Bodies That Matter: On the Discursive Limits of "Sex"* (New York: Routledge, 1993), xi–xii, 9 (Butler's emphasis). Concerning the diseuse, Shih explores "the coexistence of the corporeal and the symbolic in Cha's signifying system," calling the diseuse one who "has no voice of her own and as a medium only transmits other voices" (154, 155). L. Hyun Yi Kang argues in "The 'Liberatory Voice' of Theresa Hak Kyung Cha's *Dictée*" (in *Writing Self*) that from a "diseuse" one expects "a fluid oral performance," yet Cha presents "a lengthy description of a female subject struggling to articulate herself" (76).

10. Furth, 19–20.

11. Judith Farquhar, "Multiplicity, Point of View, and Responsibility in Traditional Chinese Healing," in *Body, Subject, and Power in China*, ed. Angela Zito and Tani E. Barlow (Chicago: University of Chicago Press, 1994), 81–82, 85.

12. Furth, 21, refers to Nathan Sivin, *Traditional Medicine in Contemporary China: A Partial Translation of "Revised Outline of Chinese Medicine" (1972) with an Introductory Study on Change in Present-Day and Early Medicine* (Ann Arbor: Center for Chinese Studies, University Michigan, 1987), 5–37.

13. Juliana Spahr, "Postmodernism, Readers, and Theresa Hak Kyung Cha's *Dictée*," *College Literature* 23.2 (1996): 30.

14. Spahr, 30; Walter Benjamin, "The Task of the Translator," in *Illuminations: Essays and Reflections*, ed. Hannah Arendt, trans. Harry Zohn (New York: Schocken Books, 1968), 79, 75, 77.

15. Julia Kristeva, *Powers of Horror: An Essay on Abjection*, trans. Leon S. Roudiez (New York: Columbia University Press, 1982), 2, 4.

Painful Bodies: Kathy Acker's Last Texts

1. Audiences at the Midwest Modern Language Association Conference, 1997 and the Twentieth-Century Literature Conference, 1999 helped to shape my thinking about Kathy Acker's work. For his intellectual rigor and incisive critiques of my work, I am grateful to Alex Hinton. My gratitude goes to Cynthia Hogue for her inspiration as a writer and a scholar. Laura Hinton's enthusiasm and encouragement about this project were invaluable. Recent conversations about Kathy Acker with Victoria Pitts provided crucial insights from a new perspective. Finally, for her long and deep engagement with my work and for her friendship, I owe great thanks to Pamela Barnett.

2. Kathy Acker, *Blood and Guts in High School* (New York: Grove Press, 1978), 97.

3. For a sustained examination of physical pain and its relationship with language, see Elaine Scarry, *The Body in Pain: The Making and Unmaking of the World* (New York: Oxford University Press, 1985).

4. Acker, "Devoured by Myths: An Interview with Sylvère Lotringer," *Hannibal Lecter, My Father* (New York: Semiotext(e), 1991), 21.

5. Paul Smith, *Discerning the Subject* (Minneapolis: University of Minnesota Press, 1988), 106.

6. Acker, "Devoured by Myths: An Interview with Sylvère Lotringer," 7.

7. Acker, "Devoured by Myths: An Interview with Sylvère Lotringer," 7. For a compelling reading of autobiography in terms of the construction of identity, see Leigh Gilmore's study, *Autobiographics: A Feminist Theory of Women's Self-Representation* (Ithaca: Cornell University Press, 1994), which speaks of autobiographical texts as "site[s] of identity production; as texts that both resist and produce cultural identities" (4).

8. Zeiger looks closely at the gender dynamics of the myth in her study *Beyond Consolation: Death, Sexuality, and the Changing Shapes of Elegy* (Ithaca: Cornell University Press, 1997), 2–3.

9. Acker, "Eurydice in the Underworld," *Eurydice in the Underworld* (London: Arcadia Books, 1997), 1.

10. Ibid., 1–2.

11. Ibid., 6.

12. Ibid., 11–12.

13. Ibid., 14.

14. Acker, "Devoured by Myths: An Interview with Sylvère Lotringer," 5.

15. Acker, "Eurydice in the Underworld," 21.

16. Ibid., 24–25.

17. Ibid., 25.

18. For Acker's developed argument about the Internet and its political possibilities, see her essay "Writing, Identity and Copyright in the Net Age" (*Bodies of Work:*

Essays by Kathy Acker. London: Serpents Tail Press, 1997). Had she lived to pursue this line of questioning, her texts might have continued to be mediated by this technology in more and more complicated ways.

19. Acker, "The Gift of Disease," "(1997) http://acker.thehub.com.au/gift/html, np.
20. Ibid., np.
21. See Diane Elam's study *Romancing the Postmodern* (New York: Routledge, 1992), in which she links Acker's plagiarism to "a postmodern understanding of reproductive rights" and reads Acker's appropriation of other texts as "an attack on literary paternity."
22. See Harold Schweizer's study *Suffering and the Remedy of Art* (Albany: SUNY Press, 1997) for an analysis of how language mediates suffering in a range of twentieth-century texts.
23. Acker, "The Gift of Disease," np.
24. Sadly, the health care industry is an integral part of this "business." Acker's lack of health insurance affected her cancer treatment. An e-mail sent out over a large literature list-serve in November 1997 noted Acker's treatment at American Biologics, an alternative therapy center in Tijuana, Mexico and described her financial crisis and asked for assistance with her large medical bills. The John Giorno Fund for Artists with AIDS in New York took contributions to help with Acker's expenses.
25. Acker, "The Gift of Disease," np (emphasis mine).
26. In another essay, "Bodies of Work," from the volume of that title, Acker explores the connection between language and the body by reading bodybuilding through Wittgenstein's theories of language games: "For bodybuilding (a language of the body) rejects ordinary language and yet itself constitutes a language . . . (*Bodies of Work*, 148).
27. Acker, "The Gift of Disease," np.

"Eyes in All Heads": Anne Waldman's Performance of Bigendered Imagination in *Iovis 1*

1. Anne Waldman, *IOVIS I* (Minneapolis, MN: Coffee House Press, 1993), 1; hereafter cited parenthetically in text as *I*, followed by the page number.
2. Gertrude Stein, "Rooms," *Tender Buttons, Selected Writings of Gertrude Stein,* ed. Carl Van Vechten (New York: Vintage/Random House, 1990), 498.
3. Anne Waldman, interview by author conducted through e-mail correspondence, 27 March 1999.
4. "Anne Waldman," *Contemporary Authors Autobiography Series,* vol. 17 (Detroit, MI: Gale Research), 291.
5. Anne Waldman, *IOVIS II* (Minneapolis, MN: Coffee House Press, 1997), 311.
6. The concept of "dissipative structures" is discussed in Ilya Prigogine and Isabelle Stengers, *Order Out of Chaos: Man's New Dialogue With Nature* (New York: Bantam, 1984), 12–14.
7. Anne Waldman, *Fast Speaking Woman* (San Francisco, CA: City Lights Books,

1996), 127; hereafter cited parenthetically in text as *FSW,* followed by the page number.

8. Charles Olson, *Selected Writings,* ed. Robert Creeley (New York: New Directions, 1966), 16.

9. The phrase "eyes in all heads" connotes for Waldman her own "confirmation" as a young poet during a 1965 marathon reading by Charles Olson in Berkeley. Olson used this phrase as follows: "No hierarchies but natural ones no such many as mass there are only eyes in all heads to be looked out of"; Waldman partially appropriated these lines in her own poem "Eyes in All Heads To Be Looked Out Of" (*Helping the Dreamer: New and Selected Poems 1966–1988,* 242–45), which was written on her birthday to commemorate her vocation and her poetic connection to Olson. For Waldman, "eyes in all heads" suggests nonhierarchical insight that can be represented through the third eyes, or wisdom eyes, of many-headed Tibetan deities. The multiplication of eyes suggests multiple subjectivities, intensities of vision, and dissolution of ego, all of which are connected to the occurrence of psychic rebirth. A more extensive discussion of the Olson's influence on Waldman can be found in my dissertation, *Spectacular Margins: Women Poets Refigure the Epic,* which examines Waldman's and Alice Notley's work in long-form poems.

10. Waldman's comments in Jerome Rothenberg and Pierre Joris, *Poems for the Millennium, Volume Two* (Berkeley, CA: University of California Press, 1998), 751.

11. Alice Notley, "Iovis omnia plena," review of *IOVIS* Books I and II, *Chicago Review* 44, 1 (Winter 1998): 129.

12. Anne Waldman, interview by author conducted through e-mail correspondence, 27 March 1999.

13. See Barbara G. Walker, *The Woman's Encyclopedia of Myths and Secrets* (San Francisco, CA: Harper & Row, 1983), 1026.

14. Alicia Ostriker's important feminist and historical study, *Stealing the Language: The Emergence of Women's Poetry in America* (1986), includes a chapter on this subject titled "Divided Selves: The Quest for Identity" (59–90). This work argues that the "quest for autonomous self-definition" catalyzed the women's poetry movement during the 1960s and 1970s, when increasing numbers of women poets claimed the cultural authority to resist patriarchal domination by empowering themselves on and off the page. While the surge of women asserting their poetic voices as a mark of empowerment and identity has had a profound effect on late 20-century American poetry, increasing numbers of women experimentalists began in the 1980s to refigure the notion of the "split" self as a critique of culturally sanctioned notions of identity or an affirmation of boundless possibility (represented, for example, through multiple subjectivity). These strategies take a more complex approach to the problem of female silence as a political, historical, and psychosocial phenomenon. Waldman's and Alice Notley's refiguring of the split self in their long and epic poems is the subject of my study, *Spectacular Margins: Women Poets Refigure the Epic.* Other poets, including Lyn Hejinian, Kathleen Fraser, Beverly Dahlen, Rachel Blau DuPlessis, and Susan Howe have taken up this issue in their experimental projects.

15. Federico García Lorca, *In Search of Duende*, ed. Christopher Maurer, (New York: New Directions, 1998), ix.

16. Shoshana Felman, *The Literary Speech Act: Don Juan with J. L. Austin, or Seduction in Two Languages*, trans. Catherine Porter, (Ithaca, NY: Cornell University Press, 1983), 148.

"Sonic Revolutionaries": Voice and Experiment in the Spoken Word Poetry of Tracie Morris

1. Morris, *Intermission* (New York: Soft Skull Press, 1998), 52.

2. Morris, preface to *Intermission*. This first full-length volume of Morris's poetry was preceded by a chapbook, *Chap-t-her Won: Some Poems by Tracie Morris* (Brooklyn: TM Ink, 1992).

3. Bob Holman, *The United States of Poetry* (New York: Harry N. Abrams, Inc., 1996); Miguel Algarín and Bob Holman, eds., *ALOUD: Voices from the NuYorican Poets Café* (New York: Owl Books, 1994).

4. Morris, *Intermission*, 50.

5. Geneva Smitherman, *Talkin and Testifyin: The Language of Black America* (Detroit: Wayne State University Press, 1986), 43.

6. Morris, *Intermission*, preface.

7. Ibid., 51.

8. Ibid., 51.

9. Interview with the author, Brooklyn, NY, 14 August, 1999 (the day after Morris's performance at the Brooklyn Academy of Music). All quotations from Morris are taken from the interview with the author, unless otherwise indicated.

10. Morris, *Intermission*, 53.

11. See Marjorie Perloff, "Language Poetry and the Lyric Subject: Ron Silliman's *Albany*, Susan Howe's *Buffalo*," *Critical Inquiry* 25 (1999): 405–34. Perloff points out that "One of the cardinal principles—perhaps *the* cardinal principle—of American Language poetics (as of the related current in England, usually labeled 'linguistically innovative poetries') has been the dismissal of 'voice' as the foundational principle of lyric poetry" (405).

12. The term "representative verse" was suggested by Charles Bernstein in his keynote talk on "Unrepresentative Verse" at the "Poetry and the Public Sphere" conference held at Rutgers University in April 1997.

13. Harryette Mullen, "African Signs and Spirit Writing," *Callaloo* 19, no. 3 (1996): 670–89.

14. Roland Barthes, "The Grain of the Voice," *Image, Music, Text*, trans. Stephen Heath (New York: Hill & Wang, 1977), 181.

15. Maria Damon, "When the NuYoricans Came to Town: (Ex)Changing Poetics," *XCP: Cross Cultural Poetics* 1 (1997): 16–40.

16. Adalaide Morris, *Sound States: Innovative Poetics and Acoustical Technologies* (Chapel Hill: University of North Carolina Press, 1997), 10.

17. Jed Rasula, in Morris, *Sound States*, 285.

18. Morris, "Project Princess," in Holman, 26.

19. Evelyn McDonnell, "Divas Declare a Spoken-Word Revolution," *Ms. Magazine* (Jan/Feb 1996): 78.

20. Damon, "When the NuYoricans Came to Town," 35.

21. Morris, *Intermission*, 36, 54.

22. Maria Damon, "Was That "Different," "Dissident" or "Dissonant"? Poetry (n) the Public Spear: Slams, Open Readings, and Dissident Traditions," in Charles Bernstein, ed., *Close Listening: Poetry and the Performed Word* (New York: Oxford University Press, 1998), 324–42.

23. Morris performed "Anthony Baez" at "Poetry and the Public Sphere: A Conference on Contemporary Poetry," held at Rutgers University, New Brunswick, NJ, on April 24, 1997.

24. Nick Yasinski, "To Make Something Happen: Activist Impulses in Contemporary American Poetry" (Ph.D. diss., Rutgers University, 1998), 158.

25. Morris performed the "chain gang" and "heaven" poems at the People's Poetry Gathering in New York City, April 1999.

26. Morris, *Intermission*, 33.

27. Elin Diamond, "Tight Spaces, Temporal Awakenings in Recent Feminist Performance," paper delivered at the Women in the Public Sphere Seminar at Rutgers University, New Brunswick, NJ, April, 1998. A version of this paper appears in *Power, Practice, Agency: Working Papers from the Women in the Public Sphere Seminar*, ed. Marianne DeKoven (New Brunswick, NJ: Institute for Research on Women, 1999).

28. Harryette Mullen, "Phantom Pain: Nathaniel Mackey's *Bedouin Hornbook*," *Talisman* 9 (1992): 37–43.

29. Ibid., 40.

30. Régis Durand, "The Disposition of the Voice," in *Performance in Postmodern Culture*, eds. Michel Benamou and Charles Caramello (Milwaukee, WI: Center for Twentieth Century Studies, University of Wisconsin-Milwaukee, 1977), 103.

31. McDonnell, "Divas," 78.

32. Anne Ubersfeld, "The Pleasure of the Spectator," trans. Pierre Bouillaguet and Charles Jose, *Modern Drama* 25, 1 (March 1982): 132, 134.

Capillary Currents: Jayne Cortez

1. Jayne Cortez, liner notes to *There It Is* (New York: Bola Press BP-8201, 1982), audio recording.

2. Jayne Cortez, *Coagulations: New and Selected Poems* (New York: Thunder's Mouth Press, 1984); hereafter cited parenthetically in text as *C*, followed by the page number.

3. *Poetry in Motion*, dir. Ron Mann (New York: Sphinx Productions and Giorno Poetry Systems, 1982).

4. Jay Wright, *The Homecoming Singer* (New York: Corinth Books, 1971), 27.

5. Leonardo Acosta, liner notes to *Irakere* (New York: Columbia Records, 1979).

6. Sascha Feinstein, "Returning to Go Someplace Else: An Interview with Jayne Cortez," *Brilliant Corners* 3, 1 (1998): 53–71.

7. Feinstein, "Returning," 61.

8. Robert Marquez, "Introduction," *¡Patria o Muerte! The Great Zoo and Other Poems by Nicolás Guillén*, ed. and trans. Robert Marquez (New York: Monthly Review Press, 1972), 13–29.

9. Quoted in Marquez, 18.

10. Quoted in Marquez, 20.

11. Nicolás Guillén, *El son entero: Cantos para soldados y sones para turistas* (1952; rpt. Buenos Aires, Argentina: Losada, 1968), 61.

Contributors

Charles Altieri teaches modern American literature at UC Berkeley. His last two books have been *Subjective Agency* and *Postmodernisms Now.* His long-projected book in progress is an effort to provide a theoretical framework for characterizing the effects in relation to literary experience.

Nicole Cooley teaches English and Creative Writing at Queens College-CUNY. Her book of poetry *Resurrection* won the 1995 Walt Whitman Award from the Academy of American Poets. Her novel *Judy Garland, Ginger Love* was published by Regan Books/Harper Collins. She is currently at work on a book about twentieth-century experimental woman writers, portions of which have appeared in *The Review of Contemporary Fiction* and *American Poetry Review.*

Kathleen Crown is an Assistant Professor of English at Kalamazoo College. Her essays on modern and contemporary poetry have appeared in *Poetics Today, Contemporary Literature, HD and Poets After, Viragina Woolf: Texts and Contexts,* and other books and journals. She is currently working on a book about postwar American poetry of trauma and witness.

Rachel Blau DuPlessis' *Drafts 1–38, Toll* will be published by Wesleyan University Press in 2001. Her *Genders, Races, and Religious Cultures in Modern American Poetries: Entitled New* was published by Cambridge in 2000 and the anthology *The Objectivist Nexus: Essays in Cultural Poetics,* co-edited with Peter Quartermain, was published by the University of Alabama Press in 1999. She also co-edited *The Feminist Memoir Project* with Ann Snitow, published by Three Rivers / Crown in 1998.

Charles Borkhuis is a poet, playwright, and critic. His fourth book of poems, *Alpha Ruins,* is forthcoming from Bucknell University; a collection of his full-length plays, *Mouth of Shadows,* was published in 2000. A former editor of *Theater: Ex* magazine, he has had plays produced in New York City, Los Angeles, San Francisco, and Hartford, CT. He was nominated for a Peabody Award and is the recipient of a Dramalogue Award. He is a professor of Literature and Languages at Touro College, in New York City.

Elisabeth A. Frost is an Assistant Professor of English at Fordham University, where she teaches contemporary American poetry, creative writing, and women's studies. She has published articles on modern and contemporary poets in *Genders, Postmodern Culture, Women's Studies,* and elsewhere. She has recently completed a book manuscript entitled "The Feminist Avant-Garde in American Poetry."

Alan Golding teaches American literature and twentieth-century poetics at the University of Louisville. He is the author of *From Outlaw to Classic: Canons in American Poetry* (1995), a CHOICE Best Academic Book selection, and of numerous essays on writing in the Objectivist, Black Mountain, and post-New American Poetry traditions. He is currently at work on two series of essays concerning issues in the sociology of poetry and on individual Language writers.

Eileen Gregory is Professor of English at the University of Dallas. She is the founding editor of the *H.D. Newsletter* (1987–1992) and author of *H.D. and Hellenism: Classic Lines* (Cambridge University Press, 1997). She has published essays on the poetry of H.D., Margaret Atwood, and Carolyn Forche.

Carla Harryman is the author of ten books of plays, poetry, essays, and fiction. Her most recent books are a novel, *The Words: after Carl Sandburg's Rootabaga Stories and Jean-Paul Sartre,* and a volume of selected prose, *There Never Was a Rose without a Thorn.* Her most recent performance project is a collaborative production of the chamber opera *A Little Girl Dreams of Taking the Veil* (San Francisco 1995, 2000) for which she serves as librettist and dramaturge. She is on the faculty of the English Department of Wayne State University.

Laura Hinton is the author of *The Perverse Gaze of Sympathy: Sadomasochistic Sentiments from* Clarissa *to* Rescue 911 (SUNY Press, 1999). She has published articles on feminist theory, film, and experimental women's writing in several journals, including *Women's Studies, Contemporary Fiction, Film Studies, Eighteenth-Century Studies, Private Arts,* as well as in book collections. An Associate

Professor of English at the City College of New York, she is currently at work on a manuscript entitled, "Reconceiving the Romance: Avant-Garde Women's Fiction and the Fetish of Desire."

Cynthia Hogue has published three collections of poetry, most recently *The Never Wife* (Mammoth Press, 1999), and a critical study of American women's poetry, *Scheming Women: Poetry, Privilege, and the Politics of Subjectivity*. For her work, she has been awarded NEA, NEH, and Fulbright fellowships. She directs the Stadler Center for Poetry and teaches in the English Department at Bucknell University.

AnaLouise Keating is an Associate Professor of English at Aquinas College. The author of *Women Reading, Women Writing: Self-Invention in Paula Gunn Allen, Gloria Anzaldúa, and Audre Lorde* (Temple University Press, 1996) and editor of *Interviews/Entrevistas*, by Gloria Anzaldúa (Routledge, 2000), she has published articles on Chicana authors, queer theory, "whiteness" studies, and Ralph Waldo Emerson.

Lynn Keller is the author of *Re-making It New: Contemporary American Poetry and the Modernist Tradition* (Cambridge University Press, 1987) and *Forms of Expansion: Recent Long Poems by Women* (University of Chicago Press, 1997). Professor of English at the University of Wisconsin-Madison, she co-edited *Feminist Measure: Soundings in Poetry and Theory* (University of Michigan Press, 1994), and is currently working on a study of recent experimental poetry by women in the United States.

Linda A. Kinnahan has explored the work of various modernist and contemporary poets. She is an Associate Professor of English at Duquesne University and the author of *Poetics of the Feminine: Literary Tradition and Authority in William Carlos Williams, Mina Loy, Denise Levertov, and Kathleen Fraser*. She has also published articles on British and American women poets such as Carol Ann Duffy, Barbara Guest, Denise Riley, Wendy Mulford, and Geraldine Monk. Currently working on two book projects, she is investigating feminist reading practices in relation to contemporary women poets and modernist women in relation to economics.

Susan McCabe teaches at the University of Southern California. She has published *Elizabeth Bishop: Her Poetics of Loss*. She is currently at work on a book on avant-garde film and modernist poetics. She has published numerous articles on modern and contemporary poets.

Jonathan Monroe is Professor of Comparative Literature and Director of the John S. Knight Writing Program at Cornell University. His book, *A Poverty of Objects: The Prose Poem and the Politics of Genre,* was published in 1987 by Cornell University Press. He has published widely on contemporary poetry within the United States, as well as on contemporary poets writing in French and German. Recent publications include *Poetry, Community, Movement,* a special double issue he guest-edited for *Diacritics,* and *Between Ideologies and a Hard Place: Hans Magnus Enzensberger's Utopian Pragmatist Poetics.* A special section he guest edited for *Poetics Today, After Shock: Poetry and Cultural Politics Since 1989,* is scheduled to appear in spring 2000. He has recently completed a book-length manuscript of prose poems, *Demosthenes' Dictionary,* and is currently finishing his second critical book, *Poetry Among the Discourses: Contemporary Poetry and Cultural Criticism.*

Aldon Lynn Nielsen is the Fletcher Jones Chair of Literature and Writing at Loyola Marymount University. His books of criticism include *Reading Race, Writing between the Lines: Race and Intertextuality, Black Chant: Languages of African-American Postmodernism* and *C.L.R. James: A Critical Introduction.* His collections of poetry include *Heat Strings, Evacuation Routes, Stepping Razor* and *Vext.* He is the editor of *Reading Race in American Poetry: "An Area of Act."* He has also taught at Howard University, the George Washington University, the University of California in Los Angeles and San Jose State University. He was the first winner of the Larry Neal Award for poetry and has also been awarded the Kayden Prize for best university press book in the humanities.

Ron Silliman has published twenty-two volumes of poetry, including *(R), Xing, Demo to Ink, Ketjak, Tjanting* and *What.* In addition, he has published one collection of essays and talks, *The New Sentence,* and edited the anthology *In the American Tree.* A 1998–99 Pew Literary Fellow, Silliman lives with his wife and twin sons in Chester County, Pennsylvania.

Heather Thomas has completed a study of Anne Waldman and Alice Notley entitled, "Spectacular Margins: Women Poets Refigure the Epic." She is the author of four books of poetry, including *Practicing Amnesia* (Singing Horse Press, 2000) and a poetry/embroidery collaboration, *The Fray* (Kutztown Publishing, 2000). Her essays and reviews have been published in *Women's Studies, TO: A Journal of Contemporary Poetry, Prose + Visual Arts,* and *6ix.* A co-editor of *6ix* magazine, she is a Professor of English at Kutztown University of Pennsylvania.

Index